BTEC NATIONAL Business

Roger Lewis
Roger Trevitt

Nelson Thornes

Wolters Kluwer business

Published in 2006 by:
Nelson Thornes Ltd
Delta Place
27 Bath Road
CHELTENHAM
GL53 7TH
United Kingdom

06 07 08 09 10 / 10 9 8 7 6 5 4 3 2 1

A catalogue record for this book is available from the British Library

ISBN 0 7487 9383 6
Cover photographs by Rob Melnychuk/Getty Images and SUNNYphotography.com/Alamy
Page make-up by Pantek Arts Ltd, Maidstone, Kent

Printed and bound in Slovenia by Korotan-Ljubljana

Contents

Acknowledgements iv

Introduction v

1 **Introduction to Business** 1
■ Business Activity ■ Strategic Aims and Objectives ■ Functional Activities ■ Survival and Growth

2 **Business and Management** 52
■ Organisational Aims and Objectives ■ Role of Management ■ Management of Resources ■ Key Management Skills

3 **Creative Product Promotion** 105
■ Promotional Objectives ■ Promotion within the Marketing Mix ■ Advertising Agencies and the Media ■ Promotional Campaign

4 **Presenting Business Information** 161
■ Relevant and Accurate Information ■ How Information can be Processed ■ Presentation of the Gathered Information ■ Creative Corporate Communication

5 **Business Enterprise** 200
■ Features of Enterprise ■ Enterprise and Legal Structure ■ Marketing Strategy and Tactics ■ Plan for a New Business Venture

6 **Business Online** 247
■ Online Presence ■ Impact of Online Presence on Customers ■ Simple Business Website ■ Opportunities

Glossary 280
Index 288

Acknowledgements

The authors and publishers would like to acknowledge the following people and organisations for permission to reproduce material:

Bob Rantaller and the Goldmajor Group; Department for Transport; Egg.com; EU Statistics UK; Friends of the Earth; Investors in People; Liverpool Culture Company; Napster; Office for National Statistics; PepsiCo Tropicana; Pirate FM; Yorkshire Tourist Board.

Crown copyright material is reproduced with the permission of the Controller of HMSO and the Queen's Printer for Scotland. Licence number: C2006009492.

Photograph credits:
Digital Vision 2 (NT), p. 156; Photodisc 54 (NT), p. 156; Jim Forrest/Alamy, p. 202; Roger Bamber/Alamy, p. 202.

Every effort has been made to contact copyright holders and we apologise if any have been overlooked.

The authors would also like to thank all those who have helped in this project, in particular the principals, colleagues and students at Southwark College and Bromley College, Lansana Keifala, Atsu Gbecki and Zara Bokhari; Jon Sutherland who provided extremely useful comments on the manuscript throughout the writing process.

We would also like to acknowledge the support and encouragement that we have received throughout from the team at Nelson Thornes and in particular from: Jess Ward, Claire Hart, Vanessa Thompson and Nigel Harriss.

Finally, we wish to thank our families once again.

Introduction

Welcome to your new course, the BTEC National in Business. Starting a new course can be exciting, but it is also challenging. This introduction will help to answer some of the questions you may have.

How does the course work?

The course is composed of core units and specialist units. It will also allow you to develop Key Skills which you may claim separately. To begin with, you will find it helpful to know the meaning of these terms.

Core units

These cover the knowledge that is needed to understand how any business works. There are three types of BTEC National course and the core units for each of these are:

Table 0.1

Core units	BTEC National Award 6 units	BTEC National Certificate 12 units	BTEC National Diploma 18 units
Unit 1 Introduction to Business	✔	✔	✔
Unit 2 Business and Management	✔	✔	✔
Unit 3 Creative Product Promotion	✔	✔	✔
Unit 4 Presenting Business Information	✔	✔	✔
Unit 5 Business Enterprise	✔	✔	✔
Unit 6 Business Online	✔	✔	✔
	4 core units plus 2 specialist units	5 core units plus 7 specialist units	6 core units plus 12 specialist units

Specialist units

These allow you to look in more detail at a particular subject or area of work. There are a total of 27 specialist units available for the Diploma, 28 for the Certificate and 12 for the Award. These focus on areas of knowledge such as: finance, marketing, management, human resources, law, economics and e-business.

Key Skills

These are the essential skills that you will need in order to succeed in your future career. They are available as a Key Skills qualification which consists of Communication, Application of Number and Information and Communication Technology (ICT). You may achieve these skills at levels 1, 2 or 3.

Key Skills should not be thought of as 'subjects', but rather as tools which will help you to complete the other core and specialist units. The publication – 'Nationals in Business Guidance and Units' suggests how Key Skills awards may be gained through the completion of the BTEC units.

How will the units be taught?

This is a matter for your centre to organise and it will vary from place to place. There may be sessions built around individual units or perhaps the course will be based on particular themes linking units. Perhaps a specialist unit will be combined with a core unit, or sessions may be set aside for a particular skill area such as ICT.

Your centre will decide how it can best offer the course to suit your needs. The 6-unit National Award will normally be offered over one year whilst the 12-unit Certificate and 18-unit Diploma will be two-year courses.

What must I do to pass?

You must complete each unit in your course and achieve points on sufficient units to gain at least a pass.

Table 0.2

	Units to be completed	Units that must be passed	Points needed to pass
BTEC National Award	6 units	6 units	12 points
BTEC National Certificate	12 units	10 units	24 points
BTEC National Diploma	18 units	16 units	36 points

Assessment

You will be assessed entirely through coursework assignments. Units 3 and 5 are assessed by an integrated vocational assignment (IVA) that is set by BTEC. These are worth double points. All other units are set and marked by your teachers according to BTEC guidelines.

Your grades will be recorded as you go along. Your tutor will provide you with the necessary course documents and will review your progress regularly, but you should make it your responsibility to keep your records up to date. Your assessment grades must be agreed by BTEC before they become final.

What grades are there?

Three unit grades are available:

Table 0.3

Pass	Awarded for satisfactory achievement of all pass criteria	2 points IVA 4 points
Merit	Awarded for satisfactory achievement of all pass and merit criteria	4 points IVA 8 points
Distinction	Awarded for satisfactory achievement of all pass, merit and distinction criteria	6 points IVA 12 points

Your final grade is awarded on completion of the course after totalling all of your points. Final grades available are:

Table 0.4

Award (equivalent to 1 A-level)	Certificate (equivalent to 2 A-levels)	Diploma (equivalent to 3 A-levels)
P(ass)	PP PM	PPP PPM PMM
M(erit)	MM MD	MMM MMD MDD
D(istinction)	DD	DDD

How will this book help me to pass the course?

The book covers the core units for the National Award, Certificate and Diploma courses.

Unit 6 Business Online is a core unit for the Diploma course and can be chosen as a specialist unit for the Certificate and the Award.

Each unit has case studies and activities to help you to develop and demonstrate your understanding. Some of the activities can be completed in class. Others give an opportunity for further investigation in private study time. In total, these activities will prepare you for the unit coursework assessments.

The assignment focus features give you the opportunity to achieve all grades from P to D. We also provide guidance and suggestions for succeeding in the IVAs set by BTEC.

A glossary of key terms is provided at the end of the book. Make sure that you know and understand these terms.

The secret of success

You will need to work hard, you expect that. You will get good advice from your tutor as you go along, but here are just a few brief pointers.

- Buy a number of files or folders. What you will need rather depends on how your course is structured, but it may be sensible to have one file per unit. You will obtain a great deal of material and make a lot of notes during the course; all of this can become difficult to manage unless you have a system.

- You will need to obtain relevant materials: try to keep up to date, but remember that collecting information is not an end in itself; it is what you do with it that is important. When you use source material, always quote the source and the date. Notice that at the beginning of each chapter we suggest items that it will be helpful for you to obtain.

- Start off with the right equipment: this includes either a set of floppy disks, rewritable CDs or preferably a USB memory pen. Remember to back-up your files, don't learn the hard way.

Whether you aim to progress into a career or into higher education, BTEC National will prove to be a valuable qualification.

Believe in yourself and enjoy it. Good luck!

UNIT 1

Introduction to Business

This unit covers:
- **business** activity
- strategic aims and objectives
- **functional activities**
- survival and growth.

This unit looks at:
- the different forms of business activity in the UK and the reasons why businesses exist
- the aims and objectives that businesses set themselves, the reasons for these and the ways in which businesses try to achieve them
- the need for businesses to survive and to grow. The use of cash flow and break-even forecasts are introduced to illustrate this.

Assessment:

This unit will be assessed through portfolio work set and marked by your teachers. You will be asked to investigate at least two contrasting business organisations, to identify the aims and objectives of each business and show how each one works to achieve these. You will also need to use financial estimates to show how businesses plan to survive and to grow.

Business Activity

What is a business?

Businesses exist to provide the **goods** and **services** that people and other businesses need, want and are prepared to pay for. Walk along any high street and you will see signs of business activity – shops, buses, delivery vans, street cleaners and builders are all involved.

All businesses are engaged in **production**. They use inputs such as materials, labour and capital equipment (such as machinery) to produce outputs in the form of the products that their customers demand. These products may be either goods or services.

Figure 1.1

Inputs and outputs in production

Inputs

Materials
Labour
Capital equipment

Outputs

Good and services

Goods are tangible objects that we can see and touch.

- Consumer goods are produced for use by individuals and households. They include: food, clothes and consumer durables (long-lasting goods) such as cars, refrigerators and DVD players.

- Industrial goods are produced for use by other businesses. These include raw materials, nuts and bolts, machinery, lorries and chemicals.

Services are activities that provide a benefit to individuals, to businesses, or to both. Unlike goods services are intangible.

- Direct (or personal) services are provided for the benefit of individuals and households. They include the services of bank managers, doctors and entertainers.

- Commercial services are provided for the benefit of businesses. These include transporting, warehousing, finance, business banking, insurance and telecommunications.

Figure 1.2 shows the commercial services that provide the **infrastructures** needed by businesses.

Figure 1.2

Infrastructures that support business

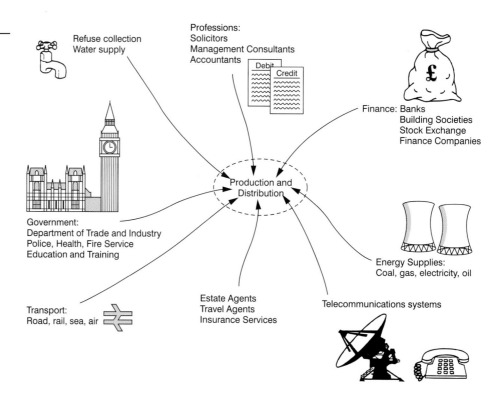

Types of business activity

There are three distinct types of business activity; each type belonging to a different **industrial sector**.

- Primary sector activities involve taking goods directly from nature. These 'extractive industries' include farming, fishing, forestry and mining.

- Secondary sector activities are manufacturing and construction. These create semi-finished and finished products by using materials extracted by the primary sector or materials manufactured from these.

- The tertiary sector consists of the service industries. These may produce either commercial services for businesses or direct services for the benefit of individuals and households.

Table 1.1 Business activities in the industrial sectors

Goods (the production industries)			Services	
Primary sector	**Secondary sector**		**Tertiary sector**	
Extractive industries: agriculture; forestry; fishing; mining; oil extraction; quarrying	*Manufacturing industries:* metals; chemicals; man-made fibres; engineering; food, drink and tobacco; textiles; footwear; clothing	*Construction industries:* building; civil engineering	*Commercial services:* wholesale and retail distribution; hotels and catering; transport; post and telecommunications; banking, insurance and finance; public administration	*Direct services:* education; health services; entertainment; police; veterinary services

Over recent decades, all industrialised countries have experienced growing employment in the tertiary sector whilst the number of employees in the primary and secondary sectors has fallen, as shown in Figure 1.3. In the UK, this trend is the result of:

■ the use of new technology in manufacturing

■ the decline of heavy industries such as ship building, coal and steel – increasingly these goods are imported more cheaply from abroad

■ a growing demand for services such as leisure and tourism.

Figure 1.3

Employment in the industrial sectors, 1979–2004

Source: Office of National Statistics

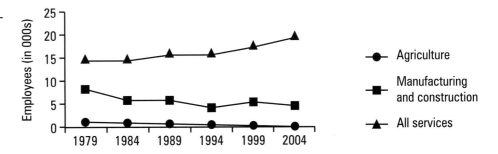

Local, national and global business activity

Local businesses tend to be relatively small and serve the surrounding area. The independent corner shop is one example. The *Yellow Pages* or *Thomson's Directory* will list others, such as plumbers, garages, hairdressers and restaurants. Remember not to confuse local businesses with the local branches of national chains, e.g. Kwik Fit may have a local branch but is a national business with branches across the UK.

National businesses have sales outlets and distribution systems reaching across the country. National Express, as the name suggests, runs coaches nationwide.

Global businesses operate in markets throughout the world. Household names such as Esso, Toyota, Avis, McDonald's and Levi Strauss are all global **brands**.

Gaining a wider market

One way in which businesses can reach a wider market is by setting up branches in different areas. Marks & Spencer, Tesco and Sainsbury all began as small local businesses. Gradually they expanded, first by establishing regional branches, then national and finally international branches.

HSBC calls itself 'the world's local bank' – what does this mean?

Manufacturers may gain access to new markets by setting up factories overseas. For example, the following now produce within the UK:

■ Japanese car-makers Nissan near Sunderland and Toyota near Derby
■ Daewoo electronics from Taiwan in Northern Ireland
■ USA computer firms IBM and Compaq in Scotland
■ Bosch electronics of Germany in Wales.

Buying into existing businesses (through **mergers** or **take-overs**) provides a rapid means of expansion. Morrisons, for example, strengthened its position as a national grocery brand by buying Safeway, Wal-Mart gained access to the UK market when it bought into Asda and for a similar reason Banco Santander of Spain took over Abbey National.

Recently the growth of **e-commerce** (or internet selling) has enabled some businesses to operate across **international** boundaries without the traditional need to set up and staff offices in these countries. Amazon is one successful example.

---

assignment focus

Before you begin:

1　Select two contrasting business organisations to study. You may choose businesses with contrasting forms of ownership, for example a plc and a **charity** or, perhaps, a plc and a public sector organisation (pages 4–8 will explain these terms).

Alternatively you may choose organisations in contrasting industrial sectors such as a manufacturer and a leisure supplier, a construction company and a retailer or a travel provider and an oil company.

Note that large UK organisations may be easier to investigate, although where you have access to smaller organisations (e.g. through employment or a family connection), these may be ideal.

2　Send for the annual report of each organisation if it has one, locate its website, scan the media for relevant topical information and if appropriate approach the organisation directly for information.

3　Title and contents
　a) Design a title page to include: the award name, the unit number and name, your name.
　b) Design a contents page – when you have completed your assignment insert the page numbers for each section here.

Who owns businesses?

The UK has a mixed economy with some businesses in the **public sector**, some in the **private sector** and some in the **voluntary sector** (see Figure 1.4).

The public sector

Public sector businesses are publicly funded and run by **central government** at Westminster or by **local government**.

Traditionally central government controlled businesses they believed to be necessary for the security of the nation (such as steel-making and ship-building) or essential for the community (such as British Rail, the gas, electricity and water suppliers). Local governments provided essential local services such as education.

In recent years, however, the public sector has grown smaller as governments have been less willing to use taxpayers' money to support business activities. Increasingly, private sector businesses are encouraged to help fund these activities or to run them altogether. Recent trends include:

Figure 1.4

Types of business ownership

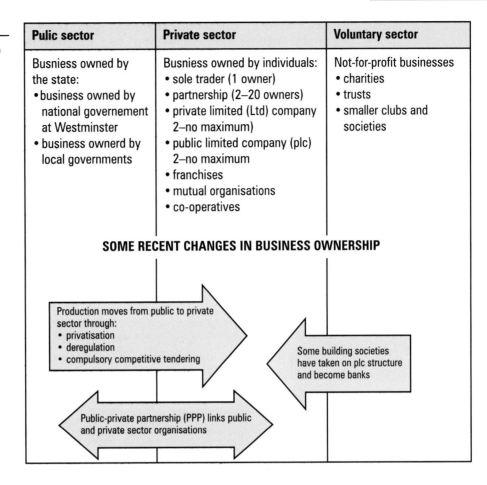

Pulic sector	Private sector	Voluntary sector
Busniess owned by the state: • business owned by national governement at Westminster • business ownerd by local governments	Busniess owned by individuals: • sole trader (1 owner) • partnership (2–20 owners) • private limited (Ltd) company 2–no maximum) • public limited company (plc) 2–no maximum • franchises • mutual organisations • co-operatives	Not-for-profit businesses • charities • trusts • smaller clubs and societies

SOME RECENT CHANGES IN BUSINESS OWNERSHIP

Production moves from public to private sector through:
• privatisation
• deregulation
• compulsory competitive tendering

Some building societies have taken on plc structure and become banks

Public-private partnership (PPP) links public and private sector organisations

- ■ **privatisation** – since 1979 many central government-owned businesses such as BT, the water, electricity and gas companies, British Airways and BP have been sold off. These now operate in the private sector as plcs

- ■ deregulation of public services – regulations have been removed to allow private businesses to run services that were previously operated by the state. Now firms such as Stagecoach and Arriva run local bus services, whilst private contractors such as Cleanaway and Accord provide local authority refuse collection (see CCT on page 39)

- ■ public–private partnerships (PPPs) – here private sector businesses help to fund public projects such as London Underground, Crossrail, NHS hospitals and prisons.

The private sector

Private sector businesses are owned by individuals, or groups of individuals. These include:

- ■ **profit-**making organisations whose owners (**sole traders**, **partnerships** and company shareholders) risk their savings and other possessions in the hope of making personal gains

- ■ mutual organisations such as building societies and some insurance providers who exist to provide a service for their members (the customers) rather than for personal gain

- ■ co-operatives, often pursuing social aims rather than outright profit.

The legal structure of private sector businesses

Sole traders, partnerships, **private limited companies** and public limited companies all attempt to create profits for their owners.

Sole trader businesses are owned by one person who may keep all of the profits but is personally liable (or responsible) for all business debts. This is called **unlimited liability**.

Partnerships (sometimes called firms) are owned and run by between 2 and 20 partners who may share the profits but are 'jointly and severally' liable for all business debts. Each partner has unlimited liability (unless stated in the partnership agreement) and a decision made by one partner becomes the legal responsibility of all other partners.

Limited liability companies are owned by their shareholders and there is no legal limit to the number of shareholders a company may have. They differ from sole traders and partnerships in a number of ways.

- A limited company exists in law and is separate from its owners. If you wished to take a sole trader or a partnership to court, you would be suing the owners of these businesses. In the case of a company, it is the company itself that is sued. It is, however, now possible to sue individual company directors where this is thought appropriate. An example is the case of 'corporate manslaughter' brought against the directors of the maintenance contractors Balfour Beatty following the Hatfield rail crash.

- All limited companies must be registered with the Registrar of Companies at Companies House to whom financial information must be sent each year. This information is available for inspection by any member of the public.

- Whereas sole traders and partners own and control their businesses, company shareholders elect a board of directors to run the company on their behalf. (In small companies, the shareholders may also be the directors.)

- Unlike sole traders and partners, company shareholders are protected by limited liability: should the business fail, their losses will be limited to the amount they have invested in the business and they cannot be called upon to forfeit their personal assets to repay business debts.

- Those dealing with a company, therefore risk not being paid. For this reason a private limited company must display the word 'Limited' or 'Ltd' in its name, whilst a public limited company must display the letters 'plc'.

The differences between private and public limited companies are shown in Table 1.2.

Table 1.2 The differences between private and public limited companies

Private limited companies (Ltd)	**Public limited companies (plc)**
These may not offer their shares for sale to the general public and they therefore tend to be smaller than plcs. Examples include local and regional businesses, such as a garage, a farm, a builder, a coach company. Some companies start as private limited companies and become plcs when they need to raise further capital for expansion. This was the route taken by Manchester United in 1991. At the time of writing the new owner has enough shares to turn it back into a private company.	These may offer their shares to the general public, through the Stock Exchange – it is plc share prices that are displayed in the daily press. Plcs have the potential to raise huge amounts of capital and most of the larger companies have this form of ownership. They include household names such as Tesco, Marks & Spencer, ICI, the high street banks, as well as privatised businesses such as British Airways and BT.

Franchises are sole traders, partnerships or companies that take on the brand and products of another business under licence. The franchiser (who owns the brand) uses this as a means of increasing its outlets and market, whilst the franchisee (who has permission to use the brand) gets a ready-made business with proven products, an established reputation and brand image. Examples of franchises include Bodyshop, BSM, McDonald's and Domino's Pizzas.

Mutual organisations, including building societies and some insurance providers, plough back all 'profits' in order to improve the service they offer to their members, the customers.

Since the early 1990s, a number of building societies have changed from being 'mutuals' into profit-making banks with plc status. The first to change was Abbey National, followed by others including Northern Rock, Woolwich and Halifax. Nationwide is the largest remaining building society.

Co-operatives operate in all sectors of the community, and they carry out a wide range of activities. They are owned by members who may be their employees or their consumers. Whilst some co-operatives have only two or three members, others have hundreds.

Retail co-operatives are owned by their customers who receive a dividend each year based on their purchases.

Workers' co-operatives are owned and controlled by their employees who share responsibilities, decision-making, profits and opportunities according to a set of internationally agreed principles. Those who depend on the enterprise can vote on how it is managed.

case study 1.1 — Rail privatisation

In 1996, John Major's Conservative government controversially broke up and sold off British Rail which until then was owned by the state. The track and stations went to a new company Railtrack plc, whilst the trains were run by separate regional operators such as Midland Mainline, Virgin and Connex.

Railtrack charged the rail companies for its services and was also subsidised by the government. However, it was in a difficult position. On the one hand, as a plc, it had to make profits to reward its shareholders and to attract new investors; on the other hand, it needed to spend huge sums to provide a safe and efficient railway network.

When a rail crash outside London's Paddington station in October 1999 led to the deaths of more than 30 passengers, Railtrack was accused of cutting back on safety standards in order to pay shareholders. In 2002 Tony Blair's New Labour government replaced Railtrack with Network Rail, a not-for-profit organisation.

activity

1　British Rail used to be state-owned. Why was this?
2　Which companies now operate the trains in your area?
3　Why did Railtrack plc find it difficult to maintain the railways effectively?
4　Write a brief argument either for or against selling off British Rail to private shareholders.

The voluntary sector

Voluntary sector organisations do not exist to reward their owners financially but to provide a service for their members or for a group in society. They rely to some extent on volunteers who agree with their aims and many are registered charities.

Charitable status allows an organisation to escape tax liability so that more of their funds can be devoted to their chosen projects. Well-known charities include Amnesty International, Greenpeace, Oxfam, RSPCA and RNIB.

Clubs and societies provide a service for their members and plough back any profit (usually called a surplus) to improve services in future. Voluntary clubs and societies include small organisations such as a local tennis club.

case study 1.2 — Nationwide Building Society: mutual benefit?

The Nationwide is the largest remaining building society now that rivals such as the Halifax, the Leeds and the Woolwich have become banks.

Building societies are mutual organisations; all profits (often called surpluses) are reinvested into the business to provide an improved service for the members (the investors and borrowers).

The Nationwide claims that, since it does not have to pay a dividend to shareholders, it is able to provide a better deal for its customers in the form of higher savings rates and lower charges for loans and mortgages.

activity

1   Check an independent personal finance site (such as moneyfacts.co.uk), or a weekend newspaper for best buys on savings and borrowing rates.
2   How true is it that building societies (usually marked as BS) provide some of the best offers?

Trusts exist where appointed trustees hold and manage assets on behalf of a group of people. The National Trust, one of the UK's largest landowners, manages buildings and land for the benefit and enjoyment of the general public.

Link

On page 52 we look at the National Trust.

The voluntary sector has a total income of over £15 billion, £4 billion of which comes from voluntary donations. The balance comes from corporate support and commercial **operations**, e.g. Oxfam runs shops and sells on eBay, the National Trust rents out properties, and local sports and community clubs run bars and social clubs.

case study 1.3   Greenpeace

Greenpeace exists to defend the natural environment and to promote peace and social justice in the world. It is a charity that employs paid officials but relies heavily upon volunteers. Activities include:

- carrying out research and providing information to make people aware of environmental problems

- direct action (getting physically involved) to prevent damaging practices such as illegal whaling or the dumping of toxic waste

- acting as a pressure group on national governments and other powerful bodies such as the European Union (**EU**) and the United Nations. The aim is to bring about a change in the law

- persuading businesses to use sustainable sourcing and 'greener' production methods. For example, builders merchants Jewson and Travis Perkins were persuaded to stop buying wood from Indonesia where rainforests are being illegally destroyed

- working with the energy company npower to set up 'Juice' – a company supplying 'green' electricity generated by wind and water power.

Table 1.3 Greenpeace's income and expenditure, 2003

Income	£000s	Expenditure	£000s
Subscriptions and donations	8,403	Campaign expenses	4,458
Profit on merchandising, publishing and commercial events	152	Campaign information costs	688
Raised by campaign groups	64	Cost of collecting subscriptions and donations	625
Interest from investing surplus funds	19	Cost of recruiting new supporters	1,035
		Marketing costs	567
		Administration and management costs	405
		Surplus retained	860
Total income	**8,638**	**Total expenditure**	**8,638**

Greenpeace has around a quarter of a million UK supporters, 2.8 million contributors worldwide and an annual income of £8.6 million. Its website can be found at www.greenpeace.org.uk.

Source: Greenpeace Annual Review, 2003

activity

1   Why would a company form of organisation not be suitable for Greenpeace?
2   Give an example of a 'greener' method of production.
3   How do you think businesses themselves might benefit from using sustainable sources (and being seen to use these)?
4   Find examples of companies that adopt environmentally friendly policies. (They are usually proud of this and may use it in their promotional materials as well as in the annual report.)

Link   You may also wish to refer to the section on business **ethics** on page 31.

assignment focus

The larger charities are keen to promote their causes and will make information available to you. You may consider choosing a charity for your unit assessment.

Researching business

To complete this unit, you will need to research two contrasting business organisations. Choose your organisations with care to make sure that they are suitable for your purpose; you must be able to find the information that you need.

You will need to use a range of information sources, which may include:

- your own experience – do not under-estimate this! You may have a part-time job, support a local sports team or support a particular charity. If so, you will have valuable first-hand knowledge

- contacts – if you have family members or close friends who own or are employed in suitable businesses, they will be able to provide materials and examples from their own experiences

- websites – national and global businesses will have websites. Increasingly small business also have a presence on the internet

remember

- If you do not know the business web address, use a **search engine**.
- Sections called 'About us' or 'Corporate information' will give information about the business itself, such as key personnel, aims and objectives, new developments, press releases, financial performance, and so on.

- annual reports – these are an invaluable source of information on companies and large charities. Plc reports are usually posted on their websites, often in the 'Shareholder information' or 'Investor information' section. Alternatively, printed versions are available from the company secretary. WILink.com also provides a free annual reports service

Link   See page 267 in Unit 6.

- promotions – some businesses advertise themselves rather than their products in an attempt to build their 'corporate image'. This certainly happens if they change their name, e.g. when Freeserve changed to Wanadoo, and British Steel changed to Corus. You may see public relations advertisements and features in the media that reveal useful information about **business objectives** and performance

- news reports – business is a living subject and you must be aware of current developments. Always listen to the news and read the daily papers (they will be in your library and you may be able to pick up one free as you travel to study). Newspaper websites not only display the daily news but contain archives that can be searched for past articles. The BBC site allows you to view video clips and listen to past features

- government statistics – the UK government collects and publishes statistical information on the state of the economy, business trends and social trends. The following should be available in your library: *Social Trends, Annual Abstract of Statistics, Business Monitors, The Employment Gazette* and *The Family Expenditure Survey*. Alternatively, visit the government statistics website at: www.statistics.gov.uk, which contains 'UK at a glance' overviews of current trends and features on selected topics. Statistics can be downloaded in spreadsheet format

Figure 1.5

The home page for the UK government's National Statistics website

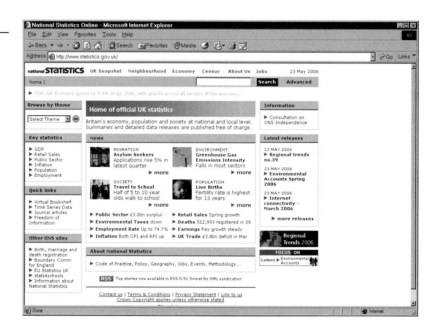

- market intelligence reports – a number of commercial organisations, such as Mintel, Dun & Bradstreet, Datastream and Verdict Research (the retail specialists), collect and publish detailed business data and reports. These can be expensive but may be available in reference libraries and in specialised business libraries. Newspapers and business magazines may carry topical summaries.

assignment focus

Select two businesses to study for your unit assessment.

1 Obtain the annual report for each. You may find a printed report more convenient than the **online** version.

2 Decide which of the other sources of information will be most useful to you and decide how you will gain access to this information.

3 If you choose a plc that has been privatised, a transport company that has taken advantage of deregulation over recent years or a building society that has become a bank, make sure that you research this aspect.

Business purposes
Why do businesses exist?

Businesses in all sectors exist to supply the goods and services that customers demand. Remember that this demand comes from individuals, households and communities, from other businesses and from central and local government via **public spending**. Demand becomes effective where customers are willing and able to buy.

Figure 1.6

Supply and demand

Supply of goods and services from public, private and voluntary sector business

Demand from customers' needs and wants

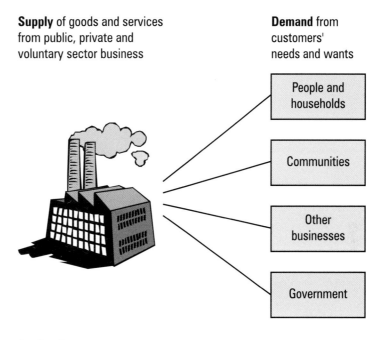

People and households

Communities

Other businesses

Government

Private sector business

The main motivation for private sector businesses is profit, so ultimately they must generate more money from selling their products than they spend on producing them.

In Unit 5, Business Enterprise, you will identify a gap in the market for a product and plan to supply this profitably.

Notice that company profit is used in three ways.

- A percentage of the profit is paid to the government's department as corporation tax.
- From the profits that remain, the directors will pay dividends to reward the company shareholders who own the business.
- The remaining profit is retained and 'ploughed back' into the business to fund future growth.

There may be occasions when a profit-seeking business is prepared to sell at cost or even below cost. In March 2006, 3 per cent of sales by the 'big four' supermarkets were below cost. Examples include:

- introductory offers – 'buy at this special low price for a limited period only'. This is a marketing tactic to encourage customers to try a new product in the hope that they will continue to buy when the price is later raised to a profitable level
- in a price war designed to steal customers from rivals and so gain a greater share of the market
- as a 'loss leader' – where one item is sold cheaply to attract customers. The hope is that they will then buy further goods at full price. A supermarket may advertise cheap turkeys at Christmas as a loss leader
- where there is no better alternative. Late on a Saturday afternoon market traders may sell off fruit and vegetables below cost to 'cut their losses' – the alternative is to throw them away

case study 1.4

Tesco plc, 'Every little helps'

In February 2005 Tesco plc announced record profits of around £2 billion. These were achieved not only through supplying customers with quality, variety and value in its core food business, but also through impressive growth in non-food items such as clothes and electrical goods, combined with expansion overseas. The company has also diversified into financial services, gas and electricity supplies. It is an **internet service provider (ISP)** and plans to act as an estate agent.

Figure 1.7

Tesco plc - profit for 2005

Source: Tesco Annual Report, February 2005

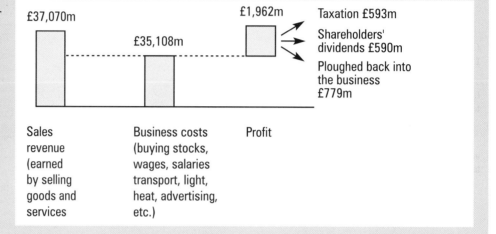

£37,070m

£35,108m

£1,962m   Taxation £593m

Shareholders' dividends £590m

Ploughed back into the business £779m

Sales revenue (earned by selling goods and services)

Business costs (buying stocks, wages, salaries transport, light, heat, advertising, etc.)

Profit

activity

Log on to the Tesco website.
1 Look at the home page and make a list of the different types of operation in which Tesco is now involved.
2 In which countries does Tesco now have stores?
3 Go to the Corporate Affairs section of the site. What are Tesco's main aims?

- end-of-season sale items where the aim is to clear outdated, slow-selling stock and make way for new products
- where the revenue is generated from sources other than the customer. Newspapers or independent television companies subsidise their products from advertising revenue so that customers pay less than the cost of production
- to enhance the service and thereby to boost corporate (or company) image. For example publishers often make a loss on poetry books, but feel that they should continue to provide them as part of their service, while local shops may provide telephone top-up cards, stamps and electricity key-charging services all for no, or minimal, profit
- where contracts or the demands of regulators specify that a given level of service is required. Rail and bus operators, for example, may be required to run an off-peak service even though this part of the service is not profitable.

In the early stages, some new projects may run at a loss because it takes time to build up a customer base. BSkyB (now Sky), Eurodisney and Eurotunnel all took some years to achieve profitability. Smaller businesses with smaller funds will need to make profits more quickly if they are to survive.

Public sector business
Public sector operations exist to provide necessary or desirable services to the community. They will need to generate sufficient funds to provide these services but will not operate for financial gain. The library and education services provided by local authorities and the

National Health Service provided by central government are subsidised by public funds so that users do not pay the full cost at the point of use. (Compare this situation with the fees paid by patients at private hospitals and students at private schools.)

Central government spends around £8,000 a year for every man, woman and child in the UK.

Figure 1.8

Central government spending

Source: HM Treasury – figures for 2004–5

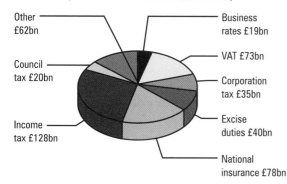

Where the money comes from
Total receipts – £455bn
(The £33bn shortfall is borrowed.)

Other £62bn

Business rates £19bn

Council tax £20bn

VAT £73bn

Corporation tax £35bn

Income tax £128bn

Excise duties £40bn

National insurance £78bn

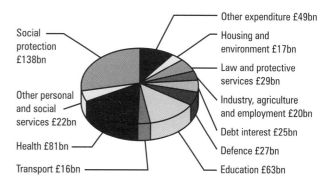

Where the money comes from
Total receipts – £455bn
(The £33bn shortfall is borrowed.)

Social protection £138bn

Other expenditure £49bn

Housing and environment £17bn

Law and protective services £29bn

Other personal and social services £22bn

Industry, agriculture and employment £20bn

Debt interest £25bn

Health £81bn

Defence £27bn

Transport £16bn

Education £63bn

Governments decide which services should be provided by the state. However, public services are costly to provide and the taxes needed to pay for them are unpopular. For this reason, recent UK governments have reviewed the way in which public money is used. There is a trend towards 'less government' so that in future the state may decide to provide fewer services, charge for them (e.g. proposed charges for the ambulance service) or target them only at the most needy. The idea is to give taxpayers 'value for money' and initiatives have included:

■ public services being encouraged to generate their own revenues or limit their **costs**. For example, the police charge for security at sports and entertainment events, the library service rents out CDs and DVDs, local authorities buy-in services such as refuse collection from private contractors who offer best value and set up local car parking schemes to raise revenue

■ public services being given strict spending targets and made accountable for the money they spend and the services they offer. Citizens' charters and school league tables are examples

See pages 21 and 37.

■ private companies being encouraged to invest in state enterprises such as transport through PPPs (public–private partnerships)

■ many government-run businesses being privatised so that the state is no longer responsible. Meanwhile public transport has been de-regulated so that it is open to private contractors.

See pages 7, 28 and 33.

Not-for-profit/voluntary sector business

Businesses in the voluntary sector raise money purely to support their chosen cause. Oxfam, for example, uses its funds to provide humanitarian aid to developing countries in the form of food, clothing, education and so on. Such organisations meet a demand from groups in the community but in many cases they provide a free service to the beneficiary.

Key stakeholders

Stakeholders are those people and communities who have an interest (or stake) in a particular business because they are affected by its activities. We can distinguish between:

■ internal stakeholders, who work within the business, including: owners (sole traders, partners and those shareholders who participate in management), directors, managers and other employees

■ external stakeholders, including customers, suppliers, bankers, financial institutions, shareholders who take no part in the running of the business, pressure groups, trades unions, employer associations, governments, commercial partners, local and national communities.

In practice, it may be difficult to balance stakeholder needs as different groups may have conflicting demands on the business.

Owners

Private sector businesses are owned by sole traders, partners or company shareholders depending upon their legal status. The owners risk their own funds when they invest in a business and may be rewarded in a number of ways.

■ Income – sole traders and partners receive a share of profits in the form of drawings, whilst shareholders receive dividends.

■ Capital growth – if the value of the business grows the owners may be able to sell their stake in the business at a profit. A rising share price, for example, will benefit shareholders.

■ Power and influence – shareholders can vote at the company AGM (annual general meeting) and influence policy decisions – environmental pressure groups buy energy company shares for this reason. A majority stakeholder can take over a company – this is how Wal-Mart gained control of Asda.

Owners are powerful stakeholders and companies often state 'adding **shareholder value**' as one of their main objectives.

Company directors

These are employees whose job is to run the company on behalf of the shareholders. They set the business objectives and take strategic decisions about the 'direction' the business will take. In a small company, such as a family business, the shareholders may also be the directors, while in a large plc the shareholders will elect a board of directors.

If directors run a profitable business, they achieve a good salary, job satisfaction and prestige. There has been recent concern about 'fat cat' salaries paid to reward some company directors. (In July 2004 Sir Peter Davis left Sainsbury with a £2.3 million performance bonus – the company reported its first-ever loss four months later.)

Managers

Managers are responsible for deciding on the **tactics** for achieving the organisation's objectives within a particular area, section or department. For example, a retailer such as Boots will appoint a branch manager to run each shop, while a college will appoint a manager to run the business studies and science departments.

Although managers have similar needs to other employees as mentioned below, they have more responsibility and are more highly paid.

Other employees

Other employees work under a manager or supervisor and are engaged either directly, or indirectly, in the production of the goods and services supplied by business. They want secure jobs, good working conditions, satisfactory pay and pensions, good career prospects and a safe and healthy workplace. Employee demands will cost the business money and may put them into conflict with owners and management (the 'us and them' syndrome).

Customers

Customers buy the goods and services that a business produces and without them the business would not exist. Customers want a reliable supply of quality products at a reasonable price on suitable payment terms. In a competitive environment, businesses must be sure to keep their customers satisfied

Suppliers

Suppliers provide either stocks of goods or commercial services such as accounting, banking, electricity, water, security or maintenance. They may supply on credit terms and will therefore want secure contracts with guaranteed and prompt payment. In 2005, the suppliers of MG Rover, knowing the company was in difficulties, refused to deliver parts unless cash payment was made. The company ran out of components and ceased production.

Bankers

Banks and other financial institutions provide various forms of funding for business. They want the business to generate a profit so that any loans and overdrafts can be repaid and investments provide a worthwhile return.

Pressure groups

These are concerned about specific issues ranging from the rights of motorists (the AA and RAC) to the abolition of foxhunting (League Against Cruel Sports). The TUC (Trades Union Congress) and CBI (Confederation of British Industry) act as pressure groups for employees and employers respectively, whilst charities such as Amnesty International (the plight of political prisoners) and Friends of the Earth (the environment) press their own concerns.

Local pressure groups may be set up to campaign on single issues such as new roads, the closure of schools, extensions to airport runways and the building of housing 'developments'.

The case of Arsenal and the Highbury Community Association is covered on pages 16–17.

Trades unions

Trades unions are concerned about the pay and conditions of employment of their members, the employees in a particular industry or workplace. Most trades unions are affiliated to the Trades Union Congress (TUC), a body representing the views of trades unions as a whole in the UK.

Employer associations

These represent the employers in a particular industry. They pass on information and set up agreements concerning matters of mutual interest such as rates of pay, conditions of work and procedures for resolving disputes. The Confederation of British Industry (CBI) represents the interests of employers at national level.

Commercial partners

Businesses frequently carry out their operations in partnership with other companies. The sponsors' logos on sports shirts are one obvious example. Other examples include:

- Liverpool will be Europe's Capital of Culture in 2008 and is linking with organisations in the public and private sectors. So far these include Hill Dickinson, United Utilities, Enterprise plc, Radiocity 96.7 and Northwest Regional Development Agency
- Newcastle airport works in partnership with airlines using their facilities
- Virgin's bank accounts operate in partnership with Royal Bank of Scotland plc.

Figure 1.9

The logo of Liverpool, European Capital of Culture 2008

Central and local governments

Central and local governments have the power to block, promote and regulate business activity. They are concerned with business impact on the local and national economy, on people and on the environment.

■ Local authorities can exercise control through local planning restrictions, the enforcement of public health and trades descriptions legislation. In turn they benefit from business rates.

■ Central government receives revenue from businesses. The Revenue & Customs department taxes business profits and collects VAT, as well as **PAYE** (income tax) and **NIC (National Insurance contributions)** deducted from employees.

Governments regulate employment, health and safety, consumer protection, competition and taxation. Help and advice to business is provided by the Department of Trade and Industry **(DTI)**.

Local and national communities

■ Local residents and local businesses are concerned about the social costs and benefits of business activity. Costs include noise, light, atmospheric and water pollution, over-crowding and traffic congestion. Communities may benefit from better job prospects, regeneration of the locality and tourism.

■ Some issues affect people across the country. The debate about the location of a new airport or the disposal of nuclear waste are examples.

Social costs (or benefits) borne by society rather than by the business that causes them are called **externalities**. This is one reason why large businesses are obliged to publish their accounts and so make them available to anyone who is interested.

case study 1.5   What a load of rubbish?

In August 2006 Arsenal leave their present ground in Highbury, North London for their new Emirates Stadium half a mile away, built on the old Ashburton Grove refuse tip. The old ground with only 38,000 seats is too small. The new 60,000-seater stadium will also generate revenue from its corporate, sports and gambling facilities.

The development was only approved after lengthy discussions with a variety of stakeholders. It involves the relocation of 50 local businesses and the council waste recycling centre, the demolition of the present industrial site and the construction of the new stadium together with 2,500 new homes (1,000 of these are affordable housing). Business and health facilities will also be built in the surrounding area and overall 1,000 construction workers will be employed and 1,800 long-term jobs created.

From 2006 the existing ground will be converted into homes and other public amenities including a health centre. This will take a further four years.

Source: www.arsenalregen.co.uk

Figure 1.10

Stakeholder groups in Arsenal FC

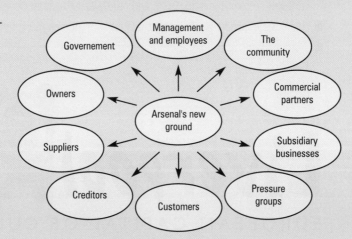

1 a) Here are some stakeholders of Arsenal FC. Fit these under the correct headings on the diagram above:

players, team manager, coaching staff, the Highbury Community Association, Robert McAlpine (the construction company), administrative staff, the fans, banks and other financial institutions, shareholders, local residents, local retailers, stadium sponsors Emirates and shirt sponsors O$_2$, Newlon Housing Trust, Islington Council, the shirt manufacturers Nike, Sky, the department of Revenue & Customs, local shops

b) Can you suggest others?

c) Identify and explain possible conflicts between different stakeholder groups over the relocation of the club.

2 Re-read Case study 1.1 on page 7.

a) Which two stakeholder groups had conflicting interests? Briefly explain the different demands of these groups.

b) Name other Railtrack stakeholders and explain why they had an interest in the business.

c) Identify the stakeholders of the businesses that you have chosen for your assessment.

Link We return to social costs in the section on business ethics on page 31.

Added value and the value chain

Businesses seek to 'add value' as they produce goods and services.

Figure 1.11

Added value

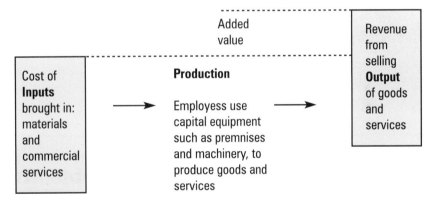

For example, a carpenter buys wood (input) costing £20. It is made into a table (output) and sold for £30:

Output £30 – Inputs bought in £20 = Added value £10

Added value must be sufficient to pay for internal production costs (mainly wages and salaries) and leave a profit for the owners.

The value chain

A whole network of organisations and processes may be needed to supply a product to the end-user. Value will be added at each stage. A typical supply chain for cereals is shown in Figure 1.12.

Procurers, producers, distributors, wholesalers, retailers and **e-tailers** all play vital roles in the value chain, as follows.

■ Procurers (or buyers) 'source' inputs, i.e. they find suitable suppliers for stocks and make arrangements to purchase them. The aim is to ensure a supply of quality goods at the right price on the right terms and conditions. For example, the baker will need the right quality grain.

Figure 1.12

A typical supply chain for a cereal

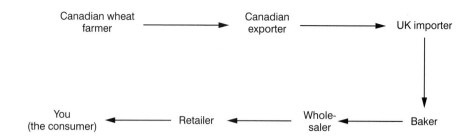

- Producers process materials into a finished or semi-finished product. Here the miller turns wheat into flour, the baker turns flour into bread.
- Distributors move products along the value chain.
- The wholesaler buys from the manufacturer and sells to the retailer.
- The retailer sells to the consumer who is the final link in the chain.
- E-tailers are electronic retailers, i.e. retailers who sell on the internet via e-commerce. In doing so, a manufacturer such as Dell can sell direct. Missing out the specialist wholesaler and retailer gives them a cost advantage – they can sell more cheaply and still make a satisfactory profit.

If a business moves into activities along the value chain, it may gain the value added at each stage for itself. This is called vertical integration.

We discuss business growth through vertical integration on page 27.

assignment focus

Write a brief introduction to each business you have selected. Include:

- the name, head office and website address
- its main area of business
- the industrial sector(s) within which it operates
- its legal form of ownership
- the various stakeholders of the business.

Strategic Aims and Objectives

Business **strategy** is about where the business is going. We can distinguish between:

- strategic aims – broad statements of intent showing in general terms what the business plans to achieve
- strategic objectives – more precise, quantified, plans of action.

Strategic aims: the mission statement

Many, but not all, organisations draw up a 'mission statement' as a summary of their long-term aims. This is a general statement of the standards, qualities and purpose of the business. For example, Arriva's vision is ' to be recognised as the leading transport services organisation in Europe'.

Strategic objectives: SMART targets

Business objectives must be quantified and ideally they should be **SMART**, that is:

- **S**pecific – they should clearly identify a product, activity, region, etc., e.g. 'We will increase sales of organic vegetables within the UK'
- **M**easurable – it should be possible to determine when the objective has been met, e.g. 'We will increase sales of organic vegetables by 5 per cent'

- **A**chievable – the target must be one that employees can hit, e.g. it must be possible to increase sales by 5 per cent otherwise employees are being set up to fail
- **R**ealistic – the target will not put unreasonable demands on employees or equipment. Sometimes the R stands for Relevant, meaning that the objective should be an appropriate one for the business to pursue and not a distraction
- **T**ime-related – the objective has a set time period or deadline, e.g. 'by the end of December'.

case study 1.6 — Manchester United

In 2003/4 Manchester United was still a plc and its mission (or goal!) was

'through **innovation**, commitment and **evolution**, to protect and develop the brand by sustaining the playing success on the field and growing the business to enhance the financial strength of the Group.'

The directors of Manchester United set out their strategic aims for 2003-4 as:

- maintaining the team's playing success – by signing and developing the right players
- developing the value of media rights – payments from world TV rights and also from MUTV, MU Interactive, MU Mobile and MU Pictures are the second largest source of income (32 per cent)
- leveraging the global brand – selling Manchester United products worldwide in partnership with sponsors such as Pepsi, Nike, Fuji, Vodaphone and Wilkinson Sword
- converting more fans to customers – signing up new members who will then be targeted in an attempt to increase sales of MU products.

The overall aim was to grow profits so that 'shareholder value' would be increased. The company was worth around £158 million in 2003, up from £137million in 2002.

Source: Manchester United Annual Report, September 2003

activity

1 Which business stakeholders are mentioned above? What interest (or stake) does each have in the Manchester United?
2 What is the difference between a fan and a customer?
3 Which stakeholders do you think the mission statement was aimed at?
4 Manchester United fans and shareholders often want different things. For example, in 1998, the major shareholders wanted to merge with BSkyB, the fans did not. In 2005, the fans opposed Malcolm Glazer's take-over of the company, but the major shareholders were eventually sold to him.
   a) Explain why these two groups had conflicting interests?
   b) Which of the two groups had the most power?
5 Suggest some SMART targets for each aim in the Manchester United mission statement.

How does a business set its aims and objectives?

The aims and objectives that one business sets itself may be very different from those set by others. This may be explained by differences in the business size, ownership or industrial sector. However, Cyert and March, in *A Behavioural Theory of the Firm*, also suggest that:

- the managers of a business may have their own personal objectives, such as trying to gain the biggest salary, or most power through 'empire-building' (building their own sections rather than the business)

- the most powerful stakeholder groups, e.g. shareholders, employees or customers, may determine the objectives. In the Railtrack example on page 7, the shareholders exercised considerable power. In a competitive market the customers will have power.

If we examine the aims and objectives of a range of businesses a number of broad themes recur. These include:

Figure 1.13

Recurring themes in business aims and objectives

Service provision

Breaking even

Profit maximisation

Growth

Ethics

Service provision

All businesses exist to meet the needs of their customers who may be the general public or other businesses.

- Private sector businesses see customer service as a way of enhancing sales. Large retailers, for example, often advertise this as a **unique selling point** (**USP**). Free delivery, bag packing, exchange of unwanted goods, knowledgeable staff are all examples.

- Public sector businesses, such as health care trusts, and voluntary sector businesses, such as the National Trust, exist to provide a service to the community or to their members.

case study 1.7 **Citizens' charters**

Public sector organisations set out their service aims in the form of a citizens' charter:

A CHARTER FOR TRAMLINK PASSENGERS

Welcome to your charter
At Tramlink we aim to give you the best possible service. The following section sets out exactly what you can expect from us and explains how to make the most of the Tramlink service.

- Trams on time
  We know that reliability is what passengers want most from our service. Our target is to keep your waiting time as short as possible by keeping to the timetables we display.
- Clean trams and stops
  We aim to keep tram stops clean.
- Clear information about the service
  We want to make sure that you never have a problem finding out when Tramlink runs, where it stops or what it costs.
- Tickets
  We want to make paying your fare on Tramlink as quick and easy as possible.

Source: Extracted from the Department for Transport Tramlink customer charter, 2004

activity

1 The Tramlink charter sets out general aims. Suggest some SMART objectives for each of these. (The real ones set by Tramlink are on page 35).
2 Suggest some SMART service targets for:
   a) a hospital
   b) the police
   c) your school or college.
3 Are there any problems in setting such targets? (For example, what if the police are set a target for arrests?)

Breaking even

Unless it is being subsidised, a business will ultimately need to cover its costs. The **break-even point** is reached when the sales revenue (or sales income) generated during a trading period exactly covers the costs so that there is neither a profit nor a loss. Sales beyond break-even will bring a profit, whereas failure to break even results in a loss.

case study

1.8

Life before break-even

Sky, EuroDisney and Eurotunnel all took some years to break even and expected to do so. They survived because they were able to raise sufficient funds either from share issues or borrowing against their assets (the land, buildings and equipment they own).

Other businesses have rich benefactors to support them. In the 2002–3 season, Fulham FC made a £30m loss, a record at the time, in 2004/5 their neighbours Chelsea FC achieved an £140m loss, after investing heavily in expensive, highly paid players. Both clubs survived because their respective wealthy owners, Harrod's boss Mohammed Al Fayed and oil billionaire Roman Abramovitch, ensured the bills were paid.

activity

1 How do you think the objectives of Roman Abramovitch might compare with those of the major shareholders of Eurotunnel?
2 Why is it important for a small business to break even relatively quickly?

Forecasting the break-even point (BEP)

In order to forecast the break-even point, we need to understand the nature of business costs and how they behave as output rises and falls.

Business costs are those items whose value is consumed (or used up) in the course of production. We can identify **variable costs** and **fixed costs**.

■ Variable costs are directly related to the units that we produce and sell. They change in proportion to the level of output and sales so that if output doubles then variable costs will double.

Variable costs include: raw materials, stocks purchased for re-sale, wages of employees directly engaged in production, direct expenses such as royalties paid to patent-holders and variable selling costs such as sales-force commission.

■ Fixed costs (or overheads) are not affected by the level of output but remain unchanged as production levels rise and fall. They are generally related to time periods rather than to production.

Fixed costs include: rent, rates, light, heat, salaries, depreciation on fixed assets, finance costs, and, for our purposes, any other costs not regarded as variable. Note that fixed costs are fixed only in the short term and within present production capacity. For example, if we move to a larger factory then rent will rise, if we employ more supervisors then salaries will rise.

Costs are not the same as payments. The following are *not* classed as costs:

■ the expense of buying fixed assets such as premises, plant, machinery, equipment and vehicles. These items remain available for future periods and are not wholly consumed in production

■ money paid to the owners for personal, rather than business, use (i.e. drawings of sole traders and partners and dividends paid to company shareholders).

case study 1.9 — Taking a break

The Students' Union want to run a day trip to the seaside. They need to know how many tickets they must sell to break-even. Research carried out by the students has provided four essential details:

■ sales price – each ticket for the trip will be priced at £15

■ fixed cost – the coach (including driver and fuel) will cost £300 for the day

■ variable cost – a meal will be included at a cost of £5 per student

■ capacity – the coach can take a maximum of 40 students.

The break-even point in units (in this case the number of tickets that must be sold) can be calculated by the formula:

$$\text{Break-even point (in units)} = \frac{\text{Fixed costs for the period}}{\text{Unit contribution (i.e. unit sales price – unit variable cost)}}$$

Therefore:

$$\text{Break-even point (in units)} = \frac{£300}{(£15–£5)} = \frac{£300}{£10} = 30 \text{ units (or tickets)}$$

The break-even point can also be calculated as revenue required (£s):

BEP in units × unit sales price = Break-even point

30 tickets × £15 = £450

A break-even chart can be drawn to illustrate the relationship between costs and sales over different levels of output. There are two stages:

Stage 1: Set out the data in table format, as in Table 1.4. The while boxes show the four essential items of data. All else is calculated from these.

Table 1.4 The data for the break-even chart in table format

	Maximum capacity 40 units	Fixed cost £300 for the day	Variable cost £5 per unit		Sales revenue £15 per unit	
Output in units (tickets)	**Fixed cost £**	**Variable cost £**	**Total cost** (Fixed cost + variable cost) **£**	**Sales revenue £**	**Profit/loss** (Sales revenue − total cost) **£**
0	300	0	300	0	(300)
10	300	50	350	150	(200)
20	300	100	400	300	(100)
30	300	150	450	450	0
40	300	200	500	600	100

estimates {

results at different levels of output and sales {

loss

break-even point

profit

Notice that:

- the output begins at zero units (the minimum customers possible) and ends at maximum capacity (40 is the most the coach can carry)
- the units are shown in steps of 10 but any convenient interval (e.g. 5 or 20) could be used. Four or five rows of data is usually sufficient.

Reading the table:

- if fewer than 30 students travel, there is a loss (calculate this for 29 tickets)
- if 30 students travel, the trip will break even, i.e. Total cost = Sales revenue so that profit or loss = 0
- if more than 30 students travel, there is a profit (calculate the profit at 31 tickets).

The table shows the break-even point shows exactly. However, often the final column may move from a loss at one level of output to a profit at the next. In this case, the break-even point is somewhere between these two points and the formula or chart can be used to find it exactly.

Figure 1.14

Break-even chart

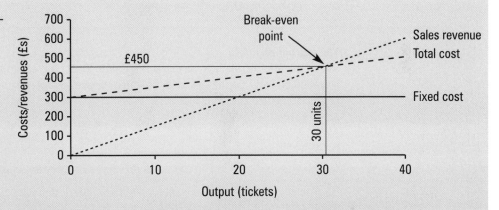

Stage 2: Plot a break-even chart using the data on the table, as in Figure 1.14.

Notice that:

- the x (horizontal) axis shows units of output (in this case the scale is from 0 to 40 units)
- the y (or vertical) axis shows costs and revenues. The scale begins at £0 and must be sufficient to plot maximum sales or costs whichever is higher (in this case £600 sales)
- for total cost and sales revenue are plotted. It is usual to also show fixed cost, although break-even can be shown without this. All lines are straight.

Reading the break-even chart:

The break-even point is located where the sales revenue and total cost lines cut (i.e. where sales revenue = total cost). Notice that the break-even point is shown:

- on the x axis as 30 units (or tickets) need to be sold
- on the y axis as £450 sales revenue to be generated.

The profit or loss of any output is represented by the vertical distance between the sales revenue line and the total cost line. Attempt the readings at 10 units and 40 units and check these against the table.

activity

1 Use the figures above to answer the following questions.
   a) What is the total cost at the break-even point?
   b) What is the total revenue at the break-even point?
   c) What will be the profit or loss if 20 tickets are sold?
   d) Would you expect there to be a profit or a loss at 25 units and at 35 units? Explain each one.
   e) Now calculate the profit or loss at 25 units and at 35 units.
   f) Why does the chart extend only to 40 units (or 40 tickets)?

2 The £15 price of the day trip is too expensive for most students. However, the committee believe they can fill the coach if the ticket price is reduced to £12. A slightly smaller meal will be provided at a cost of £4 per person. The coach will still cost £300 and seat 40 people.
   a) Produce a table showing costs, revenues and profits at 0, 10, 20, 30, 40 units.
   b) Draw a break-even chart with a suitable title and labels.
   c) Calculate the break-even point by formula. Check this against the chart and table.
   d) Explain briefly whether the trip should go ahead, assuming that the aim is to break-even rather than to make a profit.

The margin of safety

Since estimates are likely to be inexact, it is wise for businesses to build a **margin of safety** into their projects. So, for example, they may decide to proceed only where the forecast profits are higher than they require.

Margin of safety (in units) = Forecast output – Break-even output

Alternatively:

Margin of safety in £s = Forecast sales revenue – Break-even sales revenue

For example, for the students' day trip in Case study 1.9, if forecasts show that 35 students will go on the student day trip, then:

Margin of safety (5 tickets) = 35 estimated ticket sales – 30 ticket sales to break-even

Alternatively:

Margin of safety (£75) = £525 estimated revenue (£15 × 35) – £450 revenue at break-even point

Using an electronic spreadsheet model for break-even forecasting

Either set up an electronic spreadsheet model for break-even forecasing, or use the template on the Nelson Thornes website www.nelsonthornes.com/btec. It will automatically calculate the profit or loss at different levels of output, calculate the break-even point and draw the break-even chart.

If you wish to set up a spreadsheet on your own using Microsoft Excel:

1 Create the worksheet by entering all text and formulae into the identical cells as shown in the model. Check that you understand how the formulae work.

2 Link the chart by highlighting the ranges:

   Fixed cost: C8:C14, Total cost: E8:E14, Sales revenue: F8:F14

3 Now select the chart Wizard:
   a) select 'line chart'
   b) select 'series'
   c) click in the category (x) axis labels' box
   d) highlight range: B9:B14 (the units should appear as the x axis)
   e) enter the title and axis labels as shown, the legend is automatic
   f) choose the preferred option for displaying the chart

4 To use the model, enter the four items of data into cells B5, C5, D5, F5 in the input box. Do not enter data elsewhere

Try What if? scenarios by changing this data – the figures and chart will recalculate.

'What if?' analysis and 'worst-case' scenarios

Using a spreadsheet enables a business to rapidly explore different possibilities by changing key variables such as price or fixed cost. The spreadsheet automatically recalculates the figures, giving immediate answers to questions such as 'What if we need to reduce our prices by 10 per cent?' or 'What if our costs increase by 5 per cent?'

It is useful to examine what will happen in the 'worst-case scenario' – the worst that can happen. A business will want to know if it can survive in such a case.

case study 1.10 — Camelot Coaches

Arthur King, the proprietor of Camelot Coaches is planning his next trip, the Tintagel Tour. The price will include an overnight stay in a guest house and entrance to historic Tintagel Island. Estimates are:

- driver's wages: £60
- fuel: £70
- entrance to the island: £4 per person
- guesthouse: £20 per person
- administration for the tour: £600
- price: £50 per person.

The coach is a 50-seater and Arthur expects to sell 35 tickets.

activity

1 Identify the fixed and variable costs of the tour.
2 Enter all relevant details into the input box of your spreadsheet model (four items of data in all). Print this off and save it under a suitable name.
3 Will the tour break even? If so, calculate the margin of safety.
4 What profit (or loss) will Arthur make if his estimates are correct?
5 Develop the spreadsheet to show the margin of safety automatically.
6 Arthur asks you to try the following 'what if? scenarios' and to explain what they show (start each time from the original figures above).
   a) What if the fuel cost is £100?
   b) What if entrance to the island is £6?
   c) What if only 25 people buy tickets?

remember

You will need an extra input and output box.

Limitations of break-even forecasting

The usefulness of any forecast will depend upon the accuracy of the estimates used. The further ahead we forecast, the less accurate it is likely to be.

Break-even forecasting assumes a simple proportional relationship between output, variable costs and sales revenue which is why the lines are straight on the chart. In practice, this may not hold true. For example:

- we may give discounts to achieve extra sales and we may receive discounts if we buy materials in bulk (gaining economies of scale)
- it is also unlikely that wages to production staff are paid in direct proportion to production. There will usually be a basic wage and, at least in the short-term, we cannot simply lay off staff when there is less work and re-employ them as orders pick up (although employers may wish to do so).

Break-even analysis is, however, useful as a guide to future action in the short term and within present production capacity.

Profit maximisation

Traditionally it has been assumed that private sector businesses attempt to maximise their profits, i.e. to make the most profit possible by maximising sales revenue whilst minimising costs.

Businesses use a number of tactics for increasing sales revenue:

■ providing products that people will buy in preference to competing products. This may involve the use of branding to create identity and loyalty ('the real thing', 'the only flame-grilled burger'), innovation (new and more advanced products such as WAP mobile phones), providing affordable quality (John Lewis – 'never knowingly undersold'). Reducing prices may attract extra sales and will increase revenue where demand is elastic, i.e. where a reduction in price leads to a more than proportional increase in demand

■ gaining control of a market to reduce the number of competitors. This enables a business to charge higher prices because there are fewer substitutes to compete with their products. Tactics may involve setting up 'barriers' that make it difficult for new firms to enter the market (perhaps by making exclusive agreements with suppliers who then cannot supply new businesses), buying up existing firms (e.g. in the grocery market Morrison has taken over Safeway, whilst Tesco is buying up local convenience stores), putting firms out of business by taking their customers (local shops are hit when a new superstore locates nearby).

Costs can be minimised by a number of tactics, including:

■ use of new technology to replace staff – the decline of employment in manufacturing over recent years is partly due to this

■ introducing flexible working where staff are paid only when they are productive. This may take the form of part-time working, flexible hours, fixed-term contracts, home working or **outsourcing**. The idea is to convert staff wages into variable costs related to production rather than fixed costs related to time

■ locating to economies where wage rates are low, India, China or Korea for example. Increasing globalisation makes this possible

We return to this theme in Unit 6.

■ expanding in order to gain economies of scale – a large organisation can gain cost reductions. For example, it can buy in bulk so that unit costs (the cost of each item) is cheaper. Alternatively, it may install new equipment to replace staff. These measures may be too expensive for smaller businesses

■ outsourcing – it may be cheaper to buy-in services run by specialist providers (e.g. cleaning, security, maintenance, delivery) rather than running these in-house

■ economy measures – achieved by monitoring costs and cutting back on unnecessary expenses ('belt tightening')

■ delayering – flattening the organisational **hierarchy** by cutting out a layer. Middle managers are often the ones to go as their work may be carried out by computer technology or delegated (passed) to staff lower down the organisation. For example, in November 2004 Sainsbury axed 750 head office managers.

The need to remain competitive forces businesses to review their costs constantly. Savings may be achieved through genuine efficiency measures such as more efficient use of materials, conserving energy through fuel-efficient vehicles, using insulation to save heat, recycling waste, re-organising work to save time, installing new technology, and so on. However, when cost-cutting means not doing things properly, it may have serious ethical implications, that is, it may result in the damaging exploitation of people or the environment:

- people may be put at risk, paid too little or worked too hard
- animals may be kept in inhumane conditions and ill-treated
- the environment may be polluted or valuable natural resources wasted.

We deal with these issues in detail when we look at business ethics on page 30.

The importance of profit

The Tesco diagram on page 11 shows that businesses need profits in order to reward their owners and reinvest for future growth. There is evidence that in practice businesses aim for secure profits rather than maximum profits.

Growth

How do businesses grow? There are two possibilities:

- internal or **organic growth** – where a business ploughs back (or reinvests) its profits to fund future growth. This is steady sustainable growth but may take many years
- external growth – where a business either merges with, or takes over, other businesses. This provides a faster route to becoming a 'big business'.

Tactics for achieving growth may include various forms of integration:

- horizontal integration takes place where a business expands its present operations. Examples include Morrisons take-over of Safeway and the merger between Lloyds and TSB into a single, larger bank. Such tactics enable a business to increase its **market share** and gain economies of scale
- lateral integration takes place when a business diversifies its product range to gain access to different markets. For example, Philip Morris, owner of the Marlborough cigarette brand, has diversified into food products to counter the threat of legislation and compensation claims driven by anti-smoking pressure groups, and supermarkets now also sell electrical goods, clothes, financial services, gas, electricity and even property
- vertical integration occurs when a business moves into other activities along the supply chain. A retailer, for example, may expand into wholesaling or manufacturing. The holiday company My Travel (formerly Airtours) operates all along the holiday supply chain by selling tickets to holiday-makers, operating ships and planes and running its own hotels.

case study   Arriva

1.11

Arriva began as a motorcyle shop, moved into motor retailing and in 1980 bought the Grey-Green bus company. Like Stagecoach, Arriva benefited from the deregulation of local bus services. Today it is one of largest transport operators in Europe.

In 2003 Arriva stated that 'our business will grow through acquisition, better service delivery, innovation and marketing'. In other words they will take over other businesses when this is appropriate and will also expand organically.

activity

1 What sort of integration occurs if:
   a) a bus company such as National Express takes over other bus companies?
   b) a bus company such as Stagecoach also runs rail operations?
   c) an airline such as easyJet has set up a call centre to sell its own tickets?
2 How exactly did deregulation benefit Arriva?

How is growth measured?

Tesco plc

The Table 1.5 shows a number of ways in which growth at Tesco can be measured.

Table 1.5 Ways in which growth at Tesco can be measured

Year ended February	2001	2002	2003	2004	2005
Group sales, £m	22,585	25,401	28,280	33,557	37,070
Group profit before tax, £m	1,054	1,201	1,361	1,600	1,962
Number of UK stores	692	729	1,982	1,878	1,780
Business value, £m	5,392	5,566	6,559	8,043	9,057

Figure 1.15

Tesco share price, September 2004 to August 2005

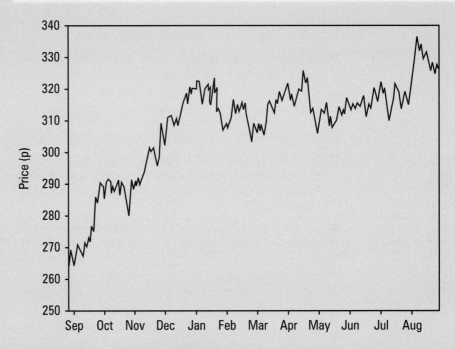

Figure 1.16

Tesco's market share, March 2005: £1 in every £8 spent in UK shops goes to Tesco

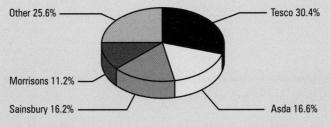

Other 25.6% — Tesco 30.4%
Morrisons 11.2%
Sainsbury 16.2% — Asda 16.6%

activity

Write, in the style of your chosen paper, a newspaper article to summarise the information above. Quote relevant figures, include at least one new chart and provide your own title. Up-date the information wherever possible and provide your sources.

■ Sales and market share – companies attempt to gain a larger share of the market by tempting customers away from competing businesses. Figure 1.16 shows that Tesco gained a larger share of the market than its rivals. In 2004, Tesco and Sainsbury could have grown by buying their rival Safeway. However, the government's Competition Commission prevented this. The Commission will usually stop take-overs leading to a market share greater than 25 per cent if they feel that this will reduce competition and customer choice. What was the result of their 2006 investigation into UK Supermarkets?

■ Level of profit – Investors expect businesses to increase profits from year to year. This can be difficult to achieve in a competitive environment. Tesco, however, has been highly successful in this respect; in 2005 they became the first UK company to make an annual profit of £2 million.

■ Number of outlets – a retailer might wish to grow by opening more stores, both nationally and internationally. A manufacturer might open factories in other countries. This should also lead to a growth in market share. In 2003 Domino's Pizza plc announced: 'Quality growth is a vision … our ambitious plans were realised with the opening of 50 new stores.'

■ Shareholder value – company objectives usually include increasing shareholder value, in other words making the business more valuable so that each share is worth more. To understand this we must look at company shares and share prices.

Why do companies issue shares?
Companies sell new issues of shares in order to raise extra capital. If the company is a plc, these shares may then be traded (second-hand) on the stock market for the going price.

Investors buy shares to gain:

■ capital growth – if the price rises, shares may be sold at a profit

■ income – if the company makes profits, the shareholders will receive dividends - a payment for each share they hold

■ influence – shareholders can vote at the company's AGM (annual general meeting) to appoint and remove directors. Sometimes those critical of a company may buy shares in order to use the AGM to protest about policies. Supporters of environmental pressure groups, for example, may buy oil company shares for this reason. Majority shareholders may exert considerable influence and may even take over the company.

See page 19 for a look at the 2005 take-over of Manchester United plc.

Why do share prices rise and fall?
Shares that are in demand by investors will rise in price, those not in demand will fall. A number of factors influence the demand for shares, including:

■ the rise or fall in company profits (Can you see a link between Tesco's rising profits and the share price?)

■ announcements about future prospects of the business - when Shell announced that its oil reserves were less than expected, the share price fell

■ opinions of experts in the media - some companies are tipped as good investments. This happened with some dot.com companies in the 1990s

■ external (**PESTEL**) factors such as the general economic climate, world events, trends and fashions. World share prices fell after the 9/11 terrorist attack on New York with airlines badly affected

PESTEL is examined on page 46.

■ take-over activity - if a firm is subject to a take-over bid, the share price tends to rise as a result of buying activity. The price of Abbey National rose when it was the subject of the bid from Grupo Santander of Spain.

Market indicators
Investors and analysts study trends in share prices over time. The most widely used indices are:

■ **FTSE-100** (or **'footsie'**) based on the 100 most valuable UK companies

■ FTSE all share index (900+ listed companies with £40m+ market capitalisation).

Measuring the value of a business

The worth of a business can be measured in two ways:

- by the bottom line on the balance sheet called the shareholders' funds. This is the 'asset value' after any debts have been paid. Asset value increases when a company 'ploughs back' profits

- by the total value of the company's shares on the stock market. This is called 'market capitalisation' and it will change as the share price rises and falls.

If market capitalisation falls below asset value, the company is under-valued, the shares are cheap and the company might be ripe for a take-over. This is one reason why company directors are concerned about a falling share price.

With the 'dot com' companies such as lastminute.com, the opposite happened; the share price was too high because internet companies were fashionable. Eventually prices crashed as investors tried to sell

Company directors aim to increase both asset value and the share price.

assignment focus

1   If one of your chosen businesses is a plc, plot its share price on a weekly basis. Look out for news items that may explain why its price rises and falls as it does. It is useful to plot the appropriate index on the same chart to see whether the price is behaving in the same way as other comparable companies. A website such as www.londonstockexchange.co.uk will do this for you.

2   Have the businesses that you have chosen to study grown? Take each of the measures of growth in turn and look at trends over the last two years. Show the five-year trend if possible.

3   Listen for the level of the FTSE-100 (footsie) each day on the news or look it up in a newspaper or on the internet.

Ethics

Business **ethics** are:

> 'moral guidelines for the conduct of business based upon what is right, wrong and fair'
> *Source*: *Collins Dictionary of Business*

As businesses strive for higher profits, or simply to survive in highly competitive markets, they may be tempted to cut costs or raise revenues by any means possible. Newspapers may print an intrusive or misleading personal story to increase circulation, a manufacturer may run a promotional campaign using sensational material that is in poor taste. Benetton, the clothing company, for example, ran an advertisement showing a man dying of AIDS.

Similarly, in the drive for lower costs a businesses may be tempted to 'cut corners', to do things 'on the cheap' and generally avoid responsibilities which may take time and cost money to carry out properly. Where this results in a detrimental effect upon stakeholders or upon the environment in general there is an ethical problem. Examples might be:

- exploiting vulnerable staff through poor pay and working conditions - an accusation levelled at a number of global clothing brands with factories in the the South Pacific

- using cheaper, substandard materials or poor workmanship with the result that customers may be put in danger. For example, poor building practices were blamed for the high number of casualties in a recent Turkish earthquake

- pollution of the environment through noise, light, damaging production methods or the dumping of waste. The actions of oil companies in Nigeria and Alaska and loggers in the rainforests of Borneo are examples of this. At a local level, builders may 'fly-tip' rubble by the roadside rather than pay council fees for proper disposal

- poor maintenance of equipment, vehicles, railway tracks, etc., which may result in injury to employees or customers.

Notice that many unethical practices are illegal, but some are not. One problem is that global businesses operate in countries with different laws.

case study 1.13 — Ethical investment

Co-operative Financial Services comprises the Co-operative Bank, CIS insurance and Smile, the internet bank. The organisation gives a high priority to ethical investment. It will not support businesses or governments which fail on human rights, the arms trade, trade and labour rights, environmental sustainability, genetic modification and animal welfare.

CIS manages £20 billion of customers' funds that it invests in shares, property and bonds. It vets companies before investing and is able to influence the behaviour of those companies in which it does invest by voting at the AGM. The CIS Ethical Engagement Policy has been drawn up after asking customers about their ethical concerns. It is the first to be published by an insurance company.

The Co-operative Bank screens customers and refuses services to businesses in conflict with its ethical policies.

activity

1 Look at the personal finance section in the weekend newspapers for information on ethical investment. Alternatively, use the nternet (e.g. moneyfacts.co.uk).
2 CIS customers are interested in ethical issues. Look at what the businesses that you are studying have to say about their approach to ethical matters.
3 a) What do you know about the conditions in which farm animals are raised and transported? Look at the website for Compassion in World Farming to fill in your knowledge.
   b) Do you think that people's awareness of these matters will change their buying habits – or is it all about cost and taste?

case study 1.14 — Safety and saving costs

Bhopal, India 1984

In 1984, lethal gas leaked from the Bhopal factory of the US chemical company Union Carbide. The result was widespread death and illness amongst the local population. The accident was caused by safety lapses but most of those affected were poor and without the means to take legal action against the company.

Union Carbide did ultimately make a one-off compensation payment, but media coverage in 2004 showed that the clean-up operation was still not complete 20 years after the disaster.

Paddington Rail Crash 1999

In October 1999, more than 30 passengers died in a collision between a Great Western train and a Thames train just outside London's Paddington station. The investigation found that a series of safety failures had contributed to the accident.

Railtrack, the company responsible for the track, had been placed in a difficult position. As a plc it had a duty to make profits to reward its shareholders, but as a provider of a public service was also required to spend millions of pounds on providing a safe rail system. There were suggestions that in an effort to keep down costs, the company had put rail passengers and employees at risk.

Chief Executive Gerald Corbett denied that the company was at fault but admitted that the crash 'had changed everything'. Railtrack was no longer able to attract funds from shareholders and the government has since replaced it with Network Rail, a not-for-profit organisation.

activity

The actions listed in Table 1.6 will all save costs. Are they ethical, undesirable but necessary or unethical? Are any of them illegal?

Make a copy of the table and complete it.

Table 1.6 Ethical, unethical or undesirable but necessary?

	Ethical	Undesirable but necessary	Unethical
Saving electricity by recycling heat from freezers			
A contractor uses less cement in a bridge than the designer specified			
A supermarket pays UK farmers as low a price as possible for vegetables knowing they have no alternative market			
Introducing fuel efficient vehicles			
Asking employees to buy their own protective clothing			
Cutting back on medical checks and machine maintenance			
Disposing of liquid waste into rivers and smoke into the atmosphere			
Relocating production to developing countries where wages are lower			
Replacing staff with computers			
Delaying payments to suppliers as long as possible			
Keeping battery hens in small cages (cheaper than free-range egg production where chickens have space to roam)			
Introducing new design techniques to eliminate materials waste			
Transporting live animals thousands of miles in cramped conditions			

Do the businesses you have chosen follow ethical or 'green' policies such as: conservation of resources, dealing fairly with suppliers, observing animal rights, protecting the environment, supporting good causes, etc? (There may be a reference in the annual report.)

The cost of unethical behaviour

In all of these cases, business activity creates **social costs** that society rather than the business has to pay. For example: where business activity results in illness or injury, there will be costs to the health service (paid for by the tax-payer), alternatively damage to the environment may reduce in the quality of our lives so that we all pay.

Business costs paid by those outside of the business are called externalities.

The government tries to encourage businesses to take their ethical responsibilities seriously. This is achieved partly through voluntary codes of practices, where business agree standards of acceptable behaviour, and partly through legislation, which can lead to fines and even imprisonment. The idea is that ethical practices are no longer the cheap alternative.

Stelios Ioannou, head of easyJet, recognised this when he said: 'If you think heath and safety is expensive, try an accident.'

However, in the global economy businesses may still avoid their responsibilities by moving production to those countries where these laws (and the associated costs) do not apply. In such cases, pressure groups such as Greenpeace and Friends of the Earth can bring pressure to bear by alerting consumers to unethical practices.

In Unit 6 we see that the Internet may be used by campaigning pressure groups to circulate negative information about businesses.

Use the internet to research the following, both of which have an ethical dimension:
- Chinese cockle-pickers drown in Morecambe Bay
- anti-capitalism, anti-globalisation and the G8 summit

There is evidence that consumer pressure is an effective means of improving business practices; sometimes more effective than the law. Shell, for example, found it necessary to have a complete re-think after its environmental record received adverse publicity in the late 1990s (the '$ – hell in Nigeria' campaign 'Shell' changed to 'hell'). Many businesses now include ethical issues in their corporate aims and objectives, and some use their ethical stance as part of their publicity. For example, the Body Shop works with people in developing countries, the Co-operative Bank will only investment in ethical projects, B&Q works with local communities in New Guinea for sustainable timber supplies, Birds Eye has stopped fishing for cod in the North Sea where supplies are at risk, and so on.

assignment focus

1   To achieve P1, for each business:
    a)   Identify the business objectives (giving your sources).
    b)   Explain the activities through which each business attempts to meet its objectives.
        - You may achieve M1 if, for each business, you clearly explain how each of the specific business activities helps to achieve particular objectives.
        - You may achieve D1 if you can effectively evaluate the success each business has had in achieving its stated objectives through the activities you have mentioned. (You must use clear evidence and give your sources for this – charts and tables of figures may be useful.)

2   This task will enable you to illustrate the calculation of the break-even point to achieve P1.
    a)   You will need to create a set of data to include: a product, a time period (perhaps a year), maximum capacity, variable costs per unit, period fixed costs, sale price per unit.
    b)   Use this data to set up a break-even forecast comprising:
        - a table of costs, revenues and profits at given levels of output and sales
        - a corresponding breakeven chart (fully labelled)
    You may provide this evidence either manually or by using an electronic spreadsheet.
    c)   Explain why a business might set up a break-even forecast and use figures from your chart to explain exactly what this technique tells a business.
        - Give examples of how and when break-even forecasting could be used by one of the businesses you have chosen to investigate and why this is so important in planning to achieve business objectives.
    You may achieve M2 when you apply break-even to a business you have studied. You must analyse how the business might use break-even calculations to set out SMART objectives.
        - In your answer, suggest items that are likely to make up fixed costs, variable costs and units of output for your business.
        - You should also mention any limitations of using the technique.

Functional Activities

In order for a business to achieve its organisational aims and objectives it will need to carry out a range of functions.

In a small business (perhaps a sole trader or partnership), the owner(s) will be directly involved in carrying out most or all of the organisational functions. A sole trader running a small cornershop, for example, will need to undertake the tasks shown in Figure 1.17.

Figure 1.17

Functions of small businesses

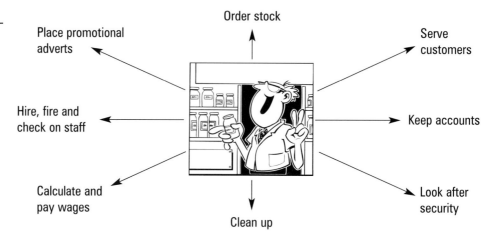

A larger business will need to employ specialist staff to look after functions such as operations, finance, marketing, human resources and administration. Separate departments, or functional areas, will be set up and the business will begin to take on a formal organisational structure.

It becomes necessary to identify how these employees will communicate, for example who is in charge, who gives orders and who carries them out. A hierarchy (a structure with different levels of authority) will develop, like the one shown in Figure 1.18. These may be tall, with many levels, or flat, with few levels.

Figure 1.18

The organisation chart of VHF Ltd, a manufacturer of radios

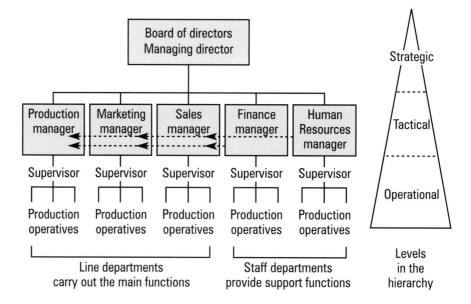

In VHF Ltd, five functional areas work together to achieve the business objectives.

- The line functions of production, marketing and sales all help to achieve the main business objectives of making and selling radios.

- The staff functions support these main functions – the finance department by ensuring that there are sufficient funds, human resources by making sure that the business has the appropriate workforce.

The organisation chart shows the different levels of authority within the hierarchy. A chain of command (the scalar chain) runs from the top of the organisation down through each line department to the shop floor. Employees at each level are managed by a line manager directly above them in their organisational function.

Turning (strategic) organisational aims into SMART (operational) targets

Notice that the hierarchy forms a pyramid shape. It is narrow at the top where the real power lies. Here a relatively small number directors make policy decisions and draw up the corporate plan showing strategic objectives. For example, a supermarket might aim to increase sales or to move into banking, a distribution company might aim to go multinational, an oil company might wish to change its corporate image by re-branding itself as an energy company so as to appear 'greener' and more 'caring'.

The hierarchy is broader in the middle where a larger number of managers devise tactics for achieving these objectives. For example, if the strategy is to increase sales the tactic might be to employ more sales staff or run an advertising campaign. Costs will be involved and budgets will be agreed together with systems for monitoring these.

The hierarchy is broadest at the base where a larger number of operatives and clerical workers run the business from day-to-day under supervision from their line managers.

Operational vs strategic objectives

In the early 1990s, following a number of breakouts from Parkhurst Prison on the Isle of Wight, opposition MPs called for the Home Secretary to resign. (The Home Secretary has overall responsibility for UK prisons.) His reply was, 'This is an operational matter not a strategic matter.' In other words, the prison governor, in charge of day-to-day operations, was responsible not the Home Secretary, who decided overall policy.

Monitoring progress

Organisations set SMART targets in order to focus their efforts and provide a way of monitoring progress. The customer charters drawn up by public sector organisations are a good example. Commitments to the public may appear as: NHS patient waiting lists, benchmarks for exam success at schools, police clear-up rates, tube and rail targets for running to timetable. These organisations will monitor their performance and report on the extent to which these targets are being achieved.

---

case study

1.15

Customer charters

On page 20, we set out Tramlink's service aims. Their SMART objectives are shown below.

A CHARTER FOR TRAMLINK PASSENGERS

Welcome to your charter

Our targets:

- 98% of scheduled tram kilometres will run.
- 97% reliability of information on 'next tram' indicators.
- 97% availability of a ticket machine at your stop.
- All stops cleaned daily.
- All trams cleaned internally and externally before starting their day's work.
- All trams cleared of litter every three hours between 0930 and 1830 on Mondays to Saturdays.

Source: Extracted from the Department for Transport Tramlink customer charter, 2004

---

activity

Obtain a customer charter for a local or national public service such as the Post Office, a hospital trust or a transport operator. Summarise the general aims and then the SMART targets that are set for each of them.

The range of functional areas

The line functions to be found across a range of businesses include those listed in Table 1.7. Notice that functional areas must work together to achieve organisational goals. The staff functions listed in Table 1.8 support the line departments.

Table 1.7 Functional areas and activities

Functional area	Activity
R&D (Research and Development)	Research and development can involve: ■ invention – discovering new techniques and products. Both large and small businesses can come up with good ideas ■ innovation – ways of applying these ideas to make a product. This can be highly expensive and generally only very large organisations have R&D sections. The largest spenders are companies dealing in: pharmaceuticals, chemicals, transport and new technology. R&D is about developing new goods. Service providers tend to carry out product development (e.g. the Halifax developed Intelligent Finance, a new bank account) as part of the marketing process.
Link with other functions	R&D will work with design to achieve higher sales and market share through 'cutting edge' products. Ethical objectives may be achieved through environmentally-friendly products such as components that can be recycled.
Design	Design translates the new idea from R&D into a product that can be marketed. It concentrates on appearance, safety, performance, cost and quality.
Link with other functions	Design will work with R&D as shown above.
Purchasing, sourcing or procurement	This section locates and buys in supplies of the right quality, in the right quantities, at the right time and at the right price.
Link with other functions	Goods must be purchased ready for production or for sale. These goods must then be delivered on time. Purchasing therefore links with production, or operations, and with distribution.
Production (or Operations)	In this context, production means manufacturing goods or assembling them from components in the factory or workshop. Notice that retailers selling own brand goods usually contract other manufacturers to make them to order. Tesco-branded mobile phones, for example, are produced by mmO2. Retailers and other service providers tend to carry out their core activity through an operations function (rather than a production function) since they do not actually manufacture.
Link with other functions	The production department of a manufacturer will produce goods to design specifications. It must purchase appropriate supplies and take delivery on time (often just-in-time). Production schedules are geared to satisfy marketing and sales targets – Dell, for example, manufactures computers to demand. The operations section of a service provider, such as a retailer, will similarly work with purchasing, distribution, marketing and sales to make supplies available to meet customer demand.
Marketing	Market research identifies customer needs and matches products with markets to achieve: higher sales and market share through clear targeting of the market, effective promotion and competitive pricing. Marketing activity is carried out through the 'Four Ps' to ensure: the right *product*, at the right *price*, in the right *place*. *Promotion* ensures that customers are informed about the product and are persuaded to buy it.
Link with other functions	Marketing should work with production, or operations, to ensure that goods sold can be produced on time and at the correct price.
Sales	The sales function involves taking and satisfying customer orders and dealing with customer accounts.
Link with other functions	Sales may be part of marketing or work closely alongside. As with marketing, sales must work closely with production (or operations) and with distribution if goods are delivered to customers.
Distribution (or Logistics)	The distribution function links the organisation with the supply chain by moving stocks of raw materials, components or finished goods into the business from suppliers. Where a business has it own warehouses, it will also move goods to factories or retail outlets within the business. Many organisations also distribute goods to customers after sale.
Link with other functions	The distribution section works closely with: ■ the production department of a manufacturer (the factory) where components are needed to meet schedules ■ the retail section of a chain of stores where the shop shelves need to be filled ■ the sales section might also need to arrange for delivery of goods to customers. Increasingly new technology and more responsive distribution systems allow businesses to save on storage costs by ordering goods for delivery just-in-time (JIT) for use. The importance of distribution can be seen when it goes wrong. In 2005, car production at MG-Rover finally stopped when the company ran out of components; suppliers had refused to leave stocks without payment. In 2004, Sainsbury's new £3bn logistics system was scrapped after it 'lost' large amounts of stock and shelves remained empty. Effective distribution, on the other hand, may improve customer satisfaction through efficient delivery times. The use of cleaner fuel, more effective journey planning and night-time journeys to avoid traffic congestion may help achieve environmental objectives. Frequently the distribution function is outsourced to specialist logistics firms.

Table 1.8 Staff functions and activities

Staff function	Activity
Human Resources (HR)	The HR function plans future staffing needs and helps maintain a suitable workforce for all sections within the organisation. HR will keep employee records, recruit and dismiss staff, comply with employment law, deal with health, safety and welfare, industrial relations, discipline and appeals, set up training and staff development and agree systems for monitoring and appraising employees.
Link with other functions	HR will help all functional areas across the organisation to get the right staff and improve their performance.
Finance	The finance function co-ordinates revenues and spending across all functional areas so that the business will have sufficient funds to survive and generate profits to reward its owners.
Link with other functions	Financial accountants record and report on the actual results of the business. They record the sales, borrowing and expenditure that take place across the various functional areas. They then draw up reports for the benefit of the shareholders. The yearly profit and loss account and balance sheet (which shows the value of the business) are required by law. Management accounting provides estimates for use by the various functional managers. We look at cashflow forecasts on page 44 and break-even forecasts on page 46. This information allows managers to plan future action, make informed decisions and control business performance.
Administration	Administration includes the office function and may also be responsible for other areas, such as premises, security, catering and maintenance.
Link with other functions	This function involves setting up organised systems and routines so that the different areas within the business can operate smoothly. For example, the office in a college may distribute post, direct visitors, keep class registers and arrange for the maintenance of photocopiers.
MIS (Management information Services)	This section gets appropriate and good quality (accurate and up-to-date) information to managers as and when they need it. The use of ICT enables them to collect and analyse data and produce detailed reports quickly. MIS will gather and process: ■ internal information about business resources, such as staff, finance, stocks etc. ■ performance, departmental targets, etc. ■ external information, e.g. industry benchmarks, competitor information, supplier prices, etc
Link with other functions	This information will keep the various functional managers informed so as to take appropriate decisions in their day-to-day work. For example, MIS in a college will provide departmental heads with details such as class sizes, student attendance figures, success rates, the ethnic and gender mix of staff and students, the hours worked by lecturers, national benchmarks (standards to be achieved) and so on.

Outsourcing: contracting-out business functions

Rather than employing its own staff to provide each function, a business may decide that it is more effective or cheaper to outsource (or buy-in) a service from another business. Thus specialist firms may be contracted to run security, catering, cleaning, payroll, delivery services and the maintenance of equipment such as photocopiers or computers. Similarly, consultants may be brought in to help set up a new MIS system or design a business website.

Local authorities use c**ompulsory competitive tendering (CCT)**, a system in which services such as refuse collection are contracted to companies, such as Cleanaway and Accord, where they offer best value for money. The Home Office has outsourced the running of some prison services to security companies such as Group 4.

Outsourcing has a number of advantages. An organisation simply pays the agreed rate and the job is done. Human resources issues such as staff training, payroll, providing cover for sickness, recruitment of new staff and redundancy are the responsibility of the contractor. However, not all outsourcing is successful. In 2000 Sainsbury set up an IT outsourcing deal with Accenture. This was scrapped in 2004 at a cost of £140m.

case study 1.16

Calling out around the world ...: call centres and the outsourcing of customer services

Call centres (telephone services providing help and information to customers day and night) have grown dramatically since the late 1990s. Since location is not important, centres can be set up away from business to take advantage of lower costs. By 2003, businesses were making further cost reductions by outsourcing to low-cost providers abroad. India with its highly educated, English-speaking, low-wage workforce became especially popular.

By 2004, 30 UK companies had call centres in India among them leading banks such as Lloyds TSB, HSBC and Abbey, insurance firms such as Aviva (Norwich Union) and the rail enquiry service – the Britain's busiest telephone number with its 50 million calls per year. Direct marketing companies also made use of cheap international calls to sell double glazing, loans and kitchens through sales staff in Bangalore and Mumbai.

Good for the UK?

British trades unions fear job losses and have campaigned against this trend. Customers have also complained about the quality of service, for example accents may be hard to understand and, it is claimed, operators do not always sufficiently understand the Western way of life.

Perhaps of more importance is the concern about security issues. Under the Data Protection Act, personal information leaving a country can only go to another country with a good level of consumer protection. However, in June 2005 the *Sun* newspaper claimed that a Delhi call centre employee had attempted to sell personal details of 1,000 Britons to one of its reporters. These details of bank accounts, passports, credit cards and medical bills would have allowed criminals to clone cards, buy goods over the internet or raid bank accounts.

The NatWest bank has tried to take advantage of these concerns by advertising 'No call centres outside the UK', whilst the GNER rail company announces that it is proud to have call-centres in Newcastle.

The future?

Studies claim that 'It's a win-win situation for countries that allow outsourcing and the countries that receive it.' The UK government says that it has no plans to prevent British firms outsourcing work to India or elsewhere.

In future hundreds more British companies are expected to outsource and the Indian industry says it will difficult to recruit enough high-quality staff to meet demand.

activity

Call centres are popular with the banking and insurance industries because costs of providing customer service are reduced.

1   What are the advantages and disadvantages for customers? (The alternative may be to go into a high street branch, write or telephone during business hours.)
2   Find out who carries out security, cleaning, canteen and maintenance services in your school or college. If these services are outsourced, why do you think this is?

assignment focus

1   Which functional activities does each of your businesses have?
2   Which of the organisational objectives does each help to achieve?

Fulfilling organisational functions in different sized businesses

The type of organisational structure used by a business will have a major impact on performance. The ideal structure will enable managers and employees to communicate effectively as they work towards business objectives.

Centralised control

In smaller businesses, sole traders and partners will provide or directly control most of the functions themselves. Small to medium companies, such as VHF Radios (our example on page 36), will set up specialist functional areas, but the board of directors still retains central control.

Centralised control allows speedy decision-making as fewer people are involved and less consultation is needed. This can be important when responding to changing business conditions.

Decentralised control

As organisations grow and diversify into different products, it becomes difficult and inefficient to take every decision from the top. Large nationals and multinationals may be conveniently split into separate product or geographical divisions; the directors retain overall control, but responsibility for specific decisions is delegated to lower levels of management.

For example, Arriva plc has created three divisions (Figure 1.19).

Figure 1.19

Arriva's decentralised control

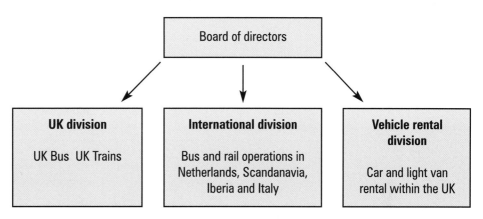

Large global organisations such as ICI have introduced a still greater degree of **decentralised control**. Figure 1.20 shows how ICI's Polyurethane division is structured. The division's managing director will still work within the guidelines set by the main ICI board, but is largely autonomous and is accountable for divisional costs and profits.

Figure 1.20

ICI's divisional structure

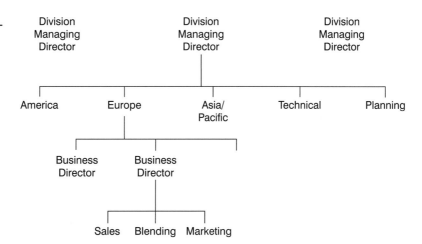

Interdependence of functional activities

When a gardener at NASA (North American Space Agency) was asked by a visiting president what his job was, he replied, 'Putting a man on the moon'. It is true that employees at all levels across the organisation must in some way contribute to the achievement of the organisational objectives. How effectively functional areas work together in doing this depends upon a number of factors and in particular:

- the structure of the organisation – this determines how well the various sections of the business can communicate. Where a business is not succeeding, the management may re-organise to create a more effective working relationship between the functional areas

- the style of management – the **attitude** of management to its employees. Successful businesses involve staff and allow them to see their contribution

- the culture of the organisation – the general way in which the management and workforce think and do things.

case study 1.17 — Sir Terry Leahy

Tesco is now the world's third largest retailer in the world (after Wal-Mart of the USA and Carrefour of France). Chief executive Sir Terry Leahy believes that a number of factors have contributed.

Listening to customers, rewarding staff and encouraging staff loyalty and progression are important; a number of people who began at the bottom have worked up into top management. The organisational structure plays a vital part. Tesco is a flat organisation with only six layers between the trolley pushers and the chief executive. This means that directors are not remote figures and communication through the organisation becomes easier.

Tesco has decentralised control. Directors recognise that decisions about stores in Thailand are better taken by people on the spot. They know the problems, understand local conditions and so can act more quickly and effectively than head office in England.

Source: Sir Terry Leahy, Speech to Institute of Directors, April 2005

activity

Tesco sells FMCGs (fast moving consumer goods) and so has to keep the shelves continually stacked.
1 Which functional areas work together in achieving this?
2 What services do you think Tesco human resources staff may provide for staff in the marketing department?

assignment focus

- To achieve P3, for one of the business organisations that you have selected, identify and describe the different functional activities carried out within the business. Say which of the business aims and objectives each functional area is designed to achieve.

- You may achieve M3 if you analyse the contribution that each functional activity makes to the achievement of specific business aims and objectives. Mention how areas work together in doing this.

Survival and Growth

The two main financial objectives of a business are:

- cashflow – a business must generate enough cash to pay its day-to-day running costs, otherwise it will not survive

- profitability – ultimately a business will aim to make sufficient profits to reward the owner(s). It will also hope to retain some profit to help with future growth.

The financial plan

Each year a business will draw up a plan for achieving its objectives. This will bring together estimated costs and revenues from all functional areas.

- The revenue of a business comes from those areas directly involved in production or operations; those with goods or services to sell, e.g. the production department of a manufacturer, the teaching departments of a college, the paint-shop of a motor garage.

- Costs are incurred by all functional areas.

Clearly the revenue must exceed the costs in order for profits to be made. The planning process is illustrated in Figure 1.21.

If there is likely to be a cash shortage, or if the forecast profit is not sufficient, the plan must be revised. An acceptable plan must strike the right balance between the various stakeholder interests. If each functional area meets its own SMART targets, the business as a whole should achieve its objectives.

Figure 1.21

The financial planning process

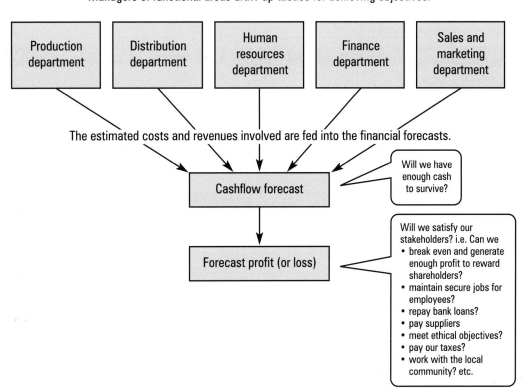

The directors set out the strategic objectives in the **corporate plan**

Managers of functional areas draw up tactics for achieving objectives.

| Production department | Distribution department | Human resources department | Finance department | Sales and marketing department |

The estimated costs and revenues involved are fed into the financial forecasts.

Cashflow forecast

Will we have enough cash to survive?

Forecast profit (or loss)

Will we satisfy our stakeholders? i.e. Can we
- break even and generate enough profit to reward shareholders?
- maintain secure jobs for employees?
- repay bank loans?
- pay suppliers
- meet ethical objectives?
- pay our taxes?
- work with the local community? etc.

The cashflow forecast: planning for survival

A business cannot survive without cash. The cashflow forecast estimates the cash available to a business over a forthcoming period – normally six or 12 months.

case study 1.18 Greenco Ltd

Greenco Ltd will begin trading in October with a share capital of £15,000. The marketing department has set a sales target for the first six months (Table 1.9). The sales price will be £10 a unit.

Table 1.9 Greenco's sales targets

	Oct	Nov	Dec	Jan	Feb	Mar	Total
Sales volume (no. of units)	1,000	1,500	2,000	2,500	2,000	3,000	12,000

The production department agrees that it can produce these goods and estimates the variable costs of production as £5 per unit, made up of:

- materials: £4 a unit
- production wages: £1 a unit.

Estimated fixed costs of the various functional areas total £44,500 as follows:

- salaries: £6,000 per month
- rent and rates: £1,500 in October and £1,500 in January
- insurance: £2,400 in October
- light and heat: £800 in December and £800 in March
- general administration: £1,000 in October, thereafter £100 per month.

Additionally, equipment costing £12,000 will be paid for in October.

The finance department at Greenco feeds all of these estimates into the cashflow forecast (Table 1.10).

Table 1.10 Cashflow forecast of Greenco Ltd, six months to March 2000

Figures rounded to £s	Oct £	Nov £	Dec £	Jan £	Feb £	Mar £	Total £
Receipts:							
Sales (of stock) @ £10	10,000	15,000	20,000	25,000	20,000	30,000	120,000
New capital	15,000						15,000
Loans, grants, etc.							0
Total receipts (A)	**25,000**	**15,000**	**20,000**	**25,000**	**20,000**	**30,000**	**135,000**
Payments:							
Purchase (of materials)	4,000	6,000	8,000	10,000	8,000	12,000	48,000
Production wages	1,000	1,500	2,000	2,500	2,000	3,000	12,000
Salaries	6,000	6,000	6,000	6,000	6,000	6,000	36,000
Rent/rates	1,500			1,500			3,000
Insurance	2,400						2,400
Light/heat			800			800	1,600
General administration	1,000	100	100	100	100	100	1,500
Equipment	12,000						12,000
Total payment (B)	**27,900**	**13,600**	**16,900**	**20,100**	**16,100**	**21,900**	**116,500**
Net cashflow (A–B)	(2,900)	1,400	3,100	4,900	3,900	8,100	18,500
add opening bank balance	0	(2,900)	(1,500)	1,600	6,500	10,400	0
Closing bank balance	**(2,900)**	**(1,500)**	**1,600**	**6,500**	**10,400**	**18,500**	**18,500**

Notice that there are three sections to the cashflow forecast:

- receipts – showing details of expected monthly cash in-flows
- payments – showing details of expected monthly cash out-flows
- a summary of the cash position, comprising:
  - net cashflow – the total receipts minus total payments for the month
  - opening balance – the balance in the bank at the start of the month. This is the previous month's closing balance. October shows zero because this is a new business and so has no previous month
  - closing bank balance – the bank balance available at the end of each month. This 'bottom-line' is the most important figure.

Reading a cashflow forecast

Warning signs might be:

- a negative figure on the bottom line, which indicates a cash shortage. This is usually shown in parentheses (brackets)

- a reducing bottom line, which may indicate that, although there are sufficient funds at present, problems may occur in future

- a large and growing bottom-line, which shows a healthy cashflow. However, it can be inefficient to build up a large surplus of cash; it may be better transferred to a higher interest account, invested in new equipment or used to pay off loans.

---

activity

Before reading on, look at the bottom line in Greenco's cashflow forecast.
1 a) In which months will Greenco have a cash shortage?
   b) In which month will the problem be greatest?
2 Which item is the cause of the problem?
3 What might be the consequences if no action is taken to avoid this problem?
The solutions to this activity appear below.

Greenco will have a cashflow problem during each of the first two months with the shortage of £2,900 in December being the worst. Unless action is taken, some bills will not be paid. Consequences of cash shortages might include: unpaid staff refusing to work, unpaid suppliers refusing to deliver, electricity being cut off, and so on.

Figure 1.22

Causes and solutions of cashflow problems

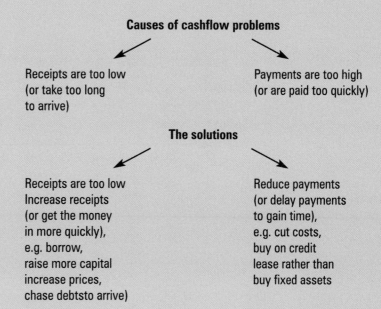

Causes of cashflow problems

Receipts are too low
(or take too long
to arrive)

Payments are too high
(or are paid too quickly)

The solutions

Receipts are too low
Increase receipts
(or get the money
in more quickly),
e.g. borrow,
raise more capital
increase prices,
chase debtsto arrive)

Reduce payments
(or delay payments
to gain time),
e.g. cut costs,
buy on credit
lease rather than
buy fixed assets

Greenco Ltd's cashflow problem

The cause of the problem is the £12,000 paid out for equipment in October. Possible solutions might be to:

- raise a loan to help pay for these fixed assets
- lease the equipment or buy it on credit so that payments are spread over the coming months
- arrange for a bank overdraft. This is not a usual way to fund fixed assets but in this case the problem is short-term and will be solved by December
- issue more shares so that the company has sufficient working capital available.

Forecasting profit

Greenco uses the same financial estimates as above to calculate the break-even point and draw a break-even chart. The calculation is:

$$\text{Break-even point} = \frac{\text{Fixed costs}}{\text{Contribution per unit}} = \frac{£44,500}{(£10 - £5)}$$
$$\text{(sales per unit - variable cost per unit)}$$

Break-even point = 8,900 units or £89,000 (8,900 units @ £10)

Table 1.11 Financial estimates

	Fixed costs for period £44,500	Variable cost Per unit £5		Sales revenue per unit £10	
Units	**Fixed Costs**	**Variable Cost**	**Total Cost**	**Sales**	**Profit/(loss)**
0	44,500	0	44,500	0	(44,500)
2,000	44,500	10,000	54,500	20,000	(34,500)
4,000	44,500	20,000	64,500	40,000	(24,500)
6,000	44,500	30,000	74,500	60,000	(14,500)
8,000	44,500	40,000	84,500	80,000	(4,500)
10,000	44,500	50,000	94,500	100,000	5,500
12,000	44,500	60,000	104,500	120,000	15,500

Figure 1.23

Greenco's break-even chart

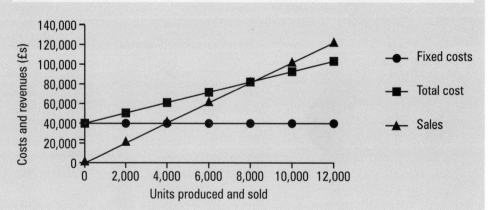

The table shows that the business will make a profit of £15,500 in the first six months thus:

		£
	Sales revenue	120,000
less	Total costs	104,500
	Profit	15,500

(Note: capital items (buying machinery, etc.) are not costs)

At the end of the year, the business will be taxed on its profits. Remaining profits can then be paid as dividends to shareholders or ploughed back into the business to increase its value.

Cash versus profit

Notice that the forecast cash (£18,500) is not the same as the forecast profit (£15,500). The two are calculated differently and so it is possible for a business to have profit and no cash, or cash and no profit. You will consider this in detail if you study the specialist financial units.

Using computer software to draw up financial forecasts

Financial forecasts may be drawn up by using either:

- commercially designed software – suitable templates are available from the **Business Link** website and from the high street banks
- a spreadsheet – a spreadsheet model that may be used for cashflow and break-even forecasts is provided on the Nelson Thornes website (www.nelsonthorne.com).

The advantages of using computer software for financial forecasting include:

- automatic calculations provide fast and accurate results once data are entered
- 'What if?' scenarios can be used – data can be varied to see the effects of different possibilities such as changing sales prices or costs
- charts can be linked to illustrate the figures. These will automatically up-date when data are changed.

activity

1. Either set up an electronic cashflow forecast or use the template on the Nelson Thornes website (www.nelsonthornes.com/btec). Enter Greenco's figures to check that it works.
2. Try out each of the alternative 'What if?' scenarios by changing the relevant figures:
   a) What if the cost of the equipment is spread evenly over the first six months?
   b) What if Greenco pays £12,000 in October for equipment but takes out a loan of £3,000?
   c) What if Greenco pays £12,000 in October for equipment but buys materials on 30-day credit? In this case, the purchases figures will be moved back a month – October to November, etc. October will read zero, and the purchases for March will appear as creditors (they will be paid in April).
   d) Suggest and try out one other solution.
3. In your opinion, which of the above is the best solution. Provide your reasons. (None of them will affect the break-even point or the final profit.)

Using the business plan to raise finance

The business plan can be used to raise extra finance. The financial forecasts provide evidence that Greenco will generate a positive bank balance by month 3 and a profit over the first six months of trading. Nevertheless, it is likely that, as a new business, it will require some security for any borrowing. This might include assets owned by the business or personal assets of directors.

Link We discuss business planning and the sources of finance in detail in Unit 5.

SWOT analysis

SWOT analysis is also known as situational analysis. **SWOT** (strengths, weaknesses, opportunities, threats) analysis is strengths, weaknesses, opportunities and threats. It is a technique used in business planning for comparing or matching an organisation's internal strengths and weaknesses with the opportunities and threats found in the external environment. This can help to identify both threats to survival and potential for growth (Table 1.12).

Table 1.12 SWOT analysis

A business can control internal factors	A *strength* is a specific asset, skill or competence found within the organisation which would help it achieve its objectives. Factors critical for success include the product that will be sold, the financial, human and physical resources available to the business and the systems that exist for managing these.	A *weakness* is a specific feature found within the organisation which could prevent it achieving its objectives. Perhaps the product is not able to compete because costs are too high, perhaps management is inexperienced or the business is unable to respond to change.
It must respond to external factors	An *opportunity* is any specific feature in the organisation's external environment (PESTEL factors) that would help it to achieve its objectives.	A *threat* is any specific feature in the organisation's external environment (PESTEL factors) which would prevent it from achieving its objectives.

PESTEL factors

Opportunities and threats from the external environment can be found under the headings political, economic, social, technological, environmental, legal, often referred to as PESTEL.

- *Political factors* relate to the actions and views of the government at Westminster, the government of the European Union and the governments of trading partners. Influences might be: raising taxes, decisions to build more homes or new transport links, providing grants to encourage regional development or declaring war.

- *Economic factors* relate to the wealth of the country. They include the level of unemployment, the rate of inflation (rising prices), interest rates, the balance of payments (between imports and exports), the level of disposable income, the level of average wages, the skills gap (the shortage of trained workers, such as plumbers, relative to demand), the price of shares on the stock market, the amount of personal debt and house prices. For example, the 2012 Olympic Games is likely to boost the economy of London.

- *Social factors* concern the views of people and their **lifestyles**. For example: businesses may be affected by fashions, the crime rate, people's aspirations, the employment of women, the religious and ethnic mix of the population, standards of education.

- *Technological factors* include new developments such as new materials, production processes, transport and communications. For example, downloaded music is replacing CDs, whilst DVDs are replacing videos. The development of the internet has been a major opportunity to businesses such as specialist retailers and a major threat to others such as record companies who find their products easily copied.

- *Environmental factors* may relate to energy needs (e.g. in 2005 hurricane Katrina disrupted the US oil supplies and drove up world oil prices), pollution of the environment by industry and the need to recycle waste. The farming industry faces threats from infections such as BSE and avian flu.

- *Legal factors* relate to the law of the land and are therefore related to political decisions. Laws affecting business include: consumer protection, employment legislation, environmental protection and health and safety legislation.

case study 1.19 | Boots Group plc: SWOT analysis

The Boots Group plc is a retail company engaged in operating drug stores. The company's business is concentrated in the UK, although it sells its products in more than 130 countries.

Table 1.13 Boots Group: SWOT analysis

Strengths	Weaknesses
■ Strong brand ownership in growth markets ■ Network of stores in the UK ■ Restructuring efforts to concentrate on 'core business'	■ Uncompetitive on pricing ■ High dependence on the UK market ■ Declining profitability
Opportunities	Threats
■ Grow local customer base through promotions ■ Trend towards self-medication ■ Growth in online retailing	■ Maturity in certain UK markets ■ Price competition has pressurised margins (medicines and pharmacies available in supermarkets) ■ Slowdown in the UK economy

Source: *Data Monitor*, 7 May 2005

activity

Complete a SWOT analysis for your school or college.

Competition – opportunity and threat

In the modern business environment, competition is the major threat to survival and being able to compete is the key to growth.

Michael Porter, the pioneer of 'competitive strategy', identified three areas in which a business can gain (and lose) competitive advantage (Figure 1.24).

Figure 1.24

The three areas of competitive advantage

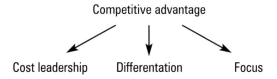

Competitive advantage

Cost leadership   Differentation   Focus

Cost leadership

Cost leadership involves reducing prices to the customer, without reducing quality. There are a number of possibilities.

■ High output reduces costs through economies of scale (see page 26) It also turns low profit margins into satisfactory profit-levels (1 million sales at 1p margin equals £10,000 profit). Large-scale organisations can also offer generous credit terms to customers ('pay nothing for six months' or 0 per cent finance).

■ Lower prices may also be achieved through more efficient production or organisation – 'getting more toothpaste out of the tube'. Tactics might include investment in new technology to cut the wage bill, buying stock just-in-time so as to cut storage and distribution costs and restructuring the organisation to improve efficiency.

Differentiation

Differentiation involves creating a unique selling point (USP) so that a product is seen as somehow distinct from the competition. Research and development may indeed develop genuinely unique products perhaps using 'cutting edge technology' such as Teflon trousers, ABS car breaking systems or mesh for filtering out mobile phone signals. Often, however, firms try to create the perception of uniqueness for products that are little different from those of competitors. Tactics for differentiation include branding to give identity ('The real thing'), quality ('lean burn engine'), customer service ('free 24-hour customer hotline') and economy ('we check our prices daily').

In Unit 3 we look in detail at tactics used by businesses to promote their products.

Focus

Focus involves identifying a particular market segment or buyer group rather than attempting to compete in the industry as a whole. A business is therefore able to reduce costs and maximise impact by targeting a selected market. For example, Saga holidays are aimed at the over-50s (the 'grey market'), magazines such as *Maxim* and *Loaded* are aimed at men in their 20s and 30s.

In Unit 3 we look in detail at how a promotional campaign may be aimed at a particular target audience.

> *remember*
>
> Fixed costs remain fixed only within present capacity. They will rise if additional capacity, for example larger premises and more managers, is taken on.

Risks associated with growth

Overtrading

Expanding a business costs money.

- If we wish to sell more, then we must produce more with the result that the variable costs of stock and production wages increase.
- If we increase capacity, then overheads such as salaries, rent and electricity are likely rise as new staff and larger premises are needed.
- We may need new capital equipment, such as larger machines.

There are dangers in growing too quickly. A small business with limited funds may find itself committed to payments it cannot meet.

Diseconomies of scale

Sometimes a business grows beyond its optimum size and becomes so large that it cannot operate efficiently. This may be true of conglomerates built up through take-overs and mergers. For example, Morrison has experienced problems after taking over Safeway, whilst Boots has sold off some of its services in order to concentrate on its core business of healthcare.

In large organisations, communication and decision-making may become difficult. One solution is to 'down-size' by selling off some of the operations in order to concentrate on the core businesses, The Hanson Group, for example, sold off a number of its interests to concentrate on its core business of construction. Other solutions might be to decentralise and set up smaller divisions, or to delayer by cutting out levels in the organisational hierarchy so as to become 'leaner and fitter'

Risks associated with inertia

Inertia in business is not changing or progressing. The PESTEL factors in the business environment are ever-changing and organisations that fail to respond will be left behind. There are many examples of this – IBM, a giant in the computer industry, lost out when it allowed a newcomer, Microsoft, to dominate the world software market. In 1993, Sainsbury was the leading UK supermarket and Marks & Spencer the leading clothes retailer. As we have seen, Tesco has seen the potential of diversification into non-food items and become market leader; M&S failed to match the designs of high street rivals such as Next and experienced falling profits.

The fall in share prices of these companies left them vulnerable to take-over bids. In 2004 M&S held off a bid from Phillip Green of BhS after putting forward a new business plan, while US retailers were interested in Sainsbury. For other companies, such as MG Rover, it is too late. The company's car designs failed to catch the public imagination and it closed in early 2005.

At the time of writing, HMV and Virgin Records are launching their own subscription-only music downloading services to fend off competition from the internet, and both M&S and Sainsbury are fighting back.

Choice of legal status

Private sector businesses may operate under a variety of legal structures:

- sole trader (1 owner)
- partnerships (2–20 owners)
- private limited companies (no limit to the number of shareholders)
- public limited companies (no limit to the number of shareholders)
- franchises (will be either a sole trader, partnership or limited company)
- co-operatives
- trusts
- charities.

The appropriate legal status for a business will be determined by the finance required, the level of risk involved and by the objectives of the owners, including their need to retain control (Table 1.14). The business plan might indicate that a different form of organisation is necessary in order to achieve survival and the desired growth.

Table 1.14 Reasons for choice of legal structure – the advantages/disadvantages of change

Problem	Possible solution	Advantages	Disadvantages
A sole trader may find it hard to survive because of: limited funds, the need to work long hours and to be an expert at all areas of business.	Take on a partner (or partners) with savings to invest and business expertise.	More funds are available, the work is shared and the business has more expertise. The financial affairs can still remain private.	Profits are now shared, decisions must be agreed, the actions of each partner are legally binding on all the others. As with sole traders the partners will have unlimited liability, this means that their private property may be used to repay debts. (Note: limited partnerships are possible for some organisations.)
A sole trader or partnership may be concerned about the level of risk.	Form a company.	This gives the owners (the shareholders) limited liability – their private property can no longer be taken to repay company debts.	Companies are often more expensive to set up and their financial affairs may no longer remain private. Under the Companies Acts, they must publish their annual accounts by sending details to Companies House where they are available for inspection by the general public.
A limited company needs extra funds to expand the business.	The company may borrow.	In this case the company remains in the hands of the present shareholders.	The loan has to be repaid with interest. which may prove expensive. Security may be needed in the form of business assets or the private property of the directors, which may be sold if the loan is not repaid.
	Bring in new shareholders	The shareholders risk their capital and have no right to be repaid.	There are more owners to share the profits. The original owners may begin to lose control of the company to the new shareholders. A family company may therefore resist this option.
	Form a plc and sell shares to the general public via the stock market.	There is potential for raising large amounts of capital. The present owners may gain financially. Plcs tend to have more prestige.	The share price may fluctuate. A falling share price may leave the company vulnerable to take-overs from other companies. Plcs are subject to extra regulations from the stock market.
An entrepreneur needs a sound business idea.	Buy into a franchise.	Less risk in using a proven business idea. Support is given by the franchising organisation.	Less freedom to pursue your own ideas. The franchisor may terminate the agreement if your service is not up to standard. Pizza Express and British School of Motoring both have franchising operations.

Other business possibilities

Co-operatives

Businesses with social objectives might consider forming a co-operative.

Workers co-operatives are growing in the UK with the assistance of the local Co-operative Development Agencies. The local CDA will provide information and support in writing a business plan.

Voluntary organisations and community groups

Voluntary organisations and community groups are non-profit-making, but will still draw up a business plan to show how funds will be raised and used. The Charities Information Bureau (CIB) provides information about setting up and funding. Sometimes voluntary organisations set up trusts that have the benefit of minimising the amount of income tax to be paid. Here a group of trustees is appointed to hold and manage the assets of the organisation on behalf of an individual or the community.

---

case study 1.20   The National Trust

The National Trust was formed in 1895 to protect coastline, countryside and buildings in England, Wales and Northern Ireland from uncontrolled development so that it is available for future generations to enjoy.

- The property that the Trust owns is either donated, left as legacies or bought using the Trust's own funds.

- The Trust is a charity and is completely independent of government funding, relying for income on membership fees, donations, legacies, and also upon revenue raised from commercial operations such as shops and holiday properties.

- There are 3.4 million members and 43,000 volunteers. More than 12 million people paid for entry to properties in 2004, and 50 million visited the free open air properties.

- In 2004 the Trust owned assets of £700 million consisting of: historic houses and gardens, industrial monuments, woods, beaches, farmland, moorland, islands, castles and nature reserves.

Source: The National Trust

activity

1 What is the advantage for the National Trust in being independent of government funding?
2 Give one major advantage for the Trust of having charitable status.
3 Why is a trust a suitable form of legal status for an organisation of this sort?

Independent advice and guidance on appropriate structures

New businesses may seek advice from a variety of sources:

- the local Business Link, a government-sponsored information and advice service. This publishes literature, provides financial planning templates, runs courses and has a website with advice on all aspects of setting up and running a business

- the local **Chamber of Commerce** which provides support and advice to local businesses

- the local bank, where the small business adviser will provide business start-up advice, literature and software. There will also be on-going support and monitoring as the business progresses

- a solicitor will draw up legal documents such as the partnership agreement or the memoranda required for company formation. They may also advise on contracts, and matters such as the registration of business names and patents.

An accountant will advise on:

■ the tax implications for different businesses, i.e. income tax for sole traders and partnerships, corporation tax for companies

■ VAT registration

■ the accounting and disclosure of information required by the Companies Acts

■ methods of raising finance.

Private limited companies may employ merchant banks to advise on a stock market flotation. The Charities Information Bureau and the Charities Commission will provide specific advice for charities. The local Co-operative Development Agency (CDA) will advise co-operatives.

We also consider sources of small business advice when looking at business enterprise in Unit 5.

assignment focus

Prepare a business plan to support the survival and growth of a business. The audience will be a financial institution that is being asked to supply funds for the project.

You may enter your figures into a commercially supplied template or design a spreadsheet for this purpose. (We supply a suitable model on the Nelson Thornes website: www.nelsonthornes.com/btec.)

The forecast should include at least:

■ details of your business including its name and legal structure, your product and business idea

■ a cashflow forecast

■ a break-even forecast together with explanations and interpretations.

Comment on the implications for the business of the forecasts you have produced.

■ You may achieve M4 if you explain the role the business plan may play in securing finance and attracting investment to secure future survival and growth. State with reasons whether your plan is likely to succeed in this.

■ You may achieve D2 if you can assess the part that particular functional areas will play in drawing up the business plan and in ensuring its success.

UNIT 2

Business and Management

This unit covers:

- organisational aims and objectives
- role of management
- management of resources
- key management skills.

This unit looks at:

- how aims and objectives may be achieved through planning and monitoring
- the role of management in improving business performance
- how a manager's role includes the management of resources
- the role of a manager's interpersonal and communication skills.

Assessment

For the assignment, you need to produce a business report using a selected, i.e. real, organisation. The report will explain how aims and objectives may be achieved, describe the role of management, describe how resources are managed, and demonstrate the role of a managers skills. To achieve a merit, you will also need to show how management can improve performance and how you can improve your own skills. To achieve a distinction, you need to evaluate the role of management in improving performance and evaluate how management functions can be made more effective.

Choose an organisation with which you are familiar, or in which you have a direct interest. The organisation should be big enough to provide evidence to cover all aspects of the unit outlined above. You can either use one organisation throughout the report, which can be fun to do, or use several businesses to illustrate your discussion. A local branch of a large company will work provided you can also get information about the company as a whole. Check with your tutor before you proceed. Keep notes on everything you do.

You will need the following to complete this unit:

- company annual reports – many available on the internet or through the *Financial Times* company report service. Look also at competitor websites
- business sections of national and local newspapers, business magazines
- websites of many companies carry excellent sections on organisation and structure.

Organisational Aims and Objectives

Aims and objectives

Corporate performance

Corporate performance is the extent to which an organisation has achieved its aims, that is how well it has done compared to the targets which have been set. The purpose of management is to improve performance.

Traditionally performance has been measured using only financial criteria such as profit. Although this is important for potential and current shareholders (owners of a financial share of the business) in private sector organisations, it is less relevant for public sector and other, not-for-profit organisations such as charities. Therefore other aims become necessary.

The main problem with an exclusive emphasis on financial rewards is that it ignores the needs of other stakeholders. These are individuals or groups who have a concern or interest (stake) in the performance and operations of an organisation. They may be consumers, local community, employees, owners, suppliers, etc.

Corporate aims

All organisations have aims, whether they are for-profit or not-for-profit, manufacturers or service providers, large or small. Long-term aims may cover a three- to five-year time period, whilst short-term aims may be set for a year ahead. Aims can change over time depending on the external environment and on internal policies.

Here are some examples of possible aims:

- survival – whilst BT and BP think in £billions, at the other extreme some businesses think only of surviving. Most new businesses have survival as the main aim of the first years of operating. The majority of business failures occur within three years of start-up

- growth in market share – the market share is the fraction or part of the market which the business controls. Generally a bigger share of the market gives more power and influence to a business. Small, local businesses could have a large share of the local market but be insignificant in regional terms (Tesco has a 28 per cent share of the grocery trade in the UK.)

- growth of sales – both sales revenue (the amount of money generated by the sales) and sales volume (the number of units sold) can be relevant. It is important that any increase in volume is not achieved too much by price cutting, such as sales and discounts, because revenue could fall

- growth of profits – although many businesses are said to try to achieve maximum profits, most will aim for a level of profits which satisfies shareholders and the internal needs of the business

- growth in donations – these are vital to charities and voluntary organisations and can come from companies, individuals and the National Lottery Good Causes funds.

Aims are general statements about the purpose of the business and the way it wants to change in the future. For these aims to become a reality, the organisation will need to create a series of objectives which show how they can be achieved.

> **remember**
>
> When you visit the website for your organisation, check out pages such as 'About us', 'Corporate', 'Core values', 'Our purpose', 'Mission', etc. Very few present their aims in a student-friendly form.

> **assignment focus**
>
> To achieve P1, you need to explain how aims and objectives may be achieved through planning and monitoring.
>
> 1 You first need to choose an organisation to investigate. Pick one in which you are interested or to which you have good access. Check out its website and any related links such as competitors. Check newspaper sites to see what the press are saying about it, e.g. *The Guardian* or *Independent*. Find out if you can get inside information. Prepare your front cover and write the introduction, say which organisation you have chosen and give reasons. Say what you are going to include in the assignment.
>
> 2 Use the resources you have found to identify its aims and objectives.
>
> 3 Later you will need to describe what planning and monitoring takes place and how these contribute to the organisation's performance.

Translation of aims into SMART objectives

Once the aims have been agreed, they need to be restated as objectives which can be used as a working guide throughout the organisation.

SMART objectives

Although we have defined these in Unit 1, it is important to look at the definition again:

- **S**pecific, e.g. 'a 5 per cent increase in sales in the East Midlands', i.e. for a particular product in a particular area
- **M**easurable – how will we know when the objective has been achieved? e.g. for the charity Age Concern, sales or profit or the number of old people helped
- **A**chievable with the right resources, good management and extra effort
- **R**ealistic/relevant – do the objectives help to achieve the aims?
- **T**imely/time-constrained – there should be a deadline.

For example, if your aim is to lose weight, a SMART objective would be 'to lose 2 lb each week for the next 10 weeks'. An initiative would be to join WeightWatchers. Performance would be measured by the weighing scales and attending the meetings every Tuesday. The strategy, once at the target weight, might be to keep fit and stop snacking!

Table 2.1 shows some of the key terms used when turning corporate or organisation-wide aims into workable objectives.

Table 2.1 Key terms

Key terms	Definition	An example from your centre
Mission	Overall purpose of the organisation based on the needs of its stakeholders	
Vision	Where the organisation wants to be in the future	To be a regional centre of excellence delivering BTEC National courses
Strategy	Long-term plans for achieving the mission and vision	Creating base rooms for business courses
Aims	Breakdown of the mission	
Objectives Tactical	Quantified specification of aims for each function or department. SMART	Recruit 40 extra students on Business Studies courses
Measures	How achievement is going to be measured	Student retention and achievement, pass rates
Targets Operational	Specific SMART objectives, e.g. for a product or area or course	BTEC National 24 students, minimum 86% pass rate, 90% retention
Initiatives	What needs to be done to put the strategy into effect	Extra tutorials in the evening! (Would you go?)
Monitoring performance	Checking to see that objectives are being met	Weekly personal tutorials with specific personal targets, e.g. Individual Learning Plans

assignment focus

1   Make a copy of the table above. Complete it for your own centre. Some ideas for examples have been included to start you off.
2   Make another copy of the table and complete it for your selected business. You need to pay particular attention to the aims and objectives. You could make suggestions for the other rows.

'HRH Prince Charles Annual Report published 30 June 2004 gives his mission as "to do all he can to use his unique position to make a difference for the better in the United Kingdom and internationally".'

Source: *Independent*, 1 July 2004

'There are "targets for using more fuel-efficient vehicles, recyclable products and more double-sided printing of documents".'

Source: *Guardian*, 1 July 2004

Strategic, tactical and operational levels of management

It is useful to think of an organisation with three levels of management:

■ strategic, or top level, management where long-term (1–3 years) corporate aims, policies, plans and strategies will be created

■ tactical, or middle level, management where aims become departmental or functional SMART objectives, such as annual sales in the South West or the number of new staff in the sales department

■ operational, or day-to-day, management, where SMART objectives are allocated for stores, teams or individuals, e.g. part-time staff in sports retailers have weekly targets to achieve.

The manager's role is to make sure that all activities are co-ordinated and organised so the organisation runs effectively and achieves its objectives.

■ Targets for each functional area should complement each other, i.e. they should not conflict. The right hand should know what the left hand is doing! This is horizontal consistency.

■ Aims need to be translated into SMART objectives for each functional area. There will need to be objectives for finance (monthly cash budgets), sales, Human Resources, etc., depending on the organisation, at each level. Objectives will need to communicated or passed down the **lines of authority**, from top level to supervisors. This process of passing down information in a sequence from the top to the bottom of an organisation is called a cascade. It gives a vertical consistency to the objectives. Figure 2.1 shows the process.

The organisation needs to be structured so that its mission and aims can be translated into SMART objectives and put into action down through all levels of the organisation. Specific targets can then be set for functional areas, departments and individuals.

Sainsbury announced in October 2004 that, because its profits had fallen, its key objective had become 'to keep the shelves stocked'. To achieve this, it was making around 700 head office staff redundant and employing 3,500 more shop-floor workers. What does this say about mission and vision? Has it improved?

Figure 2.1

Horizontal and vertical consistency

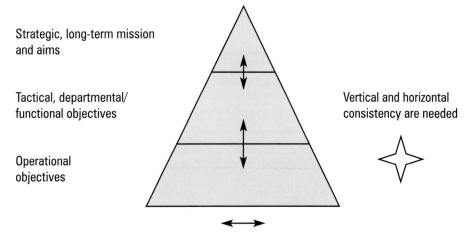

Strategic, long-term mission and aims

Tactical, departmental/ functional objectives

Operational objectives

Vertical and horizontal consistency are needed

Human Resources   Marketing Production   Administration   Finance, etc. (Functions)
People   Customers   Processes/operations   Financial (Perspectives)

Once the overall mission has been set for the organisation, it needs to be converted into SMART objectives for each department or function. These objectives will be specific to each organisation. In a school or college, for example, there may be targets for recruitment on each course (e.g. 'minimum of 24 on the BTEC National course'), completion rates, i.e. the number of students who complete the course; achievement rates, etc.

Other organisations may have objectives for product quality, reducing returns/complaints; availability of stock, delivery times, reducing the number of suppliers, market share by product and area, etc.

Table 2.2 gives some examples of tactical objectives for different departments or **functions** in two businesses. All data applies to the next financial year.

Table 2.2 Possible tactical objectives for two businesses

| Business | SMART objectives for | | | |
	Human Resources	Sales	Revenue	Finance
Clothing retailer	New part-time staff to get 5 hour' training within three weeks of starting	Increase sales of female outerwear by 8%	Increase by 12% in South Wales	Increase net profit by 1%
Local newspaper	Recruit an experienced local news reporter ASAP	Increase readership by 2,000	Increase advertising revenue by 10%	Advertising budget not to exceed £95,000

These tactical objectives can now be converted, or translated, into operational objectives at an individual store level, as shown in Table 2.3. The instructions, or directions, could cascade from head office through regional managers.

Table 2.3 Possible operational objectives in two businesses

| Business | SMART objectives for | | | |
	Human Resources	Sales	Revenue	Finance
Clothing	Training to take place each Monday morning. Store to open at 9.30. Place notice on door 'Training in progress'.	Transfer staff from other sections. Personal targets 100 items per week	The Port Talbot, Swansea and Cardiff branches to increase sales by …	Cut store costs by …

assignment focus

To achieve P1, you will need to identify the aims and tactical/operational objectives of the organisation which you are researching. If there is a website, copy and paste the mission statement, include the logo and give your source.

To be as effective as Tesco, an organisation will need to communicate its mission and vision at the corporate level down to successive layers of the business, e.g. stores, departments, teams and individuals, so that each layer of the organisation is working to the same ends, i.e. they are cascaded downwards. This vertical consistency needs to be matched with horizontal consistency across departments or functions (see Figure 2.1).

case study 2.1

The Tesco approach to corporate peformance, aims and objectives

'Our market share of UK retailing is 12.5% that leaves 87.5% to go after.' Sir Terry Leahy, Chief Executive of Tesco

Source: *Management Today* and Corporatewatch website

12.5 per cent means that £1 in every £8 spent in shops in the UK is spent at Tesco.

'The only thing that could bring Tesco down is its management, and they do not make mistakes.' Carlos Criado-Perez, a former Chief Executive of Safeway

Source: Corporatewatch website

Tesco has five measures, or perspectives, of corporate performance to 'balance' the financial criteria, illustrated in the Tesco Steering Wheel (Figure 2.2). Four of these perspectives are as follows.

1 The Learning and Growth or People Perspective. Here the focus is on the people in the organisation, the employees. Possible SMART objectives could include training and staff development, e.g. 15 per cent trained in online order processing, communications, better access to and spread of knowledge, perhaps through the use of an internal intranet. All of these could help the organisation learn.

The People segment of the steering wheel below includes 'We trust and respect each other' and 'My job is interesting'.

Link   See pages 19 and 54 for a definition of SMART objectives.

2 The Business Process or Operations perspective. This refers to the way in which the business operates internally. It could include the production of goods, with objectives about quality and the number of rejects or making work simpler and more efficient.

'Work is simpler for staff' and 'The way we operate is cheaper for Tesco' is included in Operations.

3 The Customer Perspective. Identifying and meeting customer needs is now accepted as the most important way of achieving customer satisfaction and customer focus. Putting the customer first and devising ways of measuring and improving satisfaction will help the organisation gain a competitive edge over its rivals. It could lead to an increase in sales and an improvement in market share.

'I didn't queue' and 'The prices are clear' are in the Customer segment.

Figure 2.2

The Tesco Steering Wheel. There is a unique Steering Wheel on display in every Tesco store

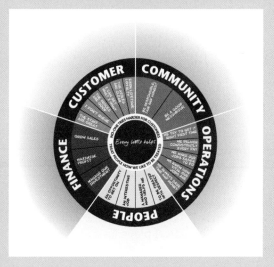

4   The Financial Perspective. Here the emphasis is clearly on profits. It may include, for example, gross and net profit or a rise in share price.

'Grow sales' and 'Maximise profit' are included in the Finance segment.

Source: www.tesco.com and Tesco Corporate Responsibility Review, 2005

 See page 27 for an explanation of the importance of profit.

---

activity

This case study can be used for the first Pass/Merit criteria.

1   Tesco is very successful. Could or should your organisation adopt this approach as its benchmark for excellence?
2   Can the aims and objectives of your organisation be classified under the four headings that Tesco uses? Should they?
3   What actions could managers take to raise performance in each of these four areas? (for M1)
4   How could the four areas be planned for and monitored?
5   How does the steering wheel help Tesco achieve its aims and objectives?

Action planning

Once the organisation has identified its aims and objectives and broken these down, e.g. by product category, regional area, customer focus, etc., it needs to plan a course of action by which these can be achieved.

Strategic planning

Top level planning

Every organisation needs to plan to achieve its aims and objectives. **Strategic planning** will help to:

- set targets and guidelines for measuring performance
- anticipate any possible problems and find solutions in advance
- allocate scarce resources more efficiently
- guide the process of change – Where are we now? Where do we want to get to? How are we going to get there?

The business plan

The majority of organisations will have a business plan which sets out their vision of what it is trying to achieve by a specific time, e.g. in one year or three years. It could include:

- a summary of its aims and objectives
- a marketing plan
- a financial plan
- a production plan
- a human resources plan.

 See Units 1 and 5 for more information on business planning.

Tactical planning

Planning, however, needs to take place at every level of the organisation and cover all its operations. There may be **tactical plans** for each department or function, for example:

■ human resources – here planning needs to include both short- and long-term requirements, such as how many extra staff are needed to cover peak periods, e.g. during the week or in the summer. What skills will be needed in the future, such as IT or customer service, and how these people are going to be trained or recruited. Do you have a part time job? When do you work?

■ marketing – a decision to launch a new product would require plans for buying advertising media, producing publicity materials, arranging distribution, etc., all of which need to be booked or produced well in advance.

Operational planning

Operational planning focuses on day-to-day activities, such as the allocation of work, lunch and holiday rotas, staff cover, etc.

Maintenance of effective operations

Once aims and objectives have been decided and strategic and tactical plans have been drawn up, the organisation would need to make sure that all resources are available when they are needed in the short, medium and long term. Does your classroom have everything that is needed? Do you?

Goods out of stock, goods not delivered on time, waiting too long to get served, computer does not work, etc. – these are examples of where management has obviously failed to provide adequate resources. You will probably be able to think of many others. Have you complained or taken your custom elsewhere?

For its operations to run smoothly, every organisation will need to make sure that it has enough of the right resources in the right place at the right time What resources are needed will depend entirely on the output of the organisation, e.g. a dry cleaners will need chemicals, plastic bags, hangers, etc. The resources are:

■ staff – a very expensive and valuable resource. Should the staff be full-time, part-time or temporary? It is normal in most retail outlets to have 80 per cent part-time staff and 20 per cent full-time staff

■ equipment, e.g. computers, fork lift trucks in a warehouse, delivery vehicles

■ materials and goods for sale – good relationships need to be developed with suppliers

■ working capital (sufficient cash to pay day-to-day expenses)

■ facilities – the buildings or premises.

Two examples will help to show how these resources need to be co-ordinated:

Question: What do your local Thai restaurant or hairdresser both need to do to maintain an effective business and achieve their objectives?
Answer: Provide quality services and products, i.e. satisfy or exceed customer expectations with an excellent meal or a good cut.

They require:

■ enough competent, trained staff, who are able and willing to give excellent customer service

■ equipment and facilities, such as ovens, scissors, heating, lighting, seating, etc., which should be clean, hygienic and well-maintained, meeting or exceeding health and safety requirements

■ everything they require to provide a service, i.e. sufficient supplies should have been purchased in advance to meet demand, weekends are the busiest (planned)

■ faultless administration, e.g. booking arrangements – 'Yes we are expecting you'!

■ sufficient working capital to pay day-to-day expenses.

Monitor, trouble shoot, problem-solve

Managers cannot stand back once the plan has been constructed and the resources have been put in place. They must be actively involved in controlling, co-ordinating and directing operations. Although some managers are never seen on the 'shop floor', there are those who manage by walking around, taking a hands-on approach. When does walking around become interference? Which type of manager do you prefer?

Ideally managers should monitor/check/control all activities. They should be able to locate/identify problems and sort them out (troubleshoot).

If they cannot, there must be systems in place to check that everything is working. There should be someone available with the authority to handle problems or sort out complaints, i.e. make decisions. Does this sound like your restaurant or hairdresser?

assignment focus

1   What key resources are necessary to ensure the success of your organisation?

2   Do managers in your organisation walk around?

3   What systems are in place to sort out problems when they occur?

Monitoring of performance and future planning

Are the aims and objectives being achieved? Are the plans still on track for success? Are all the resources in place and working? Or perhaps there are breakdowns or shortages? Have these problems been dealt with?

Figure 2.3

Planning, level of management and monitoring

There are three basic levels of management and decision-making in many organisations (see page 57). Figure 2.3 is an example of possible planning and monitoring that may take place.

Planning	Level of management		Monitoring
Long-term corporate direction, mossion Organisation-wide objectives, e.g. entering new markets, developing new products, buying new business Corporate business plan	*Strategic* top-level managers/owner, long term, non-reoutine decisions involving risk	Strategic	**Benchmarking** against best practice, competitor analysis, changes in the external environment/ market place, PESTEL strategic assessment of customers surveys, continuous improvement
Financial budgets, personal targets on recruitment/ training, sales targets by region/product group, etc.	*Tactical* Middle management decisions at departmental or fuctional level	Tactical	Comparison of actual performance with plans, e.g. quality, wastage and customer satisfaction, sales targets, store or branch **appraisal**
Daily work allocation, staffing rota, breaks, work place health and safety, arranging cover for absent staff, stock display, etc.	*Operational* Day-to-day decision, usually routine with less risk	Operational	Staff puctuality and absenteeism, stock movement and replacement, staff behaviour, customer service, team/ individual appraisal

assignment focus

You will need to investigate the planning and monitoring that takes place in your organisation and show how it helps the organisation achieve its aims and objectives.

How do organisations plan?

Do you use a diary or personal organiser to plan your life? Do activities sometimes clash because you have not planned properly? Organisations need to plan to make sure that they have sufficient resources in place to provide the goods and services needed by customers. There are several ways of doing this which depend upon what the business does and its size. A small organisation may use a year planner or calendar to show, for example, all the meetings planned for the following year with other key dates highlighted and holiday dates for staff with the staff cover available. Two useful graphical methods for planning are **Gantt charts** and **critical path analysis**.

Gantt charts

These show how a set of activities can be organised and scheduled so that a project or activity can be completed on time, within budget. Look at the Gantt chart in Figure 2.4, which shows some of the tasks needed to complete the assignment project for this unit within a time span of 12 weeks.

Figure 2.4

A Gantt chart

							Weeks					
Outcome	**1**	**2**	**3**	**4**	**5**	**6**	**7**	**8**	**9**	**10**	**11**	**12**
Collect information												D
Identify aims and objectives												E
Identify planning at the three levels												A
Identify monitoring at three levels												D
Show how these help the organisation achieve its aims and objectives												L
Outcome 2												I
Identify roles in your organisation												N
Roles of specialist managers												E

The sequence of activities is shown in column 1. The time (in weeks) needed for each activity is shown along the horizontal axis. In practice the name of the person responsible for the completion of the task would also be included. Sometimes a blank row is inserted between tasks, where the actual start and end dates for each task can be shown. In this way the consequences of any delay or hold up can be analysed and appropriate corrective action taken.

Critical path analysis (CPA)

CPA is a planning technique which is used to try to ensure that a project is completed as cheaply and quickly as possible. All the tasks/activities to complete a project are first identified and put into order to complete the project, e.g. launching a new product or ensuring that two tons of strawberries arrive every day at the Wimbledon Tennis Championships. Tasks which depend on each other and take the longest time to complete are linked to identify the critical path. These are the most important – that is, they are critical tasks and each must be completed before the next can begin. Management must focus its attention on these tasks to make sure they are completed on time. Other tasks which are less critical need less attention. They may provide a few days 'breathing space' or 'float time'.

Monitoring performance

To make sure that the organisation is achieving its targets, it will need to control and monitor (check) its actual performance regularly and compare this with what was forecasted or budgeted. There are many ways in which this can be done; the methods chosen will depend on the type and size of the business.

remember

The purpose of monitoring and control is to see whether action and decisions are necessary to achieve objectives. All planning needs to be monitored.

Responsiveness to internal performance and external 'shocks'

case study
2.2

Darwin proved right! Survival of the fittest

Marks & Spencer's (M&S) sales of women's clothing fell dramatically. The quality was excellent but they were old fashioned compared to the competition. M&S strategic reaction was to introduce the Per Una format. Do you go to M&S? Whose fault was it that styles were out of date? Why have some lines sold better or worse than expected? Have Gap and Next just been better? Was the monitoring or planning at fault?

Krispy Kreme makes and sells doughnuts mainly to supermarkets. Its sales and profits fell heavily in 2004 because it had not forecasted the negative effect of low carbohydrate diets effectively. Should management have foreseen this impact? How far could it have controlled it?

The oldest company in the world is in Japan. 'Hoshi is a Japanese Inn founded in Japan in 718. It is run by Zengoro Hoshi the 46th generation of the family to be in charge. The firm's motto is unusually practical: "Take care of fire, learn from water, co-operate with nature".' What qualities does a business need to survive this long?

Source: The Economist

activity

1   What lessons can be learned from these case studies about monitoring of performance and future planning?
2   How successful is your organisation? Search the online newspapers.

Methods of monitoring performance
Look at monitoring at the three levels of management in Figure 2.3.

Here are some ways of monitoring.

■ Competitor behaviour – continuous monitoring of competitors is necessary for any organisation if it is to achieve a competitive edge. **Benchmarking** comparisons may include price ('We compare prices nationwide so you don't have to'), customer perceptions and image, quality, reliability and profitability. A SWOT analysis of competitors could lead to new aims and objectives.

■ Changes in the business environment – look at the case studies on pages 103–4. How much of the success or failure of the business was due to factors outside management control? Much of the skill of management lies in its ability to cope with the uncertainty present in its external environment. Successful organisations will continuously monitor or audit their outside environment (environmental scanning) to identify which forces are likely to pose a threat or provide an opportunity (SWOT). In a dynamic (rapidly changing) environment this could be difficult. The organisation needs to be flexible, adaptable and willing to change, to achieve its objectives. PESTEL analysis is a useful way of environmental monitoring (see page 46), it may help to anticipate external shocks such as changes in tastes (the Atkins diet) or changes in competitor behaviour. However, there are events such as the attack on New York or the London bombs which are beyond prediction. These random external shocks, although unexpected, must be covered by contingency plans which will help the organisation return to normal as quickly as possible. (Eighty per cent of the businesses affected by the New York disaster did not have contingency (back-up) systems in place and went out of business.)

case study 2.3 — Crafty?

Kraft Foods Inc. is one of the world's largest food companies (Kraft cheese, Maxwell House coffees, Philadelphia, etc.). This extract from their website gives some of the reasons why their actual results may be different from those projected (forecast) by the company, i.e. the wide range of factors that could make the forecast wrong. Actual results may be different from forecasted results because the forecasts are not 100 per cent reliable.

These factors include:

'changes in consumer preferences, and demand for its products, including low carbohydrate diet trends, the effects of changing prices for its raw materials and local economic and market conditions. The company is subject to the effects of foreign economies, currency movements and business risks related to its customers, such as liability (compensation/damages) if product consumption causes injury, consumer concerns regarding genetically modified organisms and the health implications of obesity.'

Source: www.corporate-ir.net

activity

1   What factors in the external environment could affect your organisation?
2   Does your organisation carry out external monitoring? If you cannot find out, should it, and what should it be doing?

Link   See page 46 for an explanation of PESTEL analysis.

- Comparison against benchmarks – benchmarking is defined as the process of comparing one organisation's activities with the best practice in the industry. This becomes the standard or benchmark against which performance can be judged. It involves:
  - identifying what activities should be benchmarked for improvement, such as levels of stock or delivery times
  - identifying which organisation to benchmark
  - collecting and analysing the information, i.e. What does it do that makes it the best?
  - copying and improving upon best practice.

  Is your centre the best? What does the competition do differently?

  The process can be done either internally, where the best performing department acts as the standard or benchmark for other departments, or externally, where another organisation acts as the benchmark. Tesco is the benchmark for performance in the retail supermarket sector. Other retailers will try to find out why it is the best and then try to do better

  Are you the benchmark for your class? If not, who is and what do they do? There are national benchmarks for retention and achievement on education courses.

See www.dti.gov.uk/bestpractice for more examples

- Tracking and comparison of actual performance to plan/schedule – SMART-planned targets will initially be set for each part of an organisation's activities, e.g. sales per department, cash flow forecasts. Actual sales and cash flow can then be compared with what was expected, i.e. what was intended and what actually happened. Any deviation (difference) from the plan, whether favourable or unfavourable, will need to be investigated and appropriate actions taken. It is the planning and monitoring which enables the organisation to achieve its aims and objectives.

In retail stores there may be daily and weekly targets for each section and product. The actual sales figures are looked at daily; both favourable (sales more than expected) and unfavourable (sales less than expected) results require management action. Next for example changes shop floor displays, reallocates the staff, makes price reductions on slow selling lines, etc. The website notes that any item on display in the window (the window display is changed every three weeks) must be available in the store. Is this true?

This method of monitoring and control can be used in for-profit and not-for-profit organisations.

www.next.co.uk is worth visiting. Look at the company fact file

SWOT = Strengths, Weaknesses, Opportunities and Threats

remember

- **Exception analysis** – this is a management approach that uses the abnormal or exceptional differences between planned and actual results, e.g. planned (budgeted) and actual costs/revenues, etc. as the focus for management action and time. The technique concentrates on those areas which are a problem and require immediate attention. Activities which are running normally get less attention.

- **Continuous improvement** – many organisations now believe that the only way to achieve a permanent advantage over their competitors is to aim for continuous improvement. It can be defined as a corporate (across the board) focus on key performance indicators (KPIs), such as training, customer service, financial results, etc. (Look at Tesco.com.) It can be achieved through better management of staff and resources. For many organisations, a simple comparison of current performance with last year is sufficient. However, with the current fashion for accountability and value for money, there are league tables for schools, hospitals and local councils. This constant assessment of performance has produced the need for continuous improvement (or *Kaizen*). For example, schools are rated on the number of A–C passes at GCSE. (Do they depend on the teachers, the facilities or the abilities of the students in the particular year?).

How can a culture of continuous improvement be achieved? Firstly, the organisation needs to be focused on its customers. Does your organisation ask its customers for their opinions about the quality of service? At Homebase, this is done at the checkout, while in motorway services you can press a happy or sad face to show whether you are satisfied. The information should be used to see if targets are met, standards are being maintained or if improvements need to be made

How planning and monitoring help the organisation achieve its aims

assignment focus

1   What planning takes place at each of the three levels in your organisation?
2   Identify the monitoring that takes place at each of the three levels in your organisation, e.g. does it check sales, stock, the amount of wastage or unsold items? (You may have been involved in a stock check.)

To achieve M1, you will need to show how management activity can raise performance in your business.

In the 1990s, Robert Kaplan and David Norton devised a new way of looking at strategic/top level corporate performance called the 'balanced scorecard'. Find out more at www.balancedscorecard.org

Role of Management

To achieve P2, you will need to describe the role of management in improving the performance of a selected business.

It is useful to look back to where we started. Business organisations exist to satisfy demand for particular goods and services and in order to do this they need resources, or inputs. Staff, finance, buildings and premises, materials and information are all resources.

What is management? A typical dictionary definition of management could be:

'Management is concerned with planning, controlling and co-ordinating the acquisition/purchase and use of resources.'

Ask Yahoo what is management and there are 502,000,000 entries!

Levels of management

It is usual to think of management as a series of levels within an organisation. Each level will have specific duties and responsibilities delegated to it by the level above. The top managers in a business are the directors who are responsible for strategic decisions and policy-making. Middle managers are concerned with departmental planning and target setting. Operational managers run the day-to-day operations such as work allocation.

Figure 2.5 shows the different management activities of each level of the management hierarchy.

Figure 2.5

Management activities related to management levels

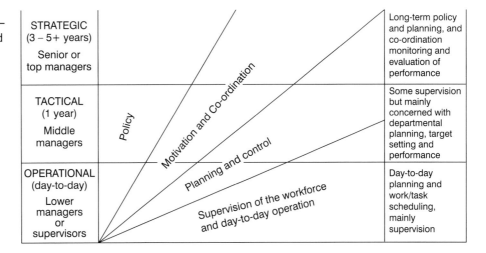

Write a brief description explaining the responsibilities of managers at each level in your organisation.

What are the functions and responsibilities of management?

There are many studies that try to identify exactly what it is that managers should do. Most writers agree that these functions would be found to a greater or lesser extent in every organisation regardless of size, objectives, type of activity or legal form.

case study
2.4

Eddie McGuiness, Groundwork Contractors

This case study shows how a real construction company puts into practice some of the topics developed in this unit.

The groundwork is the first stage of any building project. It includes the foundations and all underground pipework – 'the bits you never see,' says Eddie. 'Every building contract is treated as a project. Each stage must be completed on time before the next stage can begin. Our aims are to get the price of the job right, to control costs and keep overheads down, stay liquid and deliver on time. The first step is to meet the client and find out exactly what they need. It is important to price a project effectively, what resources are needed, how much work needs to be done, how long will it take, what materials and equipment are needed, how many workers are needed, what ground (the geology) do we have to go through. What does the client want? What can they afford? We may have to compromise. I have to make sure that all the trades have been booked and the equipment is available, I visit each job every day to make sure that everything is OK and that staff are pulling their weight.'

activity

1   What management functions does Eddie carry out?
2   What is the evidence for planning and monitoring in this business?
3   How would it help the business achieve its objectives?
4   What outside factors could disrupt this business?

Historically managers have been primarily concerned with completing their tasks or activities, paying little attention to their staff. These were their five main roles:

- forecasting – the process of predicting what will happen in the future. It is vital to the success of any organisation that it has an accurate picture of future events in order to make the right decisions when responding to change. A sales forecast, for example, would use past sales data and experience of the industry to identify future patterns and trends. The building company would need to forecast the resources it would need

See the Kraft case study on page 63 for why forecasts may go wrong

- organising – the process of arranging and being responsible for the work or jobs done by individuals to achieve the organisation's goals and objectives. People can be organised into teams or work groups to perform specific tasks. Resources need to be available at the right time in the right place to complete a job

- commanding – the process of leading by giving orders and instructions and expecting them to be carried out. There is little or no discussion or consultation with the workforce. Many managers use their position in the hierarchy as their only source of power to command and get jobs done. Do your managers command or lead because of their communication and interpersonal skills or because they are the 'boss'?

- co-ordinating – bringing the various jobs and tasks (sub-systems) together into one harmonious operation, perhaps to achieve an even flow of work without hold-ups or disruptions. Co-ordination needs to take place vertically and horizontally across functions and departments/sections. (See Figure 2.1 on page 55.) It is particularly important where one department comes into contact with another because it is here that the possibility for conflict is highest and a manager's interpersonal skills will be important. Is there departmental conflict in your organisation?

- **controlling** – directing, inspecting and regulating work. It may mean having to take remedial action. Departmental heads, for example, need to keep within spending budgets. Managers need to put control mechanisms in place so that feedback can occur; these can be as simple as 'We need to restock X because it is selling very quickly.' Do you have to report/feedback to your manager/tutor? Does it work?

People are now considered vital to the success of the organisation so that today management functions also include:

- **communicating** – being a good communicator is probably the most important ability needed by a modern manager. Good communication involves understanding, and being understood by, many groups. A manager may need to communicate with subordinates, superiors, colleagues, trade unions, government officials and outside agencies, i.e. with all stakeholders

Communication, see pages 100 and 165.

- planning – the means by which a forecast is acted upon. A plan is a detailed scheme, method or procedure for achieving an organisation's goals. In Units 1 and 5 we look at business planning; in this unit we have seen how planning can help achieve objectives. A good manager will have accumulated experience either within the organisation or elsewhere in the industry, i.e. industry-related experience to know and understand the potential risks in operating systems. The manager will have back up or contingency arrangements in place to meet possible emergencies

- decision-making – now the focal point of all management action. Managers are continuously making decisions about what to purchase and where, how much to sell and how to improve performance. The type of decisions that managers are allowed to make often depends on which rung of the management ladder they are on. For example, the bank manager of a high street branch may only be able to make loans up to an agreed amount. Anything above this will have to be referred upwards to the area manager. The outcome of a disciplinary procedure or a job interview may be a centralised management decision

- motivating – the action of getting people to do something because they want to rather than because they are forced to

assignment focus

For your assignment, find out whether workers feel motivated. Indeed are managers motivated? Ask them.

We discuss motivation, incentives and rewards on page 90.

- innovating – bringing in new ideas, routines, methods of work, products, and materials. Managers innovate whenever they change any of these

- creating – managers need to be imaginative and original. They must be able to approach problems from different perspectives in order to reach solutions. They need to synthesise or combine ideas from other disciplines

- developing – the manager's role may involve developing people either by direct 'on-the-job' training, or by 'off-the-job' training at college or elsewhere. Managers also have a role to play in developing personality

- delegating – the process of giving authority to lower level managers to make specific decisions. It is necessary because each manager cannot do all the tasks that need to be done. The senior manager needs to ensure that the subordinate can do the work and that the work gets done. Senior managers remain responsible for all delegated work; they 'carry the can'. When lower level staff are given a high level of responsibility, they are sometimes said to be empowered.

1   Which functions or roles in your organisation are carried out by:
   a) managers
   b) supervisors
   c) team leaders?

2   Which of these do you consider most important?

3   Are there too many managers?

Organisation of the workforce

A major responsibility of management is to design and structure the organisation so as to make the most effective use of its people – known as the workforce or human resources. For many organisations people, the staff, are the largest cost and always the most important resource, so it is vital to get the structure right, to enable managers and operatives to function and operate effectively.

Organisational structures

Who runs the course you are on? Which department or section is the course in? Who is responsible for the department? Every organisation needs a structure in order to achieve its objectives. Businesses are structured in different ways according to the way they operate and according to their **culture**. Would a different culture help improve performance?

The structure of a business can affect the way it works and performs. An ideal structure will enable management to perform in the most effective way, whereas an unsuitable structure can, for example, lead to poor morale among employees. Structure is continually evolving in response to both internal and external pressures. When was the last time your organisation was reorganised?

Organisation charts

It is often helpful to have a visual picture of an organisation. An organisation chart is a diagram of the structure that is used to show staff positions and levels within an organisation. The vertical lines show the hierarchy or chain of command. The horizontal lines show how the business of the organisation is allocated, for example, by function, geographical area or specialism. The chart shows:

- the formal structure and indicates the lines, or flow, of communication, information and authority both up and down the organisation
- who is responsible for whom and whom people have to report to.

Types of structure

We can identify a number of types of organisational structure. These include:

- **flat structures**
- tall structures
- **matrix** or project-based **structures**.

For your assignment you should include an organisation chart of your organisation. If it is a branch of a large business, only include the local chart and comment on the links with head office. Explain the type of structure it has.

If a chart is not available, you can construct one for a small part of the organisation.

Flat structures

Flat organisations are those which have relatively few or even just one level of management. They are frequently found in the service sector of the economy, such as the local solicitor or GP surgery.

Figure 2.6

Flat organisational structure

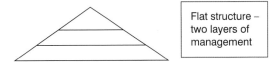

Flat organisations tend to be smaller and less complex than tall organisations. The chain of command from top to bottom is short. Many partnerships, co-operatives and some private limited companies have a flat structure with all the management at the same level. Figure 2.7 is a chart is for a small public relations company with international clients.

Figure 2.7

Organisation chart for Communication Systems SA

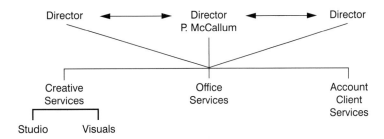

Table 2.4 Advantages and disadvantages of flat organisations

Advantages	Disadvantages
Few levels of management	People may have more than one 'boss'
Greater communication between management and workforce	Only useful for small organisations
Better team spirit	Can be difficult for the organisation to grow
Decision making can be easier	May be difficult for staff to progress

You will probably be able to suggest many others!

Tall structures

Tall organisations are those where the whole structure conforms to a tall triangle shape (Figure 2.8). It is narrower at the top where the ultimate power lies (with, say, one chief executive) and broadens out towards the base (with, say, 1,000 shop workers at the bottom).

A tall organisation has many levels of management and supervision relative to the number of employees, although it is rare to find more than seven or eight levels of management even in very large organisations of 10,000+ employees. Because there are so many managers/supervisors control at each level tends to be fairly narrow. There is a long chain of command from the top to the bottom of the organisation. Tall structures tend to be formal and bureaucratic (this is necessary because of the generally large size) with a high level of specialisation by functions such as production, sales, marketing, etc.

Figure 2.8

Tall organisational structure

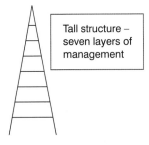

In tall organisations, there is usually a clear line of authority/command from the top of the organisation to the bottom.

Table 2.5 Advantages and disadvantages of tall structures

Advantages	Disadvantages
Narrow span of control ensures close supervision	Many layers of communication
Clear management structure	Many layers of authority can slow decision-making
Clear lines of responsibility and control	High level of overheads because managers and supervisors are expensive
Functions are clear and distinct	Subordinates have little freedom or responsibility
Clear progression and promotion ladder	Top managers may lose touch with the operatives

Can you think of any others for your organisation?

Matrix (or project-based) structures

A matrix structure is a team system which brings together people from different skill or functional areas to handle a specific project, and see it through to its conclusion. If they are to succeed, these teams need to be able to work closely together (Figure 2.9).

Figure 2.9

A matrix structure for a music company

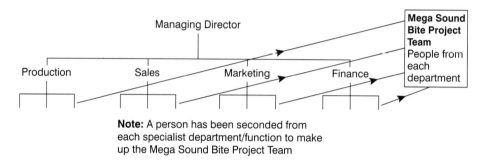

Note: A person has been seconded from each specialist department/function to make up the Mega Sound Bite Project Team

BT and Nokia both use multi-skill project teams, particularly for developing new products and services. The method overcomes most of the disadvantages of traditional types of organisation when specific projects can be identified, because:

Table 2.6 Advantages and disadvantages of a matrix structure

Advantages	Disadvantages
Communication within the team is easier	People may have more than one boss, e.g. the project manager and their own line manager, which can cause a conflict of loyalty
Can help break down barriers by bringing people together	There can be conflict between line managers and project managers over the allocation of resources
Specialists can contribute new ideas and see problems in a different way	If a matrix system is superimposed on an existing structure it can increase staff costs as more managers are created
A close team can be dynamic and enthusiastic, leading to a high level of motivation	Can be difficult to control and monitor if teams have a lot of independence
Project managers are directly responsible for completing a project on time and within the budget	
Individuals can be chosen according to the needs of the project	
May respond quicker to external change	
Can focus exclusively on individual clients/projects or issues	

■ teams can generate a high degree of loyalty, and often regret having to split up when the project finishes

■ teams can produce a high level of synergy (the whole is greater than the sum of the parts, or 2 + 2 = 5!).

Can you think of any others for your organisation?

---

assignment focus

At Nokia, a project team will research new ideas, develop and produce a business plan and create a prototype (mock-up) of the final product. Would a matrix structure be useful in your organisation?

Analysing the organisation structure

Span of control

An important feature of any organisation is the need to control all its activities. The structure needs to be designed to achieve this.

The span of control is the number of employees over whom a manager or supervisor has authority (Figure 2.11). Traditionally, the optimum number was considered to be between three and six people because this was thought to be the maximum someone could effectively control and manage. Narrow spans of control tend to create tall organisations whereas wide spans of control are more likely to be found in flat organisations. Currently there is a move to a wider span of control because this cuts costs as fewer supervisors are required. However, this is not without its dangers.

Today there appears to be no ideal span of control, both narrow and wide spans can be found in the same organisation. This suggests that the contingency approach, where the organisation responds to the current situation, seems most appropriate.

Figure 2.10

Hierarchy and line of command

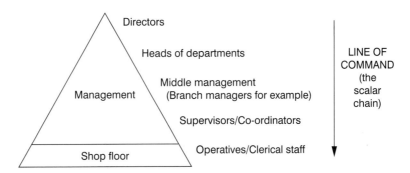

---

assignment focus

How many people in your organisation are supervisors responsible for?

The size of the span of control depends on:

■ the structure of the organisation and the degree of control and supervision required

■ the level of communication needed with subordinates – work requiring complex and frequent communication needs a narrower span of control

■ the amount of routine and non-routine work in the organisation – routine work requires relatively less hands on supervision so a wider span is possible

■ the level in the hierarchy – wider spans of control are possible lower down the hierarchy as work is less complex and more routine

■ the ability and willingness of management to delegate and subordinates to accept responsibility.

With a wide span of control, staff costs are lower as fewer supervisors are needed and there are more opportunities for delegation. However, communication and control could be more difficult. A narrow span gives better communication and control, but with higher costs.

assignment focus

Obtain an organisation chart of your centre.
1   What span of control do they have at different levels in the organisation?
2   What are the advantages and disadvantages of a wide and narrow span of control?
3   How many layers of management are there?
4   Would a different span of control improve performance?
5   How does your centre compare with the organisation you are investigating?
To achieve M1, you need to make suggestions on how management can raise performance. Would a different structure help?

Hierarchies

Two friends may set up a small business and work together on an equal footing, perhaps as a partnership with a flat structure, or as a private limited company. However, as the organisation expands and takes on employees, there will be a clear need to establish who is in charge, who gives orders and who carries them out. A structure is necessary and it will almost certainly show that there are different levels of authority, grades or status. Such a structure is called a hierarchy (Figure 2.10).

Figure 2.11

Span of control

Manager

Subordinates

Wide

Narrow

The structure of an organisation is mainly determined by the activities and functions needed to achieve its goals. For example, in a company making DVD players the main tasks would be to produce, market and sell the equipment; its structure should enable these goals to be achieved. There are three essential tasks, so it would make sense for the company to set up three specialised departments or sections to be responsible for these.

Those departments concerned solely with the main tasks of the organisation are called line departments or functions. A distinct chain of command, called the scalar chain (see Figure 2.10), runs in a line from the top of the organisation down through each department to the shop floor. This is achieved through delegation, i.e. a manager can give the authority for a subordinate to carry out a task but must accept responsibility.

Staff functions are those which support the main activities of the organisation. The DVD company may, for example, decide that it needs a specialised department to look after finance and accounts. This function may well help the business to operate more effectively, indeed it may be essential. However its role is to support the main functions (the line functions) of producing and selling. It is not in the line of command but works across the organisation to give help and advice at various points, perhaps with drawing up departmental budgets and monitoring these. The Finance Department is a staff function (see Figure 2.12). The Human Resources Department is also a staff function. Its role is to support and advise, not to produce.

Specialist function departments

Within small organisations, several functions may be carried out by one individual, e.g. finance and marketing. In large hierarchical organisations, however, these functions are frequently delegated to separate individuals, teams or departments.

See Unit 1 for more information, page 34.

Figure 2.12

Line and staff departments

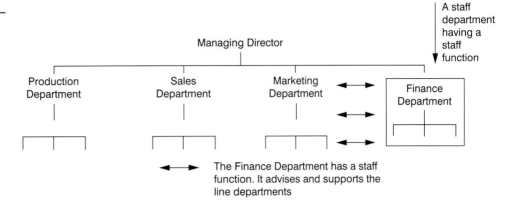

Very large companies are often organised into divisions or departments, each of which is responsible for separate product areas or geographical areas, e.g. Unilever, Nestlé and Kraft.

See page 36 for more detail on specialist functions.

ICI has an organisational structure which is based on geographical areas. Many retailers and public house chains are structured into regions with regional managers responsible for a group of outlets.

---

assignment focus

The main principles on which organisations are structured are: the scalar chain; span of control; line and staff functions; delegation; specialisation.

1 Use this terminology to describe the structure of your organisation.

  a) Does it have a flat, tall or matrix structure?

  b) Is there a regional manager?

2 What departments exist in your selected organisation?

3 What responsibilities do these departments have?

Authority and accountability

A manager's official position gives them the power, or authority, to make decisions which they can expect to be carried out. They may also have personal authority because of the expertise, skill, personality or knowledge they possess. Authority may be delegated or passed on to someone else. Do you follow orders because of the person or their position? It is important that managers with responsibility, e.g. for staff, budgets or equipment, are also given the authority to fulfil those responsibilities. Being accountable means being responsible for the actions or decisions we take. Managers can delegate authority, i.e. allow someone else to make decisions, but must remain accountable, i.e. accept full responsibility for those decisions. A cynic would say managers take credit for good decisions and never accept responsibility for bad decisions. Do you have managers like this? The organisation chart shows the lines and levels of authority and accountability.

Strategic and tactical direction

Industry-related leadership and judgement

A major responsibility of top level management is to guide the organisation through both good times and bad times when trading conditions can be difficult. Increased competition, cheap imports, changing customer demand, the arrival of a large supermarket, etc. have all been used as reasons why organisations may do badly. The ability of an organisation to respond to an ever-changing business environment depends on management competence. For example, in 2003 Hewlett Packard (HP) agreed to resell the Apple i-Pod; in 2005 the agreement was cancelled as it was no longer part of HP strategy. Fuji now supplies laser printers to Dell as a way of compensating for the fall in demand for traditional print film. Sound industry-based leadership and judgement are essential if organisations are to survive, evolve and achieve their objectives and those of their stakeholders. Judgement is insufficient without the ability to make decisions. It requires information.

Step 1: analysis
The organisation will need to carry out a complete analysis of its current situation with, for example, a SWOT, PESTEL and competitor assessment/audit. It will also need to know exactly where it wants to be at some point in the future (Figure 2.13).

Figure 2.13

Strategic and tactical decisions

Where is the organisation now? The current audit/ analysis	Srategic and tactical decisions are needed >>>>>>>>>>>	Where does the organisation want to be? How is it going to get here? Implementation

Step 2: decisions
Managers must create a clear vision of the strategic direction in which the organisation should be going, with a long-term mission for its future success. The overall strategy must have answers to these five questions:

- What business are we in?
- What are our products?
- What is our target market?
- Who are our customers?
- Where do we want to be in, say, five years' time?

Sound decisions will need to be made, for example about whether the business should grow by entering new markets or developing new products. Tesco and IKEA have grown using both strategies.

Step 3: implementation
Once a plan has been created which reflects the long-term future aims, objectives and activities of the organisation, it is essential that it is implemented effectively. There needs to be a strategy in place to recruit select and develop staff.

Tactical direction
Policies and plans need to be implemented at the tactical level and, finally, at the operational level. This requires good leadership and judgement, with systems and procedures which enable the mission to filter down through the organisation into departments, or functions, such as production processes, recruitment and service provision. For example, an organisation which claims 'we put our customers first' should be happy to deal with a customer who arrives five minutes before closing time with a complicated order!

This vertical flow of communication and information should have a positive impact on performance.

The strategic management decisions which are made would depend upon both the type of organisation and the sector in which it is operating. However, managers of, for example, charities, small businesses or public sector organisations would use a similar sequence of steps.

Consequences of effective/ineffective management
Business news is continuous, always exciting and sometimes dramatic. Familiar high street names disappear; oil companies announce huge profits or losses depending on the price of oil.

These are some possible consequences of effective/ineffective management.

- Survival in a new small business may be a major achievement. One in three new businesses fails within the first year.

- Improved performance – where do your centre or local hospital come in the government-produced league tables? 'An effective management team' is often given by Ofsted as a reason for improved performance at a centre. It is measured by better retention and achievement and a reduction in truancy/unauthorised absence. What is your role in the success of your centre?

- Market share – this is the percentage of the market held by a particular product or business. Increasing market share is a major objective of many large businesses, where competition is intense. It is less important for small local businesses such as plumbers or builders. An increase in market share is likely to be the direct result of effective management achieving a permanent competitive advantage over its rivals.

There are examples of market share on pages 110 and 177.

- Reputation/market standing – why do some retailers acquire a better reputation than others? McDonald's, Burger King and KFC all provide fast food – which do you consider to be well or poorly managed? What criteria could you use to make your decision – cleanliness, speed and quality of service, etc?

- Rising/falling share price – the effectiveness of management in a public limited company (plc) is often shown by its share price. The shares of companies which have or are expected to do well (because of rising profits, acquisition of new products, entry into new markets, etc.) are more likely to be bought than sold. Heavy buying of shares tends to drive up their price; heavy selling tends to push the price down.

- Completion of a project within the deadline and within the budget – this is a good indicator that management has in place effective systems for monitoring and controlling work throughout the life cycle of the project. If a project is completed behind schedule, this could be due to poor management or circumstances outside the project manager's control.

- Out-performance or under-performance against service delivery targets – many, if not all, organisations presumably have targets which focus on providing the best possible service to customers, such as answering all telephone calls within three rings, responding to complaints within 24 hours, delivering your take-away pizza within 20 minutes, etc. An effective management will make sure that all resources are managed to produce an effective operation. An organisation which out-performs against its targets means targets have been achieved, i.e. your meal is delivered in 15 minutes. Under-performance means your meal is delivered in 25 minutes. If an organisation continuously under-performs, or fails to live up to stakeholder expectations, its reputation will deteriorate, sales and market share could fall, leading to possible failure and eventual closure. The share price of a public limited company, such as Marks & Spencer, could fall and other companies could try to take it over by buying the shares. M&S was nearly taken over but managed to fight off the bid by convincing its current shareholders not to sell. By 2006 its fortunes had changed and £50m was paid to its 52,000 shop floor as a bonus. What is the current position?

The Administration Order (Insolvency) Act 1986 states that if a business is in financial difficulties, e.g. with large debts or insufficient working capital and cannot pay its way, an administrator may be appointed to handle its affairs and try to keep the business running (survival) as a going concern. This way assets may be worth more than if the business is liquidated or wound up, i.e. comes to an end.

We can also see the consequences of an ineffective or effective management when we examine how various stakeholder groups may be affected (Table 2.7).

Table 2.7 The consequences of effective and ineffective management on stakeholder groups

Stakeholder group	Consequences of effective management	Consequences of ineffective management
Workers/operatives	Improved morale and motivation which comes from active communication with workers who feel involved with the decision-making processes	Poor management can create a 'them and us' feeling among staff leading to conflict and industrial unrest
Customers	Improved market standing, image and reputation leading to increased sales/profits Cause-related charities could attract greater funding	May feel let down by poor customer service, lack of appreciation, goods 'out of stock', could go elsewhere, poor quality and delivery
Suppliers	A reliable network of trusted suppliers where the relationship is mutually profitable	Suppliers feel under-valued and exploited perhaps because of over-hard bargaining
Shareholders	Possible higher share price, higher credit rating which will help future borrowing, more profits distributed, further shareholder investment becomes easier	Possibly lower share price which could lead to shareholders selling shares and depressing the price even further. Other companies might attempt hostile/unwanted take-over
Local community	Good relationships/partnership with the community built up through e.g. strict controls on pollution	Community alienated by lack of concern for needs, pollution and poor work practices could lead to a boycott of the products
Achievement of objectives	Objectives achieved, growth secure, possible management and worker bonuses	Management and workers at risk, possible closure and bankruptcy

assignment focus

To complete P2, you should add some current business news for your organisation which demonstrates the efficiency/inefficiency of its management. Look at bbc.co.uk news front page, business

Management of Resources

assignment focus

To achieve P3, you must describe ways in which a manager's role includes the management of resources. You will need to visit the organisation you are investigating to find out about its **physical resources**, take pictures and make notes after your visit.

Figure 2.14

The role of management processes in managing resources

Inputs/resources ⟶ Management processes ⟶ Outputs
Physical   Co-ordinating resources   Services
Human   to produce a product or   Goods
Financial   provide a service
Technological

Physical resources

These are the buildings, equipment and facilities needed to provide goods and services. They include, for example, homes, classrooms, car showrooms, offices, shops, railway and industrial premises and your selected business. The image and reputation of a business often depends on the quality of its premises. Badly maintained premises say, in effect, 'We are an unsuccessful business'. How often have you said, 'I don't like the look of that place' and taken your custom elsewhere? Customers demand high standards. It is the responsibility of management to provide them. In large organisations, a whole department headed by a specialist premises or facilities manager may be responsible.

Management at a retail store, for example, will want to create a relaxing atmosphere for their customers so careful thought will go into the layout and design. Fixtures and fittings such as shelves and rails will be used to display goods and reinforce the brand image. Window displays will be designed to show the products to best advantage and tempt customers inside. You should look at the management of the physical resources as an integral part of the overall management process designed to achieve corporate objectives.

assignment focus

To achieve P3, you will need to look at the manager's role in maintaining and improving buildings and facilities.

For the organisation that you are studying for your assignment, answer the following questions:

1   Is the building clean, safe and healthy? i.e. Is the Health and Safety at Work Act (HASAWA) being obeyed?

2   Describe the premises:
   a) Are they old or modern, brick or concrete and glass, etc.?
   b) Where is it located?

Materials and waste

Look at how goods are unloaded. Is there a queue of lorries when you arrive to shop at your local supermarket at 9.30 on Saturday morning? How are waste materials disposed of? Is there a green policy for recycling glass, plastic, cans, cardboard? In a hospital, how does it dispose of medical waste? How often do the cleaners change the water when cleaning a ward? How quickly is spillage cleaned up in a supermarket? How are toner cartridges disposed of? Reducing waste can provide substantial cost savings.

assignment focus

1   Does your organisation make and/or sell products?

2   What waste does it produce?

3   How is this disposed of?

4   Could it be improved?

Plant and machinery

These are the assets used by the business to carry out its activities, e.g. a kiln in a pottery or a fork lift truck in a warehouse. They can include lifts and escalators, ovens in the bakery section, dry cleaning equipment, heavy lifting equipment, etc. Who is responsible for repair, maintenance and cleaning? Is it done by internal staff or by a specialist outside company, i.e. is it outsourced? Is it properly guarded or protected? The type of equipment used will depend entirely on the activities of the business, e.g. computers and printers in an office, scissors and hair dryers in a hairdressers, etc. Burns are a major cause of injury in pizza outlets.

assignment focus

1   What plant, machinery or equipment is used in your organisation?

2   Do staff appear properly trained to use the equipment?

3   Does it break down? Is it safe?

Planned maintenance and refurbishment

Does the building look cared for? Are the staff areas as well maintained as the public areas? Who is responsible? For example, do the local staff do minor repairs and maintenance? Does head office or an outside company do the major work? In a restaurant, are the outside windows clean? If not, what do you think the areas you cannot see are like?

Maintenance is carried out to make sure that:

- the premises, plant and machinery comply with health and safety legislation
- the premises are fit for the purpose they are intended
- the image of the organisation is protected/improved
- premises, plant and machinery do not deteriorate or break down.

Planned/preventative maintenance

Regular maintenance is carried out in advance to prevent any breakdown of the facilities resulting in loss of production or sales. It can either be done internally by the facilities or premises team, or it can be out-sourced.

Reactive maintenance

Repairs are carried out or parts replaced when something breaks down. This approach can result in lost production and is often less cost-effective than a planned approach.

Refurbishment

Refurbishment may simply mean brightening up the premises to attract extra customers or a complete 'makeover'. It is often associated with a change of management or ownership. For example, the new management/owners of a restaurant may want a new image for the premises. This could involve new internal layouts and designs, redecoration, new fixtures, fittings, signage, etc.

assignment focus

1 How often is maintenance carried out in your organisation?
2 How long does it take before something is repaired?

Health and safety

Emergency provisions are covered by health and safety legislation, e.g. clear fire exits, regular fire drills, clear instructions for emergency evacuation, regularly serviced fire extinguishers and emergency lighting.

assignment focus

Investigate the emergency provisions for your organisation.

1 How often are fire drills carried out?
2 Would part-time staff know what to do in an emergency?
3 Are fire exits clear? Are exit routes clearly marked?

Insurance provides financial cover or protection against, for example, the risk of fire, theft, flood, etc. Every employer must have employers' liability insurance in case compensation has to be paid to an employee who is injured or contracts a disease as a result of their work. Public liability insurance is also recommended to cover against any claims made by non-employees, such as students, patients, customers, guests, etc., whilst they are on the premises.

A certificate of employers' liability insurance must be displayed at the premises. Where is it kept in your organisation?

Security

Security is required to protect people, equipment, premises, stock, trade secrets and cash. Maintaining security is now a major concern for many organisations, with security guards a familiar sight in almost every high street. Entry and exit searches are commonplace. Many businesses search their staff.

What are the security features of your organisation? Copy the checklist below and complete it. You can amend it to suit your organisation.

Table 2.8 Security checklist

Feature	Comments
CCTV	
Security guards: How many? How often do they patrol?	
Searches on entry/exit	
ID cards compulsory	
Metal grille or shutters, e.g. shop fronts	
Fire/burglar alarms	
Panic buttons next to the tills	
Specialist features, e.g. time locks for banks	
Double entry doors, e.g. in off licences	
Internal door entry locks	
Security tags on products	
Perimeter walls and fencing, patrols, dogs	

Human resources

People, or human resources, are the most important resource in any organisation and, not surprisingly, there is a direct connection between the quality of the workforce and commercial success. To succeed, an organisation needs staff who are committed to meeting its aims and objectives, equipped to do so by adequate training and motivated by management to achieve their potential.

It is the job of **human resources management** to recruit, develop and retain quality staff. Within a small business, with perhaps one or two employees, responsibility for human resources will lie with the owner or with the partners. A small company may have one person whose job it is to look after issues relating to staff. Large organisations with many employees will have a whole section devoted to personnel.

A wide range of functions may come under human resources, although these may be organised differently from one business to another. For instance, salaries may be dealt with by a separate payroll section while many routine matters, such as booking annual leave, may be the job of the line manager. In very large organisations, it may be necessary to organise human resources into separate sections. Remember that the aim is to make the most effective use of people. Toyota put it this way: 'The key to maximising quality and productivity lies in tapping the innate judgement and creativity of employees in the workplace.' All managers at all levels have the responsibility.

Originally personnel departments were set up to look after the welfare of employees and the day-to-day administration of policies affecting them. Gradually the idea developed that a specialist understanding of issues such as recruitment, training, welfare, payments and employment law was important for business performance. The term human resource management (HRM) first appeared in the 1980s. There is still a good deal of routine administration and record-keeping, but the emphasis is now on actively helping the business pursue its goals by creating and maintaining an appropriate workforce. The idea is to maximise the use of human resources.

Recruitment and retention of staff

The first stage in the recruitment process is to identify the vacancy. New staff may be needed because:

- staff may have left the organisation because they have been dismissed or resigned
- staff have been promoted
- the business is growing
- job roles are changing.

Once managers agree a vacancy exists and authorisation is given to fill it, then the job must be defined.

The job description

Following an analysis of the job, a **job description** will be written which sets out: job title, grade, department, location, responsible to (manager's title), responsible for (e.g. staff, cash, equipment), job purpose and duties.

A person specification may be prepared which could include: physical characteristics, qualifications, experience, aptitude and motivation. (Are you a self starter, able to work on your own?)

Methods of recruitment

Internal vacancies only

The organisation may already have the right people with the right skills to do the job, particularly if the training and development programme has been effective. In this case, they may appoint internally. This may, of course, leave a vacancy elsewhere in the business.

Vacancies can be advertised within the organisation by putting advertisements on prominent company notice boards and in company newsletters, bulletins and newspapers. Note that advertisements can also be used to promote the image of the company generally, both its name and its positive qualities – 'We are an equal opportunity employer', for example.

The main advantages of making internal appointments are that it is cheap, fast and it avoids some of the problems of training and induction. The candidate is also known to the organisation. However, there are disadvantages. Existing staff may feel they have an automatic right to promotion, whether or not they are competent. Also, without new skills and ideas brought in from outside, an organisation could be resistant to change.

External vacancies

It is often necessary to make an external appointment and some organisations are compelled to advertise all posts externally. In this case, the process must be carefully planned to deliver the appropriate applicants. Advertising, together with the administrative costs of despatching application forms, checking returned forms, shortlisting and interviewing, can be time-consuming and expensive.

A firm will want to be sure that it attracts the right sort of people for the job. If it does not, then the whole recruitment process will have to be repeated, whilst the business carries on with a staff shortage. There are a number of ways of looking for staff outside the organisation.

- Job centres, once notified, will do the recruiting by sending suitable people for interview. The service is free and most useful for advertising skilled, semi-skilled, clerical and manual jobs. There are also registers for professional people.
- Employment agencies are private sector companies whose aim is to make a profit by selling a service. They are found in many high streets. For example, the Thomson Directory for the Bromley area in Kent lists 42 employment and recruitment agencies (including the job centre) covering 'accountancy', 'general personnel', 'nursing homecare', 'technical staff' and 'office staff'.

- Educational establishments, such as schools and colleges, can be a useful source of potential employees. Companies can use the centre's careers services, participate at careers events or offer work experience as a way of trying out interested students.

- Management recruitment consultants are private sector agencies used to recruit senior management. Look at the 'Appointments' section of a quality Sunday newspaper where you will find adverts for 'Chief Executive', 'International Marketing Director', etc. These have generally been placed by specialist recruitment companies.

- Executive search consultants, often called 'headhunters', are sometimes employed to recruit senior staff directly. A firm wishing to engage someone with special qualities for a top position will give the job description to the consultant, who will seek out possible candidates to approach. The consultant is able to do this by being 'in the know'. Often the 'target' will be working for a rival firm so the approach will be made in confidence. The headhunter will charge a large commission for a successful appointment but there are no advertising costs. The whole process is similar to that of an agent arranging the transfer of a footballer from one club to another.

- Online advertising – many organisations now have the capability to recruit online. Most high street stores have websites advertising for staff at all levels (from part-time sales staff to senior management), both locally and nationally. Look at Virgin.com to see the qualities it wants in its staff.

Staff retention

Some degree of labour movement into and out of an organisation is both useful and desirable because it brings in new staff with new ideas, skills and enthusiasm. On the other hand, too high a rate of movement can be expensive because of:

- recruitment, selection and training costs of new staff – e.g. it takes 18 months and costs £70,000 to train an engine driver

- efficiency costs caused by disruption – it may take some time before new staff can produce high quality work

- leaving costs – it may be necessary to make redundancy payments, pay notice periods or pay for holidays due.

The terms 'labour turnover' and 'staff turnover' are often used to describe the rate at which people leave an organisation and are replaced. It is calculated by comparing the number of people who leave with the average number of staff employed.

Organisations will interview staff who are leaving voluntarily (exit interviews). They might find that high turnover is due to:

- low morale, perhaps due to poor working conditions, unsuitable pay structures or unsympathetic management

- poor recruitment, resulting in unsuitable staff, or poor induction procedures – research shows that staff wastage can be high with new recruits

- poor career prospects, allowing little chance of promotion or simply better conditions elsewhere

- little or no effective staff development and training.

Management of staffing

One major responsibility of HR is to make sure that there are always sufficient staff with the right skills to achieve the aims and objectives of the organisation, both in the short and long term. It will have to plan ahead and match its demand for labour with the available supply.

This may involve employing a mix of full-time, part-time and temporary staff to meet its needs, e.g. extra part-time staff may be needed in a restaurant during the evenings and at weekends. Temporary staff may be employed in an office to cover annual leave. Retaining staff is important as new staff have to be trained.

Temporary staff for Christmas

Game hired 2,500 new temporary staff for Christmas 2005. They joined the 4,500 employed in the 396 Game stores in the UK and Ireland selling Grand Theft Auto, Half Life 2, Need For Speed, Underground 2, etc. They are needed to 'provide advice and assistance to customers, shorten queues, open more tills, keep shelves and displays full, work in store stock rooms, and make sure that the stores are well maintained.' Robert Quinn, Game UK Sales Director said, 'We need experts, so it's the ideal job for video games fans who like helping people.' Do you go to Game?

The recruitment agency Adecco estimated that it would cost retailers £150 million just to recruit temporary staff for the busy Christmas period. Sarah Blancke, Head of Adecco retail, said, 'Store and HR managers spend nearly 30 per cent of their time finding and managing suitable staff. The festive season is an increasingly strategic aspect of HR in the retail sector. The process can be one of a retailer's highest costs in terms of store management, time and resource.'

Source: www.theretailbulletin.co.uk

activity

1 What planning do you think is involved in recruiting Christmas staff?
2 What planning does your organisation do for Christmas or other religious festivals?
3 Why is it necessary?

It is worth visiting www.theretailbulletin.co.uk

Contracts of employment

There is a large body of law dealing with employment, e.g. **equal opportunities** legislation and minimum wage legislation. (What is the current minimum wage for under/over 18-year-olds?) Owners and managers must ensure that they obey the law because breaking the law could result in severe penalties.

By law, an employee who works for eight hours or more a week must be given a **contract of employment** within two months of commencing employment (Trade Union Reform and Employment Rights Act 1993). This is drawn up by the employer and signed by the employee. It exists to give both parties a degree of protection, certainty and security and can be enforced by law.

All contracts must include:

- the name of the company and the employee
- the date when employment began
- the date on which the employee's period of continuous service began – this may be different from the previous point if a person transfers from one organisation to another and all service is taken to be continuous (this may happen to civil servants changing department)
- pay scale, how payment will be made and at what intervals
- hours of work
- holiday entitlement
- terms relating to notification of sickness and sick pay
- pension arrangements
- length of notice which an employee is entitled to receive and must give
- job title
- disciplinary rules, or where they may be found, appeals procedure and grievance procedure.

Other conditions which may be included are: need for medical examinations, working from different locations, right to search employees, need for confidentiality and the need to obey certain specific rules of the organisation. These could be included in a separate staff handbook.

The above are called express terms, that is, they are openly agreed. There are also implied terms in the contract. These are not set out in writing and not spoken of but are assumed to hold. For example, the employee has a duty of fidelity (trustworthiness) to the employer, and is expected to exercise due care. The employee in turn will expect to be supported if in a managerial role and will not be expected to do anything unlawful as part of the job.

Personal or individual contracts

Many businesses have standard contracts setting out identical conditions and rates of pay for everyone in a particular job. This may be the result of 'collective bargaining' between trade unions and employers. However, personal contracts are sometimes offered to the senior managers of an organisation or people with specialist skills, e.g. you may have seen the term 'salary negotiable' in job advertisements.

Individual contracts are negotiated directly and privately with the individuals who are often asked not to reveal their salary to other staff. The key parts of a personal contract only apply to one employee.

They can include:

■ a personal pay package

■ personal bonus or commission rates

■ special benefits such as improved car allowances and medical services

■ hospitality and travel arrangements

■ company credit card allowances.

Part-time workers may also be on limited personal contracts, but without the 'perks' offered to senior full-time staff.

Ergonomic and safe workplace

One definition of **ergonomics** is 'the study of the relationship between people and their working environment'. People can experience physical strain, e.g. if their chairs, desks, machines, computer keyboards and VDUs are incorrectly positioned.

Work-related injuries can be caused, for example, by sitting incorrectly when keyboarding, and repetitive strain injury (RSI) may result from constantly repeating actions in the same position – on a production-line, for instance. Checkout staff in supermarkets can lift up to 10 tons during a shift as they pass goods over the scanner. Ergonomically designed furniture, correctly positioned machinery and regular breaks in routine can help prevent this.

Emergency procedures and access

Under the Health and Safety at Work Act 1974 (HASAWA), the employer has the responsibility for providing a safe and healthy workplace. Management at all levels have a direct responsibility for the health and safety of their staff and any visitors/customers on the premises whatever the size of the organisation. All staff must obey HASAWA.

remember
If you ever go clubbing, always check where the emergency exits are and whether they are unlocked. There have been several terrible fires in clubs, which have caused deaths.

assignment focus

Carry out a simple visual health and safety check of your organisation, for example:

1 Are there fire extinguishers, water sprinklers (these come on automatically when there is a fire), fire alarms, smoke alarms?

2 Are the emergency exits clear and unlocked? Do you know where they are? Have you ever been told?

3 How often are fire drills held?

4 How quickly is any spillage cleaned up?

Structuring of staff into divisions/teams

Now central to the culture and structure of many organisations, building and managing teams is an essential skill for any manager. Effective teams will have a common purpose and clear targets, such as providing great customer service; with an open and honest approach to solving problems, i.e. a 'no blame' culture. Participation and involvement in decision-making will be encouraged through empowering team members to help, encourage and support each other. The team leader/supervisor may be responsible for co-ordinating the resources available to the team, meeting targets, monitoring team performance and liaising with other departments.

The way in which an organisation is structured will have a major impact on its performance. The structure will depend on the activities of the organisation. Departments could, for example, be based on geographical area, products (in retail outlets), type of customers (**B2B** or **B2C**) or function (human resources, marketing. etc.).

See page 70.

Teams may be created inside departments, e.g. the IT or personnel team, or formed specifically to deal with particular issues/problems. These one-off project teams are often seen in matrix-type structures.

See page 69.

Lines of authority and accountability

Effective staff management requires clear and well-defined lines of authority and accountability, so that everyone knows their job roles and responsibilities. Job descriptions may need to rewritten to include any changes taking place in the organisation. Operatives will need to know who their 'boss' is and who they have to report to. Similarly, managers must know who they have responsibility for. For example, the author has had experience of being asked to do a job by one manager, then ten minutes later being told by another 'to leave that and get on with this', and being unable to complete either job satisfactorily, getting told off by both. With hindsight, it is obvious that neither manager knew the limits or boundaries of their own roles and responsibilities. The problem could be avoided with a clear and up-to-date organisation chart with well-defined job descriptions.

See page 68.

Co-ordination of team resources to meet targets

It is the responsibility of managers to make sure that the team has all the resources necessary to complete its tasks and meet its targets. Are the facilities satisfactory? Is the equipment well maintained and suitable? Or does it break down? Is there enough? Are all the materials available and in the right place? Is there sufficient well-trained staff to cope? Or is there a staff shortage? Is the financial budget sufficient?

The resources need to be co-ordinated to make sure that tasks are completed. The manager will need to plan the activities and allocate the work to the right people. What could happen if staff do not turn up, machines break down, equipment or materials are not available? These are all symptoms of an ineffective management.

Monitoring of team performance

Research has shown that an effective team is likely to have these characteristics:

- focus on customer targets and goals
- relatively small with good leadership
- high level of help, support and trust amongst members
- ideas and experiences are shared
- all team members work to the same objectives

- work roles are clearly defined and everyone knows what they should do
- absenteeism and sickness rates are low
- morale and motivation are high, members enjoy working with one another
- team members seek agreement rather than argument
- open communication with a high level of participation in decision-making.

To achieve this level of effectiveness, the team leader and team members will need to be properly trained and developed, and there needs to be a clear system of **incentives** and reward for successful teams. There will need to a balance between the achievement of any team tasks and the needs of the individual team members. Every aspect of the team needs to be monitored to ensure that it achieves optimum performance.

Table 2.9 Advantages and disadvantages of team working

Advantages	Disadvantages
Staff are able to share ideas/experience/workload	Some employees do not like working in teams
Teams can achieve synergy, i.e. a team working together can achieve more than the same number of individuals working separately or 1 + 1 = 3	Can take away individual initiative
	Decision-making can take longer as a consensus is needed
Help and support can be given to each member	Conflict can occur if the team members are incompatible
Enthusiasm, commitment and job satisfaction tend to rise	Weaker/stronger members can be frustrated
Tasks can be completed more quickly and effectively	Needs clear direction and targets
	May not be appropriate in some situations
	Team leaders need effective training

assignment focus

1   Does your organisation use teams to achieve tasks?
2   How are the teams structured?
3   How well do they perform?
4   If your organisation does not use teams, could it? Should it?

Liaison with other departments

You have probably heard people say, 'I blame the system' whenever anything goes wrong. Every organisation is a system or a set of inter-related, or connected, parts managed to achieve a common purpose. The parts or sub-systems may be departments, functions, different teams or separate locations. The boundary is the link, or interface, between sub-systems. It is here that most problems occur, e.g. between production and personnel, between chilled and frozen food, etc. It is important that managers liaise closely with their colleagues in other sections/departments to minimise conflicts and smooth out any problems. In retail clothing shops, the conflicts seem to be over the amount of display space and the number of staff allocated to each section. These could be solved by good liaison and communication to achieve good working relationships.

Grievance and disciplinary procedures

Despite the existence of employment law and attempts at consultation and employee involvement, industrial disputes do occur. There needs to be a system in place for resolving these. There will be:

- *disciplinary procedures* – to take action against employees
- *grievance procedures* – where employees have a complaint against the employer
- appeals procedures – where each side may appeal against a judgement.

Disciplinary procedures

Disciplinary action may result from:

- failure to obey work rules – particularly serious if it leads to dangerous work practices
- breaking a contract of employment, e.g. constant lateness
- unsatisfactory work performance after reasonable warnings.

Disciplinary action may result in:

- suspension – where a serious offence is alleged, it may be unwise for the employee to stay at work both from the organisation's point of view and the employee's (soldiers, police officers, teachers and surgeons are sometimes suspended, often on full pay, while allegations are investigated)
- warnings, both oral and written
- dismissal, which could be seen as fair or unfair.

There should be an agreed procedure, which should be fair, accessible, easy to understand, transparent and available to everyone.

Look at the ACAS website (Advisory, Conciliation and Arbitration Service) at: www.acas.org.uk

Grievance procedures

'Anybody working in an organisation may, at some time, have problems or concerns about their work, working conditions or relationships with colleagues that they wish to talk about with management.'

Source: www.acas.org.uk

A grievance may be caused by:

- changes in the conditions and terms of employment
- health and safety
- bullying and harassment
- changes in working practices or working conditions
- lack of equal opportunities.

This is the procedure recommended by ACAS.

- Step 1: The employee informs the employer of their grievance in writing.
- Step 2: The employer invites the employee to a meeting to discuss the grievance where the right to be accompanied will apply. The employer notifies the employee in writing of the decision and notifies of the right to appeal.
- Step 3: The employee informs the employer if they wish to appeal. The employer must invite them to a meeting and following the meeting inform the employee of the final decision. (Employees must take all reasonable steps to attend meetings.)

Source: www.acas.org.uk

assignment focus

1   Obtain the disciplinary and grievance procedures for your organisation, either from your employer or for employees at your school or college.

2   Does it follow the outline given here?

3   Is anything missing or has anything been added?

Monitoring of staff time keeping and absence

This is essential to meet targets and make improvements. Operational monitoring focuses on the individual. It will include checking and recording absenteeism, punctuality and time-keeping (arriving late and leaving early). Behaviour, attitude to work and customer service skills may be noted and could form part of a performance **appraisal**. Here the worker and line manager discuss past performance, including strengths and areas for improvement and agree the targets to be achieved before the next review. A successful appraisal can lead to a pay rise (see PRP below). At the tactical level, the emphasis is on team or departmental performance, e.g. Are deadlines kept, quality maintained and improved, targets achieved, budgets adhered to?

Performance management

A business needs to ensure that its employees are performing effectively. It will wish to:

- identify areas which are unsatisfactory
- find areas where employees need to be trained and developed
- encourage and reward good performance – perhaps with performance-related pay in the form of bonuses or pay increases.

The term 'performance management' came into use in the 1980s. It refers to the practice of setting targets, measuring performance against these and suggesting courses of action. It is forward-looking and reflects a world in which businesses are constantly trying to improve. Since the process has implications for employees' futures and sometimes for their pay, the process needs to be fair and, to use the modern jargon, 'transparent', that is, the reasons for decisions need to be made clear to all concerned. A number of methods may be used to check performance; the choice will depend upon the business in question.

case study 2.6 — Performance management at Tesco

'Our graduate programme is for those who want to excel. It is for people who want to push the limits and grow their potential. It is not for those who just accept things.'

Source: Tesco

At Tesco, performance management applies to everyone. The aim is to make sure that all employees:

- are aware of what the company is trying to achieve in its strategic plan
- make plans to focus on their own part in making the company successful
- have an on-going review of their progress.

There is an emphasis on continual improvement and staff are encouraged to develop themselves to do their jobs better.

The steering wheel

The directors set out the strategic plan for the company, called the corporate wheel or steering wheel. This shows what the company aims to achieve for the next year in each of the four main areas: customers, operations, finance and people (its employees). The plan is then cascaded down to:

- heads of department who plan to meet their departmental targets
- section managers who set out plans for their teams
- the teams on the shop floor, in the warehouses and in the offices.

Figure 2.15

The steering wheel

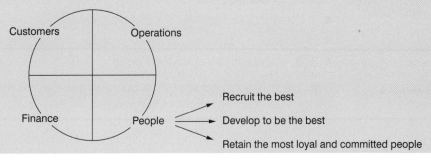

Link See also the corporate wheel, or steering wheel, on page 59.

activity

1 Read through the extract carefully then answer these questions:
   a) What does it tell you about the aims and objectives of Tesco and how these can be achieved?
   b) What does it say about the role of management?
   c) Why does Tesco consider staff development important?
   d) Why is monitoring performance at Tesco so important?
2 To achieve M1, describe the human resources monitoring and development that takes place in your organisation. Is it effective? Give reasons. Can you suggest improvements?

Investors in People

Investors in People is a national quality standard backed by the goverment. It is awarded for effective investment in the training and development of people (employees) in order to achieve business goals. The standard, which was developed in 1990, provides a framework for 'improving business performance and competitiveness'.

The standard is based upon four key principles:

Figure 2.16

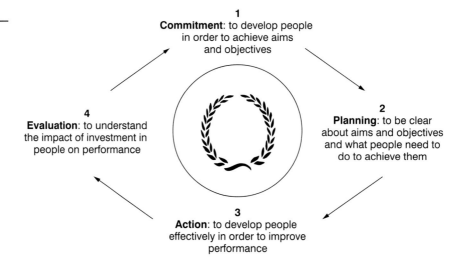

There are 12 indicators against which businesses wishing to achieve the stamp will be assessed.

assignment focus

A third of British businesses have Investors in People status. Try to find out more about the benefits, for example:

■ If you attend a college then this may have the award or be working towards it.

■ If you work in a part-time job then your employer might have the award.

■ Your local authority may have the award.

Note: the IiP symbol often appears on business notepaper. Alternatively, you could look at the Investors in People website on www.iipuk.co.uk/. Also, look at page 196.

Culture and leadership style

The culture of an organisation can be summarised by the sentence, 'It's the way we do things here.' Do your classes always start and finish on time? Do you always turn up on time? What happens if you don't? Do you care? Do the staff care?

The culture of an organisation is the set of customs, values, attitudes and behaviour adopted and shared by its members. It may be seen in the way management treat workers, how colleagues treat each other, how staff treat customers, workers' attitudes towards the product they sell or the service they provide, even the clothes people wear at work and the language they use. The culture sets the standards for the organisation; it gives support and provides guidance. Winning companies have a strong set of values which are reflected in everything they do. They strive for excellence and continuous improvement. Does your organisation do this? Do you? Do staff in your organisation say, 'Sorry, I can't do that. It's more than my job's worth'?

---

assignment focus

In your organisation:

1 Who makes all the key decisions? Are lower level staff involved in decision-making? What decisions can operatives make?

2 Does the organisation stress the rules and procedures? Or is it more flexible?

3 Do staff work in teams?

4 Do staff feel valued? Or is getting the job done more important?

5 Is there staff uniform? Do all staff wear it, or just the operatives?

6 How do managers address staff, and vice versa? Are first names used? Is there a professional culture or is it too casual? Is there a formal or informal atmosphere?

7 Do managers and operatives share the same canteen with the same menu?

8 Do managers and operatives share the same rest room facilities?

9 Are staff allowed to bring their friends to work, make private telephone calls, use the internet for private purposes or make private photocopies? Are mobile phones allowed at the workplace? This separation of professional and private activities is a cause for concern in many workplaces where staff have been sacked for sending or receiving private e-mails.

Culture, structure and change

It is important for an organisation to have a clear mission and a unifying culture. No organisation can let its culture get in the way of change. Marks & Spencer and Sainsbury, for many years the leaders and most bench-marked companies in UK retailing, have been overtaken by rivals. Commentators suggest that this was due to their inability to change their culture in line with changes in the marketplace, whereas Terry Leahy, Chief Executive of Tesco, says, 'We changed our culture by understanding customers better than anyone else and by taking care of our staff.' Tesco is now number one, and is itself a benchmarked company, i.e. a leader in best practice.

How do managers lead?

Some theories (known as trait theories) suggest a list of qualities (traits) that make an effective leader. Important qualities are: integrity, enthusiasm, warmth, calmness, 'tough but fair'. However, there are a number of such lists and none is exhaustive. The particular traits required will vary with the situation and the job in hand. People who are leaders in one situation – situational leaders – will not always be successful in all situations.

Style theories

The main styles of management leadership that have been identified include:

■ autocratic style – managers take all decisions with very little or no consultation; they expect their orders to be carried out without any disagreement or questions

- democratic style – managers take great care to involve all members of the team in discussion. It is a 'we need to find out what everyone thinks' approach. Although the style can work well with a small, highly motivated team, it can fail when the group cannot make a decision and needs real guidance and direction

- consultative style – similar to the democratic approach, but instead of allowing the group to make the decision, managers do so themselves. This approach can create a high level of motivation with good quality output and results

- *laissez-faire* (leave well alone) style – managers intervene as little as possible and allow the group to take control. The group may become leaderless

- task/activity managers – concentrate on the job to be done, e.g. some sports team managers 'take every game as it comes'

- people managers – care more about the people they lead, their emotions and feelings. The captain whose side has just lost badly would say 'We tried hard but we were beaten by the better team on the day'.

assignment focus

1 What style do managers in your organisation use? Is everyone the same? Is it the same in each department? Does it vary with the situation? Does it depend on the personality of the manager, or who is being managed?
2 What effect does style have on staff motivation and performance?
3 What type of boss or teacher do you prefer?

Incentives and rewards

An effective system of managing incentives and rewards is often vital if the organisation wants to motivate its staff and improve performance. However, the system needs to be SMART and easy to understand. For example, the London Borough of Lewisham replaced its scheme for performance-related pay and took up Investors in People instead. It felt that this would motivate staff better.

Financial incentives

For most people, pay is a major reason for going to work. Pay certainly plays a part in motivation, but it is not always clear what part. Employees may have different priorities. It could be job satisfaction or the 'fun of working as part of a team with a cheeky grin' (*source*: www.virgin.co.uk).

The manager of Greek national football team who won the Euro 2004 football competition was on £40,000 a year. Compare this with the England manager on £4m. Who was more motivated?

Pay opens the door to many other things which may motivate, such as status and self-fulfilment. Payment is usually associated with motivation where it is linked with performance. An extreme case is piece-work where there is no basic pay and payment is entirely based on output. Home-workers in the fashion trade or casual agricultural workers, such as fruit-pickers, are often paid in this way. More usually, basic pay is supplemented by performance-related pay in the form of a bonus or commission for good results. Financial incentives to sell may motivate the employee but are not always good for the customer. Can you think why?

The traditional image of the car salesperson as a 'shark' came about in this way. Someone who is desperate to sell because they need the commission is unlikely to give the customer the best advice. Linking pay to performance may give employees an incentive to work more effectively. However, it may not be appropriate for all kinds of work. Profit-sharing schemes are another form of incentive. Some companies, e.g. John Lewis, try to encourage employees by letting them share in the year's profits. In this way they can see a link between their work, the performance of the company and their pay.

Non-financial incentives

There is a growing trend for rewarding staff with non-financial incentives.

assignment focus

How are staff paid in your organisation? Are there financial and/or non-financial incentives? Do they work?

How to improve performance

Evidence seems to show that performance is improved by:

- profit sharing schemes
- increasing staff participation (involving, consulting)
- good job design
- sharing gains (not individual PRP).

Performance-related pay (PRP)

This is a method of linking an employee's pay to the work they perform or the output they achieve. Other performance indicators such as improvements in productivity or quality can also be used. PRP would normally be based on the achievement of targets set at an appraisal interview. Failing to meet targets would mean no PRP, i.e no extra pay! It could therefore be a major incentive to improving performance, both for an individual and the organisation.

Does PRP work?

The evidence is that it can work in the appropriate situation. However, its effects are not always clear. It is not suitable for all jobs because it can be difficult to measure performance, especially in parts of the service sector. It can be divisive – why did they get it and not me? Many companies are unsure what the effect of PRP is in terms of motivation.

Opponents of the system have pointed out that an anagram for performance-related pay is 'mere end of year clap trap'. They claim that assessing overall performance and sharing the rewards motivates people more. What do you think?

assignment focus

Does your organisation use PRP? Should it?

The section below will help with M1.

The future?

Winning companies recognise that people have something to offer as individuals and have gradually allowed their staff more responsibility. Examples of this include:

- open-plan offices – where all employees are on an equal footing without having to 'knock on the door'
- delayering – organisations are becoming flatter so that there is now less of a gap between the bottom and the top of the organisation (although this was often introduced as a way of cutting out the cost of middle management)
- empowerment – employees are encouraged to think for themselves and to act accordingly. Empowerment has been seen as a way of enriching the job. It has also been seen as an excuse for dumping responsibility on employees at a lower level. What do you think?
- staff as stakeholders – employees are given a financial stake in the well-being of the organisation, perhaps by profit-sharing or through employee shareholding
- staff counselling – recognises that staff have individual needs
- casual Fridays, allowing staff to 'dress-down' by wearing clothing of their choice
- improvements in training – It is now recognised that training is an investment and not merely a cost.

Creativity and initiative

Do managers encourage their staff to be creative and act on their own initiative? To achieve this, staff need to be empowered, so that they are able to make their own decisions and accept responsibility. This requires:

- staff to be fully trained
- managers who are willing and able to delegate
- a culture where staff are fully valued and appreciated.

Some organisations are now promoting themselves with the strapline 'Our staff are fully trained to deal with all your questions. One phone call is all it takes', i.e. their staff are empowered to make their own decisions. Some teams, particularly in car production, can decide on membership and the allocation of work.

assignment focus

1 Examine the ways in which your organisation attempts to encourage and assess workforce performance.

2 How much have staff been given responsibility in your organisation? Does it work?

3 Are staff encouraged to be creative and act on their own initiative?

4 Copy and complete this checklist (Table 2.10) for human resources for your organisation.

Table 2.10 Human resources checklist

Human resources management activity	Description, assessment of effectiveness, suggestions for improvement
Recruitment and retention of staff	
Contracts of employment and job descriptions	
Ergonomic and safe workplace	
Team working	
Monitoring of performance	
Grievance and disciplinary procedures	
Culture	
Incentives and rewards	

Financial resources

See page 37 for the main activities of a finance department.

In this section we look at:

- managing budgets
- bidding for resources
- **liquidity/working capital**
- resources for emergencies.

Managing budgets

A **budget** is an agreed plan that serves as a target for a future period (e.g. daily, weekly or monthly). It may be set for sales, purchases, production, expenditure, and so on. An organisation will create a budget so that it can control and monitor its operational activities. A budget will be based on past experience and forecasts of what is likely to happen.

There are:

■ quantitative budgets, which show estimated numbers of units. For example, we may estimate sales of 5,000 DVDs or that 10,000 CDs need to be produced. Sales and production budgets are often quantitative in the first instance (see Table 2.11)

■ financial budgets, which show estimated costs and revenues and are expressed in pounds. For example, we may estimate sales revenue of £50,000 a year or costs of £30,000 (see Table 2.12).

Ultimately, all budgets are expressed in financial terms.

Table 2.11 A quantitative budget

Sales budget (volume)					
April Units	May Units	June Units	July Units	Aug Units	Sept Units
5,000	6,000	10,000	10,000	8,000	6,500

Table 2.12 A financial budget based on the sales volumes in Table 2.11

Sales budget (revenue), based on sale price of £6 per unit					
April Units	May Units	June Units	July Units	Aug Units	Sept Units
30,000	36,000	60,000	60,000	48,000	39,000

Budgeting is part of management accounting. There is no legal requirement to set a budget and the figures are drawn up by managers for internal use only. For this reason, budgeted information is likely to be sensitive. It is usually only available to those who need to know and you will find it difficult to obtain real-life examples for your studies. How might this affect your analysis?

Why is budgeting needed?
The budgeting process involves managers in drawing up detailed estimates for different sections of the business and turning these into targets for the coming months. The aim is to make sure that the different sections of the business are working together, i.e. co-ordinated effectively to achieve the overall goals of the business. A large business such as Tesco will set store budgets from its head office at Cheshunt. Store managers may set budgets for each product line – fruit, fish, etc.

Planning, control and decision-making
The job of business managers involves carrying out the policies set by the directors. The managers are involved with planning, control and decision-making and the budget acts as a framework within which they can perform these functions:

Planning
The budget is part of business planning because it sets out clear objectives to be achieved in the coming period, e.g. sales to be achieved or costs not to be exceeded. Managers must use the resources within their section (staff, money, equipment, time, etc.) as effectively as possible so as to meet the targets that have been set.

Control
Managers will regularly monitor actual performance against the budget to see if the targets are being met. Any variances (differences) between the budget and actual performance will need to be investigated and explained. It may be that someone is not working hard enough,

perhaps the targets are unrealistic or perhaps the forecasts are inaccurate. Whatever the reason, questions will need to be asked and suitable action will need to be taken.

Decision-making

Decisions are taken at the planning stage and during day-to-day operations. For example, the budget may only be agreed after a number of different possibilities have been considered. When a section is not meeting its targets, the manager will need to decide what to do about this. Perhaps costs will need to be reduced or managed to keep them within the budget, or income increased.

Cost centres and profit centres

Some business may be too large to be managed directly from the top, which is why businesses are organised into different departments each headed by a manager.

The various sections or departments within an organisation may be made into cost centres or profit centres. This makes it possible to set targets for them and to monitor how well they are performing.

Costs managed to budget

A cost centre is a section within a business to which costs can be attributed. A college library, the maintenance section of an engineering works or the distribution section at a high street retailer might be cost centres. A manager will be responsible for seeing that the costs are kept within the allocated budget, i.e. that costs are managed to budget.

Income increased to budget

Profit centres are sections within a business which generate revenues as well as incurring costs. Here a manager will be responsible not only for controlling costs but also for seeing that sales targets are met. The canteen may be a profit centre if it charges for meals, the children's section in a department store or the local branch of a national company may be other examples. Income can be compared with the costs to see whether the centre is running at a profit or at a loss. If actual income is below the forecasted/budgeted target, then either income will need to be increased or costs reduced, e.g. unprofitable departments, courses, stores, etc. may be closed.

---

assignment focus

Investigate how cash is handled in your organisation. How often is it removed from the tills? How is it stored overnight – on site in a safe or collected by security guards? What theft prevention measures are in place?

The benefits of budgeting

Budgeting brings a number of benefits to a business.

■ Managers understand their responsibilities. They have clear targets, know what their departments are trying to achieve and can then communicate this information to their staff.

■ The activities of the various sections are co-ordinated so that they all work together effectively. This means that managers work towards the objectives of their organisation. This avoids 'empire building' by managers working to their own agenda.

■ It enables the business to plan for the efficient use of resources (cash, stock and staff). Business performance can be monitored against the budget. This enables managers to identify problems in time and take corrective action quickly.

■ Variances (the difference between the budgeted and the actual figures) allow managers to focus on problems rather than upon the sections which are performing well. This 'management by exception' directs effort to where it is needed.

Bidding for increased future resources

Any organisation aiming to expand will need extra financial resources. Internally, finance could be generated by more cost-effective sales, leading to higher profits which could be retained and ploughed back into the business. Externally, loans may be available through banks, whilst grants for specified purposes such as scientific development, off-shore energy and recreation could be obtained respectively via the European Union, central government and local government. Managers responsible for finance and development need to be continuously aware of these sources. Knowledge companies such as EKOT can provide information on these sources.

Many businesses, including schools and colleges, employ people with specific responsibility for obtaining funding for capital projects through the EU.

Liquidity and working capital

What is working capital?

How much money do you have in your pocket? Do you have enough for today's activities? What are your liquid assets?

Working capital represents the cash (or near cash) available to a business to finance its day-to-day activities. Without working capital, wages cannot be paid, suppliers' bills will not be settled, the mortgage will be in arrears and eventually the business may even have to close.

On the balance sheet working capital is shown as:

Working capital	=	Current assets	–	Current liabilities
Money available for day-to-day expenses		*Assets which can be quickly turned into cash*		*Those creditors who will need to be paid in the near future*

Current assets are also called 'liquid assets'. They are listed on the balance sheet with the least liquid (stock) first and the most liquid (cash) last.

The working capital cycle

The working capital cycle shows how cash circulates in a business as it trades. Current assets and current liabilities are central to trading activity, but other cash flows are also involved.

Ideally, trading activity will generate sufficient cash for all business needs through sales. However, the different demands on business cash and the uneven timing of receipts and payments may mean that cash from customers does not always flow in quickly enough. Where there is a cash shortage, it will be necessary to raise extra funds by either borrowing, delaying payments or raising extra capital.

Why do working capital cashflow problems occur?

Some common reasons are:

■ payment for purchases of stock are made ahead of sales, especially when sales are on credit

■ the business needs to invest now for some future return, e.g. an investment in expensive fixed assets

■ overhead payments coincide (all the bills come in together).

Managing working capital

It is important to forecast problems by drawing up a cash flow forecast and take appropriate action.

See pages 236 and 238 for how this is done.

Appropriate action could include:

■ reducing payments, for example by cutting costs, such as laying off staff, or finding cheaper suppliers and/or paying out lower dividends

■ delaying payments by buying on credit to delay payment until cash is available, scheduling bills by paying in instalments, renting or leasing equipment to avoid up-front capital outlays

- increasing receipts through borrowing, raising more capital through shares or increasing sales revenue through product price changes
- collecting receipts more quickly by selling for cash rather than credit, implementing rigorous credit control policies, i.e. people pay bills on time. Do you?

Provision for emergencies

Using budgets enables decisions to be made in advance by identifying when problems are likely to occur, for example in staffing or cash flow, such as a cash shortage. In this way, potential crises or emergencies can be avoided, e.g. cash reserves can be built up when the business is cash-rich or has a surplus of cash. Staff can be hired in advance specially for busy periods. Loans from banks may need to be agreed if cash flows or working capital appear to present a future problem. This process of forecasting using past experience, analysis of current trends (such as the best-selling lines) and making assumptions about the competition is an essential skill required by managers.

---

assignment focus

Describe why managers need to manage financial resources in your organisation. What could be the consequences of mismanagement?

Technological resources

What is intellectual property?

remember

You must always give the source of any quote.

The software you use, the music you listen to, this book you are reading or company names such as Virgin, Coca-Cola or EKOT are all the **intellectual property** (**IP**) of the creators of the product.

> 'IP allows people to own their creativity and innovation in the same way that they can own physical property. The owner of IP can control and be rewarded for its use, and this encourages further innovation and creativity to the benefit of us all.'
>
> *Source*: www.intellectual-property.gov

What does it say around the edge of the music CD you play? If it says nothing, it is probably illegally recorded. What about the software you use – is it legal or illegal? Your centre will need a licence for each copy of Microsoft® Word it uses. There need to be as many licences as there are computers/site users.

Anything which is unique to an organisation, its products and services gives it a competitive advantage and needs to be protected.

Boxer Muhammed Ali sold the rights to his image and name for $50m in 2006.

There are four main types of IP:

- design
- copyright
- trade marks
- **patents**.

Designs

Design refers to the appearance of the product – the lines, colours, contours, shape, feel or materials/ingredients of the product itself or its ornamentation. The design is part of the image, branding and marketing of the organisation. When a design is registered, it means that it is unique and no one else can use it. If they do, they could be liable to legal action and a claim for damages. A registered design is an important commercial asset which can be sold or licensed to another organisation. Ralph Lauren and Levi own unique designs.

In Unit 5 with your own business you can register a design, but it must be new and distinctive.

Copyright

Owning a copyright gives the creators of literary and artistic material, music, films, sound recordings and broadcasts, including software and multimedia, CDs, DVDs and video, the ability to control how the work is used, copied, performed, distributed online, broadcast, etc. The purpose of copyright is to give a monetary return for the effort and cost of creation. Without such an incentive, people may be reluctant to develop new work.

Trade marks

A trade mark is any sign or symbol, which can be used to identify a brand, perhaps to differentiate it from its competitors or to create an image. It is used as a major marketing tool by the brand/trade mark owner to reinforce customer loyalty. Do you buy brand name trainers? The sign or symbol could be a name such as Nike; a logo, the Adidas three stripes; a slogan 'Just do it'.

The trade mark can also be the use of a colour. What is the colour of your organisation's name? Is it used consistently?

---

case study 2.7

Killing the goose that laid the golden egg!

In July 2004, Irish rock band U2 announced that it might release its new album as a legal download on Apple's iTunes music store, if an illegal CD copy ended up pirated on the internet. Groups including Metallica and Eminem released albums early into stores when pirated material got onto free peer-to-peer services.

Source: Reuters Los Angeles/Yahoo News, July 2004

activity

Have you illegally downloaded music? If everyone did this, how would artists get paid? Why should they bother to record?

In the UK, a trade mark can only be registered if it can be shown graphically, i.e. in words or pictures. Companies have had difficulty registering smells and sounds.

Patents

A patent gives the sole right for a limited period (20 years) to the inventor or the inventor's employer to make, use or sell a specific invention. This must be a new product or process that can be made or used in any industry. The patent holder can stop other people from making, selling or using the product without permission. A patent gives the inventor an opportunity for making money which could repay any research and development costs.

The Patent Office in London can grant a patent for exclusive rights in the UK only. The EU Patent Office is in Munich.

 See www.patent.gov.uk

Legal protection

Copyright, Designs and Patents Act 1988

The Copyright, Designs and Patents Act 1988, protects the intellectual property of organisations and individuals. The main features of the Act are as follows.

- Exclusive rights for artistic, musical, dramatic (e.g. plays) and literary (books, song lyrics, computer programs) works last for 70 years after the death of the creator(s).
- Broadcast and recording rights last 50 years.
- Film rights last 70 years.

In 1992 the Copyright (Computer Programs) Regulations defined software as literary works so they were covered by the Act. For example, 'About Micosoft Word' on the Help menu states that any 'unauthorised reproduction or distribution of this program will be prosecuted to the maximum extent possible under the law.'

Computer Misuse Act 1990

This Act says that any unauthorised access of a computer is illegal. A person may be found guilty of breaking the Act if, for example, they use a user name or password without permission. If found guilty, the penalty may be a fine or imprisonment.

Registered Designs Regulations 2003

These regulations include new directives from the EU on the registration and protection of designs.

Trade Marks Act 1994

This Act sets out the details for registering trade marks and how these can be protected.

Patents Act 2004

This Act amends the Patents Act 1977. It applies to 'all businesses which hold patents to protect their intellectual property' (www/dti.gov.uk). The changes will help with the way patents are enforced and how disputes with alleged illegal users (copiers, counterfeiters, etc.) can be resolved.

---

case study 2.8 — Counterfeit clubs

Viagra, David Bowie music and golf clubs have all been copied illegally, allegedly by the Chinese.

Scottish golf club manufacturer John Letters collapsed in 2005. Clubs advertised as 'styled after' or 'in the style of' are a fraction of the price of the genuine article on eBay. Over 50 per cent of genuine golf clubs are also manufactured in China. Chinese authorities are investigating suspected counterfeiters.

In 2006 China made renewed efforts to stamp out software piracy.

activity

Who gains and who loses in the short and long term in this situation?

---

case study 2.9 — Polo case dismissed

In July 2004, the Court of Appeal rejected a claim by Nestle to register a trademark showing the shape of the Polo Mint without the word 'Polo' or any indication of colour or size. Mars, a competitor, said the shape is 'devoid of distinctive character'. The judge said, 'This is an appeal with a hole in the middle. It is dismissed.'

Source: Martin Hickman, *Independent*, 27 July 2004

Figure 2.17

Do you recognise this?

activity

We eat 100 million Polos a year.
1 Why did Nestle want to register the shape?
2 Why did Mars object?

McDonald's continually complains about cafes owned by Mrs McDonald. The company has announced that it would not be using the 'Golden Arches' logo on its UK advertising. Instead there will be a golden question mark with salad. Does McDonald's now have a healthy image?

Technological resources have to be managed like any other resource. Organisations continually monitor the marketplace to make sure that no one is using their IP illegally and will take strong action against anyone who allegedly does so. Large organisations would have a legal department to carry out this function, e.g. pharmaceutical companies such as GSK fight to protect their patented drugs from being copied, the European Union (EU) has stated that only ham made in Parma in Italy can be called parma ham. Should all Cornish pasties be made in Cornwall? Ginsters use this as a major feature of their advertising.

> **remember**
>
> You can use your trade mark without registering it, but it can be expensive if legal action is necessary.

case study 2.10 Victory for Bud

For 20 years, the American brewing company Anheuser-Busch, the world's largest brewer, has been trying to stop the small Czech brewery, Budejovicky Budvar, based in Budweise from using the name 'Bud' to market its own beer Budweiser. In 2003, the UK Court of Appeal ruled that both companies may use the Bud and Budweiser name. Both brewers have the right to use both the trade marks in the UK.

Source: Richard Adams, *Guardian*, 18 February 2003/www.american.edu

activity

To achieve P3:

1   What intellectual property resources does your organisation possess?
    a) Does it have any trade marks – ™? Are there any names which are registered – ® – or work which is copyright – ©?
    b) Can you include examples such as a photo of the name or logo in your assignment showing the symbols?
2   Check the web to see if your organisation is complaining or being complained about over its IP.
    a) What is management doing about it?
    b) Why is it important to protect IP?
3   Copy and complete a checklist such as Table 2.13 to make sure you have covered the main features of the IP in your organisation.

Table 2.13 Intellectual property checklist

Managing intellectual property	Examples, description and purpose
Design	
Copyright	
Trade marks	
Patents	

assignment focus

To achieve M1, you need to show how management activity can raise performance for each perspective, e.g. shorten customer queues at the checkout by using more staff or installing more tills, improving customer facilities such as car parking, introducing a home delivery service, etc. These should lead to more customers spending more money. Can you give examples of how management have helped raise performance – through praise, pay, new job roles, re-organising?

To do this, try using the four perspectives used by Tesco (Case study 2.8) and link these to different management activities, such as organising, motivating, etc.

Key Management Skills

To achieve P4, for the assignment you will need to demonstrate the role of a manager's interpersonal and communication skills, e.g. to resolve conflicts or agree targets.

Think of your teacher as a classroom manager – their interpersonal and communication skills are excellent. Which teachers do you rate the best? Why?

remember

The only constant at work is change.

Although many employees find their jobs interesting and satisfying, there are some who find their work very stressful. This may be due to their domestic life or perhaps the type of job that they do. Being able to handle people is a crucial skill required by every manager. Ask anyone who has a job, 'Does it matter if you don't get on with your manager?' The answer will usually be 'Yes', because otherwise you cannot do the job effectively.

Interpersonal and communication skills are very important when any changes are being made at the workplace. Being given a new job or working with new colleagues can cause problems. Changes to the structure of the organisation could cause conflicts as some people get promoted and others are threatened with redundancy. It is the manager's role to make sure that changes are implemented as smoothly as possible.

Good 'people skills' can motivate staff and improve morale, which should lead to increased efficiency and improved performance for all stakeholders.

Interpersonal and communication skills

Every organisation will need to be able to communicate effectively with staff at all levels for it to function smoothly and efficiently. A properly structured communication system will require clear and well-defined channels of communication, which are used by everyone in the business. For example, a manager could first communicate with supervisors, and then supervisors could communicate directly with operatives, and vice versa.

The simplest model of communication is one-to-one. These are the components of the process whatever medium of communication is used:

Sender ◊ Encoding ◊ Medium ◊ Decoding ◊ Receiver ◊ Feedback

See page 165 for more information on this model.

Communication can be **formal** or **informal**:

- Formal channels of communication are shown by the lines on an organisation chart. For example, a managing director might communicate directly with senior managers/directors. Managers communicate with supervisors, whilst supervisors communicate with operatives. This process is called vertical downwards communication and usually involves managers giving oral or written instructions/orders to their subordinates. Operatives can only communicate upwards through their supervisor. Horizontal communication takes place between staff at the same level in the hierarchy.

- Whenever a group of workers get together, informal or unofficial, channels of communication are likely to exist alongside the official ones. This is sometimes called the 'grapevine'. These channels are a significant feature of the communications network in many organisations. The grapevine which may be face-to-face or via e-mail or text is the means by which gossip or rumours are spread. Although informal links can be very destructive when rumours are untrue, they are a useful way of spreading information in a multi-sited business.

Verbal communication; meetings, interviews, face-to-face discussions and presentations are still the most important means of communications. Information about new working methods, new products, sales targets, the allocation of work, etc. can be directly given to those who need to know, with an opportunity for a question and answer session. Managers will need to use professional language which is suited to the needs of the audience and the information which is being conveyed at all levels in the organisation, e.g. a meeting on a building site will be different from an office staff meeting.

assignment focus

What formal and informal channels of communication exist in your organisation? What are the strengths and weaknesses of each?

Non-verbal communication

More commonly known as **body language**, non-verbal communication (NVC) refers to the way people communicate without the use of words. Good communicators know:

- how to use body language to project themselves
- how to interpret the NVC signals given out by others.

Body language can either be used consciously, e.g. people deliberately shrug their shoulders, car drivers give V signs, football players often fake injury; or unconsciously, e.g. people twist their hair or fiddle with their ears. Learning body language is the same as learning any language – it will enable you to understand and communicate much more easily with people.

Types of body language

- Eye contact – Do you look at people directly? Do you look away when talking to your friends, work colleagues, teachers? How do these people look at you? There are many reasons why people do not look at each other, for example:
  - they may be shy or insecure
  - they may be telling lies, e.g. 'Sorry I'm late for work, but the bus broke down.'

- Body contact – Do you shake hands when you meet people? Do you greet people with a kiss on each cheek? Is your handshake wet and limp, which indicates a lack of interest in the meeting, or firm and positive? Do you touch people when you are talking? These are all examples of body contact.

- Facial movements – when we smile, we use 15 facial muscles. The human face can change its expression more than any other creature. We can show anger, pleasure, grief, happiness, sadness, disappointment, love or compassion. How do we use these expressions?

HSBC bank ran a series of advertisements showing the importance of local knowledge – that different groups use different body language, e.g. in Bulgaria a nod of the head means 'no'!

> **remember**
>
> 'To every complex problem there's a simple solution, startling in its simplicity, piercing in its clarity, and hopelessly and completely wrong.'
> *Source*: Gore Vidal

assignment focus

Make a copy of Table 2.14 and use it to analyse the role of a manager's communication skills in, e.g. motivating staff, leadership, organising and co-ordinating work activities, meeting targets, giving praise, disciplining, etc. You can also use the table to analyse your own skills to achieve M2 (see below).

Table 2.14 Communication skills

Communication skill	How it can be used by a manager when dealing with all stakeholders	Analysis of a manager or yourself
Listening	Managers need to listen to find out needs. It improves morale and builds relationships	
Understanding	Clear understanding of a situation will help solve problems and aid decision-making	
Seeking clarification	Asking questions is important when customers/staff do not know exactly what they want	
Eye contact and facial expressiveness	Good for establishing relationships. Be genuine and enjoy helping others	
Body language	One smile goes a long way with staff and customers	
Use of appropriate language; awareness of audience needs	Bullying and harassment are illegal. Stakeholders' needs are all different. Productive work comes from effective communication	
Presentation skills	Very important in meetings, when making a case for extra resources or communicating with stakeholders	
Getting commitment from others	Gets the job done and achieves change. Carrots as simple as 'please' and 'thank you' work better than sticks!	

Task-related skills

Table 2.15 gives some examples of the task-related skills managers need to possess. How can they be used to raise performance in an organisation?

Table 2.15 Task-related skills

Task-related skill	How it can be used
Knowledge of products/services	
Effectiveness in meeting personal/team goals	
Ability to raise standards	
Experience	

assignment focus

To achieve M2, you have to make recommendations for the improvement of your own interpersonal and communications skills.

1   Make copies of Tables 2.14 and 2.15 and use them to carry out an audit, or SWOT analysis, of your own interpersonal and communication skills. For example, are you an active listener? Are you genuinely interested to hear what people have to say?

2   Identify and then prioritise those which you want to improve, giving your reasons.

3   Create a SMART action plan showing the methods you are going to take to make the improvements, be specific (S), decide how you are going to measure your improvement (M), make it achievable with some effort (A) and relevant (R), set deadlines (T).

Continuing professional development (CPD)

Many professional organisations, e.g. engineers and administrative managers, provide CPD programmes to encourage their members to gain recognition for keeping up to date and developing themselves.

Find out more at www.instam.org

Here are some examples of questions and points that need to be considered:

■   What are you likely to be doing in the next three years? Five years?

■   What will you need to know? What skills will you need?

■   What opportunities are there for acquiring the knowledge and skills?

■   What are your development needs?

■   Prioritise your needs.

■   Prepare an action plan with dates to show how you will improve your knowledge and skills.

One of the questions often asked at interviews is, 'What are your strengths and weaknesses?' Some examples might be:

Strengths	Weaknesses
Kind	Give up too soon
Ambitious	Untidy
Honest	Sulky
Friendly	Could work harder
Reliable	Careless
Conscientious	Can't take criticism
Sociable	Never meet deadlines
Determined	Always late
Hard working	Sloppy
Organised	Disorganised

Figure 2.18

How can I improve?

How can I improve

1 Weaknesses to be eliminated: 'Never meet deadlines'

Action plan

Do

- Keep a diary or year plan. Be aware of all work due – be aware of all deadlines.
- Identify immediately the main implications, for example:
  What do I need?
  Where will I get it?
  Do I have to make an appointment?
  When can I get there?
  How long will it take?
- Allocate enough time and draw up a plan. Perhaps I can leave it for three weeks, perhaps I need to write a letter now. Be realistic, remember there are other things to do as well and allow for unforeseen problems!

Don't leave everything until the night before.

Evaluate the role of management in improving business performance

Management involves trying to control as much as possible in the organisation. An average Sainsbury will take about £750,000 a week. To maintain this, there will be plans and targets for every aspect of store operations. Actual performance will be monitored daily against each target. Variances will be investigated, e.g. personnel, finance, production, sales and demand.

How much of the success or failure of a business is due to management?

To get a distinction, you will need to decide for your organisation how much of its success or failure is due to its managers' actions.

Evaluation requires you to make a judgement or express an opinion. Has performance improved? Was this due to management? Perhaps it was a failure of competitors? Or a change in business conditions (see the Kraft case study)? Is it due to location or the quality and training of the workforce?

Can we say that success or failure is 100 per cent due to the management or 0 per cent? Probably the answer is somewhere in between.

Experience shows that managers always take credit for any successes and blame the workers for any failure!

---

case study 2.11

Dasani water on tap down the drain!

On 10 February 2004, Coca-Cola launched its first bottled water in the UK with a £7m marketing campaign. Called Dasani (a major brand in the USA), it was made from mains tap water at its factory in Sidcup, Kent and was sold at 95p a bottle. Coca-Cola said that it was made using a 'highly sophisticated purification process' and it was 'as pure as bottled water gets'.

In March 2004, Coca-Cola recalled all bottles (500,000) of Dasani in the UK, after the carcinogenic chemical bromate was found to be higher than legal levels.

Coca-Cola is a large, established international company with the most recognised brand name in the world yet it lost millions on this failed launch. The bottled water market is one of the fastest growing segments in the UK, e.g. Evian, Volvic and Buxton all compete using their source as a unique feature.

activity

Was the success or failure of Dasani due to Coca-Cola management or external factors outside of their control? What do you think went wrong?

case study 2.12

The Atkins diet: Meat and two meat! With no carbohydrate, hold the bun!

Explained in every newspaper and followed by celebrities, the Atkins diet (high in proteins) once dominated the hugely profitable slimming market. Sales of Slimfast (do you use it?) slumped. The makers of Slimfast lost 50 per cent of their profits. Pasta was left unsold on the shelves. Sandwich shops advertised Atkins Breakfast. Now there is a new fad.

activity

1   How much is the success or failure of the food business due to their own management? Or is it due to factors outside their control, i.e. management has very little role?
2   Suggest other, similar examples.

case study 2.13

Tesco vs Sainsbury

Tesco is now the leading supermarket in the UK, with Sainsbury trailing well behind. Is this due to the superiority of Tesco management in improving performance or due to the failure of Sainsbury's management to compete successfully? Is the weak performance of Sainsbury due to the poor performance of its management or the competitive edge developed by Tesco?

activity

1   Who advertises Sainsbury? What image do you have?
2   Who advertises Tesco? What image do you have?
3   How important do you think marketing is in improving business performance? Or a quality product or quality staff?
4   Golden Wonder crisps went bust early in 2006. Did it fall victim to the 'Gary Lineker effect' and Walkers crisps?

assignment focus

To achieve D2, you need to say how managers can improve performance, e.g. by planning, co-ordination, control of operations, organising, etc. through using interpersonal skills and communicating more effectively. See Case Study 2.16.

UNIT 3

Creative Product Promotion

This unit covers:
- promotional objectives
- promotion within the marketing mix
- advertising agencies and the media
- promotional campaign.

This unit looks at:
- how aims and objectives may be achieved through promotional activity
- how promotion works for a specific product
- how advertising agencies contribute to promotional success
- how promotional campaigns may be designed and evaluated.

Assessment
This unit is assessed through an Integrated Vocational Assignment (IVA). Unit 5 is also assessed in the same way, i.e. Units 3 and 5 are assessed together. They are integrated. In 2006 there were four tasks for each unit. We have included the tasks as part of the activities you have to complete to achieve the unit. When you complete the activities, you will have completed the four tasks. When you have completed all eight tasks, they will be marked at your centre, then by a BTEC external assessor.

Promotional Objectives

What is promotion?
Promotion refers to any marketing communication activities that are intended to inform, persuade or motivate, current and potential customers into buying or supporting a product or service. The customer can be another business (B2B – business to business, e.g. wholesaler, retailer) or a consumer (B2C – business to consumer).

Promotion is an essential part of the marketing activities of any for-profit or not-for-profit organisation. Charities, government departments, sole traders and plcs all carry out promotion to achieve their aims. It is one of the four key elements of what is known as the **marketing mix**, the others are price, product and place. What do the four elements have in common? The marketing mix is familiarly known as the 'four Ps'.

We examine the marketing mix on page 119.

assignment focus

You need to choose an organisation which has a national promotional campaign for its products or services. It can help if the campaign is currently running (see visit4info on page 134). Download or cut out any images, photographs or graphics you can find. You will need to:

1   Describe the organisation (e.g. main products, number of outlets, whether for-profit or not-for-profit, etc.) and its aims and objectives.

2   Describe the promotional campaign.

3   Show how its aims and objectives can be achieved through its promotional activities.

4   Produce a short illustrated report.

Business aims translated into promotional objectives

We have seen in Unit 1 that an organisation could have a variety of corporate-wide aims, such as growth (getting new customers or persuading existing customers to buy more), maximising profit, providing a better service or an increase in market share (increase sales or launch new products). These would normally be set out in a corporate plan. Each aim requires a particular promotional message and a specific promotional strategy which would be implemented through individual functions or departments.

Figure 3.1 shows how a business plan can be turned into a promotional plan.

Figure 3.1

From business plan to promotional plan

| **Business plan** Corporate aims and objectives for the main functional areas, such as finance, human resources and marketing | **Marketing plan** Focus on the marketing mix, i.e. product, price, place and promotional decisions. Which price and where and how should it be sold | **Promotional plan** to achieve promotional objectives Focus on the choice of medi, TV, press, etc. (the **media mix**) and promotion activities, e.g. advertising, public relations, personal selling (**promotional mix**) |

Link

See pages 132 and 144 for further information on the media mix and promotional mix.

Figure 3.2 is an example from Unilever of how a corporate aim, e.g. 'to improve growth in all product categories' becomes a promotional objective, e.g. 'to achieve an overall increase in market share of 2 per cent'.

The corporate objectives will be turned into a strategy with objectives for each level (product category and brands) in the organisation. Action plans will be created showing how each objective could be achieved. The objectives should be SMART and vertically and horizontally consistent, i.e. integrated throughout the organisation with everyone working to the same goals. This should minimise internal conflict. Promotion and the other elements of the marketing mix will be used to achieve objectives.

An organisation cannot hope to achieve all its objectives at once. It needs to focus its promotional activities on its highest priority. Launching a new product or opening a new shop are immediate, short-term aims needing short-term promotional activities. Building up awareness or changing attitudes are long-term objectives needing a long-term financial and promotional commitment.

Figure 3.2

From corporate aim to
promotional objective

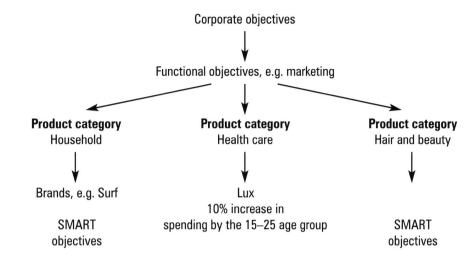

Short-term promotions such as those carried out by newspapers may result in a big increase in circulation but only when the promotion is running. Circulation tends to fall immediately the promotion stops. 'Circulation wars', when every newspaper has a continuous promotion, can be very expensive.

The acronym **AIDA** sums up the main promotional objectives. It shows the reasons for communicating with customers through promotion:

- **A**wareness – get the customers' awareness of the product through **advertising**
- **I**nterest – gain their interest and commitment through **public relations**
- **D**esire – arouse their desire through special offers and sales promotions
- **A**ction – get them to buy the product through effective selling techniques.

Raising awareness of the product/service

The most wonderful product in the world will not sell if people do not know it exists. Since earliest times, the main purpose of promotional activity has been to make the market aware of the product, e.g. where it can be bought and what is the price. This provision of information is still a main function of local newspaper and radio advertising.

With new products or when products are being introduced into new markets, the first objective of any marketing launch campaign is to make potential buyers/users aware of the product or service. With existing products, it may be necessary to remind customers of the benefits of the product. For example, Tropicana Pure Premium juice (page 115 below) changed the packaging to bring in new users and remind lapsed users of the benefits of the brand.

See page 111 for an online adverting case study of Florida orange juice.

See www.dynamic.logic.com/eyeblaster for an online case study.

All advertising media whether offline, such as TV, radio, newspapers, outdoor poster advertisers and cinema, or online, such as internet banner ads and pop-ups, claim to be able to raise awareness of the product/service if they are used as the communication medium.

case study 3.1

Spam, but not on the internet

Spam is a tinned meat product first launched in 1937. Since then over 6 billion tins have been sold. It sells about £13m in the UK each year.

Recently a £2m advertising campaign was launched 'to remind lapsed users about the delicious taste of Spam while raising awareness among new users'. The commercial featured a team of builders eating Spam sandwiches for their lunch. The overall theme was ordinary people 'celebrating all things British from camping to pantomime'.

activity

Did the campaign work? Are you aware of the product? Have you tried it? Maybe the campaign was not aimed at your age group.

'Smoking kills' and 'Don't drink and drive' are examples of public service promotion and illustrate the point that any organisation can promote its purpose and message. These are designed to raise awareness of the dangers of smoking and drinking. The action required is to stop.

Friends of the Earth, the environmental charity and pressure group, has this mission: 'Friends of the Earth defends the environment and champions a healthy and just world.' Figure 3.3 is an example of an advert for FoE designed for your age group. It is a good example of an advertisement designed to raise awareness of a current issue and was designed to be used on beer mats. It is aimed at a specific target audience, using images and text created to gain attention. Such adverts can be found in magazines like *Rolling Stone*, some 25 per cent of their readers are under 18. Phillip Morris, the cigarette manufacturers, are prevented from advertising in it.

Figure 3.3

Friends of the Earth – raising awareness

"Gasping and panting, sweat was dripping off my body…"

How is your organisation attempting to raise awareness through its current promotional campaign? Is it working?

Creating a distinctive market presence

In a highly competitive market place, it is very important for for-profit and not-for-profit organisations to differentiate or distinguish their products/message from those of their competitors. The product has to be distinctive. It has to stand out from the crowd saying choose me! Friends of the Earth, Comet and BhS are all trying to create a unique position for themselves. How do they do this? The brand name, message, **logo** and packaging can all be used to make a product stand out from its competitors. Advertising can be used to create an image, perhaps of quality, value or excellent service. The overall objective is to achieve customer loyalty.

Many organisations operate in a very competitive environment. Why should the consumer choose one in preference to another? Do you make a decision on quality, brand name, price or another criterion such as a distinctive market presence? Stella Artois is 'reassuringly expensive', i.e. premium priced and if Carlsberg (or is it Carling?) made real lager, it would 'probably be the best lager in the world'! Andrex toilet rolls are advertised by a cute little puppy which has its own website: andrexpuppy.co.uk. Churchill Insurance (owned by the Royal Bank of Scotland (RBS), the third largest bank in the world, based in Bromley, uses a nodding dog. Which company advertises using a red phone? The internet search 'Who was Flat Eric?' gave over seven million entries. (Number 174 was a BBC news item!)

See page 200 on creating a corporate identity.

What techniques is your organisation using to make its product/service achieve a distinctive market presence?

Push and pull promotion

Push promotion is where one business promotes its products to another business (B2B) to get them to stock and sell the goods, e.g. in *The Grocer*, a weekly magazine for independent retailers. Pull promotion is where a business promotes its products to consumers (B2C) to get them to buy the goods.

Check out www.thegrocer.co.uk

Beware some companies, e.g. Intel, who do not sell to consumers but still advertise heavily. Heinz spends as much money on B2B promotion as it does on B2C: 'It must be on the shelves once people have seen the adverts'. (The market for baked beans grew by 3.2 per cent in 2005 with £222m spent on Heinz. Source: www.tnsofres.com)

Promotion plays a major part in forming the image of a product which helps create a distinctive market presence. Where do you buy your clothes? Or music? Woolworths is one of the biggest sellers of music in the UK. Do you go there? McDonald's had intended to drop the 'golden arches' in favour of a golden question mark and introduce the slogan 'But not as you know it'. (Wasn't this *Star Trek*?) Did it do it? Has it worked?

Increasing market share

Market share is the proportion of the total market held by a business or product, e.g. Tesco's UK market share is 28.3 per cent. For an organisation whose primary goal is making profits, promotion would tend to emphasise those features which create and build sales. The purpose is to achieve a sustainable increase in market share so that the organisation can sell more without having to cut prices.

Many promotional campaigns are designed to keep customers loyal by reassuring and reminding them of the product, but also offering an incentive, e.g. 'Buy X and get 200 extra points at Boots'. The key purpose is to move the customer up the loyalty ladder from occasional user to being totally committed – 'Buy it again and get another 300 points' – to the point where the customer would not shop anywhere else. Loyalty cards such as the Boots Advantage card, Tesco Clubcard and the use of the Nectar card by Sainsbury are all intended to create loyal customers.

See page 118 for more information on the loyalty ladder

The ability of an organisation to increase its market share depends on its own marketing mix, the activities of competitors and whether the market as a whole is growing. In stagnant markets, where sales have reached saturation, e.g. with fast food burger chains such as McDonald's and Burger King, one of the few ways to grow is to poach customers from the competition. Unless this can be maintained, any increase can only be temporary. The key to success is to make sure that new customers become permanent by creating a relationship with them. This process is called relationship marketing. The promotional campaign for Walkers crisps fronted by Gary Lineker has doubled sales in the last ten years, but in September 2005, Walkers announced that it was closing its crisp factory in Swansea with the loss of 250 jobs. Golden Wonder crisps ceased trading early in 2006. Was this also the Gary Lineker effect?

Want to find out more? Check out www.walkers.corpex.com

Promotional activities need to be planned and implemented to reinforce the mission, aims and objectives of the organisation and to achieve an increase in market share. For example, the core purpose and values of Tesco underlie its strategy.

Tesco promotes itself with 'Every little helps' and had 28.3 per cent of the market in 2005. Asda had 16.7 per cent; Sharon Osborne currently advertises Asda with a 'Mum in a million' campaign.

Table 3.1 shows how the share of the UK grocery market changed between 1994 and 2005.

Table 3.1 Share of the UK grocery market, 1994 and September 2005

Top ten supermarkets in September 2005	% share of the market	Top ten supermarkets in 1994	% share of the market
Tesco	28.3	Sainsbury	20
Asda	16.7	Tesco	18.3
Sainsbury	15.5	Safeway	10
Morrison/Safeway	13.2	Asda	9.9
Somerfield/Kwik Save	5.7	Co-op	6.6
Co-op	5.1	Somerfield	5.5
Waitrose	3.6	Kwik Save	4
Aldi	2.3	Morrison	3.6
Iceland	2	Iceland	3.4
Lidl	1.9	M&S	3.1

These sites are very useful:
- TNS Superpanel reference library: www.tnsinfo.com
- www.theretailbulletin.co.uk

Case study 3.2 can be used as a practice run for Task 1 of the IVA.

assignment focus

1   Does your organisation have increasing market share as an objective?

2   How does it try to achieve this?

3   Find out its market share by using KeyNote reports.

case study 3.2

Tropicana

Since 1998 Tropicana has been part of the PepsICO group. Here are two extracts from the PepsICO website:

> 'PepsiCo's success is the result of superior products, high standards of performance, distinctive competitive strategies and the high integrity of our people.'

> 'Our mission is to be the world's premier consumer products company focused on convenient foods and beverages. We seek to produce healthy financial rewards to investors as we provide opportunities for growth and enrichment to our employees, our business partners and the communities in which we operate. And in everything we do, we strive for honesty, fairness and integrity.'

The 2005 promotional campaign

B2C promotion

In 2005, there was a £4.5m TV campaign, press advertising, sampling, door drops, 8 million targeted direct mail shots, a 50p-off voucher and a competition with 31 BA Club Europe weekend breaks for two, one for each day in August (pity BA at Heathrow were on strike for three days!). For a chance to win, consumers had to register online to become a member of the Tropicana Breakfast Club. The competition was heavily promoted on radio, online and through *The Sunday Times*, with direct mail and sponsorship of the Simon Bates Breakfast Show on Classic FM. Tropicana spent approximately £15m promoting its products in 2005.

B2B support and advice

Figure 3.4

PepsiCo's advertising for Tropicana

Source: PepsiCo

The company-recommended planogram (layout or graphical display of products) of Tropicana for instant consumption sales is, 'It should be located next to the sandwiches and other soft drinks to capture high value impulse purchases.' While the recommended planogram for take-home sales is, 'It should be next to milk in the dairy deck to capitalise on high footfall areas of the store and attract purchasers.'

Retailers were advised through the trade website press releases to stock up on 1-litre and 1.75-litre take-home cartons and the single serve instant consumption bottles.

What was the purpose of the campaign?

PepsiCo Trade Marketing Manager, Nicky Seal said that the: competition 'will be highly engaging and appealing to loyal Tropicana drinkers. Supported by a huge media campaign it will also drive brand awareness, reinforce Tropicana's pure premium and number one positioning and ensure Tropicana is top of mind with consumers. We felt it was the right time to give the brand new packaging with a more modern refreshing look which will attract new buyers to the brand.'

activity

1   Why was there a wide range of media selected?
2   Why was a range of promotion methods chosen?
3   What was each part of the campaign designed to achieve? What are the objectives of the promotion?
4   Why was so much emphasis put on B2B communication?
5   Can you answer the same questions for your chosen campaign?

assignment focus

Describe your chosen promotional campaign.

1   What is it selling?
2   What image is it trying to show?
3   What age is it appealing to? What gender?
4   What ethnic groups are represented?
5   Is it humorous? What emotion is it appealing to?
6   What are its objectives?
7   What promotional activities is it using?
8   Where is it advertising?
9   What media is it using?

Look at the marketing press, e.g. *Campaign*, *Marketing Weekly*. www.visit4info has all the adverts

See page 134.

Targeting of the audience

Have you been to the music festivals at Reading, Glastonbury or Leeds? Is there a difference between them?

The music industry is an excellent example of how targeting works in marketing, recording, performance, distribution, broadcasting, etc. The music industry is segmented (broken down) in many ways: age, price, singles and albums market, genre, and so on. Genre can be further split up into pop, rock, classical, dance, etc. Dance can be divided further, e.g. house, garage and trance, and these can be subdivided further into 'niche' or smaller segment markets. Once a target market has been identified, an organisation can create a specific marketing strategy directed towards meeting its particular needs.

Rock album sales are rising despite free downloads. Why? The billionth iTunes download was on 24 February 2006, *Speed of Sound* by Coldplay.

Promotional campaigns need to be directed at specific audiences. The publishers of this book, Nelson Thornes, target the Head of Business Studies in schools and colleges with their resources for Vocational Business Studies, as Figure 3.5 shows (with thanks to Nelson Thornes). This is a B2B promotion. Why haven't they targeted you as a consumer (B2C)? Can you identify the sweets?

Whilst some organisations focus exclusively on one target audience/**market segment**, others will differentiate their audiences and produce different campaigns for each group.

Figure 3.5

Nelson Thornes The B2B promotion

---

assignment focus

1 Which group is your promotional campaign aimed at?

2 Is the campaign the same in all media, press, magazines and TV?

3 Why are there changes?

Attitudes, interests and opinions

Do you watch a particular TV channel or listen to a particular radio station? Perhaps you have a favourite magazine? Other people with similar likes or dislikes will also be watching or listening. Do your friends have similar attitudes to you? All of you are a market segment or target audience defined by a range of characteristics, i.e. your attitudes, interests and opinions (AIO):

■ your attitudes (sometimes activities) could cover your views about sports, shopping, clubbing, gigs, holidays, etc.

■ your interests could include food, music, friends, etc.

■ your opinions could include those about education, your future, particular products, etc.

The **AIO inventory** is a technique which uses a set of statements to find out about people's attitudes towards a product, their interests and opinions, for example:

■ I think my BTEC course will get me a better job

■ I would only go on a beach holiday

■ I would only buy brand names.

Answers would then be rated on a five-point scale like the one in Table 3.2.

Table 3.2 A five-point scale

Strongly Agree	Agree	Don't know	Disagree	Strongly disagree

The information is used to build up a picture of a typical customer and segment the market. Promotion can then be targeted to appeal directly to a specific group.

Many campaigns have been aimed at changing attitudes or perceptions about a product. This is an image 'makeover' and can be very difficult to achieve.

assignment focus

What AIO is your campaign is aiming at: saving money? a beautiful home? value for money? a sense of adventure?

Does it appeal to you? Give your reasons.

Market segmentation

Businesses try to split whole markets into smaller units or segments so they can target their promotion and other marketing activities at specific groups of people. A target market segment is a group of homogeneous (similar) customers characterised, for example by age, income, geographical area (local, regional or national), ethnicity and/or lifestyle (e.g. taste in music). This is demonstrated by the products people buy. For example, the car market can be split into economy, family, sports cars, etc. Both consumers and businesses can be targeted in market **segmentation**, i.e. B2C and B2B (supermarkets, corner shops, etc.)

case study 3.3   ACORN

Acorn stands for Alternative Classification of Residential Neighbourhoods. It is available through CACI Market Analysis Limited.

Here is a simple way to find out the lifestyle characteristics of your postcode area: go to www.upmystreet.com. Put in your postcode and go to neighbourhood profiles.

Alternatively, if you want a full ACORN profile, where an entry would show **demographics** (age profile, socio-economic profile [level of education, type of employment], attitudes, housing, ownership of durables, leisure, food and drink), go to www.caci.co.uk. Registration is free, but you need to give details. (Get your centre to register.)

Here is an example of the amount of detail you can find:

ACORN Type 30:

> 'The striking thing about this ACORN Type's usage of packaged goods is the enormous amount of dog food purchased, more than double the average.'

> *Source*: CACI

activity

1 Find the profile for your postcode and look at each heading.
2 What could you do with this information? Do you recognise yourself, your household, or the potential for a new business?
3 Would the promotion campaign appeal to your neighbours?

Types of market segmentation

How does your organisation segment its markets?

Analyse the campaign by age, income, lifestyle, etc. You can do this with the images, words, vocabulary, etc.

There are many ways markets can be split into segments. The particular choice will depend on the type of organisation, the characteristics of the market and the type of product.

Geographic segmentation

With geographic segmentation the market is split into homogeneous (similar) groups on the basis of where people live or where customers are located, e.g. countries, regions, counties, cities, urban or rural. An organisation can then target its marketing mix at a particular group. Proctor & Gamble, for example, produces and markets different flavours of Pringles in different countries to suit local tastes; salt and vinegar flavour allegedly does not appear in Belgium.

Coca-Cola has deliberately pursued a policy of marketing the identical product worldwide, whereas Nokia has differentiated its mobile phones for different markets.

Source: Coca-Cola UK website

Demographic segmentation

Demographic segmentation uses variables such as age, gender, income, size and type of household, occupation, ethnicity, religion and family type, etc. to segment the market.

- Age – this is particularly important. Many companies now produce and sell to specific age groups, e.g. children's toys and clothing manufacturers use gender and a 1–2 year age range such as 'suitable for 3–5-year-olds'. Older drivers get cheaper car insurance, students pay more! 'We only insure careful drivers,' says one company, which presumably means that other companies only insure more risky drivers with consequently higher rates! Any complaints? Many companies have been accused of deliberately targeting their promotion at young children. Check out the alternative websites for burgers, soft drinks, sweets, etc. Do you think they should be allowed to do this?

  A Mintel report on pocket money says the UK's 7–10-year-olds get almost £417 million, while the 11–14-year-olds receive some £1.1 billion a year. 'Children are important consumers through their own purchases together with the pester power they exert over their parents,' says Jenny Catlin of Mintel.

- Gender – many products are gender-specific, such as health and beauty products or magazines. However, effective market research has shown a need for male fragrances and cars designed specifically for women drivers. Can you think of other examples?

  Some £30m is spent each year advertising female fragrances and £15m on male fragrances (*Source*: Keynote Cosmetics and Fragrances). A Mintel report 'Designerwear in the UK' shows that men are more likely to buy designer clothes than women.

- Family type – very often promotion is aimed at groups that represent the main stages in the family life cycle. Here is an example of groupings from the Advertising Standards Association survey, 'The public's perception of advertising in today's society':
  - Teenagers 16/17/18 still at school
  - Singles aged 20–24
  - Parents with at least one child aged 5–14
  - Empty nesters aged 50–60 (children have left home!)
  - The greys aged 65–75.

Source: Advertising Standards Association

A group particularly sought after are the 'DINKies' or 'dual income no kids'. Why do you think this is the case?

assignment focus

1 How does your school or college segment its students?

2 How does your promotional campaign segment its customers, e.g. who is shown in the adverts? What are they doing? How do they speak?

Link See page 113 for AIO.

Psychographic and lifestyle segmentation

Lifestyle is our way of life as reflected in our activities, interests, habits, opinions and friends. We show it in what we wear, the food we eat, the music we like. These all have implications for consumer spending. The analysis works on the assumption that people in a particular segment will have similar attitudes, desires, expectations and buying habits. Marketing campaigns can then be created which specifically appeal to their motivations. To work effectively, the target segment must be measurable, substantial, accessible and be able and willing to buy the product.

Some major market research companies have useful websites, e.g.

■ AC Nielsen: www.acnielsen.co.uk

■ www.youngandrubicam.co.uk (good for their 4Cs)

■ Taylor Nelson Sofres: www.tnsofres.com

Behavioural segmentation

This type of segmentation splits the market according to consumer behaviour, such as attitudes towards the product, buying habits, loyalty, usage and, most importantly, the benefits gained. This process examines the benefits that people hope to gain when they buy a product, e.g. do you buy toothpaste to clean your teeth or to give you 'fresh breath confidence'? (Colgate used this to create the advertising slogan 'The ring of confidence'.) What benefits do you expect from a product such as a mobile phone? Research shows fashion to be important. Does it matter to you?

Usage refers to the status of the user, e.g. first-time user, non-user, heavy user, occasional user, ex-user, etc. Identifying the category of user enables the business to create a marketing mix to target each segment. Essentially the objective is to convert non-users into users, and occasional users into regular users.

case study 3.4

Mortgages: special deals for first-time house buyers

A particular group targeted by mortgage companies are first-time buyers. This group is trying to buy a home for the first time, i.e. they are trying to get on the housing ladder. They have particular financial needs and banks compete for their business by offering low initial rates of interest. They are important to the bank because on average over a 25-year mortgage people pay back three times as much as they originally borrow.

activity

How do the aims and activities of the promotional campaign help the organisation achieve its overall aims and objectives?

How can segmentation analysis be used?

Once the segments have been identified through research, an organisation will be able to:

- create a marketing mix for each group based on the research that it has done. Each of the four Ps will be given a different emphasis. Promotion will play a bigger or smaller part in every marketing campaign
- analyse and profile customers, e.g. by age, income, consumer spending, financial status, etc., which can help with decisions about where to open new stores (e.g. WH Smith used this to identify new retail sites. Has it worked?)
- create a database structured by segments to help with marketing, e.g. the Co-op
- develop sales and market potential forecasts, e.g. Cellnet now O2, but still BT?

Branding and loyalty

Brand names are an essential part of the way a product is promoted and packaged. Every company will want the consumer to ask for its product by name. The purpose of **branding** is to differentiate products that are basically similar. It is, therefore, an important feature of the non-price competition which exists in competitive markets. Each business is trying to establish its own name and reputation in the market. For example, companies making trainers concentrate entirely on using the brand name to sell the products. They will reinforce this by putting their names and logos on carrier bags, T-shirts and sweat shirts which the consumer then pays for! Nike and Adidas are also major sponsors of sporting events. The 16–25-year-old market are major buyers of brand name fashion products.

There are about 185,000 charities in England and Wales. The top 8 per cent get about 93 per cent of the income. Each of these needs a clear and distinctive brand and message.

From the manufacturers' and retailers' viewpoint, branding is important because it helps to create consumer loyalty and increase sales. If consumers can be persuaded to only buy, for example, High Track trainers, the company has effectively achieved a fully committed buyer and can use this to adjust its prices accordingly. What can you say generally about the price of branded and non-branded goods?

case study 3.5

Big brother is watching you plc

Boots claims 15 million people for its Advantage card, the Nectar card is used by 11 million and some 10 million people have a Tesco Clubcard. (Tesco sends out 40 million loyalty letters a year.) It is estimated that 85 per cent of UK households have a loyalty card, although 80 per cent of customers say they would prefer lower prices!

A loyalty card insider says:

'We know if you have just had a baby, if you are going on holiday and how much you drink. We can suggest new products and tempt you with extra points. We can move customers along the loyalty ladder until they get hooked into shopping frequently and buying every offer. We can put electronic chips in the store card so that the retailer knows when you are in the store. We can (and some do) sew electronic tags into labels. The Nectar card allows, say, Debenhams to spot potential customers because of their purchases of petrol at BP garages. We know everything.'

activity

1 What plastic or club/membership cards does your group have? Perhaps a NUS or store card?
2 What privileges do these cards give? E.g. discounts, special offers (20 per cent off days), competitions, special 'card holder only' shopping nights (BhS), early booking for concerts and cricket test matches.
3 How do these cards help the organisation attract and keep customers?
4 Does your Organisation have a loyalty card?
5 Who benefits the most, the customer or the organisation?

The ladder of customer loyalty

Loyalty is important to every organisation from its customers, suppliers, providers of charity income, etc. It is the aim of every organisation to persuade people (consumers and businesses) to move up the loyalty ladder (Figure 3.6) and become permanent advocates, spreading the word about how good the business is.

Figure 3.6

The loyalty ladder

Advocate   Totally loyal enthusiastic customers, also known as 'apostles'. They tell others how good the business is, i.e. word of mouth advertising, or show the brand name

Supporter   Enthusiastic but still passive

Client   The first-time buyer has been converted into a repeat customer, regularly purchases and is not drawn to your competitors

Customer   Prospects who become buyers. Businesses should make this process as easy as possible and encourage them to continue as customers

Prospect   Also known as 'leads', these are people who have shown a positive interest in the business, but have not yet bought anything

Suspect   The business suspects this group might buy.

Harley Davidson owners proclaim their loyalty to the brand by tattooing themselves with the logo. Do you demonstrate your loyalty to a brand? Do you wear anything with a logo on, i.e. you are an advocate?

The objective of every marketing activity must be to convert every prospect into an advocate. However, unless the organisation continues to build relationships with its customers, they could go elsewhere.

assignment focus Check the website for your product for copies of the brand name and logo.

How to reinforce brand images

- Mention the name as often as possible without it becoming irritating.
- Use a celebrity, but take care – not everyone will like them. Sainsbury used John Cleese in its 'Shout about' campaign which did less well than expected!
- Use well-known sounds, music or slogans/catchphrases, e.g. 'Hello Moto'.
- Sell the benefits – hair and beauty products seem to be highly scientific!

Promotion is communication.

Link We can summarise Outcome 1 using the model of communication shown on page 165 and developed in Table 3.3.

Table 3.3 A model of communication for a promotional campaign

Sender	Encoding	Medium	Decoding	Receiver
Private company Sole trader Charity Government department	Creating the message to suit the audience and achieve objectives using AIDA	Mass media: TV, press, radio, cinema, posters Electronic, written, etc.	Receiver interpretation/ perception of the message; its style, tone, content, purpose, etc.	Individuals Target segments Businesses Mass market etc.

assignment focus

Go through each stage of Table 3.3 and use it to analyse your chosen promotional campaign. Use your five friends to help you: Who? What? Why? When? Where?

Promotion Within the Marketing Mix

The marketing mix

The marketing mix refers to the way in which the four key parts of a company's marketing policy are combined to achieve its objectives. The four elements, sometimes called the 'four Ps' are:

■ product

■ price

■ place

■ promotion.

Although senior management will have the responsibility for determining the overall marketing strategy of the business, the marketing department will be largely responsible for ensuring that the four Ps are used effectively. Every business will combine the four Ps in a different way depending on the:

■ type of product, e.g. convenience goods tend to be more heavily advertised to distinguish them from competitors than shopping or speciality goods

■ type and number of competitors, e.g. in highly competitive markets price may be the major factor

■ marketing mix of competitors, e.g. local double glazing companies appear to advertise continuously in local newspapers, if any one stopped promoting itself and its products/services, it probably would not survive

■ range of market segments, e.g. some businesses use a different marketing mix for each group of customers

■ type of organisation, e.g. a charity or not-for-profit organisation may emphasise different aspects of the marketing mix than a profit-centred business. Sometimes called cause-related marketing, it appeals to our emotions, e.g. 'Give just £2 a month and help save or protect …'.

Products and services

Product refers to the output of any business. This can either be tangible things, the physical goods, which you can touch, see or smell, such as a dishwasher or cod and chips; or the intangible services, such as the customer services that can be offered by the retailer. Different types of bank accounts or insurance policies are also called products. Consumers buy particular products because they expect to get utility, i.e. satisfaction or benefits from using them. This satisfaction can be obtained from any aspect of the product. For example, it could be the brand name of the dishwasher, the flavour or the 'packaging' of the cod and chips, the convenience of online banking or the security offered by insurance. Whatever the reason, it is all part of the product – the ultimate retail therapy!

Product range

The **product range** may also be called the **product mix** or product portfolio.

The product range is the total number of product/service lines and items sold or produced by a business. The term 'width' is the number of product lines and 'depth' the number of items per product line, such as ten varieties of soup. A large supermarket, for example, could have thousands of lines whereas a specialist supplier would have very few. Whitbread is reducing the width of its product range to focus on its core leisure activities such as the David Lloyd tennis centres and its hotel chains.

A brewery will make a range of beers of different strengths and quality. It will charge premium (high) prices for its stronger brands. Most large companies, for example Nestle, will aim to have a range of products that cover as many market segments as possible. Colleges do this by offering a variety of courses that appeal to a wide range of people, although each course would be aimed at a specific target group. What do all your course members have in common?

In some cases, widening the product range will be achieved by the development of new products or by differentiating existing ones. Car companies, for example, make four- or five-door cars, with or without metallic paint, sporty wheel trim, automatic gearbox, sunroof, etc. – the so-called 'optional extras'. Special editions are sometimes made. Smarties, for example, are available in five standard packs – tubes, multipacks of three and five tubes (for supermarkets), cartons and mini-cartons. Each option requires a variation of the production process and will normally be offered at a different price.

Here are some examples of strategies an organisation can follow when deciding on its product mix:

- differentiated marketing strategy – the business produces essentially the same product, which is differentiated (changed) to cater for different customer segments, e.g. shampoo for normal, dry, greasy or flyaway hair. The market is segmented by type of hair

- undifferentiated marketing strategy – one product, e.g. Dove, for 'all types of hair' is produced for the whole market, i.e. there is no attempt to segment the market. Dove, however, also supplies a differentiated segmented range

- concentrated marketing strategy – the organisation will specialise in one market segment and try to provide it with the perfect product. Which daily newspaper do you read? Newspapers are segmented. Can you say how?

---

assignment focus

1   What is the product range/mix of your organisation?

2   Which strategy has it followed?

3   Which product/service is being promoted?

New product development

Whenever there are changes in the marketplace the business should respond. For example, as the location and age structure of the population change, this creates new opportunities for **product development**, so retirement homes are built to cater for the increase in the ageing population and new pension and life insurance schemes are introduced (no medical required and no salesperson will call). TV companies are also well aware of these changes as they re-run *Thunderbirds* and *Star Trek*, first shown 20 years ago, to new audiences on new channels.

People's preferences change; for example, the growth in demand for organic products stems from a need for foods which are free from artificial pesticides and fertilisers and which promote careful consideration of the environment. This is a social trend towards a more healthy and caring lifestyle.

Why is it that organic foods are still more expensive? Is it because retailers are exploiting this segment of customers who are willing to pay higher prices?

The growth in demand for convenience foods, for example, comes from changes in lifestyles and social conditions. The demand for labour-saving devices has also increased for the same reasons.

Computer games and DVDs are examples of products that have been created in response to changes in leisure habits. Or is it these technologies that are changing habits and lifestyles? At Dixons, the electrical retailer, sales of video recorders and 35mm cameras have been discontinued due to a lack of demand and the rise in digital photography.

For an organisation to achieve its corporate and marketing objectives, it must increase or at least maintain its share of these changing markets. To be at the leading competitive edge of innovation, it will need to take risks by developing new products and improving existing ones. It will minimise the risks by carrying out thorough product and market trials before going ahead with a full launch.

Why does a business develop new products? The simple answer is that because the market is continually changing, the business must develop, acquire or introduce new products/services to keep ahead of its competitors. Here are some examples (you will be able to think of many others): new mortgage and pension schemes are created, telephone and internet banking has been introduced, even 'your old washing machine will be taken away when you buy a new one with us'!

As a Chairman of Unilever said:

> 'In the battle for competitive edge we define the need, create the brand and move it around the world at the marketing equivalent of the speed of light. Innovation is moving so fast that you need to be scouting ahead and creating markets.'

Instead of being consumer driven, i.e. responding to consumer needs, companies are now telling and showing customers what they need, e.g. Nokia.

How does a business develop new products?

Market research
A business will need to carry out market research before it develops, launches and markets a new product. The business will have to consider a number of questions:

- What are the gaps in the market?
- What are the gaps in the product range?
- What new technology is available? For example, the non-stick coating on pots and pans was developed for the US Space Programme.
- How big is the market?
- What should be the market segment or target audience?
- What is the competition doing?
- What price should the product(s) be?
- How should we advertise?
- What should our message be? For example, Highlands Airways – we aim for the top!
- How should we sell it?
- What sales can we expect?
- What profit can we expect?

You can use these questions when devising your marketing strategy in your business plan.

What are we selling?
The answer to this question will determine the thrust and direction of the business. Look at these examples:

- Is Peugeot selling cars or adventure? 'Own one and you own the road, the Drive of Your Life'
- Are P&O Ferries selling the trip from Dover to Calais or a cruise?
- Does a sports club sell the sport or the social life?

remember

Market opportunities can be spotted using PESTEL analysis.

Creative Product Promotion

The Nike campaign for trainers under the slogan 'Just do it', is intended to keep:

- Nike as a world leader in trainers
- people buying brand name trainers.

But what is Nike selling, an image, a dream, 150 million pairs of trainers or a 10k run on a cold November evening? The Nike 10k attracted 30,000 runners, all of whom visited the website and bought the orange T-shirt. It also attracted protesters carrying placards stating 'Say no to Nike sweat shops'. What does this mean? Paula Radcliffe opened the event – 'I was this close to Paula Radcliffe!'

What is your organisation selling? A fragrance or the Lynx effect!

assignment focus

1 Consider carefully what you are going to sell for your promotional campaign. Is it a product, experience, emotion, enjoyment or a promise of a better life? Take care, the Advertising Standards Authority has responsibility to make sure that adverts are legal, decent, truthful and honest (adverts for health clubs have often been criticised for failing to mention that people have to use more calories than they eat to reduce weight!).

2 What range of products does your business have?

3 Has your organisation brought out new products within the last year? Look at news or press releases on its website.

4 What is the key message of the campaign you are investigating?

Evaluating and assessing new products: product and market trials

Once the business believes it has a sound idea it will need to carry out a feasibility study to find out if it is worth putting it into production or developing further. It will need to look at:

- the costs and method of production which will directly affect the selling price and therefore its possible market
- quantity – the potential size of the market and the volume of sales. This has to be large enough to justify the development costs, which in some cases can be considerable, e.g. Cadbury's Wispa (which incidentally ended its production in 2003) cost £11 million to develop. Do you prefer Aero?
- the new product's position within the existing product range (sometimes referred to as the product mix)
- quality and style – consumer reaction. If consumers react negatively at an early stage of development, it would be a sign that they did not like the product in its present form, and it probably needs radical alteration. Quality may be associated with price but words such as 'cowboy' (high price, poor quality) and 'bargain' (low price good quality) suggest the relationship is not straightforward.

The product trial

A product trial would usually use a prototype (initial version of a product/service) to find out if the product works, i.e. the prototype will be used to test consumer reaction. Several versions may initially be made and trialled on consumer panels. These panels should be representative of the intended market segment. The winner or highest-rated version will go forward for test marketing in a selected area. This was how Yorkie, originally called Rations, was developed.

Market trials

Before new products are introduced into the market, they are usually tried out on a very small number of people to find out what changes need to be made before any further money is spent on development. Many products get no further than this stage. A careful sample will need to be chosen. What appeals to one group may not appeal to another! The main purpose of a market trial is to identify and sort out potential problems such as whether the quality is appropriate to the need of the target audience or production/service costs could be reduced to give a realistic price.

A business would run a trial of, for example, new opening hours (we'll try it for a week first and then review it), a new service, proposed changes to an existing product, etc.

A trial in a specific area could include a full press and TV campaign with promotional back-up, such as free samples. For example, the launch of Guinness's Draught Bitter in cans in the London area involved giving out free samples at London mainline railway stations.

The data which a company obtains in this way will enable it to decide whether it is worthwhile to go for a total nation-wide launch. The test area should ideally be a small version of the target audience as a whole, i.e. with a similar range of ages, income, ethnic group, lifestyles, etc.

BT tests out promotions in any one of nine regional zones to find out how well they work:

> 'By careful monitoring of what happens we can make adjustments to the product, the make up of our target group, the message of our advertising or whatever, then comes national roll-out.'

Source: BT

Field trial or test town operation

This is a miniature version of a test market in which a product, whose qualities have already been confirmed through blind placement tests (e.g. asking consumers if they prefer A or B without the consumer knowing which is the new product – the Pepsi challenge), is marketed in a limited way so that actual movement through the shops can be audited. Consumers may also be asked to return pre-paid cards giving their views on the product.

Interpreting the results

The results from these cards would not be read as if they were representative of all consumers in the test town but rather as an indication to be used to form a judgement. Therefore, if a few hundred returned cards show a consistent result, this would be sufficient justification to proceed with a wider launch. It is all a question of reconciling what is required with what is practical.

Great care needs to be exercised when interpreting the results of a test market operation, in case they are biased. Trials give the organisation the opportunity to make changes,

Product failure

For every new product that succeeds in the market there are probably 100 that fail, either because the market research was inadequate, or production faults occurred which could not have been foreseen.

Unique selling points

A major objective of promotion in both the for-profit and not-for-profit sectors is the need to differentiate the product from the competition. Charities have to compete for donations and businesses have to compete for sales. Every organisation will attempt to achieve a unique position for itself, its products or its services, in the heart and mind of the consumer. It will do this by emphasising one or other of its main features – its unique selling points (USPs) or unique selling proposition to gain the consumers' attention and interest to achieve a sale. With an ever-increasing level of competition and more products competing for our attention, it is important to promote a product so that it stands out from its competitors. However, doing this can be expensive and an organisation will need to weigh the expected cost against the expected benefits.

Here are some key features or benefits which have been used as unique selling points. As you read the list, try to think of some product examples:

- quality, e.g. 'The best a man can get'
- who makes it, e.g. 'We are the largest/smallest company so we try harder'
- price, e.g. 'Never knowingly undersold'
- product features, e.g. biggest, smallest, sweetest
- who uses it, e.g. a famous personality,
- benefits from use, e.g. cures headaches fast, makes you look ten years younger, clean fresh breath

- location, e.g. 1,000 car parking spaces on the doorstep
- value for money, e.g. 'With Fairy Liquid you get this much more'
- image, e.g. smart, attractive, friendly staff
- service, e.g. 'The smiles are free' or 'We answer every call'
- brand name, e.g. 'You can rely on x' logo
- style, e.g. cars, fashions, DFS sofas, Gap clothing, M&S summer range
- how long in business, e.g. 'Established for over 50 years'
- services, e.g. flexible payment, ten-year guarantee.

assignment focus

1   What USPs are being emphasised in the promotional campaign you are investigating?
2   What USPs will feature in your promotional campaign?

Product positioning

Product positioning refers to a specific quality or characteristic of the product which is most often stressed in its advertising and is best known to the customer – its 'personality'. In other words, what immediately springs to the customer's mind when the product is mentioned. Tropicana is '100% pure squeezed orange juice not from concentrate' (see Case study 3.2 on page 111). What image do you have of a *Sun* reader as opposed to a *Daily Telegraph* reader, of a Rolls-Royce as opposed to a Ford Fiesta?

assignment focus

1   Explain the features you will use to position your product or service in your promotional campaign. What is your unique selling point?
2   How is the product positioned in the campaign you are investigating?

Extension strategies

These are the methods that are used to try to extend or prolong the life of a product, e.g. repositioning, which means changing the customer's view or image of the qualities and characteristics of the product. Table 3.4 gives some examples of repositioning; you will probably think of others.

Table 3.4 Examples of repositioning

Product	New position
Lucozade	A sporty image and 'sweets'
Playboy	Fashions and Belgian chocolate
Baileys	New colour labelling developed to beat the 'lookalike' brands
Merrydown Cider	A premium drink in glass bottles

Companies may even change the name: Jif, for example, became Cif (a household cleaner) though the ingredients stayed the same. BP redesigned its logos. Have you noticed?

assignment focus

1   How much does the promotional campaign you are investigating stress or emphasise the product and the associated benefits in the marketing mix?
2   How is this helping to achieve the business aims and objectives?

Price

The price at which a business sells its products is an integral part of the marketing mix. Ask yourself the questions: How much would you expect to pay for a new microwave oven? Would you buy one for £40 or does this sound too cheap, i.e. it cannot be any good for that price? Do you associate price with quality? What about a £20 Easter egg for a member of your family? Does this seem expensive? What about a present for your best friend which costs £60 at Harrods in London and £20 in your local high street? Do you link the price with the place where it is bought, with quality or with value for money?

The seller of any product will have considered these and many other questions before deciding on the price at which to sell goods – 99p, £1.99, £2.99 all look and sound better than £1, £2 and £3 (actually they are only priced like this because it forces the shop assistants to open the till to give change).

Pricing policy

The pricing policy that a business adopts will depend upon many factors. Below are some examples.

- If the business is operating in a competitive market it could choose to keep its prices in line with its competitors, or try to undercut them. If the product is new and has only just been launched, a low introductory price could be chosen to tempt purchasers. Soft drinks are launched at 20p but within weeks are the same high price as other canned drinks. Marshall Cavendish, a publisher of weekly part-works, offers the first two weeks for the price of one, and a free binder!

- If the business decides to maximise profits, this will have a different effect on price than if it decides to maximise its share of the market, i.e. the company's objectives are important.

- Costs of production, both fixed and variable, can be significant, if the business chooses to adopt a cost-based pricing system. Look at the prices in your local sandwich bar – do they vary with the type of filling? Do you buy on price or the filling? Compare this with tins of paint in a local DIY, where prices are the same whatever the colour.

In this section, we will look at pricing as one vital part of the company's marketing mix.

Pricing new products

When a business introduces a new product or relaunches an existing one, it has to make a decision about which price to choose.

Penetration pricing

With **penetration pricing**, prices are set very low to enable the company to gain a foothold in a very competitive market. Once this has been achieved, prices may be progressively or selectively raised. Gillette, for example, launched a new product with a cheap razor and expensive blades. Exporters have often used this method to gain a foothold in another market – low-priced Japanese motorcycles virtually destroyed the UK industry. In 2006, China was accused of dumping shoes into the EU at below cost. The EU put a tax on all their shoes. Are you paying more?

The method is most effective if demand is elastic, so that consumers are tempted away from their usual supplier. Many new products are initially offered at a 'special introductory offer price', particularly when there are many other suppliers of similar products.

Premium pricing (perceived value pricing)

This is putting a high price on a product to give the impression that it is high quality. Some products are in demand because they are expensive. This is used where the demand is inelastic. The Belgian lager Stella Artois is premium priced and advertises with the slogan 'Reassuringly expensive'. Are you reassured by high prices?

Skimming pricing

With skimming pricing, prices are initially set very high to take advantage of some people's desire for a new product or design at any price. The term 'skim the cream' pricing is often used to describe this approach. Computer software packages, computer games, current chart music and DVDs are excellent examples of this type of pricing. The product may have a novelty or scarcity value, and the supplier may have little direct competition; perhaps because it is protected by a patent.

As with premium pricing, the high price may give extra appeal. Gradually the price will be reduced as competition appears. However, as consumers become more sophisticated, they will often delay purchasing until the price comes down. Would you buy the No. 1 chart hit six months later? Do you download?

The Competition Commission may intervene if it believes prices have been kept artificially high for too long, as happened with the makers of CDs.

Skimming is most effective if demand is inelastic, i.e. people want the product at any price. Marketers call these people 'early adopters' or 'must have' the newest mobile phone, the newest fashions in clothes or trainers. Do you consider yourself in this group?

Cost plus pricing

Pricing methods which are based on the cost structure of the business are favoured by accountants because they are supposedly more accurate and reliable. The cost of production is used as a baseline figure and the price is then marked up by the required amount. For example, if a retailer buys a product for £35 and wants a return or profit of 20 per cent, it will add 20 per cent (the margin) to the buying price to get the selling price of £42. This is the 'added value' to the product.

If the business is trying to maximise its profits, it should use a form of **cost plus pricing**. For this method to work successfully, all costs need to be accurately accounted for, particularly those associated with a change in the level of output.

In many firms this is a very difficult process, which is why the simpler mark-up procedure is used. Cost plus pricing tends to ignore the demand for the product and the competition.

Positioning pricing

With positioning pricing, prices are set which reflect the consumer's view of the product. For example, good champagne is supposed to be expensive, therefore a cheap champagne will be associated with poor quality. If the business sets too low a price, consumers may not buy the product – it is all a matter of psychology! The lowest priced tender, for example, is often not accepted. Products are often repositioned at higher prices to change their image.

Demand-based pricing

Many businesses set their prices based on what they think the consumer is prepared to pay. There are many examples of where this technique is used – consultants vary their fees according to the client; market traders will charge whatever they can get away with; jobbing gardeners will look first at the value of the property, then decide on a price; the local corner shop which buys its supplies 'cash and carry' will set the highest price it can, if the goods do not sell it will merely reduce the price. Travel companies and airlines such as easyJet work the same way, if unsold accommodation or seats exist, these are sold off cheaply, often on the internet where all pricing is dynamic, i.e. it changes with the level of demand and supply.

Competitive pricing

Competitive pricing is a situation where the business sets a price roughly in line with its competitors. Much will depend on the type of competition which exists for the product, particularly the number of sellers and the number of buyers. This process works reasonably well if the cost structures of the companies are roughly similar.

Discount pricing

In many competitive markets, e.g. office machinery or office consumables, the published list or catalogue price is only the starting point for bargaining. Buyers and purchasing officers in most businesses should be able to obtain the goods for less than the advertised price, particularly if they intend dealing with the supplier in future. Statements such as 'We definitely want to buy from you, it's only a question of price' may help get the deal you want.

Many firms can be forced into price cutting if they are short of cash or need to increase sales quickly, i.e. they have cash flow or working capital problems.

Link See page 95 for further information on working capital.

Differential pricing

A business may sometimes charge different prices for the same product at different times, e.g. peak and off-peak telephone calls, rail travel and holidays. Prices in this case will be based on the **elasticity** of demand for the product.

> **remember** A change in price could affect the sales/revenue for the product, consumers' perceptions on value, supplier and retailer margins, profit levels and cash flow forecasts, overhead costs and competitor prices. A business must always be prepared for a range of reactions when prices are changed, e.g. a competitor could follow a price change or ignore it.

Pricing strategy checklist

You can make a copy of the checklist in Table 3.5 and use it for your business plan and the marketing units.

Table 3.5 Pricing strategy checklist

Question	Answer
How competitive is the market?	
How price sensitive is the market?	
What is the existing range of prices?	
Should prices be below, the same as or above competitors?	
Should this be a permanent condition?	
Will the price achieve the business objectives?	
Will the proposed price cover costs?	
How will the other components of the marketing mix be used?	
What image is the business trying to achieve?	
What are the upper and lower limits?	

Price setting and price structures

The business will have to consider these factors.

- Identify the customers – What can they afford? What are they willing to pay? What do they think is a good 'value-for-money' price?

- Investigate competitors' prices, then decide whether to keep prices in line or undercut them. Calculate the costs and sales associated with possible price levels, keeping in mind the highest and lowest prices that could be charged, e.g. a new business will have to be able to match the lowest price available unless it is offering something extra.

- Decide on a price structure, e.g. will similar products all sell with a fixed price band? Look at prices in a fish and chip shop.

The prices of many electrical items are broadly in line with each other. This is called team or product line pricing. Check this out for yourself in an Argos catalogue.

Place or distribution

> **remember** The channel of distribution can also be called the distribution channel, distribution chain or supply chain.

The P for place is shorthand for the process of distribution – the way in which the seller gets the right goods and services to the customer, either consumers or other businesses, on time, first time, every time. To do this successfully a business needs an effective **logistics** system to place the product at the point where it is required by the customer.

Distribution is a customer service that should satisfy the actual and perceived needs of the buyer. If it does not, the producer will soon go out of business.

Distribution channels

The **distribution channel** is the method by which goods and services reach the customer at locations where customers are able to buy them, e.g. at home, work or in shops. A whole network of organisations may be needed to supply a product to end users and other businesses. The more often a product changes hands the more expensive it becomes because everyone in the chain needs to be paid, which is why buying online direct from the supplier is usually cheaper, e.g. Amazon.

The chain of distribution may have four main elements: in all cases the producer and consumer are vital – someone must produce/supply the product and someone must demand it. Whether intermediaries are used depends upon the nature of the product, where it is made, and how it is to be made available to the consumer. Examples of different chains of distribution are given below.

Figure 3.7

The chain of distribution

Producer ⟶ Wholesaler ⟶ Retailer ⟶ Consumer

<Intermediaries>

Direct selling or single stage channel distribution
Producer ◊ Consumer

This is also known as direct sales or direct supply. Examples of **direct selling** would include the local baker; doctors; hairdressers, and increasingly sales via the internet.

Table 3.6 Advantages and disadvantages of direct selling

Advantages	Disadvantages
Manufacturers can make bigger profits	It is not profitable for low value items unless there are large orders
Manufacturer can be more responsive to consumers	Goods cannot be examined before being purchased
Consumers can buy from their own homes	Manufacturers will have to pay all the storage costs
Manufacturers have total control over the product and its price	

case study 3.6 — Just a cosmetic change?

The internet is transforming the market for cosmetics and toiletries. Traditional door-to-door/home party companies such as Avon are now having to compete with store retailers and manufacturers. Ann Summers has shops, a mail order catalogue and holds parties, Clinique and Lancome (cosmetic manufacturers) now sell direct via the internet. Avon has responded by opening a health and beauty spa to change its image. Smaller companies have been able to get into the market via the internet, e.g. drugstore.com.

Source: Adapted from *Marketing Week*

activity

Why do cosmetic companies need to change the way they distribute their goods?

The internet is now firmly part of the P for place in marketing and selling goods and services in the UK. Nearly 10 million people, out of a total of 16 million home PC owners, regularly use the internet and 85 per cent of businesses. It is estimated that £40 billion of sales are now made via the e-commerce network worldwide every year, with European sales estimated at £1bn in 2006. Although sales to consumers are important, it is anticipated that its most valuable use in the future will be for business-to-business trade, e.g. finding suppliers.

Table 3.7 Advantages and disadvantages of using the internet

Advantages for the seller	Disadvantages for the seller
■ Cuts out the intermediary wholesaler and retailer ■ Can reach more people ■ A large and powerful database can be built up which enables the service to be personalised, e.g. Amazon.com the world's biggest internet bookseller will suggest titles based on a customer's spending patterns ■ Service is available 24 hours a day, 7 days a week without the need for staff ■ Provides the opportunity for small/medium size businesses to trade internationally without having to relocate or set up complex distribution channels ■ Small businesses with an effective net site can compete worldwide provided that price and delivery terms are customer focused ■ It gives access to new markets	■ Pricing structures will need to be totally transparent across the world, there can be no price discrimination between countries ■ Profit margins can be much lower than traditional distribution particularly when online costs are included ■ High level of initial start-up costs particularly the advertising needed to attract people to the site, e.g. Amazon.com. uses radio, newspaper, magazines and other websites such as Virgin.net ■ High initial technology costs but with the capacity for growth if the business expands ■ Effective storage and distribution systems are needed
Advantages for the buyer	**Disadvantages for the buyer**
■ Wide range of choice which can be accessed from home or work ■ The internet is probably a classic example of a free market, pricing is dynamic and depends on supply and demand. It should always be possible to bargain for a lower price ■ Can be accessed at any time to suit the used, e.g. airline tickets can be purchased 24 hours a day without the aggravation of phoning during office hours ■ Many people do not want to spend their free time walking around shops to find a product. Cars can be bought and delivered to your door all through a PC, with a 40 per cent price saving ■ Almost anything can be bought including a proposed site auctioning human eggs. The site is described as 'unethical and distasteful' (*Evening Standard*) ■ Provides a vast store of accessible information	■ Difficulty keeping credit card details secure (although no worse than phone systems), encryption or scrambling the data will help. A site which is secure should have an address beginning https//, a dialogue box appearing saying the site is secure and a padlock icon comes up ■ Very few sites show the small fonts! ■ What happens if goods are faulty? Need to be changed? Is there a guarantee? Warranty? Does the customer have to pay for returning goods? ■ May be nescessary to follow up a transaction with several phone calls if, for example, goods are not delivered on time ■ What after-sales services exist when goods are purchased in another country? ■ What Data Protection legislation exists, e.g. in the USA personal details are much more freely available in the UK

Short channels of distribution or two-stage supply chain
Producer ◊ Intermediary ◊ Consumer

In this chain, the intermediary can be a:

- retailer – examples are clothing and footwear manufacturers who deal directly with large retailers; large supermarket chains, such as Tesco and Waitrose, buy direct from the farms and factories which produce and manufacture goods to their specifications

- dealer – Car and motorcycle manufacturers, such as Ford, Honda and Suzuki, deliver directly to dealers for onward sale to consumers. Mobile phones are also sold through dealers. Whenever dealers are involved in distribution, there is always some concern over whether there is sufficient price competition. In the UK, the price of the original phone is subsidised by approximately £200; to compensate for this call charges are very high. Compare this with Norway, for example, where the initial costs are much closer to the real price but call charges are very much lower

assignment focus

1   Does or should your business use the internet for distribution, selling or promotion? Is the current campaign on the internet or its website?

2   What distribution channels does it use? Give reasons.

- wholesaler – these buy in bulk direct from the manufacturer, so they are able to negotiate much lower prices. They 'break bulk' and sell much smaller quantities to retailers who in turn sell individual packs to consumers. Wholesalers provide value by storing goods and making them available close to where they are needed by retailers

- agent – Tupperware (plastic tableware, mugs, etc.) and Avon cosmetics have always been sold by agents at home and office parties, although Avon have now opened a health spa in an attempt to give their image a more upmarket look

- franchise – this is a licence, given to a distributor or retailer, which gives the right to sell the products in a particular area. The franchisee (a retail outlet) will normally pay the franchiser a percentage of profits. Body Shop and McDonald's are well-known examples of companies that have grown quickly by granting franchises

- own shop – IKEA makes and sells its furniture through its own retail chain. Some of these outlets are franchises. Boots, which introduces ten new products a week, manufactures and sells its own goods. 'Forward vertical integration' is used to describe the situation where a company controls and/or owns the businesses that distribute its products.

assignment focus

A franchise could be a good way for you to open a new business (see Unit 5). Do an internet search to find out what franchises are available.

Table 3.8   Advantages and disadvantages of short channels

Advantages of short channels	Disadvantages of short channels
■ Manufacturer is able to control and monitor the supply of the product ■ Dealers get financial help and support in return for an exclusive dealership, i.e. agreeing not to sell a competitive product ■ Manufacturer is able to respond quickly to changes in the conditions of demand	■ Retailers can become very powerful and are able to negotiate very low prices. This has happened with many suppliers to UK retail chains. Lower prices, however, have not been passed on to consumers ■ The cost of distributing the product may rise (most lorries return empty from a wholesaler. Wal-Mart have been particularly successful in arranging suppliers close to wholesalers so that lorries can return full)

The long channel of distribution
Producer ⇌ Wholesaler ⇌ Retailer ⇌ Consumer

When there is a large number of small retailers, the producer will usually deal with a wholesaler who buys in bulk, stores the products and sells them on to the retailer in smaller quantities. A small grocer will usually go to the wholesaler, perhaps a 'cash and carry', to collect stock. This may be done fairly regularly to avoid the grocer having to devote space to storage.

The services provided by these intermediaries are sometimes regarded as unnecessary. However, intermediaries can be essential in creating an effective demand. For example, if we have to travel to Tokyo for a stereo, or to Canada for breakfast cereals, we may decide we do not want them after all.

Table 3.9 Advantages and disadvantages of long channels

Advantages of long channels	Disadvantages of long channels
■ Retailer gains convenience and minimises storage costs ■ Consumers are able to buy in small quantities from retailers ■ Goods are available close to where they are needed ■ Wholesalers provide valuable retailer support services ■ Transport costs are lower because the producer does not have to make as many deliveries	■ Prices tend to be higher when goods change hands many times; compare prices in your local corner shop with those in a superstore ■ Producers have less control over the way in which goods are stored and sold (many guarantees state that faulty goods have to be returned to the shop where they were bought)

Channel selection

The supplier will have to decide whether to provide the goods directly to the customer, or use an intermediary such as a wholesaler or retailer. Which decision is made will depend on the answers to these questions.

■ Who are the customers? For example, industrial users and large retailers would normally be supplied through short channels, while small retailers and consumers may require an intermediary.

■ What are their needs? For example, if the product requires complex frequent servicing then a short channel may be preferred. Long channels would work for simple products. Consumers and businesses wanting convenience and 24/7 access would need online facilities.

■ Where are they situated and what outlets are available? For example, when customers are clustered together, retailers are possible. Online direct selling can be used for national and/or international distribution.

■ What are the characteristics of the product? For example, services must be supplied directly to the consumer – there cannot be an intermediary. Do goods have to be delivered immediately or can they be stored? Products with a short 'shelf life' need short channels, whereas durable goods can be stored with a wholesaler, enabling the manufacturer to cut storage costs.

'You can buy anything on eBay, e.g. Loch Ness water or a human soul for £11.61 used?'

Source: Evening Standard

Table 3.10 Comparison of costs and benefits associated with each decision

Direct to customer	Using an intermediary
■ Gives the producer total control ■ Provides immediate customer service ■ Can be very expensive if the producer has to run its own fleet of transport ■ Can be expensive if there are many customers with small orders, widely spread ■ Producer can give the image it wants ■ Gives good customer feedback and response ■ All stock is readily available, but costly to store ■ Centralised storage can be inefficient particularly with bulky or heavy products ■ Will need to provide a range of customer services	■ Can be very expensive ■ Provides storage facilities ■ Able to provide small quanitites ■ May not give the image required by the manufacturer ■ Can be important in large areas with few customers ■ More difficult to control ■ May only carry a few popular lines ■ Intermediary or decentralised distribution is needed for high-weight, low-price goods ■ Retailers can provide services such as free delivery and installation

case study
3.7

More than one distribution channel

Many businesses now operate more than one channel of distribution in order to reach different segments of the market. For example, Next sells through its high street shops and via its catalogue; Dell computers are sold 'off the page' through the press and magazines, through telephone sales, via the internet and through a small business sales team.

activity

1   Why do businesses use more than one distribution channel?
2   Think of other examples.
3   Which channels are used by the business you are studying?

Service distribution

The main differences between the distribution of goods and services are that:

- services can only be provided direct to the customer. A dentist, for example, cannot work through an intermediary; a friend cannot go to the gym to train for you!

- because services are intangible, which means they cannot be stored and have to be provided on demand. So if you want the total experience of the Reading Festival you have to go yourself.

Service industries, therefore, have to be able to spread the demand for their services. They do this by changing the four Ps:

- price – peak and off-peak pricing is a key feature of many service industries, e.g. holidays are priced according to the season, rail travel and telephone call charges vary with the time of day. The purpose of these policies is to spread the demand

- product – administration systems have been devised which help to spread the loadings, e.g. holidays and dentists have to be booked in advance and staff are specially trained to give advice and help

- place – services have to be provided where the customers are situated, e.g. hairdressers, dentists and plumbers can be found in any reasonably populated area. The provision of services is decentralised and therefore expensive

- promotion – special promotions advertise the benefits of using off-peak facilities, e.g. no queues and no waiting at the restaurant (between 6 p.m. and 7 p.m.).

Many new businesses have been forced to seek alternative methods of distributing products when large firms have already tied up the existing market outlets. This can be a very expensive process, but also very rewarding as Häagen Dazs ice cream demonstrates. When Häagen Dazs could not distribute through traditional grocers (Walls had the rights to the freezers), it targeted off-licences!

Promotion

The promotion mix

The main methods of promotion are:

- advertising and **publicity**
- public relations
- exhibitions
- personal selling
- sponsorship
- **direct marketing**
- sales promotion
- packaging and product presentation.

Advertising and publicity

The Advertising Association defines advertising as 'messages paid for by those who send them intended to inform or influence people who receive them' (adassoc.org). It is impersonal and the messages can apply to both goods/services and ideas or causes.

See Friends of the Earth, page 108.

Publicity is concerned with gaining public attention for goods/services. It is not necessarily paid for and may be unwanted and damaging to the reputation of the product/service. TV programmes such as *Watchdog* or *Rogue Traders* publicise bad companies.

Advertising is any form of communication which is designed to inform and/or persuade businesses or consumers into taking action which meets the objectives of the sender. Remember AIDA (page 111) – the ultimate purpose of advertising is to get people to take action. On any day we will be continuously exposed to advertising in all its forms, on the radio or TV, on the bus, on posters, through logos on clothing, bags and trainers, on the internet, your mobile phone, your junk mail and e-mails, newspapers, magazines, etc. The sender/advertiser could be a retailer, manufacturer, charity or government department (e.g. anti-smoking campaign).

Advertising, in some form or other, has been in action for centuries. The red and white barber's pole is a reminder of the days when barbers doubled as dentists. Inn signs were important when customers could not read.

case study 3.8 — Using celebrities!

ANDREW FLINTOFF England cricketer

NICKNAME: Freddie (as in Flintstone)
IMAGE: Flintoff signs autographs after cricket matches, but the flood of fans approaching him is not on the scale of David Beckham
EARNINGS: Approx £1m per year. Made £341,250 on the pitch in 2005, including Ashes bonus
ENDORSEMENTS: Woodworm cricket equipment, Barclays Capital, Red Bull, Volkswagen and the *Sun*; worth a total of £650,000

DAVID BECKHAM England footballer

NICKNAME: Becks
IMAGE: Brand Beckham has world recognition. Beckham spends more time with fans than most world-class footballers, often spending 45 minutes after matches signing autographs
EARNINGS: Approx £18m per year. Made £4.5m on the pitch in 2005, plus performance-related bonuses
ENDORSEMENTS: Gillette, Vodafone, Adidas, Diesel, Pepsi and others; worth a total of £13.5m

Source: Independent Online, August 2005, 'Is cricket the new football?'

In September 2005, Kate Moss was photographed allegedly taking illegal drugs. H&M, Burberry and Chanel immediately stopped using her in their commercials.

activity

1 Why are personalities/celebrities used to promote products?
2 Why do firms advertise?
3 Does your business use celebrities? Are they the right choice? Has the campaign attracted any bad publicity?

Advertising provides information to the buyer. It can be informative when it tells consumers about the product, what it does, how it works, what it costs and where it can be bought. It is persuasive when it is intended to tempt consumers to buy a particular product in preference to any other.

To view TV and cinema adverts, find out the storyline and learn about the agency. go to www.visit4info.co.uk

The main purposes of advertising are to:

- increase demand, so that the business can sell more at any particular price
- create or change the image, for example, Kellogg's Cornflakes are in a package which conveys the image of a 'sunshine breakfast' (the 'look-alike' and 'me-too' own brand cornflakes are in an almost identical box). Adverts such as 'nothing is like' or 'the biggest small car in its class' are intended to hit a competitor's product
- create brand loyalty so that customers will continue to buy the product in the long term
- raise the profit revenue by appealing to the emotions; e.g. charities are now advertising heavily
- maintain and build the market share
- increase awareness, gain attention, create an interest or desire for the product so that receivers of the message take action
- change attitudes or the perception of the product.

Advertising is the main means by which a business can tell the public about the product and what it can do. The type of advertising medium that will be used depends on the content and purpose of the message

> **remember**
>
> Make sure you get your target market right.

assignment focus

1 Analyse the advertising being carried out as part of the promotional campaign you are investigating. What is the message? Who is it intended for? Has there been any good or bad publicity, either intentional or unintentional?

2 What advertising do your competitors use, and can you say why?

3 What advertising do you intend to use as part of your promotional campaign? Why have you made this decision? What message will you be sending?

4 If you choose TV, what programmes? What times? Can you afford it?

5 If you go for magazines, which ones and how much space will you get for your money?

Public relations

Public relations is the process of communicating a specific message to an organisation's stakeholders. Its purpose is to achieve favourable publicity.

For stakeholders, see page 14.

Every organisation will have a file which contains a record of each time it has been mentioned in the media. The public relations (PR) department of an organisation (often included in the marketing department) has the responsibility for getting this publicity. Rock groups, politicians, personalities, presenters and plcs could all have people responsible for PR. The purpose is to plan and control news to get good publicity and avoid bad publicity. Politicians use 'spin doctors' to turn or twist the adverse effects of a news story in their favour.

Public relations involves:

- keeping the media informed of new products or changes to existing products

- providing **press releases**, stories, facts, lies, photos, secrets, etc., on behalf of the client to the media. These can result in excellent free publicity. However the sender has no real control over what the receiver will do with the information. Millions of press releases are issued each year; 95 per cent are ignored by the media

- lobbying – persuading journalists, TV presenters, etc. to write or mention the client, e.g. a travel article on Poland might say at the end, 'Our reporter, Holly Day, travelled to Poland courtesy of the Polish National Airline LOT', i.e. the trip was free in return for a free 'plug'

- companies sponsoring major sporting events. Corporate entertainment is an important feature of public relations. Potential clients could be invited to Wimbledon, the FA Cup Final or an England cricket test match. Could these invitations influence their decisions?

- community relations, e.g. the local theatre could give away free tickets to the current pantomime to the winner of the 'Name everyone in the theatre last night' competition! In 2004 Avon cosmetics, famous for 'Avon calling', promised free mobile phones with an order of skin cream. Demand was much greater than expected and many people were allegedly unable to get their mobile. Is any publicity good publicity?

- organising a product launch or media event, the purpose of which is to achieve as much free publicity as possible, by inviting the press, TV, radio, the local MP, etc. Almost anything can be launched, e.g. a new album, the opening of a new crèche, a new group called 'Feel' in Bromley. Sustainable travel was the theme of the Green Canary Day media event organised by Canary Wharf and the Good Going Campaign.

It is the ultimate aim of every PR person to get a mention on the TV news. Do not do as one enthusiastic student did when set the task 'try to get your organisation mentioned on the news' – he tried to rob the place!

Managing public relations

To be effective, PR must:

- be planned and controlled so that the right message gets across to the right people, i.e. those chosen or targeted by the business

- be ready to deal with any problems. Apologising and informing people why the train is late is good PR, doing nothing loses goodwill. What is your experience?

- have a specific message or objective which can preferably be measured, e.g. in column centimetres, or air time

- be developed over the long term to build up both the image and reputation of the organisation, its products, services and/or views and ideas.

> **remember**
>
> Your definition of costs and benefits will depend on your viewpoint. e.g. sender or receiver.

assignment focus

What PR or publicity is currently in the news for your product organisation? Collect some examples.

Exhibitions

Exhibitions are big business for many sectors of UK industry. They are particularly important for B2B trading where suppliers and buyers all come together to form a market at an exhibition centre such as the National Exhibition Centre (NEC) in Birmingham or Olympia in London.

What is the purpose of exhibitions? There are many reasons why firms use exhibitions, including to:

- meet new customers
- improve their image
- launch new products
- find out about existing and possible new customers and competitors

- try out new ideas/products
- build staff morale
- network and develop contacts.

Being an exhibitor at a major trade exhibition can be used in promotional material. Being a winner at an exhibition is a selling point (the Champion Beer of Britain in 2005 was Brewers Gold brewed by Crouch Vale and now visible on its advertising). Buyers get the opportunity to compare a range of products and meet the sales staff, although they often complain that they too 'pushy or over-aggressive'. Both sellers and buyers agree that exhibitions are worthwhile, i.e. expenses are paid!

Are exhibitions value for money? Read the following information:

'Auto Sport International attracted 814 participating companies.

165,000 people attended the International Motorcycle and Scooter Show.

285 companies exhibited at the National Wedding Show at Olympia, attendance 15,855.

365,000 visited the Ideal Home Show.

Although exhibition costs can be expensive, the benefits, over the long term can be worthwhile particularly if the exhibitor can create a database of potential customers. This is best achieved by running a raffle or competition name and address required. Local Arts and Crafts exhibitions are important for both sales and recognition.'

Source: abc.org.uk

'The National Exhibition Centre in Birmingham is the busiest exhibition centre in Europe, staging more than 180 exhibitions each year, ranging from the British International Motor Show to the National Fast Food Show. Nearly 4m people visit the centre each year. There are 200,000 square metres of space, the size of a small village.'

Source: NEC website

assignment focus

1   Is your organisation participating in any exhibitions as part of its promotion campaign?

2   Check out the exhibition websites and abc.org.uk.

Personal selling

In every civilisation wherever goods/services have been sold, the sales person has been central to the promotion mix. Today many students are part-time sales assistants. Do you or your friends feel valued as a key part of promotion? Personal selling can take place face-to-face or over the telephone. Whether it's B2B or B2C, the process is the same.

Personal selling is extremely important during the desire and action phases of the AIDA concept, i.e.:

- **A**wareness – get the customers awareness of the product through advertising
- **I**nterest – gain their interest and commitment through public relations
- **D**esire – arouse their desire through special offers and sales promotions
- **A**ction – get them to buy the product through effective selling techniques.

There are three stages in the selling process (Figure 3.8).

Figure 3.8

The position of selling

Figure 3.9

The stages of the selling process

1 Opening the sale	2 Dealing with objections	3 Closing/making the sale
State the benefits, key features and USP of the product, provide information. Know the product and the customer	Anticipate what might go wrong, listen and respond, sympathise but never agree, Treat any objections as an oppurtunity to improve. Ask more questions	Fear close: 'they may be all sold if you come back later' Alternative close: 'perhaps this model would be better' Reassurance close: '300,000 satisfied customers'

The benefits of personal selling come from the one-to-one communication. The message can be tailored to individual needs and feedback is immediate. Closing (making) the sale will require good communication skills with reassuring body language. Objections can be dealt with immediately and, once trust has been established between the buyer and seller, a long-term relationship can develop, both in B2B and B2C. But how much do effective sales staff cost to recruit, train and develop?

assignment focus

1   Does your organisation use personal selling techniques?

2   Has it supported other businesses, e.g. retailers through trade promotions?

Sponsorship

Manufacturers use sponsorship as a way of advertising themselves to the public.

Sponsorship can mean giving financial support to an organisation, an event, an activity or a person. McDonald's 'I'm lovin' it' (it's first global campaign) is already signed up to be one of the sponsors of the 2012 Olympic Games in London. The International Olympic Committee (IOC) has already applied to register 2012 as a trade mark to prevent illegal use of the event and date. All advertising space within the London area will need to be secured for Olympic use for the duration of the games. Games-related words and images will only be allowed to be used by official advertisers. Ambush marketing where businesses pretend to be sponsors is strictly illegal. Banned words include Gold, Silver, Bronze (is this a sun tan?), etc.

Here is a quote taken from www.london2012.org:

'Any unauthorised use of the Olympic Marks threatens London 2012's ability to establish a successful sponsorship programme and raise the funds necessary to host and stage the 2012 Games and to fund the Team GB.'

The owner of the Olympics Hair Salon in London said he would not change its name.

remember

If you intend opening a wedding planning business, do not use five rings as a symbol!

The main purposes/objectives of sponsorship are to:

■   raise customer awareness of the organisation and its products

■   raise the company profile and brand exposure

■   create, enhance or change an image, e.g. BUPA sponsor the Great North Run, charities use the event as a fundraiser

■   generate increased sales

■   widen the audience which sees the company's logo.

Companies now sponsor sports events (The 2006 London Marathon was sponsored by _____. Can you remember the name? If you can't, who were the sponsors trying to attract?), sports stars, plays, opera and pantomimes and TV programmes, for example. *Coronation Street* is sponsored by Cadbury's (did you know?), which reinforces its family image. (Under the new EU definition of chocolate, Cadbury's with more milk and less chocolate than continental varieties will have to be marketed as 'family milk chocolate'.)

A successful sponsorship can generate millions of pounds of extra sales. Local companies are increasingly prepared to sponsor local events.

Tobacco companies are no longer allowed to sponsor Formula 1 motor racing or advertise close to schools.

assignment focus

1   Who or what is sponsored by your company as part of its PR/publicity/advertising? Why?
2   Check out the corporate responsibility section of its website.

Direct marketing

Direct marketing is any form of sales, supply or promotion made directly to the consumer. Included in direct marketing are direct mail, either off-screen or off-page mail order, tele-marketing, door-to-door distribution and direct reply advertising or selling.

There are two main advantages of direct marketing.

- The market can be precisely targeted because the business contacts a known person directly.
- Costs can be controlled and the business will know exactly what it costs to generate sales.

These are important points because most advertising campaigns tend to be hit and miss affairs, and the business does not usually know who has responded.

Direct mail

Used extensively by charities, financial services and book clubs, direct mail can be very precise. As computer databases become more efficient, individuals can be contacted directly with personalised mail. Much of the mail received is unsolicited 'junk mail', 'junk fax' or 'junk e-mail' (now known as **spam**), i.e. it is not asked for. The Data Protection Registrar is now getting an increasing number of complaints about some direct mail methods.

Agencies sell lists of potential customers. These are gained from people who have, for example:

- returned ten tokens from the *Echo* for a £1 day trip to France. The names and addresses of many *Echo* readers will, therefore, be known. Other market research will have confirmed what these people eat, drink and how they spend their leisure time. Companies which make these products will later buy these lists of names
- entered a competition and given a name, telephone number, e-mail address, etc.
- joined a club or used a credit card in any shop. (Beware store cards have very high interest rates and are being investigated.)

> **remember**
>
> Almost all the transactions you make will be recorded somewhere – 'Smile you are on camera'!

Every time someone provides personal information it adds to the information stored on a database. Mailing lists of names and addresses can be bought for about £50 per thousand. As technology becomes more sophisticated, the amount of junk mail should decrease, as it becomes possible to target individuals/households more precisely.

Mail order

Mail order companies all sell direct to the public, e.g. through catalogues. Other companies use home parties to sell children's clothes, cosmetics, jewellery, etc. These are all precisely targeted because the people who run parties only ask people with similar interests. Well-known names include Avon cosmetics, Tupperware (the odd plastic lid in your cupboard) and Body Shop, a relative newcomer to direct selling. Next has a very popular catalogue which has to be paid for.

Tele-marketing

Telephone marketing (tele-marketing) is increasing. It is cheap to set up, very persuasive on a one-to-one basis and the message can be varied.

Door-to-door distribution

In the case of door-to-door distribution, the salesperson will literally knock on every door trying to sell goods or services. Some companies leave an order form with a catalogue 'to be collected later'; in some cases the catalogue also has to be returned.

Direct reply advertising

With this method, advertisements are placed in newspapers, on TV, fax machines, mobile phones (check that you do not have to pay for receiving them), answer machines, etc. – 'You have been chosen … etc.!' Customers need to reply direct to the advertiser.

Sales promotion

Sales promotion refers to the techniques and methods used by a business to sell its products to either customers or other businesses. Its primary purpose is to get customers to take action and purchase a product.

The overall objectives of sales promotion are to:

- encourage potential customers to buy the product
- promote and/or maintain customer loyalty.

Business to business (B2B) trade promotion

The main purpose of trade promotions is to persuade businesses to stock and sell the product. There are several methods that can be used to achieve this.

- Point-of-sale (POS) displays – these are displays which are set up near the till or check-out point. Retailers will be supplied with brochures, mock-ups of the product, leaflets and shop window displays which can be used to focus the customer's attention on a particular product. They appear to be very popular in chemists. Point-of-sale methods are extensively used, particularly in supermarkets, where evidence suggests that almost 30 per cent of purchases are the result of on-the-spot decisions. How often have you heard people say 'I only came in to buy three items and have ended up with a full trolley'? Tesco has decided to become a paperless shop. It is getting rid of all paper POS materials and replacing these with TV screens in the power aisles, where most people walk and make decisions.
- Competitions – many suppliers run competitions especially for retailers, as a loyalty incentive to get them to sell more of the product.
- Discounts – these are offered to retailers when they buy in bulk or order in advance. They are particularly important when a business is trying to launch a new product. Wholesalers and retailers have to be persuaded, or induced, to stock new and untried goods with uncertain profits. On average, some 60 per cent of a sales promotion campaign budget for a consumer product, such as bottled mineral water, would be spent on point-of-sale and retail promotions.

Business to consumer (B2C) promotion

- Vouchers and coupons – these can be a very efficient way of promoting sales as they cost the company very little. In 2005 Tropicana (juices) was offering '50p off your next purchase'. This promotion was run at the same time as a TV advertising campaign.
- Samples and gifts – sachets of just about everything are now stuck to magazines, in order to tempt the consumer to buy the magazine and try the product. DVDs, CDs, floppy discs, seed trays and a bait box (this was attached to a fishing magazine) have all been available. Evidence suggests that any increase in sales due to the promotion is only temporary.

Discounts and competitions are also used to attract new purchasers or maintain the loyalty of existing customers. Why do companies offer these inducements? Do you buy products because there is a gift attached? Do you use the garage with the forecourt promotion? Crucially, do you stay loyal to your usual brand or do you switch if the competitor has a special promotion? All these offers are about keeping customers loyal.

assignment focus

1 What sales promotion is your organisation carrying out. Can you give reasons?
2 Give details of any direct marketing your organisation is doing in conjunction with its current promotional campaign. (Go into a newsagents and check a range of magazines.)
3 How can these promotional techniques help your organisation achieve its objectives?
4 How are the four Ps of the marketing mix being used in this particular campaign?

Creative Product Promotion

Packaging and product presentation

These are a key element in the process of creating a brand image. BP has 'green' garages and forecourt shops and prominently displays a yellow daffodil in its promotional literature. What does petrol smell like? Think of Toblerone and Smarties – these have all the qualities of good packaging. Packaging is an essential tool for distinguishing one brand from another.

The key features of packaging are as follows.

- colour – what colour is the Kit Kat pack? The colour associated with Cadbury's is purple, and with BP green. Some colours are said to be warm, while others such as blue are seen as cold or refreshing, e.g. toothpaste or chewing gum. Do you associate colours with emotions or feelings? The colour of the pack reinforces the image.

- Shape and design – e.g. Terry's Chocolate Orange, Ferrari – red! The shape should be instantly recognisable and enable the product to be differentiated from the competition.

- Distinctiveness or brand visibility – e.g. McDonald's arches (These are going to be dropped and replaced by a gold question mark and a bowl of salad to try and improve the image!), the Coca-Cola swirl. The graphics, logo, font style and size should all combine to give shelf 'stand out'. Look at the confectionery section in a newsagents. Which products stand out? Which do you buy? The Coca-Cola bottle is unique, distinctive and immediately recognisable. How does the pack reinforce the brand image? Do you shop in particular stores because you like being seen with their brand name on the packaging and carrier bags?

- Size – Is the pack too small, large? Can you get the spoon into the bottom of the coffee jar? Ergonomics is the study of how people and products/machines relate to each other. Do you sometimes feel that a product has been designed for someone else? Is it functional, convenient and easy to open?

- Functionality and protection from damage – during every stage of the distribution process from the manufacturer/supplier to the wholesaler and retailer. During storage and transit goods may experience a wide range of conditions, e.g. in temperature and humidity. Do you check every egg in the box? Do you find 'wrapped five times for perfect freshness' excessive? There needs to be a balance between what is environmentally friendly and what is necessary to protect the product.

- Communication – Is it persuasive with clear text and visuals? Does it provide information? Do customers want to buy it? Does it include any necessary legal requirements, e.g. 'Smoking kills', the warnings on medicines, such as 'Keep out of reach of children' or 'Do not exceed the stated dose'? Is there nutritional information? Does it provide instructions on how the product should be used?

- Message – What message does the packaging convey? Does the personality of the product show? Is the USP clearly stated, e.g. does the package and labelling convey a sense of luxury? Does it do 'exactly what it says on the tin'?

- Reinforcing the other elements of the marketing mix, packaging and the way the product is presented are vital ingredients in any promotional campaign (Tropicana, see page 115, changed its packaging to attract new users). Cosmetics companies spend millions on the packaging design. 'Our packaging can be seen everyday it is continuous promotion, one long advert. At Christmas time when most fragrances are purchased, we go to great lengths to also provide a gift wrapping service as part of the added value we offer,' said a marketing spokesperson.

Link

For IP (intellectual property), see page 96.

assignment focus

1 What are the packaging characteristics of your product?

2 Is the product fit for purpose?

3 Could it be improved?

4 Some products have excessive packaging. Does yours? Is it environmentally friendly?

case study 3.9

Changes in labelling and packaging

In an attempt to reduce binge drinking, the brewers Scottish and Newcastle (Kronenbourg, Fosters, Carlsberg) announced that it will state the number of units of alcohol in its products, urging drinkers 3 to 4 units a day for men 2 to 3 for women. Coors (Grolsch, Carling) will also have responsibility straplines. Tobacco companies already have them: 'Smoking kills'.

Coke and Pepsi intend to label their soft drinks with nutritional information such as the amount of calories, fat and carbohydrate.

McDonald's 'but not as you know it'! Conscious of accusations of allegedly contributing to obesity, 17 million homes received mail drops explaining McDonald's new healthier image. Did you get one?

Source: *Food and Drink Industry News*; www.fdin.co.uk

activity

Why do you think that companies need to demonstrate a more responsible approach in their marketing to consumers?

Advertising Agencies and the Media

Advertising agencies

International advertising agencies such as J Walter Thompson (Kit Kat and Nik Naks) or McCann-Erickson (Coca-Cola, Walls Sausages, Mastercard, but lost Bacardi) tend to work on mass market national/international brands.

i

To find out more about these agencies, go to:
- J Walter Thompson: www.jwt.com or www.jwt.co.uk
- McCann-Erickson: www.mccann.com or www.mccann.co.uk

Roles of advertising agencies

An **advertising agency** is a specialist marketing business, which will plan, create and carry out an advertising campaign on behalf of its client. The client may be a private or public sector organisation, charity or political party will generally pay an agency a percentage of the total amount spent.

A full-service agency (one-stop shop) would handle each stage of a whole campaign including:

- creative development, e.g. creating TV adverts – the agency would work closely with the client to find out their marketing needs and expectations (the creative brief is vital at this stage). Beware – an advertisement can be very creative and win awards for artistic quality, but if it does not sell the product it is a commercial failure – 'Great ad but what was it selling?'

- analysing and buying media space and time – the agency will identify client needs and match these to the types of media, e.g. press, TV or outdoor advertising. It will then buy the space in the press or the time slots on the TV. An agency should have the knowledge, experience and expertise to identify the best media mix for the product

 Link

See page 144 for more information on types of media.

- evaluating effectiveness – this stage must be carried out both before and after any campaign. Measures of effectiveness such as the number of people aware of the brand must be built in at the planning stage. An agency should have the capability to provide this research.

Other agencies specialise, for example, in media buying. Industrial agencies work exclusively with manufacturers and suppliers of industrial goods, such as the mechanical diggers seen on building sites and market these to companies such as Brandon Hire.

Small à la carte, or boutique, agencies may consist of two or three people who specialise in a particular sector or **niche market**, e.g. jewellery. Local agencies with local knowledge would be most effective for a small business with a local campaign.

Table 3.11 shows the major roles of a full service, or one-stop, advertising agency.

Table 3.11 Typical roles of advertising agencies

Production and traffic	Creative	Account planning	Media buying	Media planning
Make sure the work is completed on time to the required standard and all legal requirements are met, e.g. adverts must be 'legal, decent, truthful and honest' (asa.org)	Copywriters and art directors Responsible for creating, writing and designing the ads, e.g. slogans, text, radio and TV scripts, voiceovers Adding pictures and graphics	Responsible for analysing any market research Identifying target segment/ audience Testing and evaluating the effectiveness of the advertising	Buy time on TV and radio Buy and schedule space in newspapers and magazines Bulk buying media space and time means cheaper rates	Make decisions about which media to use based on the client's campaign objectives and the media habits of the target audience, e.g. would radio or local press be more effective?

Graphic design and typography

The creative department is responsible for designing and creating the advertisement by taking the client's initial briefing about the product, adding its own ideas and turning them into reality. It will write the words (the copy), design and select the typography (plan and choose the size and type of font which best suits the product) and prepare the advert for printing. (Go to Format in Word to see a range of styles. Be aware of **copyright** in the use of fonts.) Today these processes are often done using computer software, which can create any graphics and edit any photographs that are needed and design the most effective layout to convey the message. For a TV or cinema commercial, it would create a storyboard which literally sets out the story or sequence of images that would be used in the advertisement.

See page 157.

A **copywriter** would write any words or lyrics used in jingles, e.g. 'Washing machines live longer with Calgon'.

There are usually four elements in the design of a print advertisement which together are intended to gain attention and interest, arouse desire and promote action (AIDA).

- The headline should be dramatic, eye-catching and memorable.
- The image, photo, illustration or graphics must reinforce the headline and copy and be appropriate to the needs of the audience.
- The copy (words) are written to inform and/or persuade. These should complement the headline and image and could include a discount offer to arouse desire.
- The organisation details or signature would include the logo, addresses, telephone number, name, etc. The customer must be able to make contact to buy! The process must be easy as possible or the potential customer could go elsewhere.

Cost options

There are two major cost considerations.

- Production costs include the number of colours (full colour is more expensive), technician and studio time for production and editing, celebrity **endorsements**, etc. Generally print adverts are cheaper to produce.

- Media buying costs are determined by size of the advert, position, circulation, number of viewers or listeners, time of day (programme), number of time slots or newspaper insertions, etc. Rate cards are produced by the media to show how much an advertisement will cost according to size and position.

Additionally, the agency will need to be paid. Smaller agencies would normally be paid a fee for each project. Large agencies may be paid a commission by the media they use.

One major decision will be whether the advertisement is produced in-house or prepared by an agency.

In-house vs outsourcing

In-house means the advertising is prepared internally. If the work is carried out by an outside/external company, it is outsourced.

Table 3.12 The advantages and disadvantages of in-house and outsourcing

For and against in-house	For and against outsourcing
■ Know your own needs but can be subjective ■ Only internal resources available ■ More control ■ Could be less expensive up front ■ Experts only available in larger organisations ■ Less knowledge of specialist media and costs ■ Could work directly through the local newspaper/radio to create adverts	■ More objective with wider experience ■ Access to wide range of skills ■ Close co-operation needed between client and agency account manager ■ More expensive, but the results could be worth it. Any decision should be based on value for money, i.e. effectiveness balanced against cost ■ Wide knowledge and experience of the marketplace ■ Can produce the whole campaign

Why use an agency?

Agencies should be able to provide staff with an expert knowledge of the ever-increasing complexity of the media. They are able to provide all the functions/research necessary to see an advertising campaign through from initial research to the scheduling and buying of media space. Specialist creative staff can create all types of advertisement. Because of their size, they are able to negotiate better rates with the media. An agency should have the knowledge, experience and expertise to identify the best **media mix**. On the other hand, there may be some loss of control and the process can be expensive.

How to choose an advertising agency

- Do you like their current campaigns?
- Do they have a portfolio of work?
- Are there references/testimonials
- Who are the clients?
- Will they have time for you?
- Do they have the knowledge you need?
- What is the price and what are you paying for?
- Is the agency too big?
- Do you like them?

Advertising agencies advertise themselves in the trade press. How effective do you think they are? Check the trade press, *Yellow Pages*, etc.

1   What media are available locally? Investigate what free and paid-for newspapers/magazines (for discerning households like yours) are distributed. Find out the advertising rates.

2   What are the local commercial radio stations? Who listens to them? Is this your target market?

3   How much does advertising cost? Do they provide help in preparing the advertisement? Check their websites.

4   How much would it cost to advertise on:
    a) a local bus?
    b) at the local cinema?
    c) in your centre prospectus?
    d) in your local church magazine? Good for wedding services!

Types of media

The media mix

Whether companies advertise locally, regionally, nationally or internationally will depend upon the available budget and the market, i.e. which segments are being targeted. Generally only those products with mass market appeal, distribution and demand would be worth advertising on a large scale. The majority of businesses (90 per cent) employ less than 20 people, so for these advertising is likely to be highly selective. However, remember any website marketing has international potential.

The advertising medium is the means by which information is communicated to the public. The mass media are the means of communication which reach large numbers of people: TV, newspapers, radio and magazines are the primary mass media. The choice of medium will depend upon the product and the marketing objectives.

Television advertising

This is expensive but can be targeted at regions or specific groups according to education, age or lifestyle. Viewing panels are used to find out the nature of the audience for any particular programme and time slot. A points rating system is used to price the TV advert. Considerable information is available, for example, people who use olive oil also drink wine, read, like holidays abroad, own a car, use mayonnaise and, would you believe, watch *Sex and the City!* So if you watch it, you are likely to see adverts for these products. Specific programmes are used to advertise specific products. However, do you switch channels when the adverts are on? The Broadcasters' Audience Research Board (BARB) has introduced a new electronic system for measuring audience appreciation of TV programmes, rather than just producing numbers of people watching. The social groups C1 and C2 watch most television.

For more information on social groups see page 169.

Terrestrial vs satellite TV

There are five terrestrial TV stations but only three of these are commercial, i.e. rely on advertising revenue: ITV1 Channel 4 and Channel 5. There are now hundreds of satellite or digital stations some of which are 'free to air'.

The Broadcasters Audience Research Board (BARB) publishes weekly and monthly summary figures of audiences for all major TV channels. Table 3.13 gives the figures for the week ending 12 February 2006. Some satellite channels have fewer than 1,000 viewers.

Table 3.13 BARB viewing figures for week ending 12 February 2006

| Channel | Average Daily Reach | | Weekly Reach | | Average Weekly Viewing | Share |
	000s	%	000s	%	Hrs: Mins per person	%
ALL/ANY TV	43,186	77.5	52,532	94.3	27:13	100.0
BBC1 (incl. Brkfast News)	29,915	53.7	47,867	85.9	6:14	22.9
BBC2	19,170	34.4	40,893	73.4	2:45	10.1
TOTAL BBC1/BBC2	33,624	60.3	49,508	88.8	8:59	33.0
ITV (incl. GMTV)	25,546	45.8	45,092	80.9	5:27	20.0
CHANNEL 4/S4C	19,215	34.5	41,328	74.2	2:45	10.1
five	11,181	20.1	29,794	53.5	1:35	5.8
TOTAL/ANY COMM. TERR. TV	33,217	59.6	49,676	89.1	9:46	35.9
Other Viewing	24,377	43.7	36,254	65.1	8:27	31.1

Source: www.barb.co.uk

Want to find out more? Go to www.barb.co.uk

Adam Stanhope, who started Rapture, the channel geared to 16-year-olds, says:

'Teenagers are the most valuable demographic group in the country, targeting is important, agencies don't buy airtime from small channels to get wider reach, they buy from them to get really pure audiences.'

Source: *The Times*

What do you think is advertised during programmes about extreme sports, clubbing and computer games?

Newspaper advertising

There are national, daily and Sunday newspapers, provincial daily and evening newspapers and local weekly newspapers. Although local newspaper advertising is relatively cheap, nationals can be expensive, because of the high circulation. Newspapers can be used to target specific groups of people.

Sun readers are in the C1 and C2 category, while the A and B groups read *The Times*. It can be very effective locally. The cost of advertising in newspapers depends mainly on the size of the readership and the size of the advertisement.

Magazines

There are approximately 7,000 magazines which appeal to quite specific market segments: sports, leisure interests, railway magazines, catering and those planning a wedding (there are five Bride magazines for different ethnic groups), etc. Nike and Adidas, for example, advertise regularly in sports magazines.

Posters

Posters are generally used to display very direct messages, e.g. 'Vote for me!' Campaigns can be planned locally, regionally or nationally. They are frequently used to back up a TV campaign. Poster sizes vary from 2 to 50 square metres; the largest size gives a very large message! Nestlé use posters extensively for advertising Polo, Yorkie, Kit Kat and Aero.

Outdoor advertising

Check out the publication *Media Week* which carries details of 'roadside activity' classified by national/London posters and national/London buses. Bus stops, taxis, street furniture, telephone/internet booths, wherever there is a space there will be an advertisement. Sports events are increasingly popular – advertising space is already being sold for the 2012 Olympics in London. What does this say about the power of advertising?

Look at maiden.co.uk, the largest outdoor advertising provider and oaa.org.uk for presentations on outdoor advertising

Internet advertising

In 1997, £8m was spent on internet advertising. In 2004, the figure was £653m. This is the fastest growth of any sector and the trend is expected to continue. Existing websites can be used to advertise new products and special promotions. Banners and pop-ups can be good for increasing awareness. Do you block them?

The major difficulty for a small company is attracting new visitors to the website, even being listed in the top 50 of a web search can be very expensive. How far do you scroll down?

Good web advertising has the potential to reach 30 million people in the UK alone, with the advert available 24 hours a day. Almost all major organisations have a website and the internet is in constant use for online searching and, increasingly, purchasing. Companies such as Amazon and easyJet do all their business online. For others, selling over the internet adds another dimension to the P for place in the marketing mix. Thompson Holidays (owned by TUI, a German travel and transport business) advertise 'Click, Call, Come in, Switch on to Sky Digital'.

Cinemas

Unless you arrive late, you cannot escape cinema advertising for Bacardi, Martini, jeans and the local Indian restaurant, which never looks like the one you use! (A parody of this has been used by McDonald's in its advertising.) Cinema adverts require long lead times. Do you still have a local cinema or a multiplex in your nearest large town?

Radio

Audiences, or market segments, can be targeted locally or nationally. As with TV, specific programmes and stations attract different types of people. In London, for example, Capital Gold plays 1960s and 1970s music, while Capital Radio plays contemporary music – each appeals to different markets. As with TV, advertising costs depend on the time of day and the size of the audience. Commercial radio reaches 75 per cent of all 15–24-year-olds. What station do you listen to? What would you advertise?

Table 3.14 shows that radio advertising has grown rapidly since 1994. The reason for this growth has been the blue chip (well-known) companies such as Kingfisher who have advertised Woolworths and B&Q. Dixons says:

'Growth has been driven by our High Street retailer Link which sells our mobile communications range. Link's younger target customers match the profile of many radio station listeners. Radio allows you to target a narrow lifestyle rather than a demographic group.'

It is flexible and personal as most people listen to the radio on their own. Many radio stations will help advertisers plan and develop their campaign without the need to go through an agency.

See page 155 on Pirate FM.

How advertising expenditure has changed

Table 3.14 shows how advertising expenditure has changed over the last ten years.

Look at www.businesslink.gov.uk

Criteria for media selection

Here are some criteria that could be used to enable an organisation make its decision.

Costs versus expected coverage

The decision about which media to use is based on the cost of the advertising and the expected response. For a small local business, a *Thompson Local/Yellow Pages* telephone

Table 3.14 Total advertising expenditure by media sector at current prices, £m

	1995	1996	1997	1998	1999	2000	2001	2002	2003	2004
National newspapers	1,433	1,510	1,650	1,824	1,991	2,252	2,062	1,933	1,902	1,973
Regional newspapers	1,963	2,061	2,238	2,390	2,483	2,762	2,894	2,894	2,986	3,132
Consumer magazines	533	5,83	660	709	727	750	779	785	784	819
Business and professional	897	1,018	1,106	1,209	1,195	1,270	1,202	1,088	1048	1,082
Directories	639	692	737	780	831	868	959	990	1029	1,075
Press production costs	514	550	577	620	650	702	669	643	634	660
TOTAL PRESS	5,979	6,413	6,967	7,531	7,877	8,604	8,504	8,333	8,382	8,741
Television	3,136	3,379	3,704	4,029	4,321	4,646	4,147	4,332	4,374	4,740
Direct mail	1,135	1,404	1,635	1,666	1,876	2,049	2,228	2,378	2,431	2,469
Outdoor and transport	411	466	545	613	649	810	788	816	901	986
Radio	296	344	393	460	516	595	541	545	582	604
Cinema	69	73	88	97	123	128	164	180	180	192
Internet	–	–	8	19	51	155	166	197	408	653
TOTAL	11,026	12,080	13,340	14,415	15,412	16,988	16,537	16,780	17,411	18,385

Source: Advertising Association; www.adassoc.org.uk

Table 3.15 Local, regional, national and international advertising media

	Types of media
Local	Local paid-for and free newspapers, display and classified advertising, local radio, leaflet distribution, newspaper insertions or Royal Mail delivery, newsagents windows (good for services), local magazines and directories, buses and taxis, outdoor posters, shop window displays and signage, sandwich boards on the pavement (good for cafes), cinema, libraries, leisure centres (good for fitness clubs but check first, they might be competitors), church magazines (a target audience)
Regional	Regional terrestrial TV stations, commercial radio stations, regional editions of national newspapers, regional newspapers, e.g. *Yorkshire Post* (see regionaladvertising.co.uk and itvregions.com), outdoor posters
National	National TV and radio stations, newspapers and magazines, poster campaigns, web advertising, cinema
International	Satellite TV companies such as Sky can provide pure target audiences through their specialist channels. Newspapers such as *The Economist* and specialist magazines, e.g. *Access International* (a B2B heavy machinery magazine), have an international circulation. Internet and website promotions

entry plus a local newspaper advert could be sufficient. (A standard black on yellow whole page advert for London South East with a circulation of 253,000 costs £4,927 for the September 2006 edition.) A local car body repair business such as Heswell Bodyshop finds 'word of mouth' more than sufficient. 'We don't advertise,' said Matt the owner. What does this say about the role of promotion in the marketing mix?

Generally large businesses selling mass market products such as washing powder would use national mass media such as TV. The same advert may even be used worldwide, e.g. Coca-Cola. Small, local or niche market organisations would use local or specialist media.

Beware of using words such as' expensive' or 'cheap' when describing the cost of advertising. They should be used in the context of the objectives of the campaign and the results achieved. (See the Tropicana case study page 111 and the YTB on page 152.) Measuring the success or failure of a particular medium can be very difficult. Many organisations ask their customers 'Where did you hear/find out about us?' Direct marketing companies often include a code number in their advertisements on TV or the press, to help them find out this information.

Effectiveness of selected communication channels

Table 3.16 Advantages and disadvantages of types of media

Medium	Advantages	Disadvantages
Newspapers/magazines	Good reach and frequency, can be targeted, daily, weekly, locally, by age lifestyle, etc. complex messages can be delivered	Adverts have to compete, some magazines have to be booked a long time in advance. Newspapers are quickly thrown away
Cinema	Good for younger age groups, captive audience, can be localised	Expensive to produce Expensive for national coverage
TV	Can target nationally, regionally and by programme, mass market with high reach and frequency	Expensive to produce Expensive for national coverage
Radio	Good for local promotions, good reach and frequency, personal and intimate, relatively low cost per 1,000 listeners	Unless distinctive, may be part of the background, difficult to achieve national coverage
Outdoor	Good for geographical segmentation, good reach and frequency, wide range of opportunities (posters, buses, etc.), can be very large	Difficult to segment by age /lifestyle, can only be used for simple messages, great for graffiti!
Direct mail	Can be targeted and personalised, costs are relatively low. Quick to produce and distribute. Results are easily measured with coded response	Most thrown away as junk mail
Internet	24-hour world-wide reach and availability, can be revisited, immediate with short lead times on own website, may be personalised through database information to develop a long-term customer relationship	Pop ups may be blocked, expensive to achieve a high listing with search engines, initial development costs can be high

For any campaign, an organisation will have to decide which is the best medium to use to get its message across to its audience.

Promotional objectives

To achieve its promotional objectives, an organisation must have the right message, in the right medium, at the right time, for the right audience. Each medium has its own special characteristics, e.g. print adverts can be cut out and referred to again, internet advertss can be viewed and printed, radio and TV can be dramatic but can you remember the information? For example, the *Yellow Pages* for Bromley and Bexley has a 12-page Wedding Guide with sections on arriving in style, capture the day on film, dressing for the big day, a wedding planner checklist and helpful information on flowers, the reception, etc. An internet search produced images, video, photographs, music, helicopter rides (Matt and Helen), a country house with Thomas and Sarah, etc. Which **promotional mix** will achieve the promotional objectives requires careful analysis of the available media. Which is most likely to get the buyer to make a purchase or take action? Which would you prefer to search?

The Newspaper Marketing Agency (NMA) suggests that there are six roles for newspaper advertising:

- call to action – getting the consumer to do (or not do) something, usually short term but can be long term

- depth of information – providing new and additional information about a brand, or to show new sides to the brand

- brand values – bringing the consumer closer to the brand through associations with which they identify

- (re)appraisal – creating a stir and forcing appraisal or reappraisal of a brand by presenting it in a surprising or shocking way

- extension – reminding consumers about a brand by repeating or developing established messages seen in other media
- public agenda – raising the profile of an issue/cause by provoking reaction and thought and by creating 'talkability'.

Source: www.fipp.com

Target audience

This is the segment that the advertiser wants to reach. It could be potential new customers (the primary market) or existing customers whose profile is already known through market research (the secondary market). Every media should have details of its readership or audience, e.g. for Virgin Radio 57 per cent of listeners are male, 53.1 per cent are in the ABC1 social group (source: RAJAR/Virgin Radio).

The key to success lies in matching the message to the audience size and type. Size may be measured by the number of readers/listeners or viewers, whilst type refers to specific segments, e.g. consumers may be segmented by age, income, lifestyle, etc. Businesses may be segmented by turnover, type of retail outlet, etc.

For outdoor advertising, go to www.oaa.org.uk.

For magazine audiences, go to the Periodical Publishers website at www.ppa.co.uk.

Radio and TV stations have downloadable media packs which show the audiences.

The Business Link website (www.businesslink.gov.uk) has an interactive questionnaire to help businesses select the right media.

For newspapers, go to www.regionaladvertising.co.uk.

Focus of appeal

This can work on many levels, e.g. charities appeal to our emotions – 'Give just £2 a month and you could help.' Others work by appealing to our sense of adventure (cars), our need to be loved or part of a group (buying brand names for example – What would your friends think if you bought unbranded trainers?). Which of these images appeals to you – blue skies and warm beaches, babies and an attractive home, good food and drink, sport or perhaps an appeal to your conscience such as the advertisement for Friends of the Earth on page 108? The most successful adverts have a clear promotional message, with short simple sentences, are believable and non-humorous. Most local radio adverts concentrate on where the product can be bought. However, adverts can appeal on many levels. Children enjoy humorous adverts with cartoons and animals.

Timing (minutes)

This is critical to the success of any campaign, as frequently media time and space have to be booked months in advance. Both time of day ('Looking for a loan' advertisements always seem to be in the afternoon, whilst 'Looking for a date' commercials are on late at night!) and day of the week are important, e.g. weekend colour supplements seem to be filled with health, beauty and fashion. Holidays are advertised in January.

Media buying and scheduling are essential functions in advertising agencies, particularly as TV advertising becomes fragmented with more and more commercial channels and correspondingly smaller but purer audiences. Cross-scheduling, where the media to be used in a campaign is timed simultaneously, is important when trying to communicate an effective message and gain an advantage over competitors.

Being able to book time or space may be a critical factor in determining the choice of media for a campaign. TV and cinema advertisements have a long lead time (the time between the booking and when the advert appears) compared to local media which is more flexible.

remember

You have a very short lead time (minutes) for your campaign.

Circulation and readership figures

The *Sun* has a current estimated circulation of 3,298,000, with primarily a C1 and C2 readership of 8,897,000. TV and radio measure the number of viewers and listeners.

C1 and C2 are social grades determined by the occupation of the head of the household. C1 is supervisory or clerical and junior managerial, administrative or professional. C2 is skilled manual workers.

See the RAJAR extract on page 155 and BARB on page 144.

The figures are used to calculate:

■ reach, coverage or penetration – usually taken as the percentage of the target group who are reached or exposed to the advert at least once during a particular campaign

■ frequency – the number of times the target group have been reached.

Look at the Channel 4 website: www.in4mer.com/advertising: 50 'spots' in the Midlands with 16 per cent of the UK population cost £60,000. www.capitalradiogroup.com has information such as Red Dragon FM reaches 318,000 adults each week which is 35 per cent of the population of the area. It has a 54 per cent reach of main shoppers with kids.

Cost per thousand

Cost per thousand (CPM, where M is the roman numeral for 1,000) is a method for comparing the cost of advertising across a range of media with different viewing/listening or readership data.

These formulae show how it can be done.

Press advertising

$$\text{Cost per thousand} = \frac{\text{Cost of full page advert}}{\text{Circulation}} \times 1,000$$

For example:

$$\text{Local paper} = \frac{£1,800 \times 1,000}{150,000} = £12$$

$$\textit{The Economist} = \frac{£80,000 \times 1,000}{1,000,000} = £80$$

TV or radio advertising

$$\text{Cost per thousand} = \frac{\text{Cost of advertisement} \times 1,000}{\text{Number of viewers/listeners}}$$

Perhaps additional information, such as the number of the audience in the target market, whether or not the audience actually look at advertisements and the reputation of the media would be useful. Most media have detailed figures of their audience. Local/regional press closely followed by *Yellow Pages* are the main choice of people looking for local services.

assignment focus

Using the research you have carried out into the comparative costs of your local advertising media:

a) How have you selected and used the media you have chosen?
b) What criteria have you used?
c) How do you think your choice will contribute to the success of your campaign?

You will need to decide on a media mix and promotion mix for your campaign in the next section.

Promotional Campaign

You will need to create your own campaign for a smaller business or a local campaign. Four scenarios are given from which you have to select one:

- a local café with an Italian theme, budget £2,000 for the opening month
- a new branch of a chain of health and fitness clubs, two months pre-launch, budget £20,000
- a manufacturer of a new range of frozen deserts, three-month period with a budget of £12,000
- a new high street wedding service (with website), £8,000 over two months.

Eclipse

In this section, we outline the promotional campaign for a fictional business called Eclipse, a craft pottery based in Cornwall.

 Link

You will find more information about this business in Units 4 and 5.

The time-scale for the promotional campaign is two months (the average of the times above) with a budget of £10,500 (the average of the budgets).

Campaign brief

A campaign brief is a document that sets out the strategic requirements for the planning and management of a marketing campaign. It is a summary of the detailed research that will have gone into its production. It sets out three essential positions:

- Where are we now?
- Where do we want to be?
- How are we going to get there?

An excellent structure for a campaign is provided by the SOSTT + 4m approach, developed by P.R. Smith in the book, *Marketing Communications: An Integrated Approach*.

SOSTT + 4m

Table 3.17 SOSTT + 4m

S	Situation	Where is the organisation/brand now? What are the trends? Is there any past experience? Who are the customers? Are there any significant PESTEL influences? etc.
O	Objectives	Where do we want to get to? These could be split into marketing objectives, e.g. increase market share, and communication objectives, e.g. influencing perception and attitudes towards the product.
S	Strategy	How does the organisation/brand get there?
T	Tactics	The details of the strategy, e.g. selection of media.
T	Targets	Audience, segments, i.e. who they are, where they are, etc.
M	Men (and women)	Who does what, e.g. in the case study below some work will be done in-house by the Yorkshire Tourist Board (YTB) and some by the successful agency.
M	Money	The budget/financial resources – is it enough? How will it be spent? How much is there?
M	Minutes	What is the time-scale? When are the deadlines? A Gantt chart could help.
M	Measurement	How are the results going to be measured/monitored/evaluated? What lessons can be learned? What improvements could be made?

The case study below shows how this approach has been interpreted in practice. Every brief will be different depending on the type of organisation, campaign objectives, whether it is a product or service, size of the budget, etc. Even the layout may be different. However, in all cases, the purpose is the same – to plan and implement a successful campaign and give a framework for the creative brief.

case study 3.10 — Yorkshire Tourist Board PR agency brief

Here is an example of a public relations (PR) campaign brief created by the Yorkshire Tourist Board (YTB) as part of the 'Make Yorkshire yours' marketing campaign:

1 Position statement (situation)
The marketing campaign began in January 2005. It was scheduled to run for 18 months with a budget of £2.8m. YTB want 'an innovative and engaging PR campaign to maximise coverage of the key communication messages'.

2 Communications objectives
Some of the aims of the campaign are to:
- showcase the cream of Yorkshire tourism
- boost awareness and understanding of Yorkshire's unique qualities. Visitors are invited to 'Make Yorkshire yours'
- encourage people to find out more at the website and make more bookings online at www.makeyorkshireyours.com
- encourage visits to the region
- increase awareness of the region's outdoor pursuits and heritage.

3 Target audience
The priority is developing new audiences and reinforcing positive key messages to current visitors.
- Primary market – couples aged 45+ years, both 'traditionals' and 'discoverers' (for a more detailed breakdown such as 'affluent older families in urban areas', look at ACORN on page 119)
- Secondary market – couples aged 25–44.

4 Marketing campaign activity
This will include TV, press and magazine advertising, direct mail, online marketing through e-newsletters and advertising (an accommodation booking service will be available on the website) and public relations.

5 Key messages
'Make Yorkshire yours'. These promote Yorkshire as refreshingly modern, friendly, warm, great heritage, with something for everyone, plus log on to the website.

6 Agency activity
This sets out the time-scales (M for minutes). Both written communications, such as press releases and features in appropriate newspapers/magazines, and creative ideas, such as stunts and promotions are required.

7 Monitoring and evaluation
This will be done by measuring the amount and effectiveness of the press and event coverage using an Audit of Customer Expectations (ACE), i.e. what customers expect and what they experience.

Source: Yorkshire Tourist Board and www.makeyorkshireyours.com

activity
1 Identify the SOSTT + 4m in the case study.
2 Create a campaign brief using the SOSTT + 4m approach for your chosen business.

Creative brief

This is a brief document, no more than two written pages, which sets out simply what the promotion should do and how the target audience should respond. Table 3.18 is an example for Eclipse.

Table 3.18 Eclipse creative brief

What are the aims of the campaign?	Create and measure awareness of the Eclipse brand. Gain exposure through the media (radio and newspapers). Maximise use of the budget.
What are the objectives?	Achieve a turnover of £36,000 in the first six months. Ten stockists under contract.
How will the marketing mix be used?	The total Eclipse package consists of price discounts to the trade and online purchasers. Promotion: ongoing press and radio. Place: web, retail outlets and direct from the pottery. Product: quality Cornish image.
Who is the target audience?	A chain of vegetarian restaurants. Local craft and gift shops. The Cornish community demographics 20–30, lifestyle ABC1. Visitors to the pottery.
What is the key message in the advertising? (the content)	Looks good, feels good, hand-made quality in Cornwall, original designs, adds style to your table 'Put your Cornish food on a hand-crafted Cornish plate', 'Relive your Cornish holiday'. Inform of stockist details, website and pottery address, plus logo.
Why should the audience believe us?	Local business with local knowledge. Using local products. Supporting local community.
What do we want the audience response to be?	Raised awareness, enquiries and sales through the web/outlets/pottery. A positive image of the products.
What tone and style should be used?	Gentle graphics, expressing quality and style. With a daring edge that sets us apart.
What is the budget?	Pre-launch/launch £10,500 over two months.
Are there any constraints?	Larger budget, longer time period, need to generate revenue quickly, availability of guests, need to launch by spring. Need to include all details and instructions for washing.
What communication mix should be used?	Advertising, public relations (launch party), direct mail shots to the potential trade customers, website loyalty features, sponsorship of local tourist events, e.g. pottery demonstrations linked to the local vineyard.
What media mix should be used?	E.g. newspapers, local radio, leaflets and flyers, website.

assignment focus

Write a creative brief for your chosen business.

Campaign tactics

Reach the target group

assignment focus

The target group specified in the brief has four segments:

- a chain of vegetarian restaurants
- local craft and gift shops
- the Cornish community demographics: 20–30, lifestyle ABC1
- visitors to the pottery.

Eclipse now needs to work out how best to reach each of these target groups.

Select the media for the promotional mix

This is the way the target segments are going to be given the message. The right choice of media is critical for the success of any campaign and even more so when the M for money (the budget) and the M for minutes (time-scale/deadlines) are very tight.

Eclipse has used these criteria to make its decision:

- which media has the type and size of audience that it needs
- cost of time – national, even regional, TV commercials are too expensive as are Lifestyle TV and the home shopping channel. Radio, despite being non-visual can create mental images and a one-to-one intimacy with the product. Advertisements are cheaper and very cost effective with good reach. At the time of writing, Carphone Warehouse and Budweiser were the most easily recalled radio adverts. Which radio/TV advert can you think of now? (Look in the weekly marketing press to find out what other people recall.)

See cost per thousand, page 150.

- cost of space – the price of advertisements in newspapers and magazines depends on the size of the advert and the circulation (size of the audience). The cost of making a TV or cinema advertisement can be very high
- ability to deliver the message
- potential return and value for money.

See page 115 for more information on segments.

The media mix is the range of media used to convey the advertising message. A typical large advertising campaign budget for a nationally distributed brand could be split between posters (5 per cent), radio (15 per cent), cinema (10 per cent), newspaper and magazines (20 per cent), TV (50 per cent). As a small local business, Eclipse will spend its budget on leaflets, trade promotion, local radio, local newspapers and a launch party (for public relations and possible networking). The decision would depend on the cost/size of the budget, the promotion message, target audience and potential return/value for money

Leaflets

Leaflets, flyers and handouts are cheap and cheerful. They can be delivered by hand, by Royal Mail or distributed as newspaper or magazine inserts. Printing and distribution costs need to be checked. You will find *Yellow Pages* (yell.com) and the *Thompson Local* telephone directory will list suppliers. Eclipse will put flyers in local libraries and distribute by hand outside the pottery and the craft shops. To make the flyer worth keeping, there will be a list of useful telephone numbers, such as tourist venues, registered cab companies, etc.

You need to create promotional materials for your campaign, e.g. leaflets, flyers, newspaper advert, price list brochure with photographs of your product/service, business card, point-of-sale materials, **multimedia**, etc. The radio could want a creative brief. Be consistent: keep your font, logo and typography the same, and use it on all your materials.

Trade promotion

Eclipse has decided to spend part of its budget visiting possible retail stockists (B2B). This is called trade promotion. It is central to their policy of placing the product in craft and gift shops, but will mean giving substantial discounts on a 'sale or return' basis to persuade them to stock the tableware. The sales target could be achieved but what might happen to revenue projections? Perhaps a mini trial launch in a few selected outlets could be tried to establish possible trading patterns before going live with a full launch. Point-of-sale (POS) promotion will consist of a large cut-out lion to raise awareness and attract attention. Interest will be aroused by a prominent product display and action will be driven by a 'Special introductory offer' on the Total Eclipse (AIDA).

Local radio

Eclipse hope to use part of their budget on a local radio advertising campaign.

case study 3.11 — Local radio: Pirate FM 102

Figure 3.10

The Pirate FM logo

Figure 3.12 shows the radio listening figures from RAJAR (Radio Joint Audience Research Limited) which show Pirate having a healthy share of the radio audience in the local area. (note the west of Cornwall has a much bigger share). This would justify Eclipse's expenditure. Pirate advertising costs about £2.00 per 1,000 listeners.

Figure 3.11 Pirate FM's listening figures

	Survey period	Adult 15+ 00s	Weekly reach 000s	%	Average hours Head	Average hours Listener	Total hours	Share of listening %
Pirate FM Total	Y	608	185	30	3.7	12.3	2,272	15.3
Pirate FM 102 East	H	328	83	25	3.1	12.3	1,014	12.5
Pirate FM 102 West	Y	280	106	38	4.6	12.3	1,295	19.8

Eclipse are hoping to get publicity from inviting the breakfast show team to the high-profile launch party. Here are some of the services that can be provided for potential advertisers on the Pirate FM station. Eclipse are particularly interested in the section on 'Promotions and events':

Airtime campaigns:

- A campaign of commercials individually produced to advertise your products and services
- Short-, mid- or long-term, based on your objectives
- Use for awareness or 'call to action'

Sponsorship and promotional opportunities:

- Link your core advertising message or market positioning statement to a high profile
- Pirate FM information sequence or programming feature
- Use for short-term, high-impact advertising or for long-term name awareness

Promotions and events:

- Pirate FM can help to bring your event alive with presenter appearances or promotional crew
- Heighten the profile of, and gain maximum exposure for, your event

Source: www.piratefm.co.uk

1   Do you think that Eclipse should advertise on Pirate FM? Give reasons for your answer.
2   Should your choice of business use radio advertising?
3   Which station would you choose?
4   When would you advertise?
5   How many slots would you buy?

Give reasons for your answers.

remember

It may be expensive. Do you have sufficient in your budget?

Local newspapers

The website www.dailynewspaper.co.uk showed four local newspapers in Cornwall. Eclipse chose the *West Briton*, which is the highest selling weekly newspaper in Britain. It has a circulation of nearly 53,000 with 2.3 readers per copy and has the reader profile that Eclipse is after. Advertising costs vary with the size of the advert, number of insertions (weeks), position in the newspaper and whether it is mono or coloured.

The launch party

This will be held at the pottery. There will be a demonstration by the owners Della and Wayne, a display of the Eclipse range, opportunities to buy the products and an opportunity for guests to 'throw your own pot'. The guest list would include Pirate FM, local councillors, restaurant and shop owners, representatives from the local tourist board and business link office, plus other media. The key message will be demonstrating the product benefits of quality hand-made pottery to achieve word-of-mouth advertising (viral marketing). The invitations would need to be written into the activities in the Gantt chart. Eclipse would need an accurate estimate of guests to cater effectively. The number of guests would be strictly limited by the budget. However, any expenditure is a business expense and can be set against profits.

Suitable promotional materials and images

Eclipse will be using two images chosen for their dramatic impact and effect. They have high visibility and good 'stand out' from competitors. The images are immediately recognisable and with the logo will give Eclipse a strong brand identity.

Figure 3.12

Figure 3.13

Eclipse did not use a formal **focus group** because of budget constraints (see below). Instead these two images were chosen by family and friends (was this a good idea?) from an initial set of 12. The group was set up by Eclipse to:

- look at the images
- discuss the product and look at samples
- discuss suggestions for promotion.

The promotional message will be that Eclipse is quality tableware, hand-made in Cornwall. It looks good and feels good, with original designs it adds style to your table – 'Put your Cornish food on a hand-crafted Cornish plate', 'Relive your Cornish holiday'. It will also include stockist details, website and the pottery address.

The message could also emphasise the unique selling points of a product, e.g. Tropicana '100% pure squeezed orange juice not from concentrate', 'hp invent' or reliability, safety and performance feature in car advertisements. There is a proverb 'a good wine needs no bush', which means a good product doesn't need advertising. Do you agree?

Text and script

This needs to be written to complement the images – 'one picture is worth a thousand words'. Each medium (e.g. TV, press and magazine, direct mail, public relations) will require a different approach. Each audience will need a different focus. However, the approach should be integrated and complementary, with each medium supporting the other. Here are some issues that need to be considered.

- What are the objectives? What is the purpose? Remember AIDA.
- Is it informative, persuasive, or a combination of both?
- Gear the language to the needs of the audience. (Look at adverts in local newspapers/specialist magazines such as *The Caterer* and the range of *Bride* magazines for different ethnic groups.) Remember KISS – keep it short and simple. Use paragraphs and a good headline. For many people, the promotion may be the first contact they have with the product. It has to gain immediate attention, interest and excitement. We all see hundreds of adverts/leaflets/flyers, etc. every day. They are competing for our money. Using colour with style and pace will help to create impact and visibility, but be aware of the special needs of the audience. Try to cater for all the senses, e.g. fresh bread baked at the supermarket, leather smells pumped into the air conditioning in the car showroom!
- Is it legal, decent, truthful and honest? (See Advertising Standards Authority: asa.org.uk.)
- Sell the benefits and unique selling points (USP) rather than a specification (unless it is a technical product).
- Include the logo, **strapline** (e.g. 'Ginsters Cornish THRoUGH and THRoUGH'), contact telephone, e-mail, web address, etc. Make sure these details are accurate and available at the stated times. Word-of-mouth works both ways – 'I rang this number and it didn't exist.' If a business gets these details wrong, any promotional expenditure is worthless.
- Is it a trade or consumer promotion? Different styles, tone and language will need to be used with each audience.
- Find out how the competition/opposition promote themselves, e.g. who or what can be benchmarked as best practice in the wedding planning business?

Stages of production

Once a brief has been created and the target segment(s) identified, promotional materials can be developed which are appropriate to the needs of the audience and the selected media.

Use of storyboards

This is a sequence of cartoons or sketches which can be used to produce an advertisement, presentation or animation. A well planned detailed storyboard can save both time and money at later stages of the production process when studio time, for example, can be very expensive. The earlier in the creative process problems can be spotted the better.

Figure 3.14

A storyboard

Mock-up

This can either be a model, e.g. of a car or building, or a layout of printed materials. Leaflets, brochures, price and product lists, flyers, etc can all be created as mock-ups to see if the design concepts, such as the position of the words and images, work. When attached to an A3 sheet they make an effective display.

Mock-ups and storyboards would be shown to the client or perhaps a focus group for approval or further improvements before the final proof.

Final proof

The final version which is created must be accurate. Any text must be proof-read for spelling and grammar, accuracy and legality (e.g. copyright legislation). Any multimedia presentation should be checked for style and pace (make sure that the specific needs of the target audience are met). Use a checklist to make sure that each point in the brief has been covered.

Link   See Unit 4 on presenting information.

Commercial agencies have to pitch (make a persuasive presentation) for a contract. Below are the pitch process and timescales for the Yorkshire Tourist Board Contract.

A brief presentation should be made to outline how communications objectives will be met, what tactics will be used, creative proposals and targeting strategy. Costing and time-scales were also required.

Here are the timescales that were set:

- 10 Jan: Briefing documents sent out
- 31 Jan: Presentation by agency to YTB (3 weeks later!)
- 4 Feb: Winning agency informed
- 6 Feb: Contract starts, i.e. what the agency said it would do, begins.

Evaluating campaigns

assignment focus

To achieve D1, you will need to carry out an evaluation of your campaign and provide evidence.

Much depends on what the promotional campaign was trying to achieve, e.g. increasing awareness, improving the image, changing perception or attitude towards the product, increase membership of a club, increase donations to a charity, number of hits on a website, etc.

Here are the aims of the Eclipse campaign:

- create and measure awareness of the Eclipse brand
- gain exposure through the media (radio and newspapers)
- maximise use of the budget
- achieve a turnover of £36,000 in the first six months with ten stockists under contract.

Look at the Advertising Standards Authority website, asa.org.uk, under the adjudications section for examples of complaints made against advertisers. (High impact but are they legal, decent, truthful and honest?)

The evaluation of advertising is usually done using these criteria.

■ Does it stand out against the background, e.g. on the printed page, in a commercial break, on a web page? I.e. what is its impact?

■ Does the meaning and message come across to the target audience? Have you ever thought, 'Great advert but what was it advertising?'?

■ Brand perception with existing brands or businesses – Have the customers' views changed, e.g. from a 'greasy spoon' lunchtime café to Italian theme?

■ Has the advertisement aroused interest, created desire or led to action?

■ Has the advertisement led to increased sales, profits, charitable donations, etc?

To measure any change, the evaluation of advertising needs to take place before and after the campaign. Recall is a method used to test effectiveness. In spontaneous recall, consumers are asked to name any advert which they have seen or heard in the last few days. With prompted recall, they are asked whether they have seen or heard a particular advert, in this case Eclipse.

Developing a promotion plan

The Gantt chart

The chart (Table 3.19) can be used to:

■ identify and plan each activity

■ monitor each activity, e.g. Were individual deadlines met?

■ compare what was planned with the actual outcome/evaluation

■ identify specific media (name of the newspaper) with specific costings.

Newspapers, e.g. the *Westmorland Gazette*, specify that advertisements should be delivered as PDF files.

You can adapt this chart for your assignment.

Table 3.19 A Gantt chart for a promotion campaign

Step	Activities in weeks	1	2	3	4	5	6	7	8	9	10	11	12
1	Research and identify target group, see brief												D
2	Create the message to drive awareness, interest, desire and action AIDA												E
3	Select the media mix, e.g. local newspapers and radio depending on target group usage												A
4	Fix the timing and frequency for media exposure												D
5	Fix the budget												L
6	Select the promotion mix. Create promotion materials leaflets, with images and text.												I
7	Organise trade promotion												N
8	Organise launch party												E
9	Work on radio advert with Pirate FM												
10	Organise newspaper advert												
11	Evaluation build in SMART targets to the initial brief												

Fix the timing and frequency

For an organisation with a large budget, these details would be arranged by an agency to maximise the impact of the campaign with the target audience segment. A small business would need to plan the schedule direct with the advertising media. The launch of a new product or a re-launch should be treated as a project, with full planning and implementation, using a Gantt chart or critical path analysis to make sure deadlines are met, e.g. it is essential to have the product/service available and fully operational (in stock or in the shops) before the advertising begins.

See page 61 for more about Gantt charts and critical path analysis.

Fix the budget

Although in this example the budget has already been determined, in practice setting a promotional budget can be very difficult. Here are some methods which may help.

- Benchmark your competitors and spend the same.

- Spend whatever can be afforded – useful in small organisations with limited budgets.

- Spend what is needed to achieve objectives. How do you know?

- Spend a percentage of sales.

This sequence of activities is set for a 12-week period. Be aware of the timings for your campaign and the cost, e.g. a page in the *Sun* begins at £40,000.

The order of the activities can easily be changed. What matters is that the timings are accurate, particularly for critical activities, e.g. promotional materials must be produced before they can be distributed, launch party fully organised, etc.

Here is your invitation to the launch party!

Figure 3.15

Eclipse

Welcomes you
To our Launch Lunch Party

Cornish clotted cream
Home-made honey and jam
Locally made scones
Cornish pasties

All eaten off Eclipse original tablewear

Wines supplied by
Camel Valley Vineyards

With beers supplied by
Skinners Cornish Ales

Enjoy Your Total Eclipse Experience

UNIT 4

Presenting Business Information

This unit covers:
- relevant and accurate information
- how information can be processed
- presentation of the gathered information
- creative corporate communication.

This unit looks at:
- how to select information for a particular purpose
- how to use data/information to make presentations more effective
- how to create and communicate business information
- how to describe, analyse and create corporate information.

Assessment
To achieve a pass in your assignment, you need to produce evidence that shows you can select relevant and accurate information, which is intended for a specific purpose, process data (information) to achieve your objectives, use a range of methods to present information, and describe the use of creative corporate communications. To achieve a merit. You will also need to explain how more accurate information can be produced, analyse presentation methods intended for a specific audience and analyse a successful strategy of creative corporate communication. To achieve a distinction, you must evaluate the significance of accuracy in information and use creative communication to present business information.

Relevant and Accurate Information

Do you believe everything you read? Do you ask why information is presented in a particular way? Do you sometimes feel you are being manipulated? These are all examples of how information can be used to influence people.

'There are three kinds of lies, lies, damned lies and statistics.'
Benjamin Disraeli

'Not everything that can be counted counts, and not everything that counts can be counted.'
Albert Einstein

'I think there is a world market for maybe five computers.'
Thomas Watson, Chairman of IBM, 1943

'A little inaccuracy sometimes saves a ton of explanation.'
H.H. Munro (Saki)

'The region contains Newham, with the lowest employment rate in Great Britain (52.4 per cent), and the City of London, with the highest employment rate of 100 per cent (note this was from a sample size of just six). Published on 24 November 2004 at 9:30 a.m.'
www.statistics.gov.uk

To achieve P1, decide on a presentation topic and select information from a range of sources for a given or specific purpose, for example:

■ showing the sources of income and expenditure of a local sports club to the members

■ using statistics.gov to obtain your neighbourhood statistics to present to your centre managers for future marketing

■ giving a health and safety presentation to your group

■ presenting a business plan.

Types of information

The difference between data and information

■ Data is sometimes described as raw, that is unprocessed, information. It may be a mass of figures, which have not been analysed and have no meaning, e.g. 3, 14, 17, 21, 22, 33.

■ Data becomes information when it means something, i.e. when it has been processed, e.g. 'These are the winning numbers for next Saturday's lottery!'

There are two types of information:

■ **qualitative information** – this is 'soft' information such as the attitudes and perceptions of people, e.g. why people buy or do not buy a product or what they think about the product – 'I thought the name Mach 3 was better than Triad or Vector 3 because it showed speed' (source: Gillette Razor Focus Group). Generally, the information is collected either by interviewing small groups (focus groups) or individuals or by market research surveys

■ **quantitative information** – this is 'hard' numerical information, such as the number and type of people who use a particular product, e.g. '43 per cent of customers said they shopped at least once a week (marketing)', '10 per cent of staff have been with the organisation for more than 20 years' and '19 per cent of the resident population of Bromley are under 16, 22 per cent are over 60.' (source: www.statistics.gov.uk).

Different types of information are needed at different management levels of the organisation.

Figure 4.1

Levels of management

Strategic

Tactical

Operational

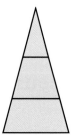

■ Strategic (top level) management will need information about the organisation as a whole. Information is provided in summary (aggregate) form, i.e. without the masses of detail that may be needed at lower levels. For example, senior executives may want the approximate sales for each individual country (e.g. the figure for Poland would be rounded down to £28,000, whereas the actual figure may be £28,109.15), while operational level staff will want to know which customer has or has not paid. A principal will require the number of students in each class, not their names and addresses.

■ Tactical (middle level) management require information about specific departments or functions, such as sales in a particular area, finance budgets, staff recruitment and training etc, so effective decisions can be made.

■ Operational staff work with detailed information, e.g. about individual accounts, customer and personnel details. This information needs to be totally accurate and up to date. What information does your centre hold about you? Is it accurate? Up to date? e.g have you changed your phone number? Is it relevant? Do you care?

Computerised databases are now an essential feature of Management Information Systems (MIS). Executive Information Systems (EIS) allow senior management to quickly interrogate the organisation database.

The employment and unemployment data for the UK allows for a 'sampling variability', i.e. a possible error of $\pm$ 2 per cent. Therefore if there are 2 million unemployed, the figure could be 2,040,000 or 1,960,000. To whom does the level of accuracy matter? The unemployed? The policy makers? The benefit office?

Features of information

Internal information

Within the business, every department and section will have its own records, which are an invaluable source of management information. Here are some of the more important sources of internal (quantitative) data that can be used to complement the external secondary material:

- sales department – sales targets, sales invoices, promotion details, orders
- finance department – invoices and prices, standard costs, customer accounts, departmental budgets
- marketing – consumer response to price, product, promotion and place decisions
- human resources department – job descriptions, time sheets, staff records
- production/operations – product records, quality data, wastage
- transport department – delivery times, delivery routes, supplier and customer details.

Qualitative data could include customer, supplier and employee feedback.

The organisation will need to have systems in place to collect (capture), store, analyse and distribute information.

External information

External information is obtained from outside the organisation. Here are two examples from *Key Note*, which is a major source of industry data:

- *Key Note Leisure and Recreation*: 'In response to the question, "In which, if any, of the following restaurant chains have you eaten during the last year?" 35 per cent of all adults said Pizza Hut, 11 per cent said Café Rouge'
- *Key Note Food Market*: '52 per cent of all females eat a savoury snack during a typical day. This rises to 71 per cent in the North!'

What can you conclude from this?

Every organisation will require external data, e.g. on market size, type of customers and buyer behaviour, legal changes including statutory government requirements, social trends, competitor analysis, etc. Its data needs depend on the size and type of business and the sector in which it operates. A PESTEL analysis would be a useful way of gathering this information.

For PESTEL, see page 46.

Primary data

Primary data is data collected for the first time, i.e. it is first-hand or primary data. External primary data can be collected in the street or in the workplace, i.e. in the 'field', not from books. Market research using face-to-face questionnaires or interviews, telephone surveys, etc. can be used to collect primary data.

The data is collected for a specific purpose. It will be original and up-to-date. It can be used to provide answers to problems or to establish a database for future operations. Although it may be expensive to collect, it is exclusive to the researcher.

Secondary data

Secondary data is data already available as hard copy or via electronic sources, which has been collected by others for their own purpose. Great care needs to be taken when using secondary sources. Always bear in mind that the data has been collected and analysed for some other purpose and this may have affected the data analysis and presentation. It is available to everyone including your competitors. When using material published by someone else, an organisation should ask:

- Which organisation collected the information?

- Is the source reliable?

- What purpose did the collectors wish to achieve? For example, statistics about the safety of smoking prepared by a tobacco company, or statistics about the safety of mobile phones prepared by a mobile phone manufacturer are likely to be biased in their favour.

- When were the figures collected? What is the date of publication?

- What do they include/exclude?

- What do the definitions mean?

- Is the data accurate?

- Is the organisation politically neutral? Biased?

- Why is the data available?

- Who is the intended audience?

- What is the key message?

assignment focus

Table 4.1 shows the key types of data held by a small business called EKOT. Complete a similar table for your organisation.

Table 4.1 Key data held by EKOT

	Primary	**Secondary**
Internal	Minutes of meetings, financial data, expenses, customer information and credit ratings, supplier information	Internal data is shared. In a large organisation data collected by one department may not be totally suitable in another
External	Market research reports (including both qualitative and quantitative data)	Keynote and EU reports, tax and insurance documents, statutory government information Competitor data

Life expectancy of information: is it up-to-date?

In business, external and internal information, such as customer account details, is continually changing, i.e. it has a very short life span. Users and presenters of information must be completely up-to-date with current information to avoid making the wrong decisions, e.g. you may have seen this on letters requesting payment, 'Please ignore this letter if you have paid within the last 24 hours.' Always check the publication date when using secondary data (both hard copy and electronic). Primary data is more is up-to-date, i.e. current.

At the time of writing, Hurricane Katrina in the USA had pushed up the price of petrol. All stakeholders with an interest in the price of petrol were complaining. What is the current price of petrol?

Means of communication

You will find this section useful for Unit 2, Outcome 4, page 100 and to provide the criteria for evaluating and creating corporate communications.

Businesses need to communicate with a range of individuals and organisations including their customers (e.g. through promotion), their suppliers, as well as their own employees. A properly structured corporate communication system requires clear and well-defined channels of communication to enable it to reach all stakeholders.

A simple model of communication

The simplest model of communication is one-to-one. Figure 4.2 shows the components of the process, whatever medium of communication is used.

Figure 4.2

The components of communication

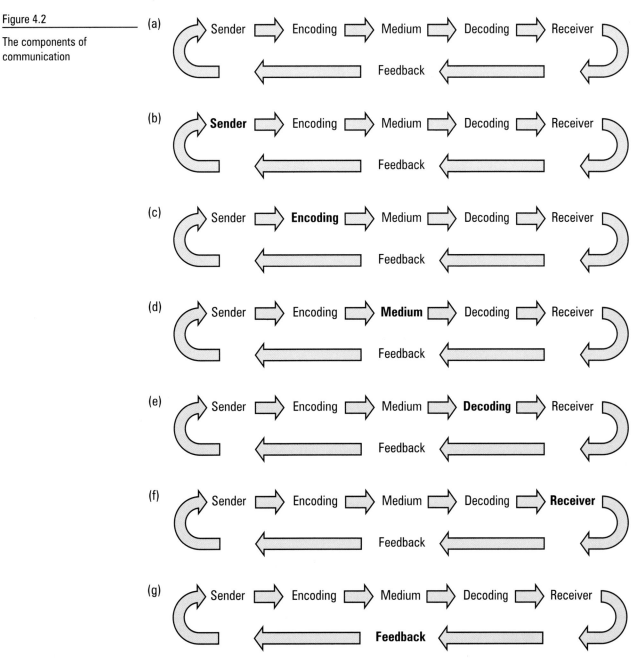

This is the person(s) or organisation originating the message. The status and relationship between the sender and receiver will determine both the content of the message and the method and style of delivery. We are communicating with you through this sentence.

Encoding means putting your thoughts into words or pictures so that the receiver will be able to understand the message/presentation. The sender will have an image of the receiver. It may be visual or just a mental picture (our image comes from teaching our own students face-to-face) and a purpose for the communication.

The process of encoding will depend on:

- the complexity of the message
- the purpose of the message, e.g. to praise or discipline, advertise, inform or create a corporate image
- the relationship between the sender and receiver(s)
- the chosen medium, e.g. face-to-face, text or e-mail, letter or telephone call.

Communication is the bond that keeps as all together. It can be a source of intense pleasure or pain. In some situations, such as rock climbing, good clear, accurate communication can make the difference between life and death. A dictionary definition is: 'the imparting, giving or exchange of information, ideas or feelings; to succeed in giving information'. There must be at least two people and the process must be a success. If it is not, there is a failure, or breakdown, in communication.

Figure 4.3

An example of a memo

Memorandum

To: You
From: Roger Lewis and Roger Trevitt
Date: Today
Subject: Templates

There are templates or examples of styles or letters, faxes, memorandum and reports in Microsoft Word, Click File, New, General templates.

For examples of how to start a letter, click Insert, Autotext, Salutation. Closing shows possible endings.

The medium is the method used to send the message. Here are some examples of methods that could be used:

- impersonal, e.g. a memo sent to 'all staff' or leaflets and flyers sent to your home. Advertising is impersonal, i.e. not addressed to a particular individual. Customer relationship marketing, which uses the masses of data accumulated on consumers, is intended to reduce the use of impersonal communication, by focusing on individuals and addressing them personally. Although it can be very effective, it can also be intrusive to the point of harassment
- personal, e.g. individually addressed letters, memos, special reports, faxes. Many companies now send out advertising material to individuals by name, e.g. 'Dear ___, We are delighted to tell you that you have been specially selected ...' For any communication to be effective, the medium must suit the message and the receiver/audience
- personal electronic, e.g. telephone, e-mail, video conferencing, texting. With these methods the relationship can be interactive and feedback is immediate
- face-to-face, e.g. interviews and meetings, informal conversations.

On the Microsoft.com home page, search for invoice template and a range of other business documents. These are particularly helpful for Unit 5

Figure 4.4 is an example of a formal report used by Identikit, an outerwear clothing company.

Figure 4.4

An example of a formal report

To: Kit Identi, Managing Director

From: K. Martins

Report on recruitment policy at Identikit PLC

1.0 Terms of Reference
This section should show the limits of the report and the precise areas which it should cover, for example: Following the meeting held on 7 May these Terms of Reference were agreed:

1.1 To examine the present system of recruitment of senior managers.
1.2 To suggest changes to the system.

2.0 Procedure
This section should show how the information was collected, for example:

2.1 A survey was conducted of all job adverts which had been placed in the last two years, and who was subsequently recruited.
2.2 A questionnaire was given to all senior managers, to find out their opinions on the present recruitment system. This had 20 open-ended questions which gave an opportunity for everyone to make a contribution.
2.3 The Personnel Manager and Deputy Manager were interviewed in depth, as a follow-up to the questionnaire.

3.0 Findings
This section should give the main findings of the report as a series of numbered headings, for example:

3.1 Survey of advertisements
Advertisements had only been placed in the two local evening newspapers, 'The Star' and 'The Echo'; these had produced only a small response.

3.1.1 Advertisements 1998–1999
Only 20% of these advertisements had produced a successful response.

3.1.2 Advertisements 1999–2000
These were marginally more successful with a response rate of 25%.

3.2 Questionnaire results
All questionnaires were returned, fully completed. The general feeling was that in order to attract more candidates it was necessary to advertise more widely.

3.2.1 National newspaper advertising
All managers felt that it was necessary to advertise in the national press, particularly when there was a special feature on the clothing industry. There was no agreement on what newspapers should be used.

3.2.2 Magazine advertising
All managers suggested that the company should advertise in the trade magazine 'COVER UP', which is published every two weeks.

3.3 Interviews
The two interviews with the Personnel Managers confirmed the general findings.

4.0 Conclusions
This section should sum up the major findings of the report, for example:

Because vacancies have only been advertised locally, Identikit PLC have only been able to attract a small number of applicants for any post. Most of the people who applied appeared to be well-intentioned but unsuitable.

5.0 Recommendations
This section should contain the main and subsidiary recommendations which can be made as a result of the investigation which has been carried out, for example:

5.1 Identikit PLC should advertise its senior management posts in national newspapers.
5.2 Identikit PLC should advertise in the trade publication 'COVER UP'.
5.3 Identikit PLC should set aside a budget to cover the increased cost this policy will incur.
5.4 Identikit PLC must ensure that a standard format is used for all its advertisements

PASS is a useful mnemonic for remembering the four key elements that should be present:

- **P** – purpose
- **A** – audience needs, e.g. Is this font too small? Is this better?
- **S** – structure, layout, design and flow
- **S** – style, e.g. formal, professional and businesslike, informal to family and friends.

Decoding is the receiver's interpretation of the message. It depends on:

- the relationship between the sender and receiver, e.g., personal, B2B or B2C
- the type and nature of the message
- the style and tone of the language
- how well the message has been encoded.

Some messages can be recognised immediately, e.g. 'It's the real thing'; 'Have a break, have a ____'. Answers: Coca-Cola; Kit Kat.

Major advertising campaigns try to make a brand instantly recognisable by constantly repeating the same message. At work getting a memo or e-mail addressed to Ms or Mr usually means trouble.

The receiver is the person(s) or group intended to receive and understand the message. With corporate communications, this could be any stakeholder. The number of receivers could range from one to millions. Should the message stay the same? Should the method of delivery change?

Feedback

Feedback is the response/reaction of the receiver to the message. Being willing and able to give feedback will greatly improve the quality of communication. Do you participate in class discussions? At gigs? Customer feedback is crucial to the success of an organisation. The real test is how much has been sold or how much given to a charity. Do you complain? People in the USA complain all the time? Do they get better service? Is quality of service linked to feedback? Is compliant an anagram for complaint?

> **remember**
> 'The average person with a complaint tells nine other people.'
> *Source*: Royal Mail website advertisement

> **remember**
> Good communication always depends on the sender.

What are the barriers to good communication?

Communication can break down because either the sender or the receiver of the information has failed to convey the meaning and/or importance of the message.

Sender breakdowns

The sender of the information could be at fault because:

- the language could be too difficult or complex
- there could be too much information ('information overload') so that the receiver misses the key points
- the sender may be using threatening verbal or body language, e.g. shouting or being aggressive, so that the receiver does not listen
- the sender could be 'talking down' to the receiver, so the latter is unwilling to listen.

Method breakdowns

When the information is very detailed or complicated, then written communication is better than verbal messages, which can be misinterpreted. The general term for a method break down is 'noise', i.e. anything which disrupts communication between the sender and receiver, such as physical noise, a crackling telephone, small print, illegible writing, long words, jargon, etc.

> **assignment focus**
>
> Much communication in business takes place in small or large groups.
>
> 1 What sender, receiver and feedback problems could occur?
> 2 How will you avaoid these possible problems in your presentations?

Receiver breakdowns

The receivers of the information could be at fault because they:

- may deliberately choose to misinterpret the message because of their attitude, e.g. subordinates might not want to be bothered to wear safety helmets because the weather is hot

- do not listen because they do not want to hear the information, e.g. people do not like to hear bad news.

---

assignment focus

You need to invite people to the presentation you will be giving. Select an appropriate means of communication, say why you have chosen it and invite them.

Hint! Consider cost, speed, security, personal touch, whether formal or informal, user friendly etc.

Purpose of information

The purpose of information is to meet the needs of the business and its stakeholders. It is a two-way process, with the organisation both a sender and receiver of information (see the model of communication above).

A business has to know the needs of its customers, the activities of its competitors and its market before it can develop its business strategy. In order to gain an understanding of the market for a product or service it needs information.

An organisation requires information for many purposes, including to:

- update knowledge, e.g. about its customers through market research, or the market in which it operates. Is there any new legislation, such as the **Disability Discrimination Act** or **Freedom of Information Act**? Are there new technologies or materials which could affect production? Keeping up to date will enable the organisation to make comparisons with past events, e.g. Are sales this week better or worse than this time last year? This historical data (or back data) is used for 'like to like' comparisons

- obtain background information to help solve problems

- gain competitive insight The main reason for a business researching competitors is that it can develop and market its own brands more successfully. It will need to find out:
  - who the competitors are by using trade directories, trade associations, website searches, local business telephone directories (secondary data)
  - whether competitors have similar products and what their prices are
  - how well they perform – most businesses check this by pretending to be customers, by observing their activities or using professional mystery shoppers (primary data), e.g. Sainsbury's used this on its carrier bags: 'Our mystery shoppers regularly check the quality of our products and the service of our staff. Are you standing next to one?'

- find out how they will react to a new competitor, e.g. cut prices or offer discounts. Following the launch of Yorkie by Rowntree Mackintosh (now Nestlé), Cadbury reacted by redesigning and relaunching their Cadbury's Dairy Milk range in a new chunky form. When British Gas announced a 14 per cent increase, npower announced a price freeze. When it announced a 22 per cent rise in 2006, how did your household react?

- find out what their customers think – this can be done informally or by asking for references (take care, they will only say good things about the company)

- to find out its strengths and weaknesses so that it can develop its own strategy and possibly use them as a benchmark

---

You can use these points to carry out the competitor analysis for the business plan in Unit 5.

- provide a foundation and guide for decision-making, e.g. on the appropriate volume of sales in targeted sections of the market

- plan for the future – the more information a company possesses, the easier it is for it to achieve its objectives

- use as a management tool to control its budgets, e.g. comparing the difference between planned and actual promotional expenditure

- make forecasts and estimates to inform future developments

- invite support for their activities – this is particularly important for charities such as Friends of the Earth or ChildLine, which need information about the scale of the problems they are attempting to solve.

All organisations, however small, have an information need.

assignment focus

What is the purpose of the information you are gathering?

Information gathering: the sources

Every business now has almost instant access to a vast amount of data. Much of the general information is free, although more specialised sources can be expensive, especially for private subscribers. Always remember that anything free on the internet is available to everyone, including your competitors. Internet data is secondary and can be provided by anyone, always ask the questions shown on page 164.

Books and journals

A major key to your success will be your ability to find information quickly. Your centre and local libraries will be your most important resources. It is essential that you get to know them as quickly as possible. Journals will have up to date in-depth information to help you.

Market reports published by KeyNote, Mintel and the Economist Intelligence Unit (EIU) are helpful

Socio-economic groups

Socio-economic groups are frequently used to target people for marketing purposes, e.g. Who reads the *Sun*? Who watches *Coronation Street*? The answers will determine what is advertised in the *Sun* and what adverts appear during *Coronation Street*. Although many characteristics can be used to classify people, such as education, age, sex, number of people in the household, or income, occupation is most frequently used to indicate which social class people belong to (Table 4.2).

Table 4.2 Socio-economic groups

Occupation	Social group	Social class
Professional managers	A	Upper middle
Middle managers	B	Middle class
Clerical/office	C1	Lower middle class
Skilled manual	C2	Skilled working class
Manual	D	Working class
Students	E	

You will need this information for the marketing units.

The internet
The Internet has transformed the way in which data and information can be collected. Information is now so readily available that you will always be expected to provide up-to-date figures and examples for every assignment. There are sites which cover every aspect of the course.

Newspaper sites enable you to access a complete range of business information on many topics, e.g.
- *The Times*: www.timesonline.co.uk
- *The Independent*: www.independent.co.uk
- *The Economist*: www.economist.co.uk

How to search the internet
You can find information by:

- typing in the web address of the site you wish to use. A number of useful addresses are given in this book

- using different search engines, such as www.google.co.uk.com or www.yahoo.co.uk. These work in slightly different ways and different search engines often give different results.

You will find that many websites are free, although you may have to register your name and address when you first enter. Other sites, such as some of the real-time financial sites and research services are only available on subscription.

There are a number of techniques for searching effectively both for sites and within sites. Tips are often provided to help you. Do not give up too easily, e.g. www.tesco.com yields tesco online and tesco insurance. Go to the online site and click on Help for corporate information or tesco.com/everylittlehelps will get what you want.

> **remember**
> - Whenever you find a useful internet site, keep a note of the address or save it on-screen (use the 'Favourites' list in MS Explorer or 'Bookmarks' in Netscape Navigator).
> - When searching, try putting the word(s) 'definition' or 'case study' after your search entry.

You will find the following particularly useful for Unit 5:
Department of Trade and Industry: www.dyi.gov.uk
Office of National Statistics: www.statistics.gov.uk
Business Link: www.businesslink.gov.uk
your local authority: www.[name of authority].gov.uk

Additionally, a wide range of information is provided by both national and international institutions, e.g. the European Union (www.Eurostat), banks (NatWest, Lloyds and Barclays are good for business plans), trades unions, trade associations, the CBI, Chambers of Commerce. ACAS (Advisory, Conciliation & Arbitration Service) covers all personnel issues.

www.companies-house.gov.uk/infoAndGuide/companyRegistration – This website is particularly good for Unit 5 where you have to start your own business.
The reference to 'sensitive words and expressions' shows words which cannot be used as a business name without permission, e.g. 'Prince', 'Wales', 'Bank', 'Royalty'.
www.bromley.gov.uk/business – This site shows the help and advice available to business from a local authority. Your local authority has similar information.
Also try:
www.startups.co.uk
www.dti.gov.uk
www.businesslink.gov.uk

> **remember**
> Beware of plagiarism and copying. When you use quotes, identify clearly where the quote begins and ends, and name your source.

1 If you are using internal/external, qualitative/quantitative or primary/secondary data, give your reasons, e.g. the strengths and weaknesses.

2 What are the sources of your information?

Look at 'Small business' on the Yahoo home page which is good for information gathering

Validation

The earth is round, although at one time the commonly held belief was it was flat. Always validate (confirm) and corroborate any statements you make. The need to ensure that any data, however it was collected, analysed or presented, is valid and reliable means that rigorous quality control checks must be in place for every step of the process. For example, if you carried out the same survey again, would you get the same results? If not, can you rely on them as the basis for a commercial decision?

Always try to include more than one source. (Use the questions on page 171 to assess their reliability. This is source checking.) Double-check any calculations and proof read any text/graphics. Be consistent, e.g. always use the same system to round numbers up or down.

Error management means learning from any mistakes you make, such as copying figures from one table to another incorrectly. Find out why you make mistakes and change your techniques.

Currency

When information, ideas or opinions are in current use and generally accepted as valid, they are said to be common currency. A valid argument must be based on evidence. If you were making a presentation on the safety of mobile phones, your opinions should be based on evidence which is supported by more than one source, i.e. you should validate and cross-check your information.

How and why have you validated your information sources?

Standards

Data Protection Act 1998

With the development of computer databases, a great deal of private information has been amassed on individuals by organisations such as hospitals, insurance companies and banks. The speed with which computers can search and sort data, allied to the fact that the data can be accessed from great distances via modems, has meant that it is increasingly easy for this information to be passed on. It was recognised that there was a need to protect the rights of those about whom data is held.

The main provisions of the Act are:

- personal data, however stored, must be secure
- businesses must notify the Data Protection Commissioner if they intend to keep and process data
- individuals have a right to be told what information is held on them (the 'data subject' provisions)
- any automated decisions should be supported by human intervention.

Source: www.open.gov.uk/dpr

> **remember**
> You could avoid the issues covered in the DP Act if you do not collect personal data in any survey you carry out, i.e. if your respondents cannot be identified.

The Act came into force in March 2000. Organisations have until 2007 to comply with all the provisions.

See the Market Research Society at www.marketresearch.org.uk

There are eight data protection principles contained in the Data Protection Act 1998. They are all concerned with the processing of personal data. The Act only applies to data that can identify an individual, e.g. name, address, National Insurance number, e-mail address, telephone number, etc.

Personal data shall be:

- processed fairly and lawfully
- obtained for lawful and specified purposes
- adequate and relevant – not excessive (no unnecessary questions)
- accurate and kept up-to-date (inaccurate or incomplete data to be erased or put right)
- not kept longer than is necessary for the purpose for which it was collected
- processed so as to keep individual data private
- kept secure against any unauthorised use, accidental loss or damage
- kept within the European Economic Area and not transferred outside unless similar protection exists. When you buy on the internet, do you know where from or what happens to your private data?

The European Economic Area is the European Union plus Norway, Iceland and Liechtenstein, which also have the free movement of services (in this instance, data).

How is it possible to get a text message which says, 'You have won £500. Please contact this number to obtain your prize' but does not say it is a premium rate number at £10 per second and calls last 2 minutes?

Freedom of Information Act
Since 1 January 2005, anyone anywhere can ask a public authority to supply any, not just personal, information it holds about them within 20 working days. Some 100,000 public authorities are listed.

Legal and ethical constraints

remember

Ethical behaviour is doing what you know is right.

Codes of practice are now available for a range of professions. For example, the Market Research Society code sets standards for how researchers should behave legally and ethically and covers the rights of respondents and clients.

There are strict regulations covering the financial sector. The Financial Services Authority (FSA) regulates the way financial products can be sold and the way information can be presented. Balance sheets and profits must be reported so that they give a true and fair view of the organisation.

The Advertising Standards Authority, now a 'one-stop shop' for all media advertising, has the responsibility for ensuring that all adverts, whether informative or persuasive, are 'legal, decent, truthful and honest'. This phrase can be used as an effective guideline for the collection, analysis, storage, interpretation and presentation of all information.

Be aware the laws on libel (written word) and slander (spoken word), which means you should not write anything, show any pictures or say anything which could be considered defamatory (attacking the good name and reputation) or unflattering to someone.

Access and suitability

assignment focus

You can use the eight points in this section to help with the merit and distinction criteria.

Accurate
Much external business data can never be 100 per cent accurate. There is always a small margin of error, e.g. in survey results and even government statistics, due to the way the data is collected. Internal data should be accurate, e.g. financial accounts, customer details. The organisation will need to recognise this and take it into account when making decisions.

For some decisions, precise information is vital, such as the number of TV advertising breaks per programme to comply with OFCOM regulations, with others an estimate or approximation to within plus or minus 5 per cent is sufficient.

Question: Which is more accurate, a broken watch or a watch which runs fast or slow?

Answer: A broken watch, because it is totally accurate twice a day.

The need for and degree of accuracy depends on the needs of the sender and receiver of the information. On some occasions an approximation is sufficient and an average can be used to describe the information, e.g. the average number of matches in a box is 40. In other situations, e.g. when inviting people to a wedding, exact and accurate details will need to be provided.

Forecasting is a good example where perfect accuracy is almost impossible. Many organisations use estimates which are based on best and worst case scenarios (situations), so that sales next year could be between £15m and £15.5m. The organisation could then make financial or staffing decisions in line with the forecast. The Advertising Standards Authority (www.asa.org.uk) requires adverts to be 'legal, decent, truthful and honest'. The financial accounts of an organisation should provide a 'true and fair' view of its financial health.

Cost-effective
Perfect knowledge or information is very expensive to obtain because of the time, money and effort involved in searching. Information must not cost more to collect than it yields in benefits, i.e. the cost of searching for the cheapest item might not be worth the saving that can be obtained.

Many people today are said to be 'cash rich' and 'time poor', i.e. they have money but no time to spend it! What are the implications for shopping habits?

Clear and concise
Too much information creates information overload and can hide the purpose for which it is intended. Remember KISS (keep it short and simple) and avoid the 'nice to know' approach to gathering and presenting information.

Up-to-date
An out-of-date timetable contains masses of information, none of which is any good! Information presented in such a way that it cannot be used or understood is a major cause of customer service complaints. Always use the most recent data that is available and give its source.

Relevant
Information must be fit for the purpose for which it is intended, i.e. relevant and pertinent. Extra information which is not necessary to solve a problem or make a decision is a major barrier to effective communication. Managers must make sure the right information reaches the right person at the right time. Too much information can cause information overload and may result in people being unable to see the wood (general overview or big picture) for the trees (the details). What is relevant for senior management may not be relevant for operational staff, and vice versa.

Appropriate
Any form of communication of information must be user-friendly. It should be easy to read, both in terms of the font style and size, e.g. **Arial**, Times New Roman, Comic Sans MS.

A useful function in Microsoft Word is the readability score which can be used to check how easy or difficult it is to read a piece of text, e.g. an advertisement. To find the score, go to Tools, Options, Spelling and grammar, Show readability statistics. With the Flesch Reading Ease score, the higher the score, the easier it is to read. The Flesch-Kincaid Grade Level score shows the reading level by year or grade, e.g. grade/year 8.

The language should not be difficult or complex, neither should it be too simple – 'Why are you talking down to me?' It is always best to present information to suit the audience, be aware of features such as age, knowledge of the language, disabilities, etc. The presentation method whether hard copy, animation, audio, multimedia or photograph ('a photograph is worth 1,000 words'), should be appropriate to the audience and suited to the information being conveyed. Many official documents are now available in large print or Braille, a method of reading and writing used by people with visual impairments. It uses a series of raised dots which are then read by touch.

Link See page 194 on W3C, the World Wide Web Consortium.

'Plain English is a message written with the reader in mind and with the right tone of voice, that is clear and concise.'

Source: www.plainenglishcampaign.com

 This site is well worth a visit: www.plainenglishcampaign.com

---

> **remember**
>
> Treat every assignment as if it was a commercial business presentation. Deadlines must be met. Thousands of pounds could be lost if materials are not available on time. In business, staff are dismissed if deadlines are not met.

Timely

Check out the notice boards at your centre. How many are out of date? An advertisement for a sale or special promotion must be in the media in advance. A business plan or marketing presentation must be available and delivered by the deadline. The right information must be made available to the right people on time.

Effectiveness or suitability

- Has the communication of the information worked?
- Was it at the right level for the audience?
- Was it sufficient?
- Was there too much or too little?
- Did it achieve its purpose, e.g. to inform or to persuade?

---

assignment focus

1. Look again at the key words and phrases we have used to describe access and suitability: accurate, cost-effective, clear and concise, up-to-date, relevant, appropriate, effectiveness, timely. Take the first letter of each to make a new eight-letter word.
2. Can you find another eight relevant words which would also work?
3. How have you ensured that your information is accessible and suitable?

How Information Can Be Processed

---

assignment focus

To achieve P2, you need to manipulate data for a range of business purposes using a range of appropriate methods, e.g. calculate averages, range and percentages.

Processing methods

One key to your success is being able to process information effectively using the appropriate method. Sometimes it is important to use a computer, on other occasions it is sufficient, or even preferable, to work by hand. You will need to use computers during the course. Remember that information technology is one of the Key Skills. We do not attempt to teach you IT skills in this book, though many of the activities are designed to develop them.

The main applications that you will use will be word processing, databases, spreadsheets, desktop publishing and PowerPoint. You may also use specialised packages, perhaps for accounting or design. There are many different products available, but in general they will work in much the same way and give equally good results. Whatever package you use, do save your work regularly and keep back-up copies (these words are written with feeling!). It may be that 'it wasn't my fault – the network crashed!', but if you have lost an afternoon's work that is no consolation. You have still lost it!

Copy and paste from source

You can copy and move graphics, text, images, etc. both within and between applications, to create the presentation which is most accessible and suitable for the audience. When copying from a website you will probably need to use the text select tool to highlight the section you want to copy. Be aware when you paste back that the formats are likely to be different.

Manipulation and data handling

Many of the publications that you will be using to gather information, both hard copy and electronic, such as the KeyNote reports or the statistics.gov website, contain many tables. To make these digestible (understandable) for your audience, you should summarise them or convert them into charts, i.e. manipulate them to suit your purpose.

Here are some of the types of graphs and charts which are available from standard spreadsheet packages or the Insert chart feature in Microsoft Word. They are each based on the information given in Table 4.3.

Table 4.3 The UK market for china and earthenware, £m, with estimates to 2007

Year	1998	1999	2000	2001	2002	2003	2004	2005	2006	2007
Value	1,220	1,260	1,270	1,280	1,294	1,300	1,305	1,315	1,330	1,345

Source: KeyNote, *China & Earthenware Market Report Plus*, 2003

For use with the Eclipse case study, Units 3, 4 and 5.

Line graphs are good for showing trends (Figure 4.5).

Figure 4.5

A line graph

Source: KeyNote

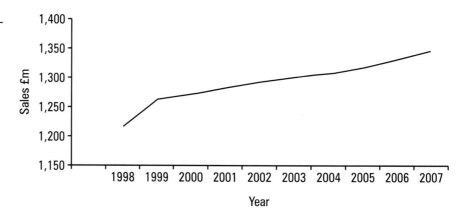

The vertical bar chart (Figure 4.6) is also called a column chart. This example shows the market for china and earthenware in £m. One year can be compared with the next.

Figure 4.6

A vertical bar chart

Source: KeyNote

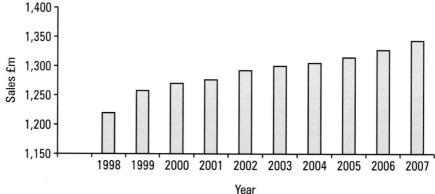

Do you prefer the line graph? If so, why? The vertical or Y axis shows the dependent variable. In this example sales vary (depend) on the year. Pie charts should not be used to show time-based data.

Mathematical manipulation and statistical analysis

The raw data of sales of china and earthenware can be enhanced by adding extra information such as:

- the average – you can find this by highlighting the sales data and copying it to Microsoft Excel. Go to Insert, Function, Average, and highlight the data with the cross cursor so the data is inside the dotted lines, A1:A11 should be showing in the number 1 box. The average is £1,286 m. This average is also called the mean or arithmetic mean

- the range – this is the difference between the lowest and highest figures, or £125 m. In this example, it is the estimated increase in sales between 1998 and the 2007 estimate. It is particularly useful in showing the extremes of any data, e.g. knowing that the average daily sale of a shop is £1,500 is useful but also knowing that sales on Saturday are £4,700 and on Monday they are £300 will help the business plan its staffing (range £4,400)

- the percentage change, e.g. the percentage change between 1998 and 2007 is the difference between 1998 and 2007 (125) divided by the original or base figure (1220) x 100 to create the percentage: $125 \div 1220 = .1 \times 100 = 10\%$, i.e. the expected increase in sales between 1998 and 2007 is 10 per cent. These calculations can add greatly to the meaning and interpretation of data.

The information in Table 4.4 is from an Allegra Strategies report on the coffee market published in Autumn 2005 (with thanks to Allegra Strategies). The web version summarised the key findings of the main report. The press reports had headlines such as 'No Grounds for Concern', 'Starbucks Grinds on', etc.

Table 4.4 Number of coffee chain outlets, 2005

Coffee chain	No. of outlets	% market share
Starbucks	420	$420 \div 1881 \times 100 = 22.3\%$
Costa Coffee	351	
Caffe Nero	188	
Bakers Oven	160	
O'Briens	142	
Pret á Manger	125	
Caffe Ritazza	95	
BB's Coffee	82	
Puccino's	77	
Cafe Nescafe	75	
Benjys	65	
Coffee Republic	59	
Amt coffee	42	
Total	1881	

Try using different chart types (MS Word or Excel) on this data, e.g. Radar, Surface, Bubble, Cone, Cylinder, Pyramid, Doughnut etc. Which are the most suitable/ unsuitable for presenting this data.

To create a chart using Microsoft Word, highlight the first two columns of the table, go to Insert, click on Chart. You will then have a range of options for chart types. We have chosen a pie chart (Figure 4.7). You will need to manipulate the charts to obtain the effects you want. The charts can also be created in Microsoft Excel and copied across to your Word file.

The pie chart is good for showing slices (segments) of the pie, but not for showing totals. It is good for a rough visual impression, but does not include figures unless these are specifically

Figure 4.7

A pie chart

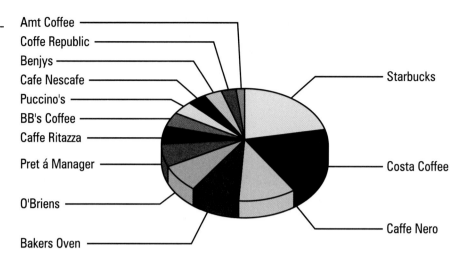

included. How does it work without colour? The chart can be manipulated to show real data and highlight a specific segment.

Charts and diagrams: the rules

The purpose of graphics is to enhance or clarify text. Whether drawn manually or by computer, they should be clear, simple and useful.

- There must be a title.
- The source of the data must be given.
- The vertical (or y) axis should show the dependent variable, e.g. sales, costs or production levels.
- The horizontal (or x) axis will then show the independent variable, e.g. months, weeks, places.
- Keep scales simple. Use units of 10, 100 or 1,000 wherever possible. A computer will scale automatically, though you can alter this.
- Use a key to show different data.
- Use shading or colours to distinguish between different parts.
- Label each axis. Make sure the units are correct.
- Stay legal, decent, truthful and honest.

Line graphs

These are good for showing historical data, but do not put more than five lines on the same graph as it becomes very difficult to distinguish them.

Pie charts

Pie charts are excellent for showing the relative proportions of data, but they do not show totals. They should not be used to show time series data, such as any figures with months, years, etc.

Bar charts

Bars can be vertical, horizontal, adjacent or separate. Individual totals can be shown.

Component or stacked bar chart

Totals can be directly compared, but parts can be more difficult to distinguish. With multiple bar charts, parts or segments can be compared but changes in the totals are more difficult to distinguish. You should decide which feature is more important, changes in the components or the totals, then use the appropriate chart.

assignment focus

You should show evidence of how you have used mathematical/graphical manipulation methods in your presentation. Give reasons for your choice.

Synthesising information

This means combining or bringing together all the information you have found to create a presentation which meets the audience's needs. Each element of the presentation text, images, graphics, charts, etc. needs to be copied and pasted into one file such as Microsoft Word, Frontpage or PowerPoint.

Once you have found the text/information you need, you will have to read through to select the main points. You can then produce a summary or edited version. Do not print the first article you find with the right title! Check the reliability of the source. If you are producing graphs or charts, check that you have entered the data correctly (your error management skills) before you proceed to the next steps. Make sure you use the correct chart for your needs and that it can be seen by the audience. Charts are an effective way of presenting financial information, as many people find large tables of figures difficult to understand. Using an average or percentage is also a useful method for summarising complex numerical tables.

You can now consider how the final version should look to achieve its purpose.

assignment focus

Include examples of how you have synthesised information, e.g. reducing a long article to a series of key bullet points or summarising changes in data by using averages.

Output requirements

What does the final document or presentation need to look like to achieve the desired effect? The answer depends on the needs of the audience, the simplicity or complexity of the message and the available budget. The first step is to have a clear idea of what needs to be said and the images/graphics that will be used to support the message. Several mock-ups could be created with different layouts.

Before you design your own presentation, find out how your businesses present their product/service. Collect their leaflets, flyers, brochures, business cards, etc. Find the best ones to use as your benchmark, then improve on them. Analyse why they are the best, e.g. Is it the font style or size (typography), pictures (best [high resolution], normal or draft quality), graphics or paper quality? Do they use graphs, charts or tables to create a better image? How many colours are used? Colour can be expensive commercially. However, it can be an important factor in the perception of the presentation.

assignment focus

Using a separate file, experiment with the range of formatting features available in Microsoft Word. For example, look at:

■ Format, Background, Printed Watermark
■ File, Page Set Up, Landscape or Portrait.

The same approach can be applied to a slide presentation. Keep editing – for most audiences, the fewer the words, the better. Be prepared for criticism and be willing to change. Between 50 and 70 words is the recommended maximum for a slide screen.

Specialist software

Pictures can be inserted from existing files, scanned in from a printer or directly from a digital camera. A software program, such as Adobe Photoshop, PhotoImpression, Dell Image Expert, Microsoft Office Picture Manager or Paint, can be used to retouch, edit, add customised edges or frames, superimpose text on to pictures, eliminate 'red eye' effects, etc. Clip art can also be directly inserted.

Figure 4.8

Using specialist software

In Figure 4.8, the Eclipse lion was given a border (chosen to suit the image that Eclipse is trying to create) and text was superimposed. The program used was PhotoImpression and the image was saved and copied into Microsoft Word.

Using a range of applications

If you are working with the Microsoft Office suite of applications, i.e. Word, Access, Excel, Powerpoint, Frontpage, you can copy and paste from one application to another. Excel is a spreadsheet program but is also good for producing charts, graphs and diagrams. Word also has a chart function – click Insert, Picture, Chart. Once the relevant data has been input, the chart area, text and axes can be changed to suit your purposes. A variety of chart types can be produced, e.g. pie, horizontal and vertical bar. Click on the chart, click Chart on the toolbar to see the types that are available.

We describe the way in which PowerPoint can be used on page 183.

assignment focus

Have you demonstrated how you have used a range of applications and combined these effectively for the audience?

Legislation and sources

In your assignments, you will rely a great deal on source material. With new technology, it is very easy to download or scan information and merge this into your work. You must be aware of plagiarism (copying from other sources such as books, the web or indeed a friend) as this will adversely affect your grades. On the other hand, using a variety of sources effectively will enhance them. Either adapt material to your needs or, where you need to quote directly, use quotation marks and name the source.

Whether you use information from books, magazines, newspapers, CD-ROMs or the web, you should always provide details of the sources you have used. Include the date of publication or the date the material was accessed from the web as a way of validating the material. For example:

Freedom of Information Act, www.dca.gov.uk/foi, accessed 12 May 2006.

The date is important because information on the site may change.

Always make sure that you are not breaking the law when you write or copy anything, for example:

- Who owns the copyright ©? It is usually the author or creator of the work who has the exclusive right to use the material. Do you need permission to reproduce it?
- Has the data been processed legally? Does it obey equal opportunities legislation on sex, race and disability? Has it been deliberately manipulated to suit the needs of the presenter?

See pages 96–98 for more information on copyright and intellectual property.

Disability discrimination and equal opportunities legislation

Disability Discrimination Act 1995

This Act makes it illegal to discriminate against someone on the grounds of their disability. Under the Act, employers have an obligation to make 'reasonable adjustments' to working conditions or working arrangements which otherwise put disabled people at a 'substantial disadvantage'.

Race Relations Act 1976 and Sex Discrimination Act 1975 and 1986

These Acts make it illegal to discriminate against someone on the grounds of race, sex or marital status. Discrimination occurs when people are excluded, i.e. assumptions are made, such as men are plumbers or women work in offices. Discrimination involves stereotyping according to race or sex.

Other legislation

Any presentation including all forms of advertising and promotion must be legal. Any individual has the right to complain if they feel they have been discriminated against. Advertisements have to be 'legal, decent, truthful and honest'.

Any text, image, graphics, photo, graph, chart, etc. which is used must obey the law. Use a variety of images in your presentation.

Code of Advertising Practice (CAP)

This says:

'Marketing communications should contain nothing that is likely to cause serious or widespread offence. Particular care should be taken to avoid causing offence on the grounds of race, religion, sex, sexual orientation or disability. Compliance with the Code will be judged on the context, medium, audience, product and prevailing standards of decency.'

Source: www.asa.org.uk

Poster advertisements, which can be seen by everyone, usually get more complaints than when the same advertisement appears in a magazine.

Britain is now a multicultural and multifaith society. There are many religions and religious organisations that are very strongly supported and whose beliefs are very strongly held. It is therefore a very sensitive area of representation.

---

assignment focus

Have you needed to change your presentation to stay legal? Have you used quotes where material is copyright? Have you shown the ™ symbol where necessary? Are your images legal?

Presentation of the Gathered Information

---

assignment focus

- To achieve P3, you must use a range of presentation methods to communicate the business information you have collected and processed. Plan your presentation carefully. Define exactly what you want to achieve, e.g. do you want to inform or persuade your audience?

- To achieve M2, you should analyse why you have chosen your method of presentation, e.g. compare it with other methods you considered and rejected, with reasons. You could analyse the advantages and disadvantages of each method using the criteria covered in outcomes 1 and 2.

Presentation methods

We are exposed to business information all day, every day, including the junk mail we get through the post, the adverts on the TV, radio and the bus – 'new route for the 227' (Half the distance, same price) – at school or college. Holiday brochures, leaflets from double glazing companies ('Just call us free now'), flyers and business cards all present business information. However, it can be difficult to distinguish information from promotion. Presentation is about communication with customers, either internal (your presentation) or external (B2B or B2C).

Every organisation, whether public or private, not-for-profit or profit-seeking will need a strategy for how it presents information. The communications mix refers to the combination of promotion methods that a business will use to promote and sell its products. For example, a typical travel company would promote its product, the holiday, by a combination of:

- advertising through national newspapers and magazines
- advertising in the trade press
- public relations events and exhibitions such as the World Travel Market, which is for trade clients, and the Holiday Show, which is for the public
- direct mail shots to former clients via its database
- website and electronic advertising
- 'free' trips for the media and travel agents.

Each of these forms of promotion will require different methods of presenting information.

Remind yourself about the simple model of communication (page 165). Figure 4.9 shows how it applies to presentations.

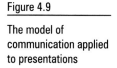

Figure 4.9

The model of communication applied to presentations

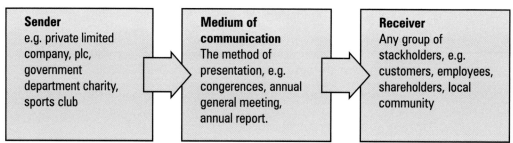

| **Sender** e.g. private limited company, plc, government department charity, sports club | **Medium of communication** The method of presentation, e.g. congerences, annual general meeting, annual report. | **Receiver** Any group of stackholders, e.g. customers, employees, shareholders, local community |

The decision always has to be which presentation method bests suits the needs of the audience and the complexity/purpose of the message. For example, communicating the importance of health and safety to a group of experienced workers requires a different approach to communicating the same information to a group of students! Would cartoons or simple, bold visual images be useful? If so, for which audience?

Documents

Traditionally hard copy print documents have been the main means of communicating/presenting business information. Internally, i.e. within an organisation, a written report would be used to present information to workers or managers. Externally a company would report to its shareholders through its annual company report, which would normally be presented at an annual general meeting (AGM) of shareholders. You should look at an annual report such as EMI to find out how it is presented.

www.carolworld.com has reports available online. It is free, but you need to register. *The Financial Times* provides a similar service at www.ft.ar.wilink.com

A good written presentation would have these features:

- a front cover with key details such as name of organisation (centre name), author name (you) and reference number (candidate number), title, company logo, the client, i.e. who the report has been prepared for (teacher) date. This may be the first contact that people have with the organisation. Do not put them off – impress them. Every report (assignment) should be presented with the same layout and it is worth spending time developing a style and format which represents the image you are trying to portray, e.g. a picture watermark may help. Once the right format has been found, use it all the time so that it becomes the house (your) style. This can be saved on the computer. What sort of image do you think is given by a poorly or badly presented front page?

- a contents page, which lists the content with page numbers for each section (in an assignment this could be the outcomes). Number each page, put in a footer with perhaps a name and reference. The presentation (assignment) should be professional. This is how many businesses make their money

- an introduction or summary page

- an acknowledgements page, which includes, for example the names of people who have given help, and written and internet sources.

> **remember**
>
> Be aware of plagiarism, i.e. do not copy and be aware of people copying you. Never lend a disk, give out a password or forget to logoff!

Binding is important – the finished presentation has to make an impact. Remember the golden rule of communication is that the responsibility for delivering the message lies with the sender. The client/receiver (teacher) cannot be held responsible for not understanding.

---

case study 4.1 · Viking Direct

A company such as Viking Direct sells a large range of products which help to create effective presentations, e.g. Cityfiles 'because first impressions count' used for estimates, quotations, proposals and presentations. With such products, you can customise and add impact to reports, e.g. by using presentation binders or report files, which have a clear cover to create an impression.

activity

Decide on your method of presentation, giving reasons for your choice.

On-screen multimedia presentations

A multimedia presentation is a combination of at least two of the following: audio, text, graphics, images, video or animation. It should appeal to the emotions and add to the value of the message. The addition of sound will help those with poor vision, but be aware that some people may have hearing impairments. Narrator converts words into speech. See Accessories, Accessibility, Narrator on the Start Up menu of your computer.

Audio

Sounds, music or speech can be added to a face-to-face or web presentation to enhance it. Keep the volume down – do not let it dominate. Make sure that sounds can be turned off, as not everyone may appreciate your choice of music, i.e. do not continuously loop the music. It is there to reinforce the images and promote the message. Most successful advertising is a blend of music, words and images. In Microsoft PowerPoint Help, search with Add Audio to see how you can add music or sound effects to a slide or animation presentation.

Sounds and music create an atmosphere. Think of the music and sounds in the films *Psycho* or *Jaws*. What images do you have?

Video

Search Microsoft PowerPoint Help with Add Video to see how video/movies can be added to a presentation.

Presenting Business Information

Since **broadband** has been introduced, with much faster download times, the facility to incorporate video into face-to-face and web presentations has greatly improved. However, when you create a website, check how long it takes before the video images appear. Most people switch off after about ten seconds! Images and video need a large amount of storage. You could find that a standard floppy is not large enough. It could be more useful copying to a CD or using a memory stick. If you do not have a choice, split your files. Whenever you make a presentation, whether professionally or as a student, check that the software used to create the presentation is compatible with the system for the presentation. What do you have at home? What is the presentation software, e.g. Windows 98/Windows XP/Apple for preparation, Windows for presentation?

Animation

Animation is the process of adding movement or effects to text, graphics or images. Animation can add character, interest, drama, etc. to make a presentation unique. A well-animated presentation is a very effective way of communicating a promotion message, delivering a business plan (Unit 5) or showing the profit and loss account for the last year (animate so that each item is brought in separately and explained using Microsoft PowerPoint).

If you are using Microsoft PowerPoint creating an attractive animated slide show is a relatively straightforward process.

Figure 4.10

Creating an animated slide show using PowerPoint

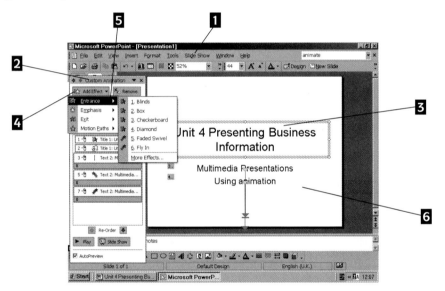

1   On the menu task bar, click on Slide Show (Figure 4.10):

2   Click on Custom Animation.

3   Type in a title.

4   In the Custom Animation side panel, click on Add Effect.

5   Four choices are given
    - Entrance: where text or graphics enter the slide
    - Emphasis: to add effects to an existing slide
    - Exit: which adds effects to text/graphics leaving a slide
    - Motion paths: enables text/graphics to move around the slide

    Each of these is further subdivided so that you can personalise the slide show.

6   Run the slide show and your animated text appears.

Images

Images add excitement to any presentation – 'a picture is worth 1,000 words'. Images can quickly get the attention of an audience. Look at Figure 4.11.

1   Click Insert.

2   Click Picture, then choose one of the options. Alternatively you could add a diagram chart, etc.

3   Clip Art images have been added in Figure 4.11.

Figure 4.11

Inserting clip art using
PowerPoint

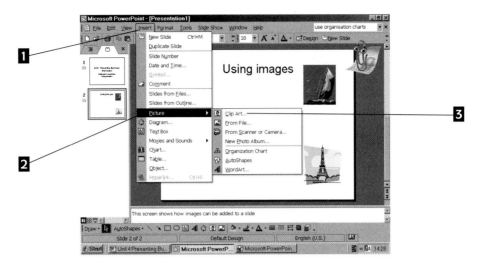

Images can also be added from a scanner or camera, or direct from a mobile phone if you have the infra-red transfer facility. Which would you prefer: a lengthy description of how a hairstyle looks or a picture of the model?

Web-based presentations

Images on a website can sell products. However, before they can be used, they must be in the right format. JPEG (Joint Photographic Experts Group) and GIF (Graphics Interchange Format) are the most common. These are compressed files, which means they can be downloaded quite quickly and require less storage space. They are also available on most computers. JPEG is usually used for photographs. If images/video clips, e.g. those available on Yahoo, are copyright, either permission must be obtained before they can be used or the copyright owner must be thanked.

See Unit 6 for more information on building a website.

Hints on **web-based presentations**.

■ Find out all you can about the possible users, e.g. Are they beginners? Or highly competent users? Young or old?

■ Do not use too many different fonts.

■ Use different font sizes to show the importance of the information being presented.

■ Use bullet points rather than large blocks of text.

■ Keep the background simple, so that it does not detract from the message. Red is considered a warm colour, whilst blue is said to be cold.

■ Keep the colour scheme simple, both for the text and the background.

■ Do not use too many colours and make sure the text is readable over the background. Yellow on white is very difficult to see!

These points also apply to slide presentations.

World Wide Web Consortium guidelines on accessibility

If you are unfamiliar with accessibility issues relating to web page design, remember that many users may be operating in contexts very different from your own. They may:

■ not be able to see, hear, move, or may not be able to process some types of information easily or at all

■ have difficulty reading or comprehending text

■ not have or be able to use a keyboard or mouse

■ have a text-only screen, a small screen, or a slow internet connection

■ not speak or understand fluently the language in which the document is written

- be in a situation where their eyes, ears or hands are busy or interfered with (e.g. driving to work, working in a loud environment, etc.)

- have an early version of a browser, a different browser entirely, a voice browser, or a different operating system.

Source: W3C

Multilingual support

There are 20 official languages in the European Union (EU). There are only six at the United Nations (UN). Only meetings of EU leaders or ministers get full interpreter coverage, but the majority of documents are translated into all 20 languages.

If you need to work alongside an interpreter, stop after every two or three sentences to allow for translation. Use subtitles and the translation facility on the computer if you are using a computer presentation.

If you are presenting to an audience which needs **multilingual support**, make the presentation visually interesting by using pictures, cartoons and objects with positive and constructive body language, e.g. smiling, hand gestures, etc. These will complement and reinforce the verbal delivery and help understanding. The text (words) should be kept simple and relevant. The context and examples should be geared to the age group.

Make sure that any interpreters or signers for the hard of hearing are fully briefed. Documents may have to be translated.

---

assignment focus

'*Croeso Y Cymru*' means' Welcome to Wales' in the Welsh language. '*Witamy*' is 'Welcome' in Polish. '*Konichiwa*' is 'Hello' in Japanese. '*Ni hao*' is 'Hello' in Chinese. World Hello Day is held in November. How many languages are spoken in your group? You could put the words for 'Hello' and 'Welcome' in as many languages as possible on a large sheet of paper or on a slide to begin your presentation.

Audience requirements

Special needs of the audience

Here are some statistics for the UK:

- visual impairments: 1 million
- hearing impairments: 7.5 million
- mobility problems: 0.5 million wheelchair users
- learning difficulties (including Down's Syndrome):1 million+.

Some 31,000 students are classified as disabled, for example:

- dyslexia: 10,500
- visual impairment: 1,100
- hearing impairment: 2,100.

Source: www.worc.ac.uk

Try the search 'How to make a good presentation' in Ask Jeeves

---

Presentations

Face-to-face presentations are a popular method for communicating with sales staff. When new or updated products are introduced, the sales manager may make a presentation to demonstrate the features of a new range by using a variety of audio-visual techniques, e.g. films and videos.

Table 4.5 Audience characteristics and presentation requirements

Audience characteristics	Presentation requirements
Age	For a younger audience use cartoons, simple graphics, few words in a large font, use colour. With an older audience, make it relevant. Think carefully about any music. Their tastes may not be the same as yours. Slow down the delivery.
Gender	Be aware equal opportunities. Do not use stereotypes. Use a variety of images. Use examples which appeal to both sexes.
Ethnicity	Value cultural diversity. Cater specifically for different needs, e.g. are translation facilities needed? Do not use stereotypes. Use a variety of images. Find out about your audience in advance, e.g. in China the colour white is associated with death, whilst red represents pleasure.
Special needs (presenter and/ or audience)	Do materials need to be written in Braille or large print? Is an audio loop needed for people with hearing impairments? Is sign language required? With lip readers, make sure they can be seen and can see you. Check the lighting. Does the language need to be simple? Comic Sans is the recommended font for slow readers.
Readability and legibility	Is it interesting and able to be read? Is it clear enough to be read easily? Consider fonts style/size/lighting. Two slides can be better than one! Be aware that not everyone has perfect vision. The bigger the font, the better. Use a simple font (Arial or Comic Sans).
Attention span	How long can your audience concentrate? Do not change slides/OHTs too quickly – people need time to read. Watch the audience's body language. Check if they need more time, or is it OK to move on?
Distraction avoidance	Make sure you get the main message across to your audience. Do not overload with too much detail. Make sure there is nothing in the room that would cause distraction, e.g. mobile phones should be switched off.
Audience experienced/ inexperienced	The experience of your audience will determine the content and knowledge level of a presentation. Presenters are the experts because they have business/industry-related experience and knowledge and carried out the research.

assignment focus

Create your presentation taking into account the needs of your audience. Say and give evidence to show how you have catered for their needs.

Making a presentation

1   Collect the information. Make sure it is accurate and up-to-date.

2   Obtain the evidence. You must be able to support any arguments you make.

3   Prepare all the materials you will need, e.g. notes, pictures, videos specifically for the audience.

4   Try to think of what questions you might be asked. Then find the answers.

5   Try to think of where people could disagree with you. Then find the answers.

6   Make your presentation clear, interesting and simple. Would you like to listen to yourself?

7   Look at your audience and do not be afraid to smile. Use positive body language, stand up straight and do not slouch as it sends out a negative image.

8   Use visual aids such as an overhead projector (**OHP**) or multimedia computer linked to a projector and screen.

9   Always be positive.

10   Rehearse and practise your presentation several times.

11   Do not rush a slide show. People need time to look at it.

12   With a computer presentation, make sure you face the audience and position the computer carefully.

13   Use a large font on transparencies/slides, with few words.

14   Check that everything works before you begin. (Have the speakers been stolen?)

remember

Have a contingency or back-up plan in case something goes wrong.

remember

Be prepared for questions. They show that people have listened to you.

case study
4.2

Goldmajor Group

The four slides below show the launch strategies for Esprit Jewel in the UK presented by the Goldmajor Group as part of their marketing and distribution plan. Prepared six months in advance, it is clear, readable and legible. It only contains necessary vital information with no extra or extraneous information which could distract the audience. It is a business to business (B2B) presentation.

Slide 1 shows the planning necessary to prepare for the launch. POS is the point-of-sale material such as posters and photographs of the jewellery. These would be displayed where the jewellery is sold. PR is the public relations required, e.g. journalists, buyers and designers connected with the jewellery.

Slide 2 concentrates on four points which demonstrate industry research, experience and knowledge. Note the importance of the exhibition.

Slide 3 shows the intended market positioning of the launch.

Slide 4 shows how the jewellery will be advertised during the first six months.

Figure 4.12

Slide 1

LAUNCH STRATEGIES

- ✍ 1. Prepare collection
- ✍ 2. Finalise retail pricing
- ✍ 3. Prepare POS and printing materials
- ✍ 4. Order stock quantities
- ✍ 5. Prepare PR and media activities
- ✍ 6. Launch February 2004

Figure 4.13

Slide 2

LAUNCH

- ✍ Goldmajor Group would aim to launch the Esprit Jewel range in February 2004 at the Birmingham International Spring Fair.

- ✍ This is one of the major events in the UK jewellery calendar, attracting some 80,000 UK as well as international visitors each year.

- ✍ The Goldmajor Group have been very successful exhibitors here for the last 27 years.

- ✍ Purpose designed exhibition stands will be commissioned for displaying the brand and professional photographs will be taken and used for display purposes.

Figure 4.14

Slide 3

MARKET POSITIONING

- The marketing of Esprit Jewel will be tied in closely to the Esprit clothing brand.
- Esprit clothes are popular with those in the 19-39 age bracket and are viewed by the UK consumer market as a simple and modern brand.
- The clothing attracts consumers who dress in a stylish and classic but contemporary way and is perceived as being of high quality whilst still being reasonably priced.
- The brand enjoys a loyal customer base in the UK and has good brand awareness. In this way, the Esprit Jewel collection with its modern and simple lines will be warmly received.

Figure 4.15

Slide 4

ADVERTISING

- The PR mix will involve both business to business and business to consumer.
- During the first 6 months, advertising and promotion will mainly target business to business. This will be done by means of exhibitions and direct mail shorts using Goldmajor Group's existing and well-established client base which currently stands in excess of 2000 customers. There will also be advertising in the trade press.
- During this period and the subsequent 6 months, promotions will focus on the retailer to establish the Espirit Jewel brand in a retail environment, creating confidence and sell-through.

Source: With special thanks to Bob Rontaller and the Goldmajor Group

activity   What do you consider to be the strengths and weaknesses of each slide?

 Link   You need to produce and deliver a presentation for Units 3 and 5.

Try to avoid:

- over-running your time so you have to speed up
- forgetting any of your presentation materials on the day
- not checking that the disk you created at home works at your centre
- too much chatting and laughing with your friends
- drying up because you are nervous. Take a deep breath, smile and carry on. Remember everyone else will probably be nervous
- being too casual.

Facility management

Any office supplies outlet would have a wide range of materials and equipment for preparing an effective professional document-based presentation. Two pieces of equipment that a small business or home office would find useful are:

- a heat seal laminator for covering photographs, menus, certificates, handouts, maps, etc. with a plastic pouch or wallet. This process improves the appearance whilst also protecting the document. The finished product looks and feels more professional

- a comb binder, which is particularly good for binding documents with a large number of pages.

Overhead projector (OHP)

When you prepare a transparency, check that the 'paper type' facility on the printer has been correctly set. If a photocopier is being used, check that:

- the transparency is photocopier-safe

- the correct photocopier tray is used.

Before you begin a presentation, switch on the OHP. Put the transparency on the glass stage of the OHP, check the image size and make sure it is in focus. You can do this by moving the mirror up or down. Make sure the glass is clean. Can everyone see? Do the blinds need to be closed? Should the lights be switched off? Always practise before any presentation and check that the equipment works. Be aware of health and safety issues, e.g. tape down any trailing leads.

During your presentation, look at your audience, not the screen. Look at the transparency on the OHP and use a pen or pencil pointed at the transparency to emphasise each point. Be aware that the whole of a transparency can be seen as soon as it is displayed. Use a piece of card to gradually reveal the points you want to make.

Remove each OHT (overhead transparency) when you finish. If there are long gaps, switch off the OHP. Keep the same sequence of OHTs in case someone wants to see one again. Put a sheet of paper between each transparency to avoid them sticking together.

Computer projector

With this system, the computer is linked to a projector. Practise using the system before making any presentation. Become familiar with the controls, particularly the use of the wireless mouse and how to manually run the slides, as someone in the audience will always ask to see a particular one again. The key to success is practice and more practice and do not get flustered if something goes wrong. Remember Murphy's Law, which says that if something can go wrong, it will. So be prepared. If you are using a laptop, check all leads and connections.

Flip chart and display boards

Do you have good clear legible handwriting? Enough pens and paper? Flip charts can be prepared in advance or created during a presentation to summarise the discussion. Large display boards can be excellent as they allow any participants, guests, etc. to look at your materials in their own time at their own pace and, if you are available, ask any questions.

> **remember**
>
> What are the needs of your audience? Keep it simple. Do not put too much on each OHT. What do you need to do for the hearing and/or visually impaired? For those with dyslexia?

Relative costs/benefits of different presentation methods

Presentation costs need to be calculated under three headings.

- Pre-production – this includes researching and collecting information, preparation and mock-ups of any drafts, the administration costs, including inviting the participants and organising the facilities; writer/technical costs, etc.

- Production costs – this includes slides, documents, paper, binding, printing, acetate/copier charges (should this be done in-house or outsourced?). For a commercially produced multimedia presentation, the price would be based on running time, number of words, number of screens, whether animation, video clips or voiceover is included, programming and design features such as an interactive component, etc. A typical cost would be £1,000–2,000 per minute.

- Delivery – this can include costs of the presenter, transporting and setting up equipment, facilities/accommodation. Audience costs for a large meeting/conference could be expensive. Perhaps a web conference where the audience participate over a web camera link would be cheaper?

These costs need to weighed against the benefits of each presentation method. A well produced, professional document can be handled, re-examined at a later time, used to take notes, etc. When presented face-to-face, immediate questions and answers can clear any problems and the latest updated information can be included easily and quickly.

Computer-based PowerPoint presentations using a video/data projector can look superb with music and video, providing the message is not overpowered by the animation/special effects, e.g. individual letters and separate words arriving continuously. Take care when using colour, some people are colour blind, yellow text on a blue background is very difficult to read. The audience cannot normally take the presentation home, which is why many speakers/presenters provide a printed copy of the slides. Updating means adding or changing slides, with additional information provided by the speaker. Slides cannot be changed during a presentation. The major benefit of these presentations is their ability to reach large audiences.

assignment focus

Enjoy your presentation. Give out a feedback form to get audience reaction and treat any criticism as an opportunity to improve.

Creative Corporate Communication

assignment focus

- To achieve P4, you must describe the use of creative corporate communication techniques in a particular organisation, e.g. if you have a bank account, how effective is your bank statement? As a communication, does it include the logo? How does it address you? Is it available in Braille or large print? How does it write to you? What is the logo? What image do you have of the bank? Collect samples of its literature. What image does it present to savers/borrowers? How does it treat you if you are overdrawn? Does the website work (online activity)? Can you make a payment to another bank?

  You should work through each point, e.g. logo, livery, etc.

Information can be obtained from company annual reports, *The Times 100* website, marketing magazines, watching TV advertisements.

- To achieve M3, you need to analyse a successful strategy of creative corporate communication. Carry out a SWOT analysis. How effective is the communication? Who is the target audience? What is the message? What is the image? What age groups are shown? How does it show images which cover equal opportunities issues, e.g. disability, gender, ethnicity, age, sexuality? Does it matter? What has made the corporate communication successful? How is it linked to the four Ps of marketing?

- To achieve D2, you will need to use creative communication techniques to enhance/improve the presentation of business information, e.g. by including sounds, music, video, voice, pictures, graphics or animation, you could change the image of an Annual Report such as EMI.

Corporate communications

Corporate communications are any form of communication used by an organisation in its contacts with stakeholders to create a **corporate identity** or **corporate image**. This suggests that the way in which it portrays itself to employees is just as important as the way in which it deals with customers or suppliers. The corporate image should reflect the personality of the organisation, i.e. its mission, vision and core values. It is expressed through its logo, packaging and literature, its staff **uniforms**, the sounds used in its advertising or the celebrities used in its promotions.

Our own image is formed by what we wear, how we behave, how we speak, our hairstyle, perfume or aftershave, etc. It is about how others see or perceive us. It can be created through any of the senses. What image do you have of your friends, family or teachers? Why? What image do you have of the local shop or restaurant? What creates the image? Is it the attractive and friendly staff, the facilities, cleanliness, advertising, smell or taste of the food, or its ethical or green policies?

> If you want to know more about which companies are ethical and which are not, check out the *Rough Guide to Ethical Shopping*, which names and shames many well-known high street stores

Corporate image

Some organisations focus their attention on developing the image of individual brands, products or services. Others such as HP (with the strapline 'invent'), Cadbury's or Greenpeace concentrate on their corporate, or organisation-wide, image. This is done by sending a consistent message to all stakeholders, the target audiences, at all times. It is a strategic level process which is demonstrated by its relationships with employees, consumers, the media, etc.

Logo

This is the emblem, or symbol, of an organisation used in its stationery, advertising, display materials, etc. to continually reinforce the image. It must be used consistently on all internal and external communications. For example, Figure 4.16 shows the corporate logo of Nelson Thornes, the publishers of this book.

Figure 4.16

The corporate logo of Nelson Thornes

assignment focus

1 Does your organisation have a logo?

2 Collect examples of when and where the logo is used.

3 How effective is it in establishing the corporate image? What is your interpretation of the logo, its design, colour and font?

Livery

Livery includes the colour and design of the vehicles, the facia of the stores/premises, i.e. the colour and design of the shop fronts is standardised to make them readily visible in any high street. It also includes the signage on its vehicles, such as aeroplanes (easyjet and BA – Concorde was once painted blue for the launch of Pepsi in cans as part of a £175m promotion), trains (Virgin Trains are red and black with white branding and stripes on the lower bodyside – with thanks to thejunction.org.uk) What image does the design and facia of the premises create? Why does every high street now appear to look the same? Does the address matter? Perfumes appear to come from Paris.

assignment focus

1 Does your organisation have a livery?

2 Give examples and explain its value and purpose as part of the corporate image. What image does it give?

Uniforms or corporate clothing

Staff in major supermarkets, retail outlets, banks and public houses all wear corporate clothing. The obvious reason for uniforms is to identify staff. However, they can also be used to create a professional image for the organisation and reinforce the brand. In some organisations, e.g. the uniformed public services, police, fire brigade and nursing, everyone wears uniforms. How much attention do you pay to the style, design and colour of staff uniforms/corporate clothing? If you have a part-time job, do you wear uniform? A uniform is often considered to be part of the livery. Do you wear school uniform? Are there 'dress down days' or non-uniform days? Why? Corporate clothing can often be a great motivator and team builder, creating a feeling of pride and belonging.

assignment focus

1   Do staff in your organisation wear uniforms or corporate clothing? Do you like/dislike it? Give your reasons, e.g. Is it colour, style, material or suitability?

2   How do they help the corporate image?

3   If they don't wear uniforms, should they?

    The Cable and Wireless website at www.cw.com is superb

Corporate message and vocabulary

What words are always used to describe the organisation – 'cutting edge', 'reliable', 'cheapest'? The **corporate message** and the vocabulary are used to position the organisation in the mind of the consumer. They form its personality and enable it to distinguish itself from its competitors.

assignment focus

Collect examples of the corporate message/vocabulary of your organisation. Do the same for some of its competitors. How do they compare?

Supporting promotional statements or straplines

This is the key message or phrase that the organisation wants to put across to its **target market**, e.g. 'Just do it', 'The real thing', 'Every little helps', 'A Mars a day helps you work …' (Why is this not used this any more?), 'Have a break, have a Kit Kat', 'The future's bright, the future's Orange'.

The strapline should be immediately associated with the brand name. Its main use is to distinguish a product/service from its rivals. Along with the signature, it is the most important part of the communication.

assignment focus

1   Does your organisation have a strapline?

2   What is it and does it work?

3   What image does it give of the organisation?

4   If it doesn't have one, can you write one?

Target markets

Does the organisation portray the same image in each of its markets? For example, the makers of trainers use different words and images when they advertise in different publications. In men or women's magazines, they emphasise style and fashion. In specialist sport magazines, it is sport, power and cutting edge technology.

assignment focus

Does your organisation have a similar strategy for creating its corporate image?

Endorsements and affiliations, using personalities

Does David Beckham play football or appear in TV adverts? Choosing a celebrity to endorse (advertise) a product can be very successful, e.g. Gary Lineker and Walkers crisps. Gary has done 50 adverts and doubled the sales of Walker's crisps in the last ten years. However, a wrong choice could destroy the image of the product. The *Evening Standard* reported that some celebrities who have been seen unflatteringly in a particular design have ruined the sales.

When England regained the Ashes by beating Australia in the 2005 test cricket matches, the sponsor npower must have been delighted. (It advertised the next day by saying British Gas had been 'hit for six'.) Freddie Flintoff, the 'Player of the Series' became a celebrity and can be expected to be seen endorsing a range of products. 'He is not gender-specific or age-specific. Women and men love him and people, young and old, love him,' said the managing director of True North.

All products/services want to be associated with England's success. Channel 4 televised the test series with huge audiences (potential advertising revenue). Sky has bought the rights to the next series.

case study 4.3 — 'Materi ale Girl'

Madonna, in an interview with Jonathan Ross, said that her favourite alcoholic drink was a real ale, Timothy Taylor's Landlord. Sales jumped and the brewery was able to fund a major expansion. Celebrity endorsement obviously works.

In the James Bond film *Die Another Day* advertisers spent nearly £50m getting their products seen or mentioned in the film. James even changed his car from a BMW to an Aston Martin!

Source: With thanks to www.thepublican.com

activity

Does your organisation use a personality to promote its corporate image? Who is it? Does this help, e.g. what do they do, what do they say? If it does not, who would be suitable and why?

Multimedia associations

Websites, radio, TV and cinema advertising all provide opportunities for an organisation to use creative corporate communications to target and influence its chosen market(s). The ingredients of an effective approach include images which can be used to reinforce the consumer perception of the product.

Adding music, other sounds and voiceovers all contribute to mood and atmosphere. Do you associate a corporate image/advertisement with a tune or voice? Some personalities/famous names can be heard regularly on TV and radio commercials. Do you purchase because a product has been endorsed? The Tropicana orange juice New York adverts featured the song 'How do you like your eggs in the morning' with Dean Martin and Helen O'Connell. Music can be a very powerful marketing tool. How much does it cost to download the ring tones on your mobile? Always check that you haven't signed up to a subscription service.

The Advertising Standards Authority (www.asa.org.uk) has received many complaints about mobile phone and associated businesses and their methods of selling.

 Try www.commercialbreaksandbeats.co.uk to find out more about which songs accompanied particular adverts

Guinness are promoting an image where they 'are committed to responsible drinking'. If you try to enter the website, you will be asked which country you are in and when you were born because different countries have different age limits. How would you reply? Who is being responsible?

assignment focus

1 Is music associated with your organisation?
2 Who is the singer(s)?
3 What is the genre, e.g. jazz, folk, etc.?
4 How does the music create or reinforce the corporate image?

Corporate literature

This includes all communications sent to stakeholders (target audiences), e.g. letters to employees, the annual financial report sent to shareholders, press releases to the media (check the website), flyers and messages sent to consumers. It should be consistent and the vocabulary should clearly convey the image and personality of the organisation.

assignment focus

Collect and analyse the corporate literature sent out by your organisation. What corporate image of your organisation does it present? Include photographs, letters, brochures, copies of the logo, straplines, images used in its advertising, annual report, website print screens, etc. What are the strengths and weaknesses? How would you change/develop it?

Use of communications media

Registration with a range of internet service providers (ISPs)

In many ways online corporate communication is similar to offline, e.g. search engines such as Google and Yahoo, perform the same functions as directories. Press releases are similar to e-mail newsletters. Banner adverts are advertising online. It is important for an organisation to use **communications media** to establish a corporate image across both its offline and online activities.

A corporate website is now an essential part of the online corporate communications of most medium to large organisations.

Benefits of a clear corporate image

What can a good corporate image achieve? It helps to:

■ provide distinctiveness from potential competitor products and organisations. In an increasingly competitive marketplace, corporate image is a major determinant of how people spend their money. Even the most powerful brands can lose their direction and require a fundamental corporate makeover to recover. Can you think of some examples, e.g. has your centre changed its logo and image? Should it? Even charities compete for our donations

■ increase sales, e.g. a clear brand image makes people aware of the product and enables customers to identify with it. Teenagers tend to buy brand names because other people buy them, i.e. they are popular and fashionable and they are not the only one buying the product. A strong corporate brand image also helps to position the product in the mind of the consumer

■ establish an image and reputation – Which university do you want to go to? Where do you shop? Where would you like to work? Are your answers determined by the corporate image? Politicians are often accused of 'spin' which is manipulating the media to create a favourable image!

Below is the front cover of the *Eurostat Yearbook 2004* as Reuters and Yahoo news reported in October 2004. Wales has been omitted, i.e. Shropshire has acquired a coastline! What image do you have of Eurostat, the statistical branch of the European Union (EU)?

Figure 4.17

The front cover of *Eurostat Yearbook 2004*

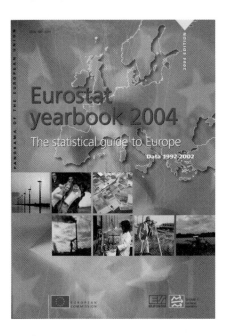

case study 4.4 — Investors in People

Go to the Investors in People (IIP) website at www.iipuk.co.uk. Click on About Investors in People, and then Corporate Guidelines.

This website shows how the Investors in People brand, logo and image should be portrayed by organisations which are entitled to use it.

Figure 4.18

The correct way to use the IIP logo

The Investors in People Logo is a registered trademark of Investors in People UK and is reproduced with their permission.

activity

Why is Investors in People so particular about the use of its logo?

  www.Jetix.net is a good website directed at a specific younger market

assignment focus Case study 4.5 is designed to show how D2 can be achieved. It will also help with other outcomes such as Using Creative Communications.

Corporate identification guidelines

These would include instructions and guidance on font size and typeface style, use of logos, including the exclusion zone; stationery including letterheads, compliment slips, business cards, envelopes, brochure covers and product literature.

case study 4.5 — Eclipse

For the business plan in Unit 5 we have created a fictional business called Eclipse. In Unit 6 we develop its website. Here we give some ideas for creating and/or changing its corporate image/communications.

Initial information gathering

Eclipse first used the Key Note China & Earthenware Market Report Plus to investigate buyer behaviour and the brand strategy of the major companies. It found that 'brand recognition and brand loyalty are strong in the ceramics industry' which meant that they would need to create a powerful corporate image. They had intended to use a celebrity such as Jamie Oliver to endorse their tableware, but discovered that he was already linked with Royal Worcester. They wondered whether they could afford Rick Stein who has a restaurant in Cornwall. Eventually they decided they would approach 'Wire Daisies', a Cornish group who came together after an eclipse party in Cornwall in 1999. See www.wiredaisies.com. Their album 'Just Another Day' would be ideal for Eclipse!

The big companies such as Wedgwood or Denby Pottery spend an average £250,000 on media advertising. Eclipse could not afford it.

It needed to establish a niche with a strong local flavour.

Internet search

An internet search under 'creative corporate communications case studies' produced a list of commercial companies which could develop and design a corporate image based around the Eclipse brand and its values. Many of these sites had useful examples.

Using case studies after a general search usually produces good results with practical examples.

Corporate stationery/website/presentation image

Eclipse needed business cards, letterheads, compliment slips, invoices, a brochure/publicity materials. The design and style would need to be consistent and reinforce the image they were trying to create. It would also need to work on their website and be represented in any presentation they made to possible corporate buyers/stores, etc. It needed to be distinctive and unique to give it shelf standout from possible competitors.

Eclipse discovered that there were only 216 web-safe colours, which did not distort or dither.

Possible straplines:

- 'Eclipse – Out of this world'
- 'Eclipse – Puts everyone else in the shade'
- 'Eclipse – Quality on a plate'
- 'Eclipse – A once in a lifetime experience'
- 'Eclipse – Not just for pasties!'
- 'Eclipse – The crème of Cornwall'
- 'We Eclipse the competition'.

Multimedia presentation

This would include images of the tableware being used by various groups of people (20–30 somethings – Would you agree that this is the right age group?) to create atmosphere and add style to the surroundings. The image should be of total quality. The music still has to be decided. Perhaps Iris Litchfield 'light contemporary classical piano'?

Figure 4.19

Font style and size

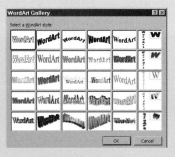

Figure 4.20

Examples of WordArt

These styles can be accessed from View, Toolbars, Drawing, Insert WordArt. You can highlight the word you want to change in WordArt.

In Figure 4.21 the insert WordArt icon is highlighted. This Print Screen is also interesting because it shows the draft version of the page you are now looking at!

Figure 4.21

The WordArt options available

Promotional literature

Figure 4.22 shows some examples of the promotional literature for Eclipse. You will probably be able to do much better for your organisation as part of your assignment.

Figure 4.22

Promotional literature

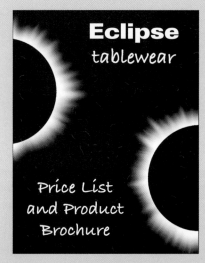

activity

1 Which strapline would you choose, and why?
2 Are the photographs suitable or appropriate to the Eclipse image?
3 Which font styles do you prefer?
4 How would you evaluate our attempts at creating a corporate identity? Give your reasons. Be as critical as you want, but be constructive and make alternative suggestions.

assignment focus

1 How could you enhance the image of your organisation?
2 When you have completed the improvements on the presentation of business information in your organisation, you could display them on coloured sheets of A3 paper (remember background colours can be warm or cold). You could include a multimedia slide show to run on the computer. Include both the before and after versions. You could link this to the promotion plan in Unit 3, the business plan in Unit 5 and the website in Unit 6. Good luck and enjoy!

UNIT 5

Business Enterprise

This unit covers:

- features of enterprise
- enterprise and legal structure
- marketing strategy and tactics
- plan for a new business venture.

This unit looks at:

- the reasons for being self-employed and the need to plan for this
- ways of identifying a suitable business idea for today's market
- suitable legal structures and appropriate sources of finance
- drawing up a marketing plan and financial forecasts
- how to interpret forecasts and review the plan if necessary.

Assessment

The unit assessment is by an integrated vocational assignment (IVA) set by BTEC, marked by your teachers, then checked by BTEC.

To complete this unit, you will need:

- access to IT for presentation, calculation and research purposes
- electronic spreadsheet or commercial business planning software for the financial forecast (ideally).

You will find it helpful to speak to professionals such as people in business, small business advisers from a local bank and representatives from organisations such as the Prince's Trust, businessdynamics or Shell Livewire.

To gain a merit, you will need to conduct market research. Secondary data is available from sources such as trade associations, Business Link, the local authority, the Office of National Statistics (ONS, available from the UK government statistical website) and related publications such as *Social Trends*, *Annual Abstract of Statistics* and *Business Monitors*.

As always, keep up with the news for latest developments.

To gain a distinction, you will need to evaluate the **viability** of your planned business venture.

We illustrate the various stages in business planning by looking at a small pottery called Eclipse. The complete business plan for this venture is included at the end of the unit.

Features of Enterprise

Features

According to businessdynamics (the business education and enterprise charity), 'One in three young people want to work for themselves.' Is this true of the students in your group? Are you one of these?

Why work for yourself?

Your answer to this is likely to include:

- 'To be my own boss'
- 'To get job satisfaction'
- 'I can make more money that way'
- 'Can't get a job that I like'
- 'There isn't much work round here'.

Can you suggest any others?

businessdynamics concludes that, 'Enterprise certainly isn't for everyone. It is insecure, frustrating and exhausting, but it's also exciting, challenging and rewarding.'

Are you the right sort of person?

An entrepreneur is a person who undertakes the risks of establishing and running a new business enterprise. Being your own boss is likely to be very hard work.

You need to be sure what you want from self-employment and whether you have what it takes to succeed. What being your own boss does not do (at least at first) is give you lots of time off.

case study 5.1

Nothing ventured, nothing gained

When Justin Cooke set up his media company he was 25. In the early stages, he frequently worked so late at the office that he took his sleeping bag and slept under the desk.

Gap in the market

In 1993 Claire Owen lost her job. Despite having a young child her response was to set up her own award-winning marketing recruitment agency, 'Stopgap'.

Claire believes that any new entrepreneur must have personal self-confidence and enough cash to survive for the first 18 months without drawing money from the business. In her experience, banks are unlikely to lend cash to a brand new business unless it can provide security to guarantee repayment.

activity

1. Your boss would not expect you to work as long as Justin. So why do you think Justin did it?
2. What sort of qualities do you feel you will need to run your own business?
3. What sort of things might be used as 'security' for a loan?
4. Is there anyone in your group whose family owns a business? If so, ask them to give a brief talk on: type of business activity, form of organisation (sole trader, partnership, etc.), the pros and cons. Why did they set up on their own? Are they pleased that they did?

What are the opportunities and risks?

When newspapers print lists of the richest young people, there are the usual well-paid employees such as Wayne Rooney and David Beckham, but many are young entrepreneurs working hard on their own ideas.

What does a successful entrepreneur look like? What line of business are these entrepreneurs in?

Figure 5.1

Richard Branson

Figure 5.2

Anita Roddick

case study 5.2 — Innocent Drinks – a case of organic growth

Key people

Innocent Drinks was set up in August 1999 by three friends, Adam Balon (sales director), Richard Reed (marketing director) and Jon Wright (operations director). At the time, they all had jobs but were looking for a business idea. They had previously looked at (and rejected): a plastic alternative to house keys (they kept losing theirs) and a way to stop baths overflowing.

The product

They finally came up with an idea for 'smoothie' drinks made only from crushed fruit.

The USP (unique selling point) was that they would use pure ingredients, with no artificial sweeteners or concentrates. They are 'not made from fruit – they are fruit'.

A gap in the market

This is a lifestyle product based on people's increasing interest in healthy eating, and their willingness to pay for it. The three friends found from experience that many of the smoothies they bought in the shops used fruit concentrates rather than whole fruit. They knew that they could make better drinks at home using a blender, but this was very time-consuming and left a lot of washing up. Perhaps people would pay for 'natural, fresh goodness' made easy.

Market research

The friends bought £500-worth of fruit, made up a batch of smoothies and took them to the Jazz on the Green festival in West London.

Instead of a questionnaire, they asked punters to put the empty bottles either into a YES bin (yes they should make the drinks full-time) or a NO bin. The response was overwhelmingly 'yes', so they gave up their jobs next day and formed the company Innocent Drinks.

Funding

The owners' savings did not provide enough capital and they spent nine months looking for backing. No banks were interested. They e-mailed all of their friends and work acquaintances. Eventually they found an American **business angel** (or financial backer), Maurice Pinto; he believed in their idea and supplied the funds.

Development and growth

Innocent sold its first smoothie on 28 April 1999. They had planned to raise more finance but sales grew so quickly that the company immediately became self-financing.

Performance

The figures show that this has been a smooth operation. In 2004 (after the first five years of trading):

- 46 people were employed
- annual sales turnover was £10.6 million – and growing at 50–60 per cent p.a.
- the company was the UK market leader with 40 per cent market share (the UK market buys 50 million bottles each year)
- best sellers were yogurt, vanilla bean and honey 'thickie'.

Opportunities and threats

The UK market for natural lifestyle foods and drinks is growing and Innocent has plans to freeze the smoothies to produce desserts – a healthy alternative to ice cream. There are also ideas for cosmetics.

Supermarkets have seen the potential and are producing own-label copies.

Corporate image

The company has a strong set of principles. It will not compromise on quality, bottles are 25 per cent recycled plastic, the labels are made of mango-leaf paper. They have also set up a charity, The Innocent Foundation, to fund projects in those areas of the world where the company sources its products.

They use an electric car with the Innocent logo on the side.

The future

Global firms are bound to be interested in buying a strong growing brand such as Innocent and the owners might be tempted by the money on offer.

There is a precedent: Ben & Jerry's, the American ice cream manufacturer, developed on similar lines and with very similar principles to Innocent. Although their advertising retains the small, friendly, home-made feel (the number of nuts you get depends on who threw them in ...), they are now one of the many brands owned by the Anglo-Dutch giant Unilever.

Source: Adapted from *The Guardian*, August 2004

activity

1 What suggests that the three friends were the right types of people to form a business?
2 Do you think that they planned the business start-up well, or were they lucky?
3 What is a 'business angel' and why was this one so important?
4 Was primary or secondary market research carried out at the Jazz on the Green festival?
5 Was this a suitable venue for the market research? Why do you think it was chosen?
6 Conduct a SWOT analysis for the company (see Unit 1, page 45).
7 Explain the term 'lifestyle product'. Give examples of such products that you use (not necessarily food).

Innocent Drinks: www.innocentdrinks.co.uk

Business failures in England and Wales

Setting up an enterprise inevitably involves risk and, as Figure 5.3 shows, many businesses do fail, often leaving their owners in financial difficulty.

Figure 5.3

Business failures in England and Wales, 1999–2004

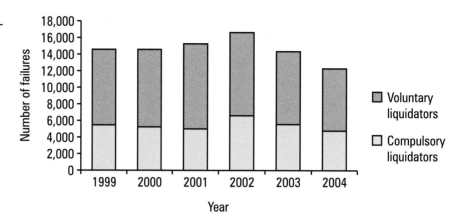

Below we look at how drawing up a business plan will help avoid some of the more predictable problems.

Is self-employment right for me?

Setting up in business requires a considerable investment of time, funds and energy. Before going ahead, it is sensible to be sure that you really have what it takes.

Business Link, the business support organisation, suggests that would-be entrepreneurs rate themselves against the list of key qualities shown in Table 5.1 (the rating scale is ours).

Table 5.1 Is self-employment right for me?

Desirable personal qualities	Strong	Satisfactory	Weak
Are you prepared for the personal demands of setting up a new business?			
How well do you handle uncertainty?			
Do you have a positive attitude?			
Are you prepared to take chances and gamble on your own ideas?			
Do you have any of the key qualities of a typical entrepreneur? (e.g. initiative, dedication, energy, the right attitude)			
Do you have an absolute determination to succeed?			
Can you bounce back from setbacks and take criticism?			
Are you able to delegate?			
Do you have core business skills? (e.g. communication, number and ICT skills, financial ability, judgement, etc.)			
Are you prepared to spend time carrying out in-depth market research?			
Do you have sufficient funds to set up a new business? (Funds needed can vary considerably.)			
Are you willing to draw on expert help when you need it?			

Source: Adapted from Business Link

Maximise your strengths

Very few entrepreneurs are strong in all of the areas required.

- Karan Bilimoria made a success of Cobra beer despite his father's opposition.
- Lena Bjorck arrived in the UK from Sweden with no qualifications. Whilst working as a kitchen porter, she realised that service to customers was poor and that she could do it better. She now runs one of the country's most successful catering companies.

The key is to make the most of your assets and take action to address any gaps.

Figure 5.4

Make the most of your assets and take action to address any gaps

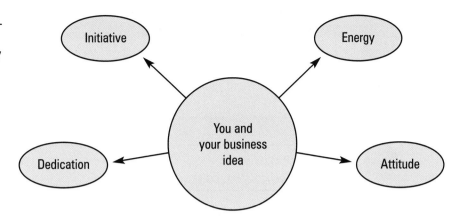

To summarise, succeeding in business is about ideas, motivation and ambition. However, you also need the confidence to sell yourself and your ideas; this is clearly easier when you believe that your idea is a good one. Finally, you must know your own strengths and weaknesses and know when to take advice.

Contribution of SMEs to the UK economy

Small and medium enterprises (**SMEs**) can be identified in various ways. Here we identify them by the number of employees:

- small enterprises – 0–49 employees
- medium enterprises – 50–499 employees
- large enterprises – over 500 employees.

case study **Strength in numbers**

5.3

In his budgets since 1997 Chancellor Gordon Brown brought in a number of measures to help and encourage small enterprise. The chart shows why he believes that SMEs are a vital part of the UK economy.

Figure 5.5

The importance of SMEs to the UK economy

Source: © Office For National Statistics, 2002

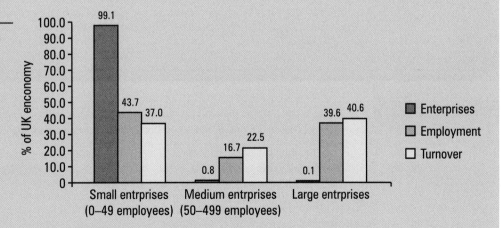

It is the job of the UK government's Department of Trade and Industry (DTI) to promote SMEs through the Small Business Service. This service liaises with local Business Links in England, Business Gateway in Scotland, Business Eye in Wales and InvestNI in Northern Ireland. It also links with organisations such as the Prince's Trust, Shell Livewire and the Patent Office.

The DTI supports businesses by providing grants, loans, guarantees and consultancy to help with a range of business issues.

activity

1　Use the information in the chart to explain why the government is keen to support SMEs in the UK.
2　Find the website of your local Business Link. Briefly summarise the services that it provides for SMEs in your area. Use a spidergram to illustrate this.

- www.dti.gov.uk
- www.businesslink.co.uk

Innovation and creativity

Setting up a successful small business is about spotting a gap in the market that you can fill, or seeing potential before anyone else does.

Although certain types of R&D (research and development) require huge investment, it is equally true that small businesses constantly introduce effective new ideas, or new applications for existing ideas.

Keep it simple

Many of the best ideas have been very simple (think about Innocent Drinks), but have succeeded because they answered a particular need. You have a good idea if you can explain it in simple terms so that people can immediately see the point.

case study 5.4

Re-inventing the wheel: a revolutionary idea?

One of James Dyson's first projects was a wheelbarrow with a ball in place of a wheel. This was a very simple but effective solution to wheeling over uneven ground without tipping over.

Dyson not only solved a problem, but spotted a growing trend. Gardening ('the new rock and roll') has become a multi-million pound industry over recent years thanks partly to Friday night TV 'lifestyle' programmes such as *Groundforce* and *The Flying Gardener*.

activity

1　Dyson's wheelbarrow was the start, but he is best known for the Dyson vacuum cleaner, now a big seller in the USA as well as in the UK. What was the USP (unique selling point) that enabled this to compete with established brands such as Hoover?

2　Even successful companies have failures. The Dyson washing machine (USP twin drums) sold poorly and was withdrawn from the market. Find out why. What does this tell you about the importance of market research?

The Dyson website (www.dyson.co.uk) and the archives of newspaper websites should help with this activity.

Eclipse Pottery

What's the idea?

Della Moon lives in Cornwall where she has been making pottery for a number of years. For some time, she has exhibited in local galleries and taken on small commissions. Recently, Della's work has attracted growing interest and she is now considering turning her hobby into a business.

Why set up in business?

Della is attracted by the idea of being her own boss and having the freedom to work on her own ideas. She realises that there are risks, that she will have to work hard and that, to begin with, she will almost certainly make less money than in full-time employment. Della's son, Wayne, has a number of business contacts and is thinking about joining his mother in this project.

The business idea

Della will design, produce and sell her award-winning Della-Ware six-piece dinner sets.

Training and development needs

Della brings a range of skills to the business, although she feels that she needs to learn computerised accounting and is looking for a suitable evening class. Della is also aware that she will need to seek expert advice at certain times particularly about finance and marketing and has made contact with her bank and the local Business Link.

Della knows why she wants to work for herself. After completing the personal skills checklist on page 204, she discovers that she is well equipped to run her own business.

The business name

Della has decided to trade under the name 'Eclipse'. This fits with the natural image that the business will promote, it links with Della's surname and also suggests that Della will put the opposition 'in the shade'.

Della's completed business plan is shown on pages 249–56.

---

assignment focus

Choosing a business venture

To achieve P1, identify the attributes that you have to offer and your aims in setting up the business venture

For this task you should:

- state your aims in setting up in business

- complete a personal skills questionnaire, such as that on page 204, and identify the skills and qualities that make you right for self-employment

- suggest further training that you might need and how you might gain this.

This will form part of the introduction to your business plan and will help you to choose a suitable business idea.

Business trends

The business environment is dynamic (constantly changing). This can threaten existing products, but provides an opportunity for new ones. Successful businesses are those most able to identify and support new trends

PESTEL analysis

PESTEL analysis is a useful way of looking at the factors that cause changes in the business environment. It uses six headings to examine the ways in which businesses are influenced by the outside world.

We also discuss PESTEL on page 46.

- Political factors – the policies and actions of governments may favour or harm the business, e.g. governments may decide to encourage smaller cars, tax smoking or cut public expenditure.

- Economic factors – these affect our ability to buy goods and services. The level of unemployment, the rise in house prices, inflation and wage rates are examples.

- Social factors – these are about the way that people live. Our attitudes, views, beliefs and lifestyles influence our buying habits. Our clothes, music styles, leisure pursuits and the food we eat are all influenced by social factors.

- Technological factors – manufacturing processes, materials, storage techniques, communications methods are all constantly evolving. For example, products and production methods may go out of date as new products arrive, the internet is changing how we shop and the world is facing the challenge of creating clean energy.

- Environmental factors – these include the effects of climate change (e.g. on farming), and the pressing need to recycle and avoid pollution. Legislation is forcing businesses to adopt 'greener' policies, e.g. leaded four-star petrol has now been phased out.

- Legal factors – governments may influence business behaviour in a number of ways. Certain activities such as discrimination in the workplace (through employment law) and unsafe working practices (through health and safety law) are illegal.

Figure 5.6

PESTEL analysis

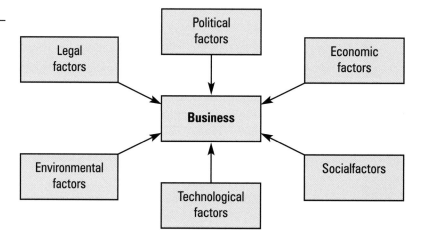

Other activities may be either encouraged or discouraged by the use of taxation, financial penalties or incentives. Examples might include the use of grants to encourage location in development areas or the use of congestion charges and airport taxes to discourage unnecessary journeys.

The PESTEL factors create opportunities and threats to businesses. Banning smoking in public areas, for example, threatens cigarette manufacturers but may provide pharmaceutical companies with an opportunity to sell nicotine patches.

We will consider PESTEL factors further when we conduct a SWOT analysis into our proposed business on page 221.

Sources of information on business trends

A wide range of sources can be used to identify business trends including the following.

Specialist market reports

Market research reports from firms such as Verdict (retail trends), Mintel and Dun & Bradstreet can provide invaluable business information at a price. Specialist business libraries and some reference libraries will make these available.

case study 5.5 — John Lewis hit by bombs and G8

The second week in July 2005 was marked by protests against the meeting of world leaders at the G8 conference at Gleneagles, Scotland. In the same week, terrorist bombs exploded on the London transport system.

John Lewis reported a 33 per cent fall in sales at their Edinburgh branch and a 28 per cent fall in their London Oxford Street store as a consequence. However, sales at johnlewis.com rose 77 per cent as many stay-at-home shoppers logged onto the internet. Overall, total turnover for the week was up by 1.8 per cent.

On the day of the bombing, it was claimed that some London hotels doubled their prices to commuters unable to get home when the underground system was closed down. Meanwhile the Mayor of London suspended the congestion charge designed to keep motorists off London streets.

Source: Adapted from *The Guardian*, 16 July 2005

activity

1   Identify the PESTEL factors mentioned in the case study. To which category does each belong? (Some may fit into more than one.)
2   Is the response of the hotels unethical or just good business?

Government publications

The government collects data and publishes statistics on the state of the nation. The following should be available in your library or the local reference library:

- *Social Trends* – looks at how we live and covers lifestyle issues such as working hours, patterns of work, access to the internet, spending habits, use of leisure time, and so on
- *Family Expenditure Survey* – shows how we spend our money in the UK
- *Regional Trends* – compares the economic activity within different parts of the country
- *Annual Abstract of Statistics* – provides a selection of the major economic trends
- *Business Monitors* – provides specialist reports on specific industries
- *Key Note* publications – also report on specific industries.

Websites

The UK government's Office of National Statistics (ONS) website at www.statistics.gov.uk provides free statistics in spreadsheet format together with extracts of reports.

Biz-ed is an educational site that brings together relevant business material including case studies, company reports and selected official data.

The media

Websites for the BBC and the 'quality' papers contain a wealth of business information. The newspaper sites have archives through which back copies can be searched.

- www.bbc.co.uk
- www.guardian.co.uk

Local sources might include the local authority, the local Business Link, the local Chamber of Commerce and trade associations.

Eclipse Pottery

Find the gap

Della and Wayne conduct a PESTEL analysis to identify trends that are likely to provide a business opportunity. They use the following information sources:

- the local Business Link
- the local Chamber of Commerce
- local trade directories and the local press
- their bank's small business adviser.

They also visit the local reference library to view *Key Note* publications and *Business Monitors*.

The partners come to conclusions under each PESTEL heading.

- Political factors – the unstable world situation may lead to an increase in visitors to the area as more people choose to holiday in the UK away from cities. Council tax rises in the West Country and rising petrol costs may make visiting Cornwall more costly.
- Economic factors – the Cornish tourist trade is seasonal, based upon summer holidays and outdoor activities. It is too far to travel for short-breaks out-of-season. However, the introduction of cheap flights from Stansted to Newquay will cut travelling times and may attract short-break visitors.
- Social factors – the 'natural feel' of Eclipse products will appeal to the A–C1 target market.
- Technological factors – there is potential for reaching a niche market via the internet. However, competitors may also use the internet as a means of entering the market.
- Environmental factors – the 'natural wholesome' image of Eclipse pottery fits well with a growing awareness of environmental issues. Unpredictable climate change (e.g. the Boscastle flood of 2004).
- Legal factors – the partners must be aware of the various forms of legislation with which a business must comply. Health and safety is a particular issue.

 Link

Della and Wayne include these external opportunities and threats in their SWOT analysis shown on page 240.

analysis shown on page 240.

---

assignment focus

Choosing a business venture

To achieve P1, identify the business venture you have chosen with reasons, addressing risks and opportunities.

When you identify a business venture:

- play to your strengths. Choose an activity that you are interested in and for which you have the right skills. You may mention other ideas that you considered and why you rejected them
- keep it simple, small-scale and local. Avoid unrealistic, over-ambitious plans needing vast amounts of funding and specialised knowledge.

When you address risks (or threats) and opportunities use PESTEL analysis as a framework. You will need to find a gap in the market, so be aware of current (especially local) trends. Perhaps you can produce a set of figures or a chart to show that there is likely to be a demand.

At this stage you may wish to change your business idea.

Enterprise and Legal Structure

Business formation and legal status

The choice of legal status for your business will depend upon:

- the funds required to set up and run the business
- the type of business activity (e.g. some professional associations do not allow their members to form limited companies)
- the level of risk involved (limited liability may be needed)
- whether you wish to keep control (e.g. a plc may be taken over by another business).

We also look at legal status in Unit 1.

You may decide to start up a new business or to buy an existing business. Either way your enterprise will be small-scale so that your choice of legal status is likely to be one of those listed in Table 5.2.

Table 5.2 Advantages and disadvantages of different legal status

Legal status	Advantages	Disadvantages
Sole trader one owner	■ The simplest and cheapest form of business to set up ■ You will have complete control and can keep all of the profits ■ Your business affairs remain confidential	■ The initial capital comes from your savings ■ It may be difficult to raise extra finance without some form of security ■ You will have: – personal unlimited liability for all business debts – a heavy work load – all of the responsibility and you cannot afford to be ill
Partnership Two–20 owners	■ Simple and cheap to set up ■ Partners bring extra capital, and perhaps valuable experience and expertise ■ The work-load and business liabilities are shared ■ Business affairs remain confidential	■ You are no longer in overall control; decisions and profits are shared ■ All partners have unlimited liability for business debts and a contract made by one partner is legally binding on all others ■ Problems may result if: partners cannot work well together or if one wishes to leave
Private limited company No maximum number of shareholders	■ Business affairs are separate from the affairs of the shareholders (the owners) ■ Extra capital may be raised by selling shares ■ Shareholders have limited liability for business debts so that their personal property is not at risk ■ Shares can only be sold by permission of existing shareholders; this avoids unwelcome take-over attempts	■ Usually more expensive and complex to set up than a sole trader or partnership ■ Under the Companies Acts, a company must: – register their details with the Registrar of Companies at Companies House – submit an annual financial summary to the Registrar for inspection by the general public
Public limited company (plc)	Not appropriate for a small business start-up	
Franchise May be sole trader, partnership or limited company	■ Sells an established branded product trusted by the consumer; this minimises the start-up risk ■ Support from the franchisor may include help with setting up premises and regional or national advertising	■ Disadvantages depend upon the legal status chosen by the franchisee ■ The franchisor will monitor the franchisee for quality and may withdraw approval to operate
Charitable status	■ Organisations providing certain services to the community may gain charitable status to reduce the tax liability of the business	■ Charitable status is not available to all businesses

Eclipse Pottery

Legal status – what form of business organisation?

Three forms of business organisation will be appropriate for Della: a sole trader if she sets up alone; a partnership or private limited company if Wayne joins her. Structures that would not be appropriate are: public limited company because the business will not be large enough; a franchise because Della designs her own property; a charity because Della intends to make a profit to live from.

Della and Wayne decide to form a partnership for the following reasons:

■ finance – Della will not have enough capital of her own. Wayne will provide additional funds

- support – Della will not have to run the business alone. Wayne will bring in his business expertise to complement Della's design skills

- confidentiality – it would not be possible to keep business affairs confidential if they formed a limited company. A company also involves more paperwork, more cost and more regulation. Company details and a copy of their annual accounts would be open for inspection by the general public at Companies House

- risk – the venture is not high risk, therefore limited liability is not essential.

Registering the business name
The partners will trade under the name 'Eclipse', which they must register with the Companies Registration Office to comply with the Business Names Act.

Partnership agreement (or deed)
Della and Wayne ask their solicitor to draw up a formal partnership deed (Figure 5.7).

---

assignment focus

Choosing a business venture

To achieve P2, you should include the proposed legal structure of the business explaining why it is appropriate.

For this task you should:

- identify and describe the appropriate legal structure for your business

- give the reasons for your choice by explaining why it is more appropriate for you than other structures.

Figure 5.7

The formal deed of partnership for Eclipse

> ### Principal terms for the Partnership Agreement for Eclipse
>
> Capital to be invested thus: D. Moon £5000 W. Moon £10 000
>
> **Profit sharing:**
> Each partner to take drawings of £1000 per month.
> Otherwise profits to be retained in the business.
> Both partners to have unlimited liability.
>
> **Roles:**
> D. Moon to design and manufacture pottery.
> W. Moon to provide contacts and administrative support.
>
> **Security:**
> The house belonging to D. Moon will be pledged as security for any external finance that is necessary.
>
> **Decisions:**
> All business decisions must be unanimous.
>
> **Cheques:**
> All cheques to bear the signatures of both partners.
>
> **Death of a partner:**
> Partners agree that if either dies then their original capital will remain in the business for use by the other for a maximum of 2 years.
>
> **Disputes:**
> To be resolved by arbitration.
>
> **Duration of partnership:**
> Minimum of 3 years; then to continue at will
>
> **Retirement:**
> No retirement during the first 3 years, thereafter a partner may retire on giving 6 months' notice.
>
> **Alterations**
> The partnership agreement can be altered only by mutual consent.

Sources of finance

When does a business need to raise finance?

Ultimately, a business will aim to become self-financing with sufficient sales to pay its costs and generate a profit. Ideally, like Innocent Drinks, it will also hope to plough back some of the profits to fund future growth.

In practice, however, many businesses will need to raise extra finance at various times.

- A new business will need start-up finance for equipment, stocks, and so on before it can begin to trade.

- Whilst trading, a business may experience periodic cash shortages. Perhaps trade is seasonal or perhaps unexpected problems arise such as late payment by customers, strikes by workers, difficulties with suppliers or the loss of a major order.

- An established business may seek new finance in order to expand into larger premises, buy more sophisticated equipment, employ more staff, and so on.

Types of financial need

We can identify two types of financial need (Figure 5.8) and the finance is different for each.

Figure 5.8

Types of financial need

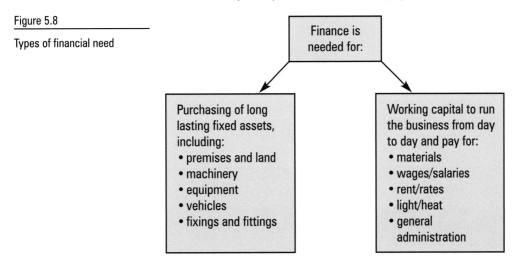

The sources of finance

Finance may be raised from within the business or externally (Figure 5.9).

Figure 5.9

Sources of finance

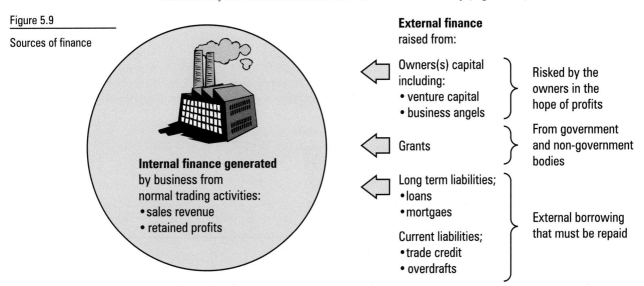

The appropriate form of finance depends upon the financial need.

Capital provided by the owners

Owners' capital can be used for either the purchase of fixed assets in the start-up phase, or as a source of working capital used for daily running costs.

The amount of capital required is a major factor in determining the appropriate form of business organisation. Whilst sole trader status can support a small organisation, a project such as the Channel Tunnel will need access to the millions of pounds that only a plc can raise.

Capital is regarded as permanent in that it does not have to be repaid. Instead, the owners risk their savings in the hope that they will be rewarded from future profits. Sole traders and partners will take their share of the profit as drawings whilst company shareholders will receive dividends.

case study 5.6 — Sweet success

For many years the shareholders of Ben & Jerry's, the niche market ice cream, received no dividends at all. The firm ploughed back all profits, with the shareholders' approval. It grew as a result into a valuable premium brand. The shareholders were rewarded when the company was bought by Unilever.

On the other hand, Thornton's, the chocolate company, after a disappointing 2003, paid out virtually all of its £4.4 million profits as dividends. This left only £1,000 to plough back.

activity

1   How would ploughing back profits help Ben & Jerry's to grow? Why would the shareholders agree to this?
2   Why do you think that Thornton's chose to reward its shareholders rather than plough back profit?

As a business grows, extra capital may be raised by changing the form of business organisation. A sole trader may bring in partners or form a limited company. In turn, a limited company may 'float' on the stock market as a plc. Tesco has been through all of these stages as it has grown.

case study 5.7 — Nothing ventured ...

New and developing companies may raise further capital with the help of **venture capital** trusts or business angels.

Venture capital trusts (VCTs) are companies that will purchase shares in new or expanding businesses. Potentially large amounts of new capital can be raised in this way. 3is (formerly Investors in Industry) is one of the major providers of venture capital to UK businesses.

Figure 5.10

3is

Business angels are individuals with funds to invest (see the Innocent Drinks case study). To protect their investment, they may wish to take some part in the management of the business and they normally have considerable skills and experience to offer. As a reward for their risk, business angels will be interested in gaining a return of perhaps 25–30 per cent on their investment. They may also put a time limit on their involvement.

activity

1   What percentage interest would you get from investing in a bank savings account? Use the weekend newspapers or a bank website to find out.
2   Why does a business angel require a much higher return?
3   Refer to the 3is website for further details of its activities.

Borrowing

Borrowing, unlike owners' capital, must be repaid at some point.

Long-term borrowing is suitable for the purchase of fixed assets.

■   Bank loans are offered for a period of between one to ten years and repaid in regular instalments at an agreed rate of interest. A new business may need security for any borrowing, i.e. a guarantee that the loan will be repaid.

■   Loans from friends and relatives may be offered for lower rates of interest or even interest-free. The time period for repayment may also be more flexible.

■   Commercial mortgages are long-term loans used to buy land or buildings. The property acts as security and will be repossessed and sold if the borrower cannot repay. Repayment may be over 25 years.

Short-term borrowing is suitable for providing working capital.

■   Trade credit is offered when suppliers agree to accept payment for goods or services at a future date. The typical credit period is 30 days.

■   Bank overdrafts enable a business to overspend (overdraw) on its current bank account. Overdrafts are repayable on demand (at any time the bank wishes).

Other methods of financing

■   **Leasing** – a business can hire rather than buy a fixed asset such as vehicles or machinery. The main benefit is that the asset is made available for immediate use without the need to buy it outright.

■   Factoring – a business that allows its customers credit may run short of cash whilst awaiting payment. Here a bank will pay 80 per cent of all invoices immediately. It will then collect the debts as they become due. At this point, it will pay the remaining 20 per cent, less a commission for providing the service.

■   Debt funding (or borrowing) – allows the owners to remain in control of the business, assuming that they can repay with equity funding (selling a share in the business, perhaps to venture capitalists or to business angels) the original owners rise losing control of the business.

Eclipse Pottery

Start-up finance

Della and Wayne draw up a list of their start-up costs (Table 5.3). They will fund these from their savings and by means of a bank loan secured against Della's house.

This will leave an opening bank balance of £1,000 (£20,000 funding less £19,000 costs = £1,000 bank balance).

Della and Wayne include this information in their business plan as follows:

■   the assets required under 'physical resources' in the operational plan (page 242)
■   the financial details in month zero of the cashflow forecast (see page 244).

Table 5.3 Start-up costs and sources of finance for Eclipse

Start-up requirements	£	Sources of finance	£
Fixed assets		*Partners' capital*	
'Jet Heat' electric kiln	9,000	Della	10,000
Multi-rev potter's wheels	4,000	Wayne	5,000
Specialist tools	2,000		15,000
Computer, laser printer, software	2,400	*add*	
Office furniture	1,600	*Long-term liabilities*	
		Bank loan	5,000
Total required:	19,000	Total finance:	20,000

---

assignment focus

Choosing a business venture

To achieve P2, identify potential sources of finance, explaining how these fit with the legal structure and aims of the business venture.

For this task you should:

- identify the start-up costs of your business, and the sources of funding you will use to meet these. Clearly itemise all figures

- explain how the sources of finance you have chosen fit with the structure and aims of your business venture.

---

remember

You will include these items when you create your business plan:
- Start-up costs will appear in your operational plan under physical resources.
- The start-up costs and sources of funds will be shown in the cashflow forecast in the financial plan.

Additional sources of finance and guidance

A number of other forms of support are available to new businesses depending upon their size, activity, geographical location and the age of the entrepreneurs.

Government and European Union support

The UK government will provide grants for up to 50 per cent of the cost of some projects and a variety of development programmes some of which contain financial help. Government support for UK business is co-ordinated by the Department of Trade and Industry (DTI).

www.open.gov.uk

Small Firms Loan Guarantee Scheme (SFLGS)

The government Small Business Service guarantees a percentage of a bank loan. The aim is to encourage banks to make loans available to small businesses which would otherwise have difficulty in borrowing.

Small Firms Training Loans (SFTL)

Some banks make loans available for certain training costs that could otherwise not be afforded.

Export Credit Guarantee Department (ECGD)

This is a UK government department that insures UK exports sold on credit against non-payment. It also provides long-term cover for certain foreign investment projects. The aim is to encourage firms to export by removing some of the risks.

Regional development grants

The government provides financial assistance for firms setting up in certain regions of the country. The aim is to encourage businesses to relocate into areas where employment is needed.

Objective One funding

Objective One was devised to help reduce differences in social and economic conditions within countries of the European Union. It targeted regions with prosperity at 75 per cent or less of the European average, with £350m of European investment made available to the UK. As an example, Cornwall and the Isles of Scilly (a region suffering from the decline of traditional industries such as mining, farming and fishing) used Objective One funds to assist local businesses and improve the prosperity of the region.

From 2007 to 2013, Objective One is replaced by a Convergence Programme. This will continue economic development in the regions by investing in skills to help people into work; helping develop a knowledge-based economy and aiding business productivity and innovation.

Business Link

This is a local source of help and advice to small businesses. The website has a comprehensive section on starting a business with spreadsheet templates useful for financial planning. All aspects of starting up and running a new business are covered.

LLSCs, ELWa and LECs

Government tries to co-ordinate educational provision to the future needs of industry. It also aims to encourage investment and foster economic growth and development throughout the UK.

Much of this work is carried out regionally by:

- Local Learning and Skills Councils (LLSCs) in England
- the regional offices of Education and Learning in Wales (ELWa)
- Local Enterprise Companies (LECs) in Scotland.

These bodies help businesses to set up, grow and evolve. They also provide training and support for the unemployed and fund vocational qualifications. (No similar body exists for Northern Ireland.)

Non-governmental sources of support

The Prince's Trust

The Trust was set up in 1983 by Prince Charles to provide business support and advice for people aged 18–30 who are starting up their own businesses. It offers low interest loans of up to £5,000 and pre-start marketing grants of up to £250.

www.princes-trust.org.uk

Shell Livewire

Shell Livewire runs a Young Entrepreneur of the Year Award Scheme. It also gives free business advice covering business planning, sales, marketing, finance and funding.

www.shell-livewire.org

Business dynamics

Founded in 1977 (as Understanding Industry) by 3i to provide information and events for 14–19-year-old students interested in business enterprise.

www. businessynamics.org.uk

Protecting the business idea

Businesses will wish to prevent competitors from copying their ideas. Options include the following.

Patents

The Patent Office exists to help inventors register their new ideas so that they cannot be legally copied by rivals. They must be tangible and capable of accurate description.

Trade marks ™

The logos or brand names that differentiate the goods and services of one trader from another can be registered. Nike, Canon and HP Sauce are examples.

Copyright ©

This covers musical, artistic, and written works, films, broadcasts and computer programmes. You are automatically covered if you create something original.

The free transfer of information over the internet has led to a debate as to what should be freely available and what should not. For example, the unregulated copying of music onto formats such as MP3 is a threat to record companies and the artists they represent.

Registered design ®

This protects the appearance of a product if it is new and distinctive.

---

case study 5.8 — The French connection

FCUK® products were protected by registered design. The brand created by Trevor Beattie in 1997 became very popular. However, by 2004 the novelty was fading – 'tired and tacky' was how the ad industry described it. A £3m campaign was launched to replace it using the new slogan 'Something beginning with F'.

activity

1 Why was the FCUK brand so successful initially?
2 To whom did it appeal – which target market?
3 Such an image may not have been acceptable some years earlier. Which PESTEL factor has changed to allow its use?

www.frenchconnection.com

Eclipse Pottery

Protecting the business idea

Della will need to register her distinctive designs that are sold under the Eclipse name.

Figure 5.11

The Eclipse logo

assignment focus

At this stage you may wish to create a distinctive business name or a logo for your business venture that you will complete for P4 and M1. Alternatively you may wish to trade under your own name.

Marketing Strategy and Tactics

Strategy is about where a business is going. Tactics are about how it will get there

Remember that a business can only succeed by selling goods and services to its customers. The marketing function has the crucial tasks of:

■ identifying exactly what customers want by conducting market research and analysing the results

■ satisfying customer demand by providing the right products, in the right place at the right time.

The business plan will include both the marketing strategy of the business and the tactics it will use to achieve this:

Figure 5.12

The business plan workflow

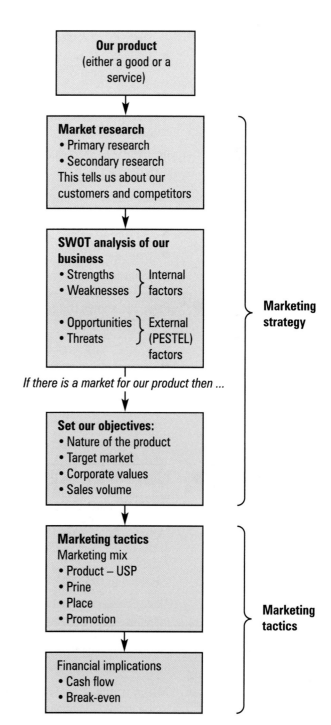

The starting point – our business idea

Is there a market for our product?

Can our business take advantage of this market oppurtunity?

Our marketing objectives, What sales do we hope to achieve?

How will we achieve these sales?

Will we survive? Will we be profitable?

Link We also cover marketing activities in Unit 3.

The marketing strategy

The marketing strategy is based upon the information gained from market research. It sets out the marketing objectives, which include:

- the goods or services to be produced – it may be that market research causes the original idea to be changed
- the target market, e.g. the product may be aimed at a specific age group, at males or females, at those with a certain lifestyle or at a particular economic group. Mobile phone companies are targeting students – how are they doing this?
- the values we will use to help us to compete, which include the image and reputation we wish to be recognised by. Ethical or green issues could be important here. In our case study, for example, Eclipse creates hand-crafted natural products
- the scale of operation and the level of sales we hope to achieve, expressed as either volume (units) or turnover (value).

Market research

Market research investigates the potential customers of a business and the competition it may expect.

Primary (or field) research collects data for the first time. Here researchers try to discover the likely demand for a new product through a number of methods, including:

- interviews
- direct observation
- questionnaires and surveys
- trialling products
- sampling the population.

Link Page 221 shows the primary research methods used by Eclipse pottery.

Secondary research uses existing information such as:

- government publications
- local sources, including the local authority, Business Link and Chamber of Commerce
- trade or industry sources such as **trade associations**, CBI (Confederation of British Industry), trades unions
- specialist market reports.

Link Pages 9–10 and the BTEC 'Guidance and units' also provide sources of secondary research.

Market research should show us whether there is a gap in the market for our product (think of the Yes/No bins for Innocent Drinks). We may find that our product needs to be adapted, or perhaps we need to develop a different product altogether (remember the earlier ideas discarded by the Innocent Drinks team before they developed 'smoothies').

Market research should also confirm the nature of our target market. For example, will our potential customers be male or female? How old are they? What is their occupational group? Ethnic group? Geographical area? Post code? Such knowledge will enable us to market our products more effectively. Innocent Drinks trialled their drinks at a music festival because the age and lifestyle of the audience represented their target market.

Mass market versus niche market

Whilst large corporations have the resources to mass market their products, a smaller business may need to concentrate on a more specialised 'niche' market. In the car industry, for example, multinational household names such as Ford, Toyota and Renault compete fiercely to maintain huge sales worldwide. Morgan, on the other hand, succeeds by supplying a small number of premium-priced vehicles each week to the sports-car market.

Eclipse Pottery

Marketing strategy

Della has some local market experience. However, she and Wayne decide to gather more detail. They use three methods of primary research:

- sending samples of pottery to local craft shops to get feedback
- holding focus groups – meetings with selected local restaurants and pubs to discuss the potential for customised dinner sets
- asking the opinions of customers at craft fairs via a questionnaire – respondents will be entered in a prize draw to encourage participation.

Competitor analysis will involve:

- looking at dinner sets already stocked by craft shops
- observing the two local potteries, Pot Pourri and Cassius Clay's, and acting as 'mystery shoppers' to see the product range, prices and means of payment
- scanning the local press to find out how competitors are promoting themselves.

For secondary research, the partners consult:

- the local Business Link via the internet
- the local Chamber of Commerce
- the local trade directories – to find out about competition
- Key Note publications and *Business Monitors* – to look at the trends in the sector
- the local press.

The partners use the research data to draw up the marketing strategy shown on page 240.

SWOT analysis

A SWOT analysis (Table 5.4) looks at the internal strengths and weakness of the business itself and at the opportunities and threats from outside. This shows how a business is placed to take advantage of the demand for its product.

Table 5.4 SWOT analysis

Strengths	Weaknesses
This section looks at the internal resources of the business and how effectively they are used including: ■ physical resources – quality and suitability of equipment, premises, vehicles ■ human resources – quality of employees, motivation, organisation, communication systems ■ financial resources – the funds available to the business ■ effectiveness of the functional areas and communication between them ■ effectiveness of leadership and management ■ suitability of business location, quality of products, effectiveness of corporate image.	
Opportunities	**Threats**
These are the external PESTEL factors (political, economic, social, technological, environmental and legal) that we discuss on page 46. Remember that businesses cannot control these but must respond to them.	

The SWOT analysis that Della and Wayne conduct for the pottery is shown in the business plan on page 240.

Eclipse Pottery

Marketing objectives

The partners use the results gained from market research to set out precise marketing objectives. They will aim for sales of 300 dinner sets in the first six months priced at £120 each (Table 5.5).

Table 5.5 Sales budget

	Apr	May	Jun	July	Aug	Sept	Total
Sales volume (units)	30	40	50	60	70	50	300
Sales revenue (@ £120 per unit)	3,600	4,800	6,000	7,200	8,400	6,000	36,000

The complete marketing objectives of Eclipse appear in the business plan on page 240.

The danger of overtrading

A business must be realistic when setting its sales targets. Chasing high levels of sales will involve extra cost. If sales revenue does not grow quickly enough, severe **cashflow problems** may result.

Marketing tactics

The tactics are the means by which the business will achieve the objectives in its marketing strategy. The key is to create an effective marketing mix through use of the four Ps:

■ product – the good or service that we will sell must be perceived as somehow attractive or desirable. It may, for example, be unique, high quality and so on. Customer service, guarantees and after-sales support are also part of the package

■ price – the amount that we will charge for our products including credit terms and discounts. Price will be determined by a number of factors such as the quality of the product, the target market, and the strength of the competition

■ place – where the customers can buy the products. We may sell from a shop, via the internet, by mail order, by telephone, on the doorstep, etc.

■ promotion – the means by which we will tell our customers about our products and persuade them to buy. We might use a variety of methods including: advertising in the appropriate media, branding to present the right image, sponsoring a personality, organisation or event, trade promotions to get our goods into the shops, public relations to gain favourable publicity or sales promotions perhaps involving discounts, competitions or special offers as an incentive for retailers to stock the product.

Unit 3 examines promotional activities in detail.

All businesses will need to develop a USP (unique selling point) – a reason why people will buy our products rather than those of our competitors. This might be:

■ competitive pricing – 'never knowingly undersold', 'find it cheaper and we'll refund the difference'

■ outstanding customer service – 'no quibble returns policy for unwanted purchases', 'same day delivery', '2 year warranty on parts and labour'

■ the product – 'hand-crafted', 'pure wool', 'smooth and creamy'

■ the location – 'at a high street near you', 'beat the queues buy online now'

or any combination of these and other factors.

The tactics the partners of Eclipse will use to sell their products are shown in the business plan on pages 240–1.

Producing a detailed business plan

To achieve P3, produce a marketing strategy including information on products/services to be offered, market research and marketing activities proposed.

For this task you should:

■ produce a marketing strategy for your chosen business idea. Include details of your product (either good or service), the market research that you will undertake, the scale of operation including your sales target (this could be in units of good to be sold, or revenue to be generated by providing a service)

■ give details of the marketing tactics you will use. Here you will need to identify your USP and explain how you will use each of the four Ps in the marketing mix.

A Plan for a New Business Venture

At this stage, it is useful to look at how the components of a business plan will fit together (Figure 5.13).

Notice that all costs and revenues from marketing and operations are brought together in the financial plan. This will tell us whether the business can achieve its fundamental business aims of survival and growth. If the plan is not viable, it will need to be revised.

So far we have considered the business idea, the legal structure of the business, start-up finance needed and the marketing strategy and tactics.

We know what we will sell, we now need:

■ an operational plan to show how we will run the business

■ a legal plan to identify our responsibilities in law

■ a financial plan to see if the business will be viable, i.e. if we can survive and whether it will be worth the effort.

Almost inevitably a new entrepreneur will need help and support from a network of outside agencies when drawing up this plan. They will also need to identify their own development needs.

The operational plan

This shows how the business will produce and distribute the goods or services it intends to sell. The plan will therefore identify the physical and human resources needed and their cost. A manufacturing business may include a production schedule detailing exactly how sales targets will be met.

Business inevitably involves risk ('nothing ventured nothing gained'). However, within its operational plan, a business should include strategies to identify and minimise risk wherever possible.

Physical resources include:

■ capital items – long lasting fixed assets including premises, equipment, furniture, fittings and vehicles. It is useful to draw up a capital budget listing all capital items required

■ stocks, consisting of either:
  ▪ the materials used in production by a manufacturer or
  ▪ the goods a retailer will buy in order to re-sell.
  A production schedule will help to identify exact requirements and their timing (the Eclipse example appears below). Details of suppliers should be provided together with terms of delivery and payment

■ other consumables, such as cleaning materials, stationery, etc. should be listed, again with the cost.

remember
Fixed assets purchased by the business are not included as business costs when calculating break-even. Depreciation on these items is a cost as is the leasing or renting assets.

remember
Neither drawings nor dividends should be included in business costs when calculating break-even.

Figure 5.13

How the components of a business plan fit together

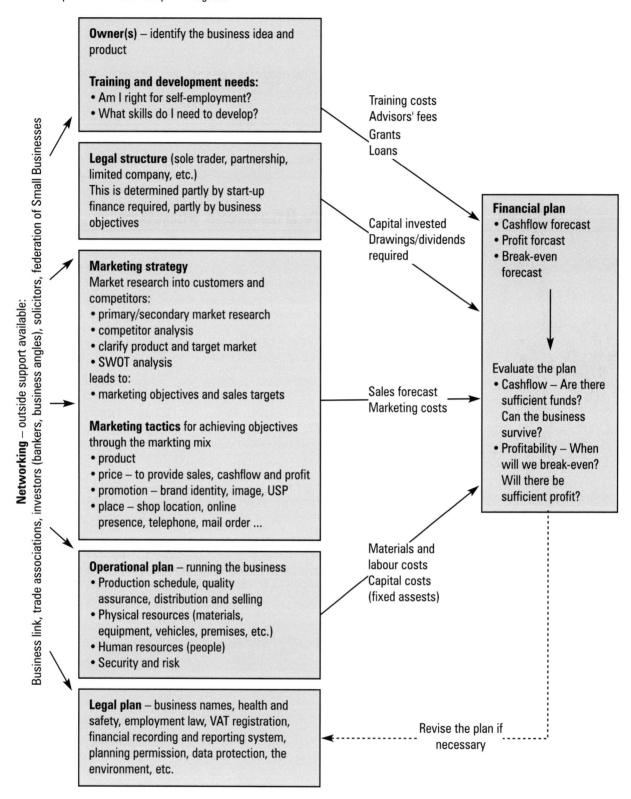

Human resources (or people) may include:

- the owner(s) – either sole trader, partners or company shareholders. Sole traders and partners will be rewarded by drawings usually paid monthly in the same way as a salary. Company shareholders are rewarded by dividends usually paid annually

- employees – the number of employees, their roles and the likely wage or salary bill should be included. There may also be recruitment and training costs. We examine the legal requirements of employers below

- outsourced staff – rather than employ staff directly, a business may choose to engage outside providers such as sub-contractors, accountants, solicitors, security firms, and so on. This will avoid the legal responsibilities of employment and may provide flexibility if demand rises or falls. Staff may be a fixed or variable cost, depending on their role.

Other operating costs

The operational plan will itemise any other costs involved in running the business, including the overheads of rent and rates, maintenance, light and heat, insurance, telephone and post, water, vehicle running costs, etc. These are fixed costs.

Eclipse Pottery

Operational planning

As part of their operations plan the partners draw up a production schedule to show how they will meet their monthly sales budget. Maximum capacity is 60 units a month and so some items must be made ahead of time to spread the workload (Table 5.6).

Table 5.6 Production schedule to meet monthly sales budget (no. of units)

	Apr	May	Jun	July	Aug	Sept	Total
Sales budget	30	40	50	60	70	50	300
Production schedule	40	45	50	60	60	45	300

This, together with costs of production, appears in the Eclipse operations plan (page 242).

assignment focus

1 If your business is a manufacturer, draw up a production plan to show how your own business will meet your sales budget.

2 Whatever your business, draw up a production cost budget. You will need this later for your cashflow forecast.

Some hints:

- If you are a manufacturer proceed as above. You may need to take an average cost per unit depending upon what you produce.

- If you are a retailer, decide on your mark-up – the relationship between the purchase price of your stock and your sales price. For example, if each item you buy for £1 you sell for £2, then your monthly purchase cost will be half of your monthly sales revenue.

- If you provide a different type of service (perhaps a gig as a DJ, a sports **coaching** session, baby-sitting, car servicing), you will need to establish what (if any) the variable costs of your service are.

The business must be able to operate with the resources available. The costs of the business operations and their timing will be entered into the financial forecasts.

Legal planning

Legal requirements are many and complex, and they vary from business to business. The Business Link website provides an electronic questionnaire to show individual entrepreneurs the laws applying to their own particular businesses. Here we provide general details.

Consumer law

- The Supply of Goods and Services Act (1982) states that goods must be of 'satisfactory quality' and 'fit for the purpose for which they are sold'. A buyer who has a genuine complaint about faulty goods can ask for money to be refunded by the supplier or for compensation if the goods are retained. It may be costly to take a supplier to court although the small claims court will make this less expensive.

- The Consumer Safety Act (1987) protects the consumer from harmful goods.

- The Trades Descriptions Act states that goods must 'as described' including any weights and measures. For example, 'ice cream' must contain a given amount of cream and a 1 kg bag of sugar must contain 1 kg. Inspectors from the local town hall enforce this Act.

Employment law

Relevant laws include the Employment Act (2002), Sex Discrimination Act (1975), Equal Pay Act (1970), Race Relations Act (1976), Disability Discrimination Act (1975), European Working Time Directive (2002).

The most important legal provisions are as follows.

- Discrimination on grounds of race, sex, disability, sexual orientation, religion or philosophical belief is illegal.

- You must be prepared to make 'reasonable adjustments' to enable disabled people to work or continue working.

- You must provide a secure, safe and healthy working environment.

- Within the first two months of employment, an employee must receive a written contract of employment showing terms and conditions.

- Most employees are entitled to work a 48-hour maximum average working week and minimum rest periods.

- Employees are entitled to a minimum of four weeks' paid leave a year and may also be entitled to maternity leave, paternity leave, adoption leave and leave for family reasons.

- Part-time workers must be treated no less favourably than full-time staff.

- Your employees have the right to the current national minimum wage. At times they may be entitled to statutory sick pay (SSP) or statutory maternity pay (SMP).

- You must deduct income tax and National Insurance (NI) contributions from your employees' wages under PAYE (Pay As You Earn), and send these to HM Revenue & Customs. Employees must be given a payslip itemising pay and deductions.

Data Protection Act 1998

If your business holds any personal information about clients or employees, you may need to notify the Data Protection Commissioner and abide by their conditions.

Health and safety

The Health and Safety at Work Act (HASAWA) makes a business owner responsible for the health and safety of everyone affected by their business and its activities. This includes:

- employees working at your premises, from home or at another site

- visitors, such as customers or subcontractors

- members of the public (even if they're outside your premises).

You are also responsible for anyone affected by products and services you design, produce or supply.

HASAWA is enforced by the Health & Safety Executive (HSE).

www.hse.gov.uk

Record-keeping and taxation

All businesses must keep accurate financial records to enable them to send an income statement (showing profits or losses) and a balance sheet (showing the value of the business) to HM Revenue & Customs at the end of each financial year.

These annual accounts enable taxation to be calculated: sole traders and partners are charged income tax and National Insurance on an individual basis, whilst companies pay corporation tax. Company directors are employees and are taxed on PAYE in the normal way.

Where a business exceeds the annual turnover (sales revenue) allowed in the Chancellor's budget, it must charge **VAT** on its sales and make a VAT return every three months (or, for smaller businesses, every year).

Under the Companies Acts (1985 and 1989), limited companies have additional legal responsibilities. They must also:

- publish an annual report and accounts
- present this to the shareholders for approval at the AGM (annual general meeting)
- send a copy of the report and accounts to Companies House where they are made available to the general public (for a small fee).

Accounts of larger companies must be audited (checked) by an independent firm of chartered accountants.

Strategies for minimising risk

These might involve insurance and contingency planning.

Insurance

It is not possible to insure against being a bad entrepreneur. However, it is possible to insure against a variety of business risks.

Liability insurance will help pay any compensation and legal costs that occur if an employer is found to be at fault. Examples are:

- employers' liability insurance, covering damage to employees
- public liability insurance, covering damage to the public
- product liability, covering damage resulting from a faulty product.

Other insurances are available for:

- premises and contents – covering buildings, stock and equipment
- consequential loss (business interruption) – to help with ongoing fixed costs if a disaster, such as a fire or flood, closes the businesses for some time
- theft from buildings and vehicles
- breakages including goods in transit
- fidelity – what if an employee runs off with the money?
- personal insurance, e.g. income protection and critical illness insurance
- motor insurance – the law requires at least third party insurance to protect innocent bystanders and their property
- life assurance – in a partnership each partner will have an insurable interest in other partners.

Contingency planning

A business is wise to prepare for the unexpected. One way is to look at a 'worst-case scenario' (the worst that can happen) and see how it will react. Insurance alone may not be enough. For example, investigations following post-2000 terrorist attacks showed that:

- 80 per cent of businesses directly involved in incidents closed within 18 months
- 90 per cent of businesses losing data as a result of incidents closed within two years (source: BBC).

In an information-led economy, businesses are wise to at least keep back-up copies of data on a separate site.

case study 5.9 — Boscastle

On 16 August 2004, the Cornish coastal village of Boscastle was devastated by a flash flood when heavy rain caused local rivers to overflow.

The main livelihood of the village is tourism and many businesses including gift shops and restaurants had their stock destroyed. Vehicles were washed into the sea and premises badly damaged or even destroyed.

The reconstruction work was still going on more than a year later.

Figure 5.14

activity

The events at Boscastle in 2004 show the importance planning for the unexpected and in particular the need to insure.

1 Which insurance policies would protect businesses affected by such a disaster?
2 'Self-assurance' exists where a business chooses not to insure, but instead to bear the risk itself. Can you explain why a business may choose to do this for certain risks?
3 Name some risks that must be insured by law. Why is this?

The environment

A business will need permission from the local authority to use its premises for business purposes and planning permission for any new building work. There will also be local regulations about noise, pollution, parking and access, delivery times and out-of-hours working.

Additionally, the 1990 Environmental Protection Act applies to all businesses.

Licensing

Some types of business, such as those dealing in food, gaming, animals, caring and the entertainment business, will need a licence from the local authority before they are able to trade.

case study 5.10 — Nemesis for Alton Towers?

Tussauds Theme Parks Ltd, owners of Alton Towers in Staffordshire, have been found guilty of statutory noise nuisance under the 1990 Environmental Protection Act. The judge agreed that the 'the screams and mechanical noise' were a nuisance to neighbours and gave the owners three months to come up with a plan to quieten things down.

Source: *The Guardian*, August 2004

activity

As well as theme parks, pubs and clubs, sporting events and late night shopping venues may create disturbance for nearby residents.

1 What (if any) environmental problems are likely to be posed by your chosen business?
2 What laws apply?
3 What are the solutions?

Eclipse Pottery

Legal planning

The partners have decided to keep things simple.

■ They will not to directly employ staff. Instead Debbie will work with a local self-employed potter who will charge on the basis of items produced. They will therefore not be affected by employment law.

■ The partners will keep their accounts on a small business integrated software package. They will enter customers' names and addresses, and in future may need employee payroll details. They will check their position with the Data Protection Registrar.

■ The public will not visit the showroom although this may change if the business expands.

■ The pottery trade does not yet need a licence, although in time the partners may open a café.

Della and Wayne balance the cost of insurance premiums against the expected risk. Finally they opt to cover premises, contents, breakages, product liability, public liability and personal accident. Both partners already have private life assurance policies.

Self-development planning

On pages 204–5, we suggested that an aspiring entrepreneur should identify their strengths and weakness and general suitability for running a business. The business plan should address ways in which any personal development needs are to be met. This may involve self-study, **mentoring** or coaching, or support from the agencies mentioned below.

Networking and accessing external sources of help and advice

We have mentioned that an entrepreneur must be prepared to seek help and advice as and when it is needed. The range of local sources of information available to small businesses includes:

■ high street banks – the small business adviser has the role of interviewing small businesses when they apply to the bank for financial support. Template business plans and information packs are made available and the adviser will consider business proposals to decide whether the bank will be prepared to help. Finance may be provided in the form of loans, overdrafts or factoring arrangements on condition that the adviser continues to visit the business to provide ongoing monitoring and support

■ the local Business Link –provides a variety of forms of support for businesses at a regional level

■ trade associations – provide information, help and advice to businesses engaged in particular types of activity. Associations cover a diverse range of industries ranging from the well-known Association of British Travel Agents (ABTA) to the Association of British Orchestras, the Aromatherapy Trade Council and even the British Christmas Tree Growers Association

■ investors – for a small business these may include family members, venture capitalists and business angels

assignment focus

Identify the appropriate trade association for your proposed business by referring to the Trade Association Forum website (www.taforum.org)

We discuss venture capital and business angels on page 214.

■ solicitors – provide help with legal matters such as conveyancing (purchase of property), drawing up contracts, e.g. the partnership agreement prepared for Eclipse (on page 212) and setting up companies

■ accountants – assist with financial matters including planning, setting up recording systems, tax advice and auditing accounts at the end of each financial year

■ local Chambers of Commerce – represent local businesses of all sizes and from all sectors. Their aim is to promote, help and support the businesses within their area by providing information, arranging events and pressing for changes that they feel will stimulate economic activity

■ Federation of Small Businesses – exists to support to small businesses within the UK as a whole.

www.fsb.org.uk

Financial planning

The financial plan brings together all of the costs and revenues forecast in the marketing plan and the operational plan. It tests the viability of the business by estimating both cashflow and profitability (Figure 5.15).

Figure 5.15

Cashflow and profitability

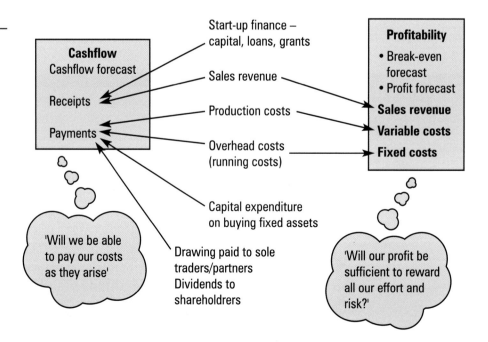

Some businesses will also include a forecast balance sheet as a check on the accuracy of the calculations and to estimate the value of the business at the end of the period. A balance sheet is not required to achieve this unit.

Notice that all estimated receipts and payments are entered to the cashflow forecast. However, only certain of these items are used when we calculate profits. Not included in the profit calculation are:

■ capital expenditure on fixed assets – not regarded as a cost because these assets will last longer than the trading period in question.

■ drawings and dividends are personal, rather than business, expenditure

■ finance from owners' capital or borrowing is not a trading income.

Cashflow monitoring

The cashflow forecast shows the monthly receipts and payments that will result from business operations and the cash position at the end of each month. At this stage you may wish to re-read pages 42–3 in Unit 1.

Remember that:

■ cashflow is about survival – without cash, bills do not get paid

■ the purpose of the cashflow forecast is to anticipate future cash needs. This will allow a business to anticipate cash shortages and arrange to deal with them

■ in the cashflow forecast, receipts and payments are entered to the months in which money will be received or paid. This is not always the month in which a sale or purchase is made

■ the bottom line of the forecast estimates the cash available each month. A negative bottom line indicates a cash shortage.

Eclipse Pottery

Anticipating cashflow problems

The sales forecast and cashflow forecast are part of the financial plan drawn up by the partners at Eclipse (Table 5.7).

See page 246 for the interpretation of the Eclipse cashflow forecast.

This will enable them to anticipate potential cashflow problems.

The cashflow cycle

Cashflow is not just a matter of the value of receipts and payments, but also of their timing. The **cashflow cycle** determines when receipts and the payments will occur as production takes place.

Clearly, the longer the interval between stages 1 and 2 (buying stocks and using them in production) and stage 4 (receiving payment), the more likely it is that a business will have cashflow difficulties. For example, a difficulty for many new businesses (including Eclipse) is that they must buy supplies for cash whilst allowing credit to customers.

Notice that as well as production costs, businesses also need sufficient working capital to pay overheads, to purchase fixed assets, to repay loans and to reward the owners.

Managing the cashflow cycle

A business will try to adjust the timings within the cashflow cycle to its advantage by delaying payment and bringing forward receipts. Tactics might include:

■ buying JIT (just-in-time for production) – this prevents unnecessarily tying up cash in unwanted stocks. It will also minimise the costs associated with storage such as: warehouse wages, rent, damage and obsolescence

■ buying on credit – it may even be possible to sell the stocks before payment is due. Supermarkets do this and are 'cash rich' as a result

■ selling for cash wherever possible ('cash' means immediate payment and so includes plastic cards and cheques)

Table 5.7 Sales and cashflow forecasts for Eclipse

Sales forecast	Apr £	May £	Jun £	July £	Aug £	Sept £	Total £
Sales	3,600	4,800	6,000	7,200	8,400	6,000	36,000

Notes	Cashflow forecast Figures to nearest £	At start £	Apr £	May £	Jun £	July £	Aug £	Sept £	Total £	Notes
	Receipts									
	Cash sales								0	
30 day credit	Cash from debtors		3,600	4,800	6,000	7,200	8,400	30,000	6,000	Debtors
	New capital	15,000							15,000	
	Bank loan	5,000							5,000	
	Total receipts (A)	20,000	0	3,600	4,800	6,000	7,200	8,400	50,000	
Materials	Payments									
	Cash purchases		800	900	1,000	1,200	1,200	900	6,000	Creditors
	Cash to creditors									
	Drawings		2,000	2,000	2,000	2,000	2,000	2,000	12,000	
	Production wages		600	675	750	900	900	675	4,500	
	Transport/distribution		40	40	40	40	40	40	240	
Fixed assets	Capital items	19,000							19,000	
	Rent/rates		2,200			1,100			3,300	
	Insurance		2,000						2,000	
	Light/heat				700			700	1,400	
	Advertising		1,200						1,200	
	Loan repayments		80	80	80	80	80	80	480	
	Interest charges		10	10	10	10	10	10	60	
	General admin		50	50	50	50	50	50	300	
	Total payments (B)	19,000	8,980	3,755	4,630	5,380	4,280	4,455	50,480	
	Net cashflow (A-B)	1,000	(8,980)	(155)	170	620	2,920	3,945	(480)	
	add Opening balance b/d	0	1,000	(7,980)	(8,135)	(7,965)	(7,345)	(4,425)	0	
	Closing balance c/d	1,000	(7,980)	(8,135)	(7,965)	(7,345)	(4,425)	(480)	(480)	

- exercising effective credit control so that where customers do demand credit their payments are collected on time
- making a factoring arrangement with a bank to get some of the money immediately.

 Link　See page 215 for details of factoring.

Attracting extra funding

Even when a business is operating efficiently, the cashflow forecast may still indicate periods where there will be cash shortages. In general, further cash can be generated by:

- equity, i.e. new capital from the owners. This may mean changing the legal status of the business from a sole trader to a partnership, whilst a company may sell new shares
- debt, i.e. borrowing from a friend, relative or financial institution. Purchase of fixed assets will be financed by long-term borrowing in the form of loans and mortgages, whilst daily working capital needs can be financed by short-term borrowing such as a bank overdraft.

Figure 5.16

The cashflow cycle

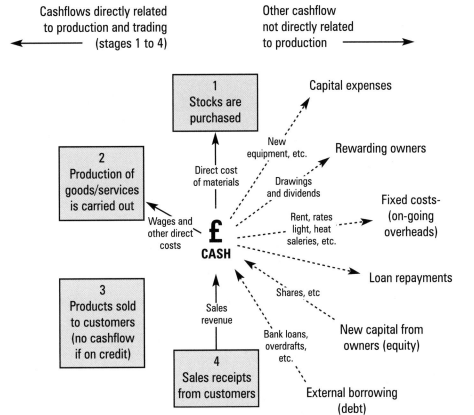

Cashflows directly related to production and trading (stages 1 to 4) ← | → Other cashflow not directly related to production

Profitability

The break-even forecast shows the sales needed to cover costs and break-even.

You may wish to remind yourself by re-reading pages 22–24 in Unit 1.

The profit forecast (or income statement) shows the profit or loss the business can expect to achieve at the predicted level of sales. Remember that these profits will be used to reward the owner(s) in the form of drawings or dividends. Any remaining profits will be 'ploughed back' to finance future growth.

Eclipse Pottery

The break-even point

The partners produce and sell a single unit – a dinner set made to a standard design. Their estimates for the first six months are:

- maximum capacity: 360 units over six months (operational plan)
- forecast sales: 300 units over six months (marketing plan)
- sales price: £120 a unit (marketing plan)
- fixed costs: £8,500 for the six-month period (operational plan)
- variable costs: £35 per unit (operational plan) (i.e. potter's wages £15 per unit and raw materials £20 a unit)
- contribution: £85 per unit (i.e. £120 sales revenue per unit less £35 variable cost per unit).

The partners draw up a table of costs, revenues and profits for different levels of production and sales (Table 5.8).

The partners calculate the exact break-even point by using the formula:

$$\text{Break-even point} = \frac{\text{Total fixed costs}}{\text{Contribution per unit}} = \frac{£8,500}{£85} = 100 \text{ dinner sets}$$

Table 5.8 Break-even point for Eclipse

Maximum output	Period fixed costs	Unit variable costs		Unit sales price	
360 units	£8,500	£35		£120	
Units	**Fixed cost £**	**Variable cost £**	**Total cost £**	**Sales revenue £**	**Profit/(loss) £**
0	8,500	0	8,500	0	(8,500)
60	8,500	2,100	10,600	7,200	(3,400)
120	8,500	4,200	12,700	14,400	1,700
180	8,500	6,300	14,800	21,600	6,800
240	8,500	8,400	16,900	28,800	11,900
300	8,500	10,500	19,000	36,000	17,000
360	8,500	12,600	21,100	43,200	22,100

Alternatively:

Break-even point = 100 units @ £120 each = £12,000

They use the table to construct a break-even chart (Figure 5.17).

Figure 5.17

The break-even chart for Eclipse

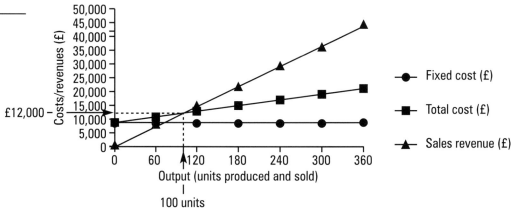

Table 5.9 Profit forecast (or forecast income statement) for the period from April to September

	£	Notes
Sales	36,000	(300 units @ £120 each)
Variable production cost	10,500	(300 units @ £35 each)
GROSS PROFIT	25,500	
Fixed cost	8,500	
NET PROFIT	17,000	
less Partner's drawings	12,000	
Retained Profits	5,000	Ploughed back into the business

Break-even for a service business and multi-product businesses

Eclipse sells a single product. However, many businesses sell a variety of goods and services at different prices. For these 'multi-product' businesses, it may be possible to calculate an 'average unit' and find break-even in the normal way. However, where this is not realistic an alternative method is illustrated below.

Top-Crust: a multi-product business

Top-Crust provides a variety of take-away sandwiches, rolls and drinks. There is no standard unit so we estimate monthly sales revenues instead. Estimates for the first six months are:

- sales: £2,000 per month

- variable costs (bread, fillings, tea, etc.): £800 per month

- fixed costs for the six-month period: £5,000

It is important to understand that:

Sales £2,000 – Variable cost £800 = Gross profit £1,200

We can now calculate two essential percentages:

- variable cost will be 40 per cent of sales (£800 variable costs ÷ £2,000 sales × 100)

- gross profit will be 60 per cent of sales (£1,200 ÷ £2,000 sales × 100)

In our table sales revenues replace units:

Table 5.10 Break-even point for Top Crust

Maximum sales revenue	Period fixed cost	Variable cost as % of sales
12,000	£5,000	40%

Sales revenue £	Fixed cost £	Variable cost £	Total cost £	Sales revenue £	Profit/loss £
0	5,000	0	5,000	0	(5,000)
2,000	5,000	800	5,800	2,000	(3,800)
4,000	5,000	1,600	6,600	4,000	(2,600)
6,000	5,000	2,400	7,400	6,000	(1,400)
8,000	5,000	3,200	8,200	8,000	(200)
10,000	5,000	4,000	9,000	10,000	1,000
12,000	5,000	4,800	9,800	12,000	2,200

| Break-even point in sales revenue | | £8,333 | | | |

Figure 5.18

Break-even chart for Top Crust

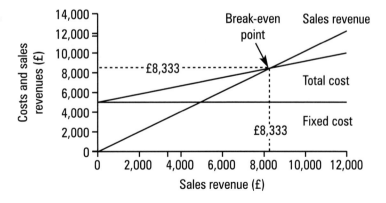

Notice that break-even is achieved when sales reach £8,333. The formula used here is:

Break-even point (in £s) = Fixed cost £5,000 ÷ Gross profit percentage 60%

What if? and electronic spreadsheets

A business may wish to consider a range of possibilities, called 'What if? scenarios', before finalising their financial plan. For example, they might ask: 'What if sales in August are 10 per cent lower than predicted?', 'What if suppliers increase the cost of materials?', 'What if strong competition forces us to reduce prices?'

remember

Your plan must be coherent so that, for example, the financial forecasts clearly relate to the marketing and operational plans.

A common technique is to look at a 'worst-case scenario' (the worst that could happen) to see if the business could still survive.

An electronic spreadsheet model will enable a business to carry out these operations quickly and accurately. As the key variables (such as the sales price, materials costs, etc.) are changed, the spreadsheet will instantly recalculate the figures. Charts can be linked to a spreadsheet model to illustrate the figures. These will adjust automatically whenever data are entered.

The Microsoft Excel template used for the Eclipse financial plan is supplied as a resource on the Nelson Thornes website at www.nelsonthornes.com/btec. This will generate a cashflow forecast, a break-even forecast and an income statement.

assignment focus

1 Construct the spreadsheet using the template on the Nelson Thornes website. You should use exactly the same cells or the formulae will not work. Depending upon your expertise and needs you may wish to adapt this template for your own use.

2 Test that the sheet works by entering some data into the receipts and payments sections of the cashflow forecast.

   Note: If you enter the receipts and payments from the Eclipse cashflow forecast on page 32, the break-even and profit forecasts should appear automatically.

3 You can now construct your own financial plan. Any changes to the original data will update the rest of the sheet automatically.

   At a later stage you can examine the strength of your business idea by setting up What if? scenarios. These can be used in the evaluation of your business plan to gain grade D1.

assignment focus

Producing a detailed business plan

1 To achieve P4, provide documents related to realistic financial planning for the business.

   For this task, you should draw up the financial plan for your business for a six- or 12-month period. You should include:

   a) a cashflow forecast

   b) a break-even forecast and break-even chart

   c) profit forecast.

   You may design a spreadsheet for this purpose or enter your figures into a commercially supplied template (we supply a suitable model at www.nelsonthornes.com/btec).

   You should now be in a position to assemble your business plan.

2 To achieve M1, your plan must be professionally presented and you should also include a summary of your proposals in your final plan that show how you have carefully analysed your options giving justifications for the decisions you have taken.

Evaluating the business plan: Is the business plan viable?

We need to be sure that our business plan is a realistic guide to what will happen when we start trading. We need to examine all sections of the plan to ensure that it is viable. Here are some questions we might ask.

Marketing strategy and tactics

■ Is our market research accurate, up-to-date and sufficient? Have we really established that there is a market for our product?

■ Do we really have a quality product that can compete in the marketplace?

■ Will our marketing mix generate sufficient demand for our product?

Operational plan

- Can we deliver quality products (goods or services) to our customers on time? Do we really have the resources, systems and expertise to operate the business effectively?

- Have we covered all of the legal angles?

- Are we suitably insured and do we have **contingency plans** for the unexpected?

Financial plan

- Will we generate enough cashflow to survive? How will we fund any shortages? The unexpected can happen, have we planned for a 'worst-case scenario?'

- Will there be sufficient profit to reward the owners and make all of the effort and risk worthwhile? For example, how does the reward compare with the safer option of investing savings in a bank and taking up employment?

If aspects of the plan are unsatisfactory, then changes will need to made. Perhaps there is a need to carry out further research, raise more finance, raise prices, sell more, cut costs, and so on. Once the plan is finalised the business will adopt the sales forecast, production schedule and financial forecasts as targets (or budgets) for the period.

Monitoring the plan

Each month, as the business trades, the actual results will be monitored against the budgets set in the business plan. Any differences (or variances) will be investigated in an attempt to correct problems before they become serious.

Eclipse Pottery

Is the business plan viable?

Della already has experience as a potter and of the market she will enter. Wayne has business expertise. The partners believe that their plan is based upon sound research and exposes them to little risk.

However, the financial forecasts (pages 243–5) show that there is a potential cashflow problem in the first six months. It is hoped to negotiate a suitable overdraft facility using Della's property as security.

Contingency plans

In the event of costs being higher than expected, sales falling below predicted levels or the bank not agreeing the overdraft facility, then the partners can make the following adjustments:

- cut down start-up costs by buying capital equipment on credit or leasing it

- arrange for the bank to factor the debts (see page 215). Once the business is established, it should be able to negotiate credit terms with suppliers

- reduce drawings. The partners are committed to their business idea and have sufficient savings to operate without drawings for the first year if necessary.

Risk is further reduced because:

- only limited stocks and finished goods will be stored at the property

- each partner will hold a back-up copy of data

- there will be no employees

- suitable insurance will be taken out.

1 *Presenting your plan*

To achieve M2, you must now present your plan to a bank manager who may provide funding for your venture. You should:

- prepare and deliver a short oral presentation to support and justify your business idea

- use visual aids, such as OHP (overhead projector), a flip chart or Powerpoint slides to illustrate the main points

- structure your presentation clearly, e.g. the business idea, key people, USP, the cashflow forecast, profitability

- invite questions and be prepared to answer them. This means that you need to have a good understanding of your idea and the research it is based upon.

You might wish to devise a structured feedback sheet with closed questions to cover both the quality of your presentation and of your business idea. This will help later with your evaluation for criterion D1.

2 *Evaluating and improving your plan*

Following your presentation, a number of points will have been raised. You must now produce a short, formal report (see Unit 4) that could be used as an annex or a handout to your main plan. You should cover:

a) criteria you have used to further evaluate the viability of your business plan. This will be the introduction to your report to show what you will cover. Examples might be:

- the business idea and USP

- the form of ownership

- the key people

- the financial viability – cashflow and profitability

b) an assessment of the strengths and weaknesses of:

- your proposed business (using the criteria above)

- the quality of your planning (including your research)

- how you have presented the proposals (both written and oral)

c) recommendations with justifications for how your plan or proposals should be strengthened so that you can start a viable business.

If you make suggestions for improving the financial forecasts, it will be useful to provide What if? scenarios to demonstrate the likely effects of these. If you have used a spreadsheet model, these can be produced automatically after changing relevant data.

Della Moon and Wayne Moon, trading as Eclipse
The Wheelhouse, Wateringham PL14 3CN
Tel (010101) 820541 Fax: (010101) 820557
E-mail: moon&son@netprobe.net

BUSINESS PLAN

Contents

Introduction
Marketing strategy
Marketing tactics
Operational plan
Legal plan
Sources of information
Financial plan
Evaluation
Appendix

Introduction

Business idea and aims

The business will produce and sell earthenware/ceramic 6-piece dinner sets to a standard design registered as 'Eclipse'. The finish will be to the specification of individual clients with whom we will work closely.

Our mission is to:

- provide a quality product supported by a quality service for customers
- establish a reputation for excellence initially at an area level
- establish the presence of the 'Eclipse' trade mark in the marketplace
- maximise profits through operations in a niche market
- concentrate on quality rather than quantity.

Management details

Key people: Della Moon (Design and production)
Date of birth: 18/08/51
Experience: Local government finance officer 22 years
Qualifications: 4 O-levels, OND Business and Finance
Expertise: Pottery exhibitions locally, won local design award 2004, sales to local business
Address: 23 Factory Row, Wateringham PL6 2QF
Tel: 01010 454545

Wayne Moon (Marketing)
Date of birth: 07/10/76
Occupation: Commercial artist (freelance)
Experience: 6 years of working on major contracts
Qualifications: 2 A-levels, Higher Diploma in Art & Design, Crossley College of Art
Expertise: Has working relationships with numerous potential business clients
Address: Roundwood, Warren Place, Penleigh
Tel: 01101 663410

Legal structure

The business will operate as follows:

Legal structure: Partnership
Partners: Della and Wayne Moon
Trading as: Eclipse
Business address: The Wheelhouse, Wateringham PL14 3CN
Tel (010101) 820541   Fax: (010101) 820557
E-mail: moon&son@netprobe.net

The partnership structure will enable the owners to pool their capital and skills whilst keeping regulatory requirements to a minimum. The partners do not foresee any significant risk in the venture that would necessitate limited liability.

Sources of start-up finance
Start-up finance will be raised as follows:

	£
Partners' capital:	
D. Moon	5,000
W. Moon	10,000
Bank loan	5,000
Total	20,000

It is intended that the Moon family retain control of the business. A bank loan secured against the property of W. Moon is therefore preferred to raising further capital by bringing in new partners.

Marketing strategy

Primary research has been concentrated on local businesses which we see as our initial market. Our investigations have taken the form of:

- a survey by questionnaire of a representative sample of potential consumers
- a survey of local businesses – we used a combination of visits, telephone calls and mailshots to ask a series of key questions.

Secondary research into the existing competition and the economic prospects for the area has used a variety of sources including the *Yellow Pages*, the local *Thomson Directory* and local statistics supplied by the local Business Link and Chamber of Commerce. In addition we have consulted the *Population Census*, *Labour Force Survey*, *ONS Unemployment Rates*, *Social Trends* and *Business Monitors*.

The trends that we have identified in tourism, local employment and population all support our belief that there is a gap in the market for our product.

Customers
We expect our customers to be:

- local restaurants
- local craft and gift shops
- one-off contracts for special commissions.

The market is expected to grow by roughly 5 per cent a year and we believe that there will be a continuing demand for quality pottery items that are distinctive and hand-crafted.

Competitors
The tableware that is generally available from retailers is not a substitute for our goods, which are differentiated by the quality of the designs and the image. We would therefore expect to have a local **monopoly** with all the benefits this would give us.

SWOT analysis
See Table 5.11.

Marketing objectives
Our objectives are to:
- establish a reputation in our niche market as a provider of distinctive, quality products
- achieve a turnover of £36,000 in the first six months by selling 300 units at a guide price of £120 for each dinner set:

Sales forecast

	Apr	May	Jun	July	Aug	Sept	Total
Sales volume (units)	30	40	50	60	70	50	300
Sales revenue (@ £120 per unit)	3,600	4,800	6,000	7,200	8,400	6,000	36,000

Marketing tactics
We will achieve our objectives through the following marketing mix.

Table 5.11

Strengths:	Weaknesses:
■ We are a local business. We understand our customers and will sell personalised products. ■ Our emphasis on quality and concentration on a niche market allows a potentially high mark-up. ■ A relatively small capital investment is required and we will incur little financial risk. ■ We have excellent premises, new equipment, and low running costs. ■ The flexibility allowed by sub-contracting production to a local potter will allow us to respond to market demand in the short term and to keep down fixed costs.	■ 30-day credit terms are necessary to gain sales but cash purchase of stock means that the business will need external finance in the early stages. ■ The business is initially dependent upon one large contract. ■ Maximum production is limited to 60 units per month at present. ■ Increasing turnover will require expansion and may bring the danger of overtrading.
Opportunities:	**Threats:**
■ The trend towards eating out will continue (source: *Household Expenditure Survey*) providing the potential for increased sales to restaurants. ■ The South-West tourist season may lengthen as cheap flights from Stansted to Newquay encourage short-break visitors. ■ There is potential for reaching a niche market via the internet. ■ Eclipse pottery with its natural wholesome image is well placed to benefit from consumers' growing preference for organic foods and a green lifestyle. ■ Our premises allow for future expansion and eventual workshop sales. ■ Students from the art college could be employed on a casual basis during peak times to provide additional flexible labour.	■ Increased legislation from the European Union in: health and safety, employment, the environment and consumer protection may place a burden on small businesses. ■ New competitors may enter the market via the internet.

Product

We will specialise in dinner sets bearing the distinctive 'Eclipse' motif. Our USP (unique selling point) will be our emphasis on personal designs using local knowledge, quality materials and craft.

We will concentrate on quality rather than volume in order to secure a niche in the market.

Price

In discussion with potential clients, we have identified an optimum unit price of £120. Potential sales are likely to fall sharply above this and there will be no significant rise with lower prices. Trade sales will be on 30-day credit.

Although we believe that people are willing to pay premium prices for goods, our low operating costs enable us to set prices that will deter new entrants to the market.

Promotion

All promotion will be geared towards portraying an image of quality.

The business name 'Eclipse' and logo have been carefully chosen to appeal to the ABC1 groups who will be our target market.

The business launch will consist of an open evening at 'The Wheelhouse' by invitation only with a guest list of local dignitaries and business people who may be potential clients. The local press have agreed to write a feature.

Della Moon's work is well known locally and examples, together with business contact details, are displayed in galleries in the area.

Eclipse will exhibit at craft fairs and exhibitions to gain exposure and we anticipate that much custom will come from reputation by 'word of mouth'.

The business name and telephone number have been entered in the *Yellow Pages* and *Thomson's Directory*, and we will build a database of all enquiries to add to Mr W. Moon's existing contacts.

We have produced a brochure of sample designs for mailing to interested parties together with business stationery. A 'brochureware' website is currently in preparation.

Promotional costs will be relatively modest with initial outlay likely to be:

■ launch evening: £500
■ brochures, business cards, stationery and mail-shot to selected customers: £700.

Place

Initially we intend to sell within a radius of approximately 50 miles. Sales will be on the following basis:

- direct to some customers such as the chain of vegetarian restaurants with whom we have already had discussions
- batches commissioned by selected local retailers
- individual commissions from customers at craft fairs, shows and exhibitions within the area. Where customers cannot collect the goods themselves, we will arrange delivery by independent carrier
- our website will act as a promotional brochure initially, although there will be a facility for contacting us about commissions.

We will not be dependent upon passing trade, although potential customers can come visit our workshop by arrangement. In future we may develop a showroom on the premises perhaps with a cafe.

Operational plan

A unit of production is one place-setting (six pieces of pottery).

Maximum production capacity is 60 units per month. This means that some orders must be produced in advance so as to meet sales deadlines.

Unit production costs will be:

- raw materials: £20 per unit
- labour: £15 per unit.

Production schedule

Table 5.12

	Apr	May	Jun	July	Aug	Sept	Total
Production volume (units)	40	45	50	60	60	45	300
Production cost (£)							
raw materials (@ £20)	800	900	1,000	1,200	1,200	900	6,000
labour (@ £15)	600	675	750	900	900	675	4,500

Quality assurance

Each batch will be inspected carefully before distribution to customers. Items will be carefully, sealed in boxes and stamped and dated as 'passed'.

Since our aim is to establish a reputation for quality, all 'seconds' will be destroyed – nothing is to be sold off cheaply.

Physical resources

Capital expenditure:
The following fixed assets will be purchased at start:

Table 5.13

	Cost (£)
'Jet Heat' electric kiln	9,000
'Multi-rev' potters' wheels	4,000
Specialist tools	2,000
Desk-top computer, laser printer	2,400
Office furniture	1,600
Total capital expenditure:	19,000

Premises:
'The Wheelhouse' premises with appropriate workshop and storage facilities will be rented.

Raw materials:
Raw materials (clay, glaze and paints) will be purchased on a JIT, cash-on-delivery basis from a local supplier who provides same-day delivery. Stocks will not be held as supplies are guaranteed.

Financial resources

£20,000 of start-up finance will be raised as shown in the introductory section.

Ultimately the partnership hopes to secure credit from suppliers, although this may not be possible in the early stages of the business.

Properties owned by both partners may be used as security against further loans or overdrafts. If necessary the partners will forego their drawings for the first year.

Overhead costs:
Estimates for the first six months are:

Table 5.14

	£	Details
Production overheads:		
Rent/rates	8,000	Rates £2,000, rent £3,000 quarterly (Apr/Jul) in advance
Light/heat	1,400	Paid quarterly (Jun/Sep) in arrears
Insurance	2,000	Paid in advance
Administration overheads:		
Transport/distribution	240	£40 monthly
Advertising	1,200	Cost of initial launch
Interest charges	60	£10 monthly
General administration	300	£50 monthly
	13,200	

Human resources
D. Moon will concentrate on design, W. Moon will run the marketing and finance aspects of the business. Initially each partner will take drawings of £1,000 a month.

Pottery production will be carried out by a contract potter working to D. Moon's design instructions. Production will be carried out on the firm's premises to ensure quality control. Payment will be £15 per saleable unit.

Legal plan
The premises are already designated for commercial use and comply with health and safety regulations. The remote location means that there will be no disruption to neighbouring properties and there is ample space for parking and loading.

Advice has been taken from the local authority concerning health and safety issues and the workshop is passed as safe.

Employment laws are not applicable as the potter is self-employed and works on a sub-contract basis.

Initially the business will not register for VAT as annual turnover will be below the Chancellor's most recent threshold.

All financial transactions will be recorded by D. Moon on an integrated computerised accounting package. An accountant will be engaged each year to draw up the business final accounts for the Department of Revenue & Customs.

No licence is required to operate a pottery although this will change if it is decided to open a cafe. The partnership will not need to register under the Data Protection Act.

After balancing the cost of insurance premiums against the expected risk, cover has been arranged for: premises, contents, breakages, product liability public liability and personal accident. Both partners already have life assurance policies.

Sources of information
In drawing up this plan the following sources of information have been invaluable:

- Business Link for Devon and Cornwall: www.blinkdandc.com
- JMB Solicitors, Bodmin
- Accounting Associates, St Austell
- Federation of Small businesses
- St Austell Chamber of Commerce: www.staustellchamber.org.uk.

Financial plan

Table 5.15

Sales budget (units)	Apr	May	Jun	July	Aug	Sept	Total
Sales	30	40	50	60	70	50	300
Sales revenue budget (£)	**Apr**	**May**	**Jun**	**July**	**Aug**	**Sept**	**Total**
Sales @ £120 per unit	3,600	4,800	6,000	7,200	8,400	6,000	36,000

Note: please see the marketing plan for details.

Receipts will be 1 month later than above owing to 30-day credit.

Table 5.16

Production budget (units)	Apr	May	Jun	July	Aug	Sept	Total
Production lovel	40	45	50	60	60	45	300
Production cost budget (£)							
Raw materials @ £20 per unit	800	900	1,000	1,200	1,200	900	6,000
Direct labour @ £15 per unit	600	675	750	900	900	675	4,500

Note: please see the operational plan for details.

Payment will be in the months shown above.

Notes	Cashflow forecast Figures to nearest £	At start £	Apr £	May £	Jun £	July £	Aug £	Sept £	Total £	Notes
	Receipts									
	Cash sales								0	
30-day credit	Cash from debtors		3,600	4,800	6,000	7,200	8,400	30,000	6,000	Debtors
	New capital	15,000							15,000	
	Bank loan	5,000							5,000	
	Total receipts (A)	20,000	0	3,600	4,800	6,000	7,200	8,400	50,000	
Materials	Payments									
	Cash purchases		800	900	1,000	1,200	1,200	900	6,000	Creditors
	Cash to creditors									
	Drawings		2,000	2,000	2,000	2,000	2,000	2,000	12,000	
	Production wages		600	675	750	900	900	675	4,500	
	Transport/distribution		40	40	40	40	40	40	240	
Fixed assets	Capital items	19,000							19,000	
	Rent/rates		2,200			1,100			3,300	
	Insurance		2,000						2,000	
	Light/heat				700			700	1,400	
	Advertising		1,200						1,200	
	Loan repayments		80	80	80	80	80	80	480	
	Interest charges		10	10	10	10	10	10	60	
	General admin		50	50	50	50	50	50	300	
	Total payments (B)	19,000	8,980	3,755	4,630	5,380	4,280	4,455	50,480	
	Net cashflow (A-B)	1,000	(8,980)	(155)	170	620	2,920	3,945	(480)	
	add Opening balance b/d	0	1,000	(7,980)	(8,135)	(7,965)	(7,345)	(4,425)	0	
	Closing balance c/d	1,000	(7,980)	(8,135)	(7,965)	(7,345)	(4,425)	(480)	(480)	

Note: Please see the marketing plan and operational plan for details.

Column one shows the start-up funding required.

Table 5.17 Forecast income statement (profit and loss) for period ending 30th September 200X

	£	£
Sales		36,000
Variable production cost		10,500
GROSS PROFIT		25,500
Fixed cost		8,500
NET PROFIT		17,000
less Partner's drawings		12,000
Retained profits		5,000

Table 5.18 Break-even point

	Period fixed costs	Unit variable costs		Unit sales price	
	£8,500	£35		£120	
Units	**Fixed cost £**	**Variable cost £**	**Total cost £**	**Sales revenue £**	**Profit/(loss) £**
0	8,500	0	8,500	0	(8,500)
60	8,500	2,100	10,600	7,200	(3,400)
120	8,500	4,200	12,700	14,400	1,700
180	8,500	6,300	14,800	21,600	6,800
240	8,500	8,400	16,900	28,800	11,900
300	8,500	10,500	19,000	36,000	17,000
360	8,500	12,600	21,100	43,200	22,100

Break-even point = 100 dinner sets

or £12,000 (100 units sold @ £120 each)

Figure 5.19

The break-even chart for Eclipse

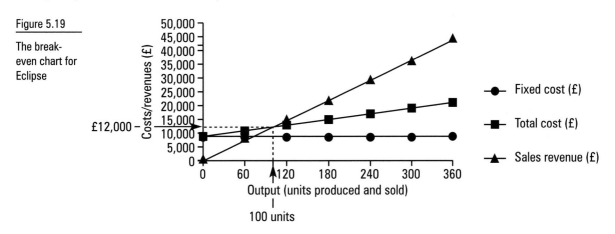

Evaluation

Marketing

The sales estimates are based partly upon firm orders and partly upon enquiries from prospective customers who have shown genuine interest in the products.

Operations

The production budget shows that orders can be produced to time under present constraints. Should there be further demand, the business has capacity to produce an extra 60 units worth £7,200 revenue.

Finance

Cashflow:

There will be a cash shortfall over the period partly due to start-up costs and partly to the need to pay production costs immediately whilst giving customers 30 days credit. Additional funding of just over £8,000 is needed in the initial stages and it is hoped to raise an overdraft using one partner's property as security. When the September customers pay the £6,000 due in October, the bank can be repaid.

Profitability:

The business will break-even at 100 units and generate a net profit of £17,000 for the six-month period. This will enable the partners to take their drawings of £12,000 and to plough back £5,000 for future growth.

Assuming that the bank overdraft is forthcoming, the business plan is viable. It is acceptable to the partners who are prepared to operate with minimal drawings in the first year.

Monitoring and review

The financial forecasts will be monitored on a monthly basis and any significant variances investigated.

This business plan was submitted for and on behalf of Eclipse by the partners:

Della Moon .... Date: 20 Jan 200–

Wayne Moon .... Date: 20 Jan 200–

Business Online

This unit covers:
- online presence
- impact of online presence on customers
- simple business website
- opportunities provided by an online presence.

This unit looks at:
- the range of businesses that conduct business via the internet
- the reasons why businesses set up an online presence
- the impact of online presence on customers
- the design and creation of a simple business website
- the ways in which an online presence helps achieve business aims and objectives.

Assessment
This unit will be assessed through portfolio work set and marked by your teachers. You will be asked to investigate the impact of business online presence on businesses and customers. You will design a simple business website; you may also create and evaluate this site. Finally you will describe business opportunities arising from an online presence.

To complete this unit, you will need to use search engines and business websites.

The internet
For some businesses, the internet is an additional means of communicating with their stakeholders, to others it is the main means of communication – the 'dot.com' businesses would not exit without it. For the purposes of this unit, a business with an **online presence** is a business with its own website.

The internet is a vast international electronic network allowing users to share information and communicate directly. It links computers worldwide in organisations such as businesses, government departments, charities, universities, libraries, schools and private homes.

A brief history of the internet
1966 The US military began to use the system to connect defence laboratories. It was later extended to the major US universities.

1982 William Gibson coined the term **cyberspace**.

1991 Sir Tim Berners Lee developed the World Wide Web (www) to enable researchers to send and receive scientific papers via the internet.

1991 The first free web-browser (MOSAIC) finally opened the World Wide Web to businesses and the general public.

Since 1995, the traffic on the web has grown rapidly. Private users are attracted because it is free and uncensored, business users because it provides a global opportunity for marketing and e-commerce.

The popularity of the internet has been helped by, among other things, the increasing availability of low-cost high-specification computers, government initiatives aimed at computer literacy, the development of faster access (e.g. broadband). More recently mobile phones and portable notebook computers have given travellers remote 'wireless' access via the use of 'hot-spot' locations.

The growing popularity of online buying (or e-commerce) is one of the notable internet trends.

case study 6.1   Internet use

These charts are taken from the *Family Expenditure Survey*, 2002.

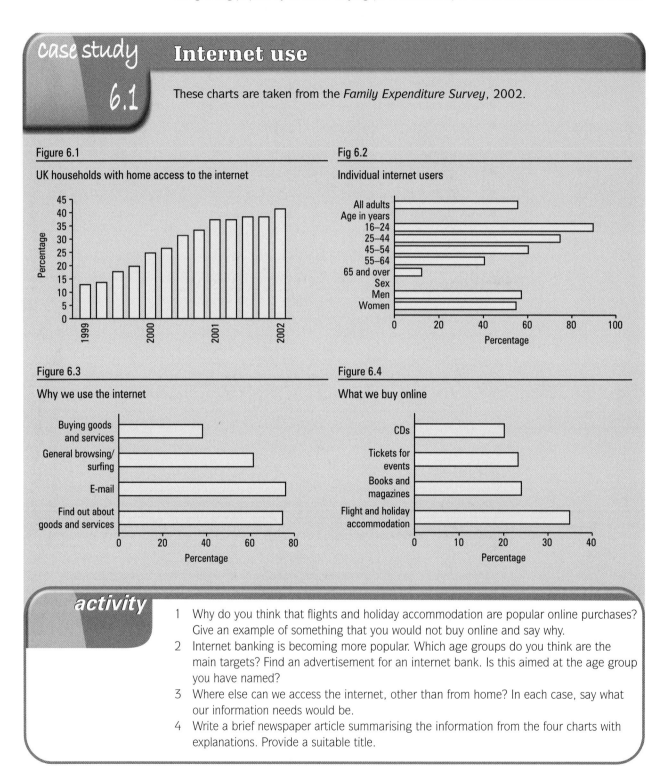

Figure 6.1

UK households with home access to the internet

Fig 6.2

Individual internet users

Figure 6.3

Why we use the internet

Figure 6.4

What we buy online

activity

1 Why do you think that flights and holiday accommodation are popular online purchases? Give an example of something that you would not buy online and say why.

2 Internet banking is becoming more popular. Which age groups do you think are the main targets? Find an advertisement for an internet bank. Is this aimed at the age group you have named?

3 Where else can we access the internet, other than from home? In each case, say what our information needs would be.

4 Write a brief newspaper article summarising the information from the four charts with explanations. Provide a suitable title.

Unravelling the net – some internet terms:

- e-mail – electronic mail, a service provided by an ISP (see below) or by Usenet

- Usenet – a collection of bulletin boards set up by subject matter

- ftp (file transfer protocol) –the principal protocol (set of rules) used to download files from the internet, especially from websites

- **web browser** – an application used to request and read pages from the World Wide Web. The best known are Netscape Navigator and Microsoft's Internet Explorer

- www (World Wide Web) – a set of technology standards that enables multimedia documents (text, images, sound, video) to be read by anyone with access to the internet. The 'web' organises its contents by subject matter to enable advanced information retrieval

- search engine – used to locate relevant information on the World Wide Web, e.g. MSN, Ask Jeeves, Yahoo and Google.

Figure 6.5

Some internet terms

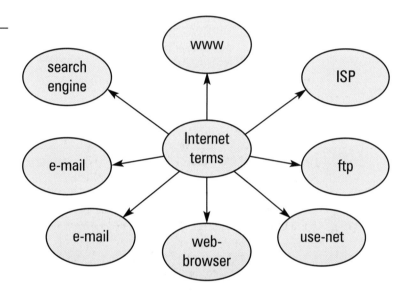

Connecting to the internet

- Direct connection – large organisations and government agencies set up their own connection and pay to have a full-time link.

- Internet service providers (ISPs), such as BT, AOL, Virgin, allow a link for smaller organisations and individuals. This is dialled up as needed or connected by broadband.

- www.statistics.gov.uk, together with industry sources to identify trends in e-commerce
- Business annual reports for objectives and assessment of their online presence
- The media for current developments and concerns – back copies of newspapers can be accessed via the archive feature on their websites, e.g. www.guardianunlimited.co.uk, www.times-online.co.uk

Online Presence

The range of businesses with an online presence

Look at the details businesses provide on their headed notepaper, their business cards, advertisements and on the sides of vans. Which have an e-mail address alongside the telephone and fax number? Which ones also have a website address?

Businesses with their own websites range from large global concerns, for whom an internet presence is regarded as essential, to small sole traders who increasingly see the potential benefit to their business.

---

case study

6.2

Online presence

The advertisements have been adapted from a village magazine:

A

> **Tawny Owl Guesthouse**
> All rooms en-suite
> Breakfast and evening meals available
> Stunning moorland views
> Tel: XXXX 452498 for details or visit www.tawnyowl.co.uk

B

> **JJS Painters & Decorators**
> No job too small,
> competitive rates, references
> available
> Tel: XXXX 450672

C

> J.JSPD@virgin.net
> Tim's Taxis
> Tel: XXXX 450672
> Mobile: 0789 XXXXXX

---

activity

1. Why will a website be useful to A, but less useful to B and C?
2. What sort of information might Tawny Owl Guesthouse post on their website?
3. Think of at least five services that you use locally and name the businesses concerned. Examples might be: hairdressing, motor repair services, taxi services, a cafe, a club, bus services, the local library, banking, etc.
   a) Which of these businesses has an online presence? What is its purpose?
   b) Why do the remaining businesses not have a website? Could any of them benefit from developing a site?

2B or not 2B?

In 1993 few businesses had a website and very few allowed goods and services to be ordered over the internet. Now both businesses and consumers increasingly see the potential of conducting business online.

Business websites may be:

- B2B (business to business) sites – aimed at other businesses with whom they trade
- B2C (business to consumer) sites – aimed at the users of their products.

B2B sites are used by businesses providing industrial goods and commercial services for use by other businesses. For example, JCB makes earth-moving equipment for the construction industry, the haulage company Eddie Stobart delivers stock to retailers, wholesalers and manufacturers Rolls-Royce enables industry to order parts via its sourcerer site.

B2C sites are used by those businesses selling directly to the end-user. These include retailers of consumer goods such as Dorothy Perkins and Woolworths, and providers of direct services such as Royal Mail, HSBC, Stagecoach and Thames Water.

Some businesses operate as both B2B and B2C. Which of the businesses above does this?

Figure 6.6

B2B and B2C

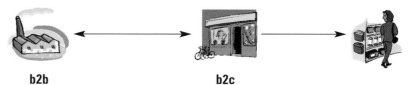

| Business trade with other businesses as they carry out PRODUCTION in the primary, secondary and tertiary sectors | Businesses market consumer goods and direct services and direct services to the consumer | CONSUMPTION of goods and services by the consumers (end-users) |

b2b ⟷ **b2c** ⟶

The extent to which businesses have an online presence varies. Local businesses serving a local market (the local newsagent, DIY shop or dentist) may see little benefit. However, businesses serving a wider market such as the larger retailers (Tesco, PC World, JJB Sports, etc.) or those selling specialist products, are almost certain to have a web presence. As the case study shows, these sites increasingly enable online selling.

case study 6.3 The rise and rise of e-commerce

In 2004, the Office of National Statistics (ONS) surveyed 10,000 firms representing businesses of different sizes and from all sectors. They found that:

- 31 per cent of all businesses have a website. The main use is to convey product or company information to stakeholders. Increasingly these businesses now direct customers to their website rather than to their telephone number

- 1 in 20 of all business websites also provide online selling. This rises to 1 in 3 if we look at larger businesses with 1,000+ employees.

The value of e-commerce is rising, the main users being the manufacturing, wholesale, retail, catering and travel sectors:

		2002	2003	2004
B2C	Retail sales to households	£6.4bn	£11.4bn	£15bn
B2B	Sales to other businesses	£12.6bn	£28.1bn	(not yet
	Total internet sales value	£19 bn	£39.5bn	available)

- There are now 16 million internet shoppers in Britain with women accounting for 56 per cent and men for 44 per cent of the total.

- Two-thirds of money spent is on goods; clothes retailing is the fastest growing sector.

- One third of sales are services and digital purchases with holidays, travel and music (through legal download sites such as Apple's i-Tunes) all growing.

In 2004, the e-tailing group the Interactive Retail in Media Group (IMRG) rated the best three e-retailers as: Amazon.co.uk, Tesco.com, figleaves.com. What does 'figleaves' sell?

The future?

IMRG says that internet sales are growing between five and eight times faster than high street sales every year.

- B2C: In 2004 internet shopping was 6 per cent of all retail sales; by 2014 it is likely to be 33 per cent.

- B2B: 29 per cent of businesses buy online, especially office consumables such as stationery. Although large businesses are most likely to do this, small business use is growing. Manufacturers report that large retailers (supermarkets) demand that they supply online.

Why is e-commerce so popular?

More people and businesses have access to the 'net' (36 per cent of employees have access at work) and shoppers appear to have overcome their reluctance to use credit cards online to pay for goods. Businesses see it as more efficient, because the electronic processing storage and retrieval of information saves time and staff costs. It is also open day and night.

However, there are two potential problems:

- The 'net' is being weighed down by spam – unwanted emails which account for 65 per cent of e-mail traffic.

- Fraud is costing the financial services sector billions of pounds. This cost will eventually be passed on to customers.

Unless these problems are tackled, the internet may become unusable by 2008.

Source: Adapted from the 'ONS E-commerce Survey of Business', *The Guardian*, 23 November 2004/*Metro*, September 2005

activity

1. Produce a two-paragraph newspaper article to summarise the trends in:
   - B2B internet use
   - B2C internet use.
   Include at least one example for each.
2. Construct two charts to illustrate information from above, provide a one-sentence caption to explain what each one shows.

remember

Investors paid high prices for internet company shares in the belief that, since the internet was the coming thing, anything dot.com was guaranteed to make high profits. In fact many of these companies struggled to survive and their share prices on the stock market fell. The dot.com bubble had burst.

From bricks to clicks …

Traditionally businesses have traded from 'bricks and mortar', i.e. a physical base, such as a factory, warehouse or shop. Internet trading enables a shift towards 'clicks' (electronic trading by clicking on a mouse) so that location is becoming less important.

This gives rise to two new possibilities:

- 'clicks and mortar' businesses operating part physical and part electronic trading. Increasingly B2C businesses, such as the major supermarkets, the high street banks and a growing number of other retailers, sell both from their premises and via the internet

- 'clicks' only businesses. These are the new 'dot.com' organisations that only sell online. Examples include book and music retailer Amazon, travel company lastminute.com, computer retailer e-Buyer. One of the most dramatic success stories is the internet-only auction site e-Bay (see page 260).

Why do different businesses choose to operate in these different ways?

In the last chance saloon?

The dramatic fall in share prices that took place after the millennium was in part due to the poor performance of some of the earlydot.com companies – lastminute.com founded by Martha Lane Fox and Brent Hobeman was one dramatic example.

<table>
<tr><td>

case study

6.4
</td><td>

Internet banking aims for net profits
</td></tr>
</table>

The financial services industry provides a good example of how e-tailing (online retailing can open up new markets for business). Traditionally any business wishing to enter the banking industry would need to acquire and maintain a network of branches in expensive high street locations.

From the 1980s the growth in popularity of postal and telephone accounts showed that there was a market for home banking. Internet banking is a logical extension of this trend.

In recent years new players such as Virgin, Tesco, Sainsbury and the Prudential (through Egg) have entered the market as 'clicks' only banking businesses. The existing banks have responded by moving into 'clicks and mortar' through their own e-banking brands such as: Cahoots (Abbey National) and Smile (Co-operative Bank).

Advantages of e-banking to the banks:

There is an initial cost of setting up the site but thereafter:

- e-banking avoids the expense of running branches in expensive high street locations

- staff costs are reduced – the customers browse the site and serve themselves. The site processes transactions automatically

- the sites have a global presence and are always open to take business

- more competitive offers result from lower costs

- the site is maintained centrally and so should be up to date.

Figure 6.7
_____

Why e-banking is
attractive to customers

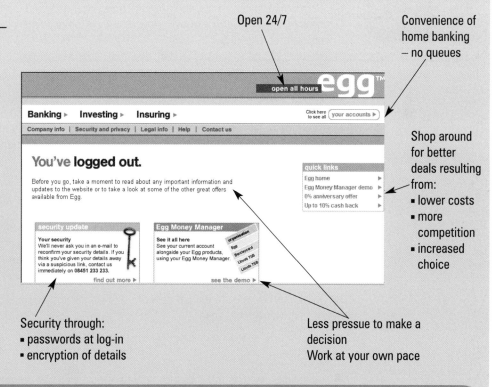

Open 24/7

Convenience of
home banking
– no queues

Shop around
for better
deals resulting
from:
- lower costs
- more
  competition
- increased
  choice

Security through:
- passwords at log-in
- encryption of details

Less pressue to make a
decision
Work at your own pace

activity

1 Not all consumers will have access to e-commerce.
   a) Which groups in society are less likely to have internet access? (See the chart on page 248.)
   b) Which groups may have internet access but not the ability to buy online? (Think what you need to make an online purchase.)
2 Explain any other disadvantages of buying online from the customer's viewpoint.

Almost a nice mess, Stanley!

Credit card company Morgan Stanley have over a million customers worldwide. In November 2004 they found a security loophole in their website that could have allowed people to access account details and move money about. The problem arose from a 'user-friendly' feature that remembered a user's password when the first number of their credit card was entered.

Four days earlier the internet bank Cahoots closed its site for 10 hours when a customer discovered that it was possible to see other customers' details.

Source: Adapted from *The Guardian*, 10 November 2004

Gone phishing – with the net

Phishing is a multimillion pound problem. It involves criminals gaining passwords in order to steal funds from internet bank accounts.

The usual method is to send an e-mail that appears to come from your bank asking you to confirm your password on a fake website set up by the thieves. The internet security firm Messagelabs says it is intercepting 50,000 such emails and more than 80 new phishing websites every day. Around £4.5m has already been refunded to about 2,000 customers.

The problem for banks is that the crooks are getting smarter. Cyber crime experts have warned internet banks to take more care with security or run the risk that people will stop using their services.

activity

1 Banks tend to keep quiet about cyber crime. Why do you think this is?
2 Look at the Egg website above. How do they attempt to alert customers about the problem of 'phishing'?

Security and e-commerce

Security fears were initially a barrier to e-commerce in general and e-banking in particular. However, the accelerating growth in popularity suggests that customers now have confidence in new forms of **encryption** for protecting personal details and credit card numbers. Nevertheless, problems remain.

Delivering the goods

There is a distinction between buying physical goods and digital products online.

Physical goods (printers, CDs, cars) need to be physically transported to the buyer in exactly the same way as goods bought from shops, by mail order or by telephone shopping. The Post Office were quick to spot an opportunity and launched a TV advert for Christmas 2001 showing Elton John internet shopping and then receiving the goods by Royal Mail.

By 2004 internet sales to the UK generated 400 million mail consignments (around seven for every man, woman and child).

Digital products on the other hand can be both purchased and delivered online. Examples include:

- e-banking – we can instantly view and print details of our account, make payments and transfer money (although we cannot get cash)
- digital music (as opposed to music on CD, cassette or vinyl) can be downloaded and saved via formats such as MP3
- electronic journals, newspapers and annual reports can be saved to file or printed
- subscription information services from companies such as Mintel, Reuters and Dun & Bradstreet also provide immediate downloads in various formats.

case study
6.6

Legal downloads charge ahead

Figures from the International Federation of Phonographic Industries showed that music fans legally downloaded 200 million music tracks from the internet in 2004 (up tenfold from 20 million tracks in 2003). Music downloads were worth £177 million across the UK and Europe in 2004. The figure for 2005 is expected to double.

In 2004, 1.5 per cent of record company revenue came from downloads; by 2008 it is predicted to rise to 25 per cent.

In response to increasing demand, a separate download music chart is now drawn up. This differs from the traditional singles chart because some tracks are not available online, whilst the online buyers tend to be 'older and richer' according to computer consultancy Ovum.

The Apple i-Pod portable music player was designed to take advantage of the new market for downloaded music. It has been a runaway commercial success.

activity

1 Why was the Napster website prosecuted? (Hint: read page 273.)
2 What is an MP3 file?
3 Which sites now enable legal downloads of music files and how much do they charge?

Purpose of an online presence

Having a business website is not an end in itself but should help the business to achieve its aims and objectives by communicating effectively with the business stakeholders.

Most websites are designed primarily for marketing and sales purposes. However, they will often have a number of other aims.

case study
6.7

Sainsbury's website

Figure 6.8

The content of Sainsbury's website

Shareholder information	About us	Marketing
Financial details, profits, share price	Sainsbury's history What the company stands for	About Sainsbury's products

e-commerce	Sainsbury's website	Contact us
Online shopping and delivery		Postal and e-mail address

Corporate information	The community	Recruitment
Details of directors and policies	Social responsibility e.g. links with charities, schools	Posts, vacancies and how to apply for them

activity

1   Re-read the section on key stakeholders on pages 14–17 of Unit 1.
2   Identify the stakeholders targeted by Sainsbury in each section of its site shown above. If you log on to the Sainsbury site (www.sainsburys.co.uk) you will be able to give specific examples of content to help with this task.
3   What do you think is the main purpose of Sainsbury's site?
4   Whilst you are on the site, think about the usability. For example, Is the site easy to navigate (can you find your way around)? Does it load quickly? Is it interesting? Is the information helpful to its audience in each case?

assignment focus

1   Log on to the website of another business and produce a diagram (as above) to show what the site includes. (The site plan will help you.)
2   Which stakeholders are being targeted?

Note: This assignment will help you plan your own site.

Potential advantages to a business of using a website

An online presence may provide a number of specific benefits to a business:

- round the clock promotion to a global audience. A website is open for business 24/7 (24 hours a day/7 days a week)

Remember the Egg website on page 253.

- increased flexibility of location – a dot.com business can locate so as to gain cost savings

On page 253, we saw how internet banks were free from the need to maintain a 'bricks and mortar' presence in expensive high street premises.

- reduced reliance on traditional means of communication.

Online communication has the effect of reducing the level of interpersonal contact between business and customer. Traditional retailers, for example, provided personal service whereas e-commerce provides a form of remote electronic self-service.

The reduction in staffing, the freedom to locate in less costly areas and the global reach afforded by an online presence bring efficiencies and economies of scale for those business that can compete.

Assuming that they have internet access, are confident with it and the technology is working, the customer should also gain. The internet is a 'one-stop shop' that can be used at any time, from home, office and, increasingly, on the move. There is no need to travel and should be no need to queue. Information can be retrieved from sources across the globe, downloaded, printed or saved.

The ONS survey into e-business (pages 251–2) noted that many businesses now routinely refer customers to websites rather than to their address or telephone number. We can see the advantages for business in educating us to do this and in discouraging us from contacting them directly. (If you telephone or write to a business as part of your research, you may well be told 'It's all on our website' – how helpful this is depends upon the site itself and how good you are at searching it.)

remember

A significant number of people still do not use the internet and many continue to prefer the reassurance of personal service.

Effective cross-cultural communication

In communicating globally, websites give the potential to reach across cultural boundaries. This may be facilitated by using images that have universal appeal. However, there are dangers. Some images have very different meanings in different cultural contexts – a point made by the HSBC 'the world's local bank' advertisement.

Some sites offer a choice of language (e.g. Edexcel specifications are also available in Welsh), whilst others link with a sister site tailored to language or cultural needs (e.g. Manchester United's Mandarin chinese website).

Figure 6.9

A website provides an effective means of capturing and storing customer data

Name	Age
Lee J	32
Mo R	23
Phu S	29
Rowe T	45
Simon P	60
Timms B	39

The 'Front-End' – the web page on screen is the interface between the user and the web-site software

Customer details

The 'Back-End' – the part the user cannot see. This may include a database of user details on the web-server

Connection to customer databases

Successful marketing involves targeting customers effectively and a website provides an effective means of capturing and storing the necessary data.

Customer details are recorded as they use the site, e.g. when they register, when they make enquiries or make purchases. This information is then stored in a database to build up a picture of what the customer might buy in future.

The database of customers and visitors can also be used to attract revenue from other companies that might wish to advertise on the site.

Capturing data is possible whenever a site allows for user interaction. For example:

- the 'contact us' facility allows users to make queries or pass on opinions about the business
- on sites where goods and services can be ordered and paid for by plastic card, the customer will have to create an account by inputting a password and a user ID, input details of the order, the delivery address and debit or credit card details for payment
- sites providing free information such as newspapers, educational sites, football clubs, etc. may still require users to register, to monitor site usage. Users will need to log in at subsequent visits using their ID and password.

Using cookies to gain follow-up to sales

A **cookie** is saved onto a user's hard disk when they first access a website. The cookie enables the site to recognise the user whenever they log in. The site can then welcome customers by name and track the searches they make and what they buy. These details are added to those already in the database. Some customers object to cookies as an 'intrusion' and most web browsers allow them to be disabled.

The customer details in the database are used to encourage further purchases. Ebuyer, for example, e-mails details of new offers, Amazon identifies books or CDs likely to be of interest when the user logs in.

Connection with the supply chain

It is possible to make online connections with the various links in the supply chain taking a product from the producer to the consumer. For example, a business selling on the internet can take an online order from a customer, use the internet to source the product from the supplier (either a manufacturer or wholesaler), arrange with a courier (such as UPS or Royal Mail) for delivery, provide delivery dates and enable the customer to track the progress of the order.

Rapid search and retrieval of data

Search engines, such as Google, MSN, Yahoo, Alta Vista and Excite, play a vital role in locating web pages for users. We may have a website in mind but do not know the address, alternatively we may not have a site in mind and are just 'surfing the net' to see what is available.

Once a site has been located further searches may be possible via an in-site search facility.

---

case study 6.8 — Search engines

Search engines look for keywords. A search may be refined by linking key words together and by narrowing the geographical area, e.g. searching the UK only.

Search engines do not search the whole web, rather each has an index of sites that it will search. This is why, for example, a particular search in Yahoo will turn up different sites from an identical search in Google, Excite or Alta Vista.

At the time of writing, Google has the largest index. You can check its home page to see how many sites it will use.

For a website to be successful, it must be included in the index of the major search engines otherwise surfers will not discover it. In order to improve their chances, many businesses will pay to submit their sites to search engines. The website designers can also help by using **metatags** to include keywords that search engines are likely to recognise.

activity

1   How many sites does Google currently search? (Look at the home page.)
2   Conduct an identical search in three different search engines.

Connection to call centres

Call centres are large telephone-based advice centres staffed 24 hours a day. Many businesses offer a combination of online and telephone services with the help-line number shown on the website. For example, a query about a website function may require a telephone call – perhaps it will not accept a credit card, or perhaps the user is unsure how to perform an operation.

Businesses such as Egg (see page 277) and easyJet began with call centre sales and have subsequently attempted to move much of their business online.

User-friendliness and responsiveness to demand

Ideally a website will be user-friendly and responsive to the needs of the user. The image it should give is of a quality business and one that cares about its customers.

A dated, slow, unfriendly site may be worse than no site at all. In a competitive market, a business cannot afford to alienate customers by sites that only operate with the latest equipment, leave you wondering what to do next and are painfully slow to load and navigate.

 Link

We look at effective site design on pages 266–9. We also consider how to ensure equal opportunities for web-users with disabilities.

Mind the gap – is your website any use?

Every day the gap between what people want and what the web offers gets wider.

Today's websites are complex and many users are inexperienced. Whilst sites need to be more usable, many are actually getting worse because they are driven by the needs of their advertisers. They are also designed by former graphics professionals and newspaper and magazine lay-out artists using **web-authoring tools** and effects that get in the way.

User experience is better if the system responds in less than a second but pop-up adverts are actually making it slower.

remember

Later, when you design your own site, try to remember the issues raised here. Think about what the site is for.

The real secret is to work out the usability issues first, before you design the site (if the plane won't fly what is the point of putting blue and white stripes on the wings?). Experts believe that fewer than 1 per cent of sites get any usability testing before they are launched. On one building society site, 80 per cent of attempts to make a purchase failed because two words 'apply here' needed amending. Research costing £2,000 identified the problem – and paid for itself in a weekend.

Source: Adapted from the *Guardian* article 'Second Sight' by Jack Schofield

assignment focus

■ To achieve P1, explain with examples how an online presence may support the achievement of business aims and objectives.

To do this you will need to select a number of businesses, each with an online presence, and search their websites. Try to choose contrasting businesses, e.g. businesses in different sectors or charities, as well as profit-making businesses. It is also helpful if you are interested in these businesses and are a customer of at least some.

a) Identify the aims and objectives of each of your chosen businesses. You may first wish to review business aims and objectives in Unit 1 (page 119).
b) Give examples of how an online presence helps these businesses to achieve their aims and objectives.

Remember to identify the various stakeholders at whom the business objectives, and the site, are aimed.

■ To achieve M1, you will need to explain with examples how an online presence may support the achievement of business aims and objectives by attracting customer interest.

Explain here how your chosen business sites attract customer interest in order to achieve their aims and objectives. You will need to identify how these sites promote the business.

Impact of Online Business Presence on Customers

There are businesses with an online presence in all three sectors of the economy. Remember that their customers include both private individuals (B2C) and other businesses (B2B). Table 6.1 gives some examples.

Table 6.1 Online presence in the industrial sectors

Private sector	Public sector	Voluntary (not-for-profit) sector
Customers use business websites for: ■ buying goods and services (e-commerce) ■ servicing online bank accounts ■ information about services, e.g. train times ■ information about business activities, e.g. ethics, profits, etc.	*Local government* Customers use websites for information about services, e.g. libraries, education, leisure centres, parking schemes, housing, etc. *Central government* Customers use websites for: ■ information about the economy and government activities ■ calculating and paying tax online, advice on running businesses	Customers use websites for: ■ making donations ■ checking on activities ■ buying goods and services

A business online presence brings a number of advantages to customers including:

- increased variety of goods and services
- constant global availability
- increased range of suppliers
- increased quantity of information
- quality information
- increased speed, facility (usability) and flexibility of information seeking and transaction arrangements
- **accessibility**
- increased opportunities for comparative analysis of products and services
- increased range of interconnective hardware
- increased opportunities for discussion of specific products and markets
- opportunities for negative comment and criticism of business
- competitive product prices
- reduced scope for brand loyalty in an enlarged global market.

Increased variety of products and services

The internet provides customers with access to an ever wider variety of goods and services. Individual providers, such as Amazon, have access to a vast range of stock justified by their global reach, whilst collectively online providers offer customers a huge choice.

e-Bay is a sort of a global car boot sale where people (37 million by 2004) pay to sell their goods electronically. The range of products is endless – all of those things that people and businesses have no more use for. Customers have included a country singer from Maidstone looking for a Dolly Parton outfit, NASA looking for replacement parts for the space shuttle and Tube Lines buying computer chips for London Underground. e-Bay has also investigated claims that illegal guns have been sold on the site – once again proving that the internet is only as good as the people who use it.

The global reach and searching capabilities of the internet give customers improved access to specialist items; those things that are difficult to find in the local high street because they are rare or because they are a minority taste. For example, Meccano is a metal construction kit comprising metal plates, rods, nuts and bolts, pulley wheels, and so on, which can be assembled into an endless variety of working models: windmills, trains, bridges, etc. Meccano is out of fashion, but still has lots of devotees spread across the world. Globally there is a market but there is no ideal shop location because there is little prospect of passing trade in any particular area. Until recently one Meccano shop survived in the UK. The shop has now closed – but the business remains; it has gone online.

Niche retailers have traditionally relied upon mail order to reach their far flung customers. The internet is the perfect medium for such businesses.

assignment focus

Try to identify other niche markets for which the internet is an ideal means of trading. Search for a supplier for each.

Constant global availability

The World Wide Web is just that – worldwide. If one supplier does not have the product we need then, unless the item is very rare indeed, we should be able to locate another supplier who does – and they will always be open. This was the initial appeal of businesses such as lastminute.com.

Type 'cheap laptops' into a search engine and see what happens – how many suppliers are listed?

case study 6.9 — Net cord

Tennis becomes a national obsession for two weeks each year during the Wimbledon lawn tennis championships. However, the Wimbledon All England Club website provides the 'brand' with constant, year round, global availability.

activity

Visit the site of the Wimbledon All England Lawn Tennis Club, or if you prefer, the site of another sports club.

1 To what extent is the club engaged in e-commerce?
2 What other financial benefits will the site bring to the club?

Increased range of suppliers

A search for a product (depending upon the search criteria) can bring up a huge variety of suppliers. These might be online retailers or agencies listing the suppliers of particular items.

Bookfinder.com, for example, will search secondhand bookshops across the UK and the USA for rare and out-of-print editions. This site recently located two copies of an out-of-print book for the author – one copy in Chicago, Illinois, the other in Scunthorpe, Lincolnshire.

Gone fishing – but without the net

Before the internet became widely accessible, *Yellow Pages* ran an award-winning advert showing a fictional character called J.R. Hartley trawling secondhand bookshops in search of a copy of *Fly Fishing*; an out-of-print book that he had written many years before.

His problem was solved by the 'Good Old *Yellow Pages*' which supplied a list of secondhand bookshops in the area. He still had to telephone each shop on the list, and even then his search was restricted to the local area. He was lucky to find a copy.

Had the internet existed, JR could have searched for the book itself across the world. The traditional *Yellow Pages* has now been supplemented by an online version (Yell) that enables users to search locally or nationwide for businesses, contact details, maps, car parks and consumer advice.

Increased quantity of information

Remember that the internet developed as a means of sharing information between libraries, universities and research laboratories; only later was it used (some would say 'hijacked') by businesses for e-commerce.

The wealth of information now available can be of real benefit to customers whether their requirement is educational, recreational or commercial. We can locate information, products and suppliers, judge specification (although we cannot try out goods), compare prices, availability and delivery dates. It is also possible to research the ethical record or environmental commitment of suppliers – factors that may influence our decision to buy.

If you look in the BTEC National specifications, you will find a wide range of internet resources that you might find useful for business information – 34 web addresses are suggested as references for this unit alone.

Quality information

Remember that information is not useful for its own sake (a US sports commentator once remarked, 'That's the highest anyone has ever jumped on a Thursday'). We only benefit where information is relevant to our needs and of good quality, that is, authentic, accurate, unbiased and up to date. It must also be accessible.

- Relevant information – it is important to search precisely – if a query turns up 5,000 results, we certainly have a choice, but in practical terms it is unhelpful. In order to avoid information overload we must be discriminating and search for what is relevant.

- Authentic information – the internet is unregulated and anyone can set up a website (you may do so as part of this course), advertise products and write anything about anything. We need to have some way of validating what we find – Where has the information come from? Is it accurate? Does the author have a particular point of view? One internet bookseller has reportedly asked authors to write their own book reviews – will these be useful for customers?

Customers purchasing on the web need to be assured that they are buying from a legitimate trader. Dell is an e-tailing success story. Their computers are not available in the shops but they do have an established reputation as a quality brand. How do we judge the quality of brands we have never heard of?

- Accurate information – is the information provided correct? Some sites police their contributors, e.g. there are strict guidelines for those contributing learning materials to educational sites. However, for other sites there are no such assurances.

- Up-to-date information – it is good practice to show when a site was last up-dated. Figure 6.11 shows that around 28 per cent of business websites are poorly maintained.

Figure 6.10

Quality of website maintenance
Source: Netvention Inc., 2004
(www.netvention.com)

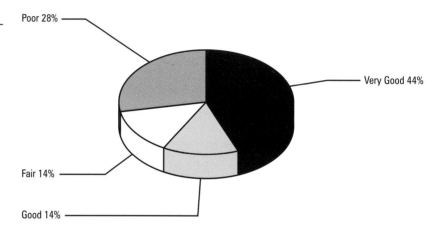

Poor 28%

Very Good 44%

Fair 14%

Good 14%

Increased speed, facility (usability) and flexibility of information-seeking and transaction arrangements

At its best, the internet is fast, effective and convenient. This can give the web distinct advantages over more traditional methods of information-seeking.

Accessibility

The internet is accessible to more and more people through cheaper hardware and availability in schools, colleges, libraries and internet cafes, as well as in the home. The development of wireless technology (see page 274) now makes access available to those on the move.

Although users with older systems and those with physical disabilities (such as visual impairment) may not have full access, website design is increasingly subject to codes of practice and increasingly to the law, in an attempt to make the web generally available.

We look at these issues on page 272.

Increased opportunities for comparative analysis of products and services

How do we compare prices of products and services? Traditionally we might telephone a number of providers, physically visit shops and showrooms, read up details in newspapers,

case study 6.10

Get the train online

If we have the right timetable at home (and can find it), then we look up our train. Where this is not the case, the internet may have the solution.

A search engine will help us to find a relevant site such as The Trainline or one of the regional rail companies.

- Input: We enter our journey details – date, time of departure, destination, single or return.

- Process: The system will search the company timetable database and locate relevant services.

- Output: A tailored response appears on-screen, showing a choice of suitable trains with times of departure, details of any connections and times of arrival.

The site should operate in real-time, so that any last-minute changes (cancellations etc) are shown – something our printed timetable will not have.

Further services include pricing information and online ticket booking paid for by credit or debit card.

As with any site, the usefulness will be dependent upon the amount of traffic on the line (which may affect speed), site design (which affects facility) and the effectiveness of delivery – will your ticket arrive on time for example?

One regional rail operator sends out tickets three days before travel (leaving time for panic if there is a postal problem) and will not make changes to reservations booked online.

A more satisfactory solution is to e-mail a booking confirmation with a number that can be used to obtain an electronic ticket. Travelocity, the online travel agent, uses this system.

activity

1 Find a site providing booking arrangements such as those above. You may use a rail site, a cinema or theatre, a sports club, etc. Take the booking arrangement up until the point that you pay.
2 Briefly describe the site.
3 Evaluate the service in terms of: speed, usability (facility), flexibility, transaction arrangements.

magazines and advertising literature, or seek independent advice (perhaps insurance brokers, mortgage brokers or *Which?* magazine). This takes time and energy.

The speed, convenience and range of sources on the internet increases the opportunity for effective comparisons. ONS research indicates that a growing number of websites now offer price comparisons for goods and allow shoppers to hunt out bargains.

Increased range of interconnective hardware

New technology is providing customers with more and more ways of getting online. Developments include:

- wireless application protocol (**WAP**) – this enables users of mobile phones and portable computers to receive e-mail and web-based information whilst on the move. 'Hot spots' are being set up as areas where wireless (not plugged in) applications, such as notebook computers can access the internet

- personal digital assistants (**PDAs**) – John Scully of Apple computers first used this term to describe the Newton pocket computer. PDA now describes any pocket personal organiser that combines a calendar, diary and address book.

Increased opportunities for discussion of specific products and markets

Groups with common interests may take part in discussions via:

- Usenet and newsgroups – newsgroups are online discussion forums that make up the Usenet network (this started in 1979 before the internet). Discussions take place in text-only format and cover a wide range of subjects. ISPs such as BT, Virgin and AOL allow their subscribers to access newsgroups. Access is also possible through search engines such as the 'Groups' option on Google

- bulletin boards and forums – some websites allow users to post messages for other users to read. The BBC website, for example, provides the 606 board (six minutes past six was when the radio programme was originally transmitted) where football fans can give their views

Some companies provide online forums to encourage stakeholders to discuss company policy, e.g. Shell has the Tell Shell Forum www.shell.com/tellshell.

- chat rooms – here users can discuss of topics of common interest. They have become the subject of public concern recently as a result of abuse by certain users. Chatrooms are available via ISPs.

Opportunities for negative comment and criticism of business

Internet content is unregulated. Just as the internet gives businesses an opportunity to promote their products globally 24/7, it also allows dissatisfied customers to get their own back by setting up 'revenge' sites.

Whilst some revenge sites are just personal rants (or blogs), others are more professional.

- Sites directed at specific big companies are the most common. In the UK, these can often be recognised by the word 'hell', as in NTLhell.co.uk. In the US, the names are more hard-hitting: FordReallySucks.com and F***General Motors.com being two examples. Site-owners risk being taken to court on the basis that they are infringing company trademarks.

- Some sites such as moneysavingexpert.com and grumbletext.co.uk highlight poor products and service across a range of business.

- Pressure groups such as Greenpeace and Friends of the Earth have long been critical of the environmental record of big business. Businesses are conscious of their brand image and adverse publicity can be a powerful weapon for change. In 2004 Greenpeace actually congratulated a number of businesses on the improvements they had made.

moneysavingexpert.com is run by Martin Lewis, the TV and radio broadcaster. The site cost £80 to set up and tells 750,000 consumers a month what to buy, what not to buy and how to take revenge on companies.

Lewis says that companies spend billions on marketing to us and his site allows us to fight back. The bank First Direct accused him of 'consumer terrorism' when the site encouraged people to open a bank account, take the £25 offered to new customers, and then to cancel the account without using it.

Each week the 'vent board' allows consumers to 'name and shame' a different company.

Source: Adapted from *The Guardian*

Competitive product prices

Insurance from Churchill ('give the dog a phone') is 10 per cent cheaper if bought online, the interest rate earned from Abbey's online bank, Cahoot, is higher than on their other accounts. Why is this?

For many products the operating costs of internet trading are likely to be lower than those for conventional high street trading and these can be passed on to the customer in the form of lower prices. There are a number of reasons for this.

- Clear savings can be made in staff salaries where transactions are conducted electronically.

- Storage and premises costs are reduced. Since location is less important, less expensive areas can be chosen. Furthermore some countries will provide tax advantages, e.g. Tesco is able to offer cheaper CDs from its Jersey-based site because VAT can be avoided.

- Global sales introduce economies of scale. Where fixed costs (such as rents, electricity and salaries) are spread over more products, each product becomes cheaper to process. There are also economies from bulk-buying where orders are large.

- Direct selling may be possible in which case there is no 'middleman' to pay. Dell is a good example of a manufacturer selling directly to the consumer via the internet. Dell products are not available in the shops – no retailer is involved. In a similar way, the low cost airlines easyJet and Ryanair sell their flights directly from their own call centres thus avoiding the travel agents' commission.

- Where retailers decide to sell online, their costs are likely to be lower than their in-store prices because of efficiencies in the supply chain, although customers may have to pay delivery costs. For digital services, there is a distinct price advantage, as we have seen, internet-only banks, for example, tend to offer the better deals.

- With internet selling, it is much easier for new businesses to enter a market so that customers have more choice; we saw this in our study of the banking industry on page 253. This increased competition keeps prices down.

Reduced scope for brand loyalty in an enlarged global market

Branding remains highly important for many goods because it is an assurance of quality and image. However, if we can be assured of quality we may be prepared to change brands more frequently if products are available. The increased choice offered by the internet is therefore likely to break down brand loyalty, where image is not a factor but price is.

'Credit tarts' want jam on it

Despite being one of the more expensive credit cards at the time, Barclaycard used highly effective advertising to become a leading brand.

It used to be said that people were more likely to divorce than change their bank – not any more. In the new competitive environment credit card companies are making highly attractive offers to tempt new customers; usually with 0 per cent interest for the first six months. In a society with so much personal debt, this can represent a considerable saving.

The internet makes it fast and painless to switch accounts so that a significant number of customers – so-called 'credit tarts' – make the change, and then after six months, move on again to the next free offer.

assignment focus

To achieve P2, you need to describe, with examples, the impact on customers of the online presence of a selected business.

Study a selection of business websites and identify the different ways in which customers are affected (they may be good or bad). For each, provide examples to illustrate the points that you are making.

Simple Business Website

Creating an online presence

A commercial business website can be expensive to set up (probably £100,000 upwards) and requires continuous maintenance to ensure that it is functioning effectively and is up to date. It must be worth the expense; a poorly designed or badly maintained site is worse than none.

A business must be clear of the purpose the site is to serve, and it must be effectively planned to achieve this. We must take account of:

- the contents of the site
- the usability of the site
- any conventions that must be followed
- laws that we must comply with.

Planning your site

First decide what your site is for. For example, is it for information, marketing or selling? Do you want the user to simply read the site or to use it to communicate with you?

Eclipse Pottery

In Unit 5 we looked at Della and Wayne Moon who have set up a partnership to manufacture and market pottery. Della and Wayne have now decided that a website will enable them to promote their brand more effectively.

They decide that the site will provide information about the business, a brochure and price list of the pottery they produce.

The site will not provide online buying facilities, but there will be a form to be used by customers for making enquiries and placing orders, together with contact details.

Ideally the site will use a counter to monitor 'traffic'. It will not simply record total 'hits' since this does not give an indication of real interest – people may visit by accident. Instead, it will monitor navigation through the site.

The business aims to:

- provide a quality product supported by a quality service for customers
- establish a reputation for excellence initially at an area level
- establish the presence of the 'Eclipse' trade mark in the marketplace
- maximise profits through operations in a niche market
- concentrate on quality rather than quantity.

The site will help the business to achieve these aims.

Designing the website

Della and Wayne speak to a consultant who draws up three charts to show how the website will operate. There is:

- the navigation chart – this shows the different pages and how they are linked
- the storyboard chart – there is a chart for each page showing the code to be used
- the **cascading style sheet (CSS)** – this shows the standard formats that will be applied across the site.

The navigation chart shows how the user will move around the Eclipse website (Figure 6.12).

The storyboard chart shows the code that will be used to structure each page. The code used for the home page is shown in Figure 6.13.

Figure 6.11

The navigation chart for the Eclipse website

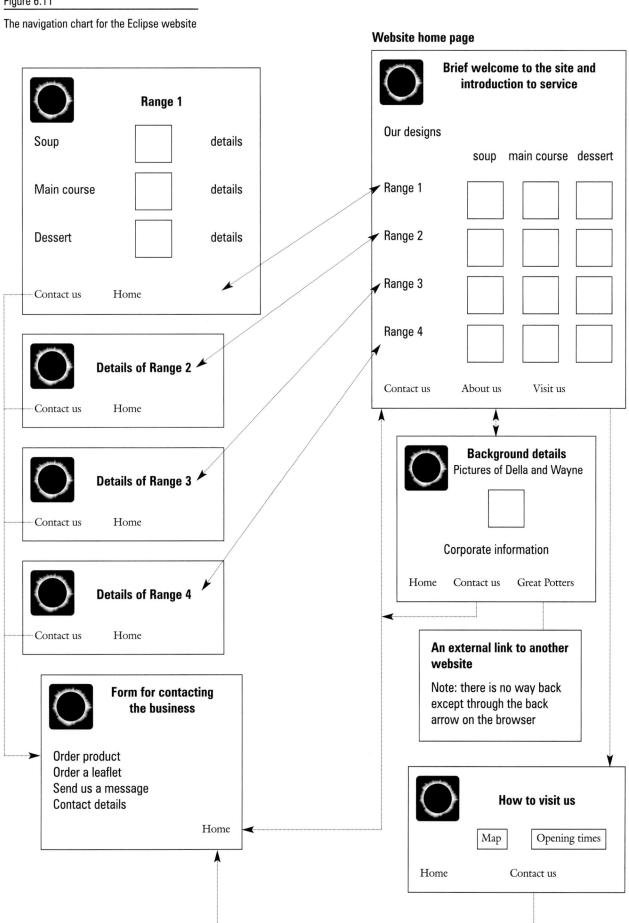

Figure 6.12

The storyboard chart for the Eclipse website

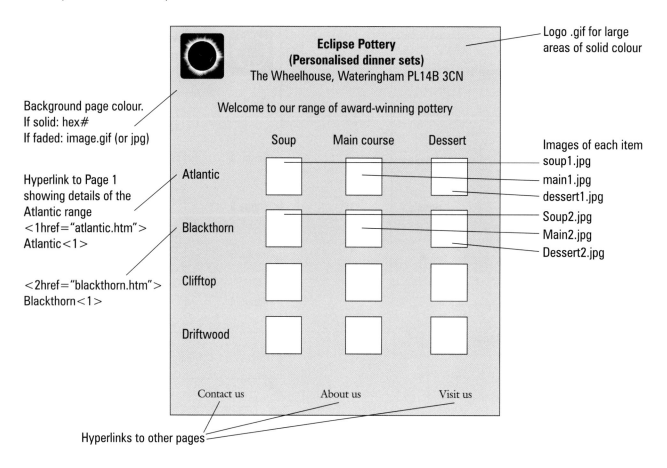

The cascading style sheet (CSS)

Your website will need to make appropriate use of colour, image and text. In particular, it is important to adopt a 'house style' so that your web pages have a consistent appearance. (Look at the pages of a professional site to see this.)

As it is time-consuming to format each page separately, the answer is to use a cascading style sheet to set up the font styles, font sizes, colours, etc. that you will use throughout your site. These can then be applied (or cascaded) to the web pages where they are needed by means of 'tags'. For example, H1 refers to a style of heading.

Since all formats are set from the code in the style sheet, any changes to the site format, e.g. changing a blue background to green, can be made simply by changing the appropriate code. All pages to which this code has been applied will then also change.

To achieve P3, you will need to plan the creation of a simple business website.

It may be useful to plan a website based upon your business idea from Unit 5. In this way, you will have a clear business idea, together with aims and objectives you hope to achieve.

a) Describe the business for which you will create a site. Clearly identify the aims and objectives and the stakeholders who will view the site.

b) Plan the creation of the site using the three stages outlined above.

c) Identify the colours, font styles and any distinctive lettering or logo that you will use to reinforce your corporate image.

Creating the website

Once the website has been planned, it can then be written. We do not cover the technical details of website writing here. The possibilities open to you will depend upon the technical expertise of your teachers and the precise facilities available in your school or college. In general, however, there are two approaches:

- writing the site using code such as **HTML** (hypertext markup language) or **Javascript**, a language used to create interactive elements on websites. This requires a degree of expertise and support

- using a web-authoring tool. This will simplify the process in that it will write HTML for you. The most popular tools include Microsoft Frontpage and Macromedia Dreamweaver.

Images can be created by:

- using a graphics package such as Adobe Photoshop or Macromedia Flash

- importing a photograph taken by a digital camera

- importing existing graphics from an existing file, perhaps from clip art or from the internet (however, be careful of copyright). In a similar way a chart could be imported from a spreadsheet

- scanning an image and importing this to the web page.

Testing and usability

To ensure that the site works effectively it is necessary to check its content, appearance, navigation and accessibility.

Content

A site must contain the appropriate information and communicate this through effective language, images and possibly sound.

Appearance

The format should be easy to read. This means that text should be clear and uncluttered using a plain font of reasonable size. Memory-consuming effects (spinning balls, moving text) should be used sparingly, if at all. Images should be small and simple, and colours should be used carefully.

It is generally accepted that no web page should contain more than seven different sections or it becomes confusing.

Accessibility

A website will be viewed globally by users with different computers of different specifications, using different operating systems and different browsers. Additionally some users may have disabilities. Good design will take all of this into account to produce a site that can communicate effectively across the target audience.

It might be reasonable to assume that users will have at least Windows XP, 1024 x 768 screen resolution, a 56K modem. The site should be designed so that it performs effectively on equipment with these minimum specifications.

It is a convention of the World Wide Web Consortium that websites must be accessible to the visually impaired. This is achieved by coding images with alt text (alternative text) to enable them to be read by a screen reader.

Sites must also have **cross-platform compatibility** – we discuss this on page 272.

Navigation

Users must be able to find the information they need and move easily from page to page. They will be impatient with a site that leaves them unsure of the next step or a site that is slow to load. As a rule of thumb, the user should be able to access a page within a maximum of three mouse clicks or 7 seconds, any longer and they may give up and move to another site.

All aspects of the site must comply with site conventions set out by W3C, as well as ethical and legal standards.

Refer to page 273 for further details of W3C guidelines.

Figure 6.13

Usability checks

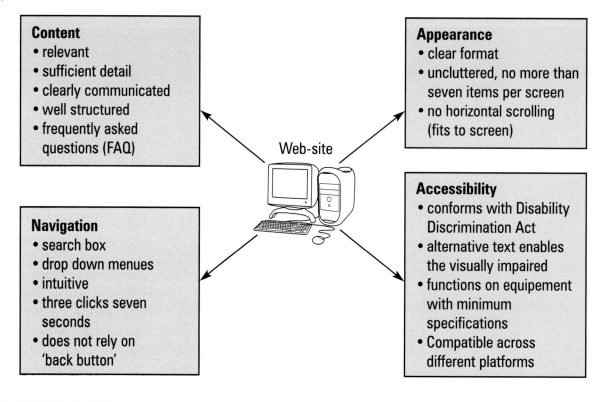

Content
- relevant
- sufficient detail
- clearly communicated
- well structured
- frequently asked questions (FAQ)

Appearance
- clear format
- uncluttered, no more than seven items per screen
- no horizontal scrolling (fits to screen)

Web-site

Navigation
- search box
- drop down menues
- intuitive
- three clicks seven seconds
- does not rely on 'back button'

Accessibility
- conforms with Disability Discrimination Act
- alternative text enables the visually impaired
- functions on equipement with minimum specifications
- Compatible across different platforms

assignment focus

To achieve M2, you need to create a simple business website.

a) Select a website of your choice and test it for usability against the criteria shown above.

b) Create your website using either one of the authoring tools or by writing HTML. Make sure that you stay with your plan, or note down any changes.

c) Check the site for errors in text, spelling and grammar. Check also for legal and equal opportunities issues.

d) Test the site to ensure that it can be easily and effectively navigated by all potential users.

Launching the site

Once a website is written and tested, it is ready to be launched so that other internet users may gain access to it. Launching a site involves three stages:

Figure 6.14

Launching the site

3 Upload the site

2 Find a suitable host

1 Create a domain name

Stage 1: Create a domain name

Your website must have a name, for example www.levistrauss.com is the **domain name** of the Levi Strauss site. You will need to:

- choose a suitable name, but make sure it is original. The site www.networksolutions.com will help you check this

- register your domain name so that it appears on the internet domain name system (or DNS). This lists all of the domain names on the internet together with their owners. http://rs.internic.net/alpha.html provides a directory of Accredited Registrars. You can register as .com, .org or .net.

Top level domain names include:

- .co.uk or .com (for the USA) – sites belonging to commercial, profit-making organisations. Some UK organisations now also use .com

- .org – a not-for-profit organisation

- .ac.uk or .edu (USA) – an academic institution

- .gov.uk – a government site

- .mil – a military site

- .net – an organisation, such as an ISP, whose activities are related to the internet.

With the exception of the USA, countries are usually identified within the domain name, e.g. .uk for the United Kingdom, .au for Australia, etc.

Stage 2: Find a suitable host

You will need to find an ISP (internet service provider) to 'host' your website. The host will provide space to store your website on its server and enable you to connect to the internet. It may also provide facilities such as security features and e-mail addresses. ISPs will usually host your website free of charge but they will receive a share of the call charges involved when the site is accessed.

In the example below, the ISP is Plusnet, there are many other examples including BT, Virgin and Geocities.

A web address is an example of a **URL** (universal resource locator), see Figure 6.16. This is a string of characters used to find a resource on the internet.

Figure 6.15

What the parts of the address mean

http://www.eclipsepots.plus.com

Protocol request/ response

World wide web

The name of your website is already taken, you will need to choose another

ISP (internet service provider) hosting the site

The extension given. Other ISPs might offer: .co.uk

A specific page within a site can be located by adding the appropriate page address to the end of the web address. For example:

http://www.eclipsepots.plus.com/contact — The page showing contact details

Large business web addresses rarely show the ISP, for example Iceland.co.uk. This is because they may have their own server and they may pay the ISP for the hosting service.

Stage 3: Upload the site
This involves transferring the website onto the host's computer so that other web users are able to access it.

Maintaining your website

Creating and uploading a site is just the start. Your site needs to be maintained so that it is up to date and works effectively. Any links with other sites should be checked to ensure that they are still appropriate. The date of the most recent up-date should be shown. The domain name registration must also be renewed.

---

case study 6.11

Poetry Society impotent over Viagra

The Poetry Society's award winning website, www.poetrysoc.com, used to attract 300,000 hits (visits) a month. Suddenly subscribers noticed that, instead of verse, they received a directory of online services ranging from casinos to hair-loss treatment to Viagra.

The ISP had not renewed its registration of the domain name, thus allowing a different company (Ultimate Search Inc. of Hong Kong) to purchase it.

The Poetry Society, which is a charity, had spent five years building up its website and promoting its web address. The mistake is likely to cost them £20,000 and there is little they can do.

activity

1   What sorts of costs do you think the Poetry Society will now have, i.e. what sorts of things is the £20,000 cost likely to involve?
2   For some businesses, an outcome such as this would be a complete disaster. Name three of these and explain your choice.

Firewalls: protecting data

A **firewall** is software that monitors signals passing between a business network (linking the business computer with the ISP) and the outside world (the World Wide Web). The job of the firewall is to filter out dangerous or undesirable traffic from other users on the World Wide Web (e.g. hackers) in order to prevent security breaches and damage to business data.

Suitability for use

Cross-platform compatibility
Web users do not have identical hardware and software; a website must function effectively across a range of specifications.

- The site will need to be trialled on different browsers; it must work on both Internet Explorer and Netscape Navigator.

- Some users will have broadband (a faster internet connection), while others will have a slower telephone link. Your site needs a suitable dial-up speed, so that it loads within a reasonable time; complex graphics and special effects will slow it down.

- Remember that some functions, such as audio material, may not be accessible to all users, in which case this should be an optional enhancement rather than central to your message.

- If your site is to be displayed on a WAP phone, it will need to be coded in WML (wireless mark-up language) to make it compatible. It will also need to be simply presented to take account of the limitations of a small screen.

■ Your website must be included in the index of the major search engines so that internet surfers are able to discover it. To improve the chances of 'hits', it is possible to register with search engines for a fee. Alternatively, keywords that the search engines will recognise can be placed within HTML metatags when the site is coded.

Screen readers and text-only browsers

The site should be designed to work with a screen reader; software that visually-impaired people use instead of a monitor to get their computers to talk to them. The problem is that the arrangement of the typical web page, with boxes, columns and graphics, is such that the screen reader cannot make sense of it. One solution is to tag images with descriptive text that can be read. Alternatively text-only browsers (such as Betsie developed at the BBC) will remove all images and convert the page into plain text that the screen-reader can understand.

Legal constraints

It is important to understand that there are laws and conventions relating to the use and design of websites.

World Wide Web Consortium (W3C)

The **World Wide Web Consortium** is based at Cambridge, Massachusetts, USA. Its purpose is to develop and maintain common technology standards for use on the World Wide Web. These include the use of the HTML language for web pages, acceptable graphics formats and new standards for use with interactive television and mobile phones.

The Royal National Institute for the Blind (RNIB) is a member of W3C and has helped draw up the conventions for site design that will enable screen-readers to perform effectively.

World Wide Web Consortium: www.w3.org

Data Protection Act 1998

The Act covers data held about individuals in written records as well as on computer files. Users of personal data must register with the Data Protection Registrar at the Data Protection Agency where they are put on a register of data users.

The law states that all personal data held must be: fairly and lawfully processed, relevant to its purpose, accurate, kept securely, not kept for longer than is necessary, used for limited purposes and in accordance with the rights of the data subject (the individual on whom information is kept). The data must not be transferred to countries that do not have adequate protection. This final point is an issue for businesses outsourcing their call centres to overseas locations.

Individuals have the right to see the information held on them and, if it is inaccurate, to have it corrected or deleted. They can complain about the misuse of personal data and, if necessary, sue for damages in the law courts.

The global nature of the internet means that this and other laws cannot always be fully enforced because of the different legal systems across the world. Users must be aware of this.

Intellectual property rights

In Unit 5, we saw how businesses could legally protect their ideas (their intellectual property) by patent, registered design, registered trademarks and copyright. Anyone who then uses these ideas without permission is acting illegally.

Whilst it has been customary for internet users to share and download files online (shareware software, for example, was freely distributed by the originators), more recently the issue of unauthorised file-sharing via the internet has become the subject of legal battles. The unauthorised downloading of software, digital music and films is illegal and court cases have been brought by companies in the software and music industries. Napster, a popular download music site set up by a college student, was the first to be sued by the major record companies.

Figure 6.16

Napster's logo

Despite their victory in court the music industry has realised that downloading is here to stay and has instead decided to regulate the trade:

- record companies have set up their own music download sites with payment per track or by subscription
- the Apple i-Pod has become a huge success on the back of the popularity of both legal and illegal downloading
- high street music retailers, such as Virgin and HMV, recognise the trend and in 2005 launched their own download sites (although their files cannot be played on the i-Pod)
- digital music is so popular that digital charts are now compiled alongside CD charts.

Napster now operates as one of the growing legal download sites. Unlimited music is available only to members who have a current monthly subscription.

Consumer protection legislation

Certain laws are relevant when businesses sell goods and services, whether by traditional means or via the internet. The situation is confused by the global nature of the internet and the laws below are those relating to the UK.

Trades Descriptions Act 1968

This states that goods and services offered for sale must be described accurately. Descriptions must include:

- accurate quantities, i.e. a litre must be a litre
- accurate ingredients, e.g. chips must be made of real potato, otherwise they are called French fries.

Sale of Goods Act 1979

This was amended by the Supply of Goods and Services Act (1982) and the Sale and Supply of Goods Act (1994) to cover most goods and services. Goods must be:

- fit for the purpose for which they are sold, e.g. walking boots must be suitable for walking over rough ground
- as described. This means that goods with imperfections can be sold as long as they are honestly described as 'seconds', 'pure new wool' must be just that
- of mechantable quality, i.e. they should be fit be sold, or of reasonable quality.

Services sold over the internet include travel and banking. They must be at a reasonable charge, carried out with reasonable care and skill, and within a reasonable time.

Contract law and the internet

Whenever goods and services are sold, a contract is made between the supplier and customer and there are obligations on both sides.

The law of contract is crucial to trading over the internet. Some important points are as follows.

- Most internet sites require that terms and conditions are read and accepted by the customer who then ticks a box before proceeding to the checkout. However, there is usually a consideration period before a contract is formally agreed.
- On the internet, goods are bought unseen, hence there is usually a short period for consideration to allow for returns.

Your right to cancel:

At Amazon.co.uk we want you to be delighted every time you shop with us. Occasionally though, we know you may want to return items. Read more about our Returns Policy at: http://www.amazon.co.uk/returns-policy/

Further, under the United Kingdom's Distance Selling Regulations, you have the right to cancel the contract for the purchase of any of these items within a period of 7 working days, beginning with the day after the day on which the item is delivered. This applies to all of our products.

Source: Amazon website

- Financial agreements on the web are no different from those conducted face-to-face.
- Contracts dealing in illegal goods, such as banned substances or stolen goods, cannot be legally binding.
- Customers buying from countries with no consumer protection laws are not protected.
- Buying a product legally but bringing it into a country where it is illegal leaves the buyer open to prosecution.
- Agencies exist which allow consumers to establish the credibility of internet traders.

Opportunities Provided by an Online Presence

Opportunities for greater processing efficiency

If you buy a new laptop online, the procedure will be as shown in the diagram below.

Figure 6.17

Buying goods online

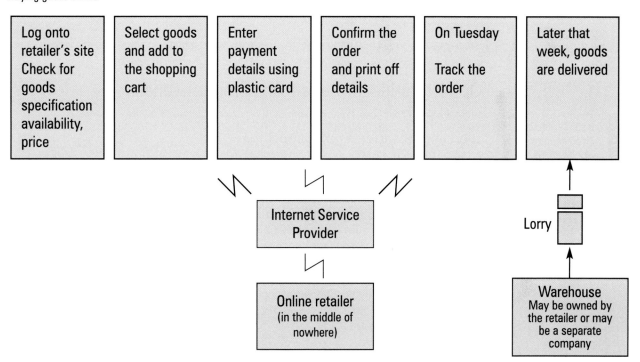

There are a number of ways in which online trading introduces efficiencies for both B2C transactions, as illustrated above, and B2B transactions.

Online order tracking and progress monitoring

Goods bought online are bought unseen and are delivered in the conventional way. To reassure customers, it is usual to have an order tracking facility (also provided by delivery companies such as UPS). An e-mail will be sent to confirm that the order has been dispatched and the customer will be invited to check the progress of the order on the website.

Integration of supply chains

Business to business (B2B) online communication enables the sourcing of goods and services through more responsive links with the supply chain (the chain of businesses involved in bringing a product from the producer to the customer). This allows delivery from the supplier just-in-time (JIT) to meet customer demand.

As a result, e-tailing businesses do not need to carry large stocks – sites such as Amazon and e-Buyer show their stock levels online. Where stock levels can be reduced, so too can associated storage costs such as rent, insurance, warehouse staff, damage to goods and obsolescence.

Improved cashflow
Online sales are paid for immediately by plastic card, either a debit or credit card. In either case, the validity of the card will be checked and the seller receives immediate payment. There will be no debt chasing or bad debts and cashflow is improved.

Greater freedom of location
We have seen that, whereas conventional retailers pay high costs for high street sites, location is less important for online retailers. The business is free to locate where the costs of labour, premises and tax are low. For example, UK companies working from the Channel Islands are able to avoid VAT charges.

Rationalisation of human resource requirements
An online presence is based upon the use of technology rather than of people and this leads to changes in the number of staff employed, their role and their methods of working.

Since online customers interact with a computer rather than face-to-face, there is likely to be a reduction in the number of customer service staff. For the supplier the saving on salaries, training and other employment costs can be significant. On the other hand, a smaller number of new staff with specific IT skills are needed to design and maintain systems.

Since location is now less important, there may be a movement to allow staff to work from home, or to outsource to independent providers with cheaper labour costs.

Opportunities for enhanced competitiveness
An online presence may make a business more competitive in a number of ways.

Increased awareness of competition
A business may use the web to check on the standard and scale of competition either locally, nationally or globally. Yell (see page 261) and upmystreet, for example, will both identify competing business within a given area.

Capacity to monitor competition
Once we have established who our competitors are, we can use the internet to monitor what they have to offer. This can either be done through logging onto their websites, much as a mystery shopper would do to check the prices charged, the variety, specifications and quantity of stock, the terms of delivery and other aspects of customer service. More conveniently, we could use a specialist site that has already done this research. Moneyfacts, for example, will give best buys in personal finance, whilst service providers such as AOL list sites that regularly scan the web and compare prices.

Lower barriers to market entry
The lower costs associated with online operations means that it is now far easier to break into certain markets. We have seen examples of this from the personal finance industry, where Virgin, Tesco and Sainsbury have all entered retail banking by using 'clicks not bricks'. Traditionally, a new business would need to acquire high street premises, fit these out at considerable expense and then employ and train an army of new staff. Technology has changed the rules.

Costs saved on staff and premises allow savings to be passed onto customers giving online providers a price advantage that allows them to get a foothold. The customer may also be attracted by the convenience: there are no queues or travelling, the transactions are confirmed instantly and the line should always be open (unlike the telephone which may be engaged, or the branch which may be closed).

Tesco has now also used the internet to diversify further into the gas supply and estate agency markets.

For small businesses the internet offers access to a global market without the need to establish physical bases overseas.

remember

Constant visibility – with an internet presence there is no closing time and no global boundary, the business remains open everywhere, 24/7.

case study

6.12

Egg cracks the UK market

Egg was set up by the Prudential in the 1990s. The Pru was a traditional insurance company that decided to expand into banking and also develop a younger customer profile.

Egg began as a telephone banking operation aimed at those 20–30-somethings with good careers and high earning potential. Wacky advertising and attractive, loss-leading, savings rates were used to built up a customer base.

The aim was always to move into internet banking when the market was ready. The UK operation worked well and the company is now listed on the stock market. The expansion into France, however, made huge losses.

activity

1 Explain the choice of Egg's target market.
2 Compare the interest rates offered for the Egg telephone savings account with the internet-only account. Which is the better deal? Why do you think this is?

Awareness of changing customer preferences

Web technology enables businesses to monitor sales, build up a profile of their customers and analyse how they navigate their website – how customers arrive, how long they stay and the point in the site from which they leave. This is more sophisticated and helpful that merely counting 'hits' (site visits only), many of which are random.

The back-end database can provide essential marketing information including details of product sales and customers. For example, it will show who the customers are and what they buy.

All of this information should enable a supplier to respond to demand, perhaps by making changes to stocks, prices and services, e-mailing customers with new offers or suggesting purchases when they next visit (on page 257 we discuss how cookies are used to do this).

Delivery of goods

Earlier we discussed the need for punctual delivery of goods and the opportunity that the Royal Mail recognised in the growing volume of online sales. We have also seen how e-tailers such as Amazon and e-Buyer reassure their customers that all is well by providing an order-tracking facility. Clearly the ability to deliver goods safely and on time is central to the success of e-commerce.

A wider product range and diversifying sourcing

Traditionally businesses sourced products by sending out buyers to identify appropriate suppliers and products, making orders and arranging delivery. This could be time-consuming and costly, and inevitably a number of potentially excellent suppliers were never discovered. Online links provide results of global searches instantly. The increased knowledge of what is available and the speed of online buying has inevitably led to businesses stocking a wider range of goods.

Branding and logos

A website is primarily a visual tool so that there is potential for the development of corporate image through use of branding and logos. The reach of the internet provides an opportunity to bring the brand of even a small business to a global audience. For example, the website for Eclipse pottery will use colours and images to reinforce the natural and quality aspects of the product.

Increasingly, sites are becoming more sophisticated and entertaining as technology improves. Companies use them as marketing vehicles alongside the promotions placed in other media such as the press, billboards and TV. The French Connection site, for example features music and video and is all about lifestyle. Lucozade Sport provides case studies and research to support their claims that the product enhances performance in sport.

assignment focus

Log on to the French Connection and Lucozade Sport sites:

1 What methods are being used here to enhance the two brands?

2 What is the brand image of each product? Who is the target market in each case?

Portals and ISPs

A **portal** is a website, often run by an ISP. It offers screens full of free links to other websites. For example, Yahoo, Lycos and MSN will offer links to sites under headings such as sport, news or finance. Traffic to a site will be increased if it can be included in such links.

Opportunities for service support

An online presence may enable a business to provide a better service to both its employees and customers.

Working away from the office

Increasingly, new technology allows employees to stay in touch whilst working away from the office. They may, for example, be at a meeting, a conference, on the road selling or working from home. In all of these situations, the business website provides a two-way information link between the employee and the business. For example, it may allow e-mails, remote access to the company database or to details on the intranet, printing of documents, and so on.

The use of portable 'notebook' computers or PDAs, together with wireless technology, has facilitated access from a wide range locations.

Online instructions

When you buy a new PC or printer, you will find technical support information on the maker's website. This may involve instructions for setting up the equipment, trouble-shooting or registering for warranty purposes. This online facility is now replacing the telephone help-line because it is cheaper to provide (no staff needed), is always available and should be free from human error.

Support may also be offered in the form of interactive online tutorials.

Downloads of firmware, software and product updates

New editions of software may be downloaded from the supplier's website as they become available – the latest version of Internet Explorer might be an example. These are usually free of charge for existing users. Firmware (something between hardware and software originally held in a ROM chip) is now stored in such a way that it too can be updated by loading from the internet.

Frequently asked questions (FAQs)

Businesses often provide their customers with answers to FAQs on their website. These may deal with matters such as common faults in equipment, essential product information or details about business operations. The idea is to provide basic information so that this will not have to be repeated and explained constantly.

Good **netiquette** (etiquette on the net) demands that FAQs, together with the answers, are read before asking further questions.

Customer feedback pages

Suppliers ask for customer comments in order to provide customer information and feedback. Almost every page on BBC Online has a link to a feedback form.

Links to related sites

Business websites will often contain hyperlinks to other, related sites. For example, the website of Oxfam has a link to the *Daily Mirror* site – the two organisations are partners in an attempt to help the people of Rwanda.

Oxfam also links with the BBC website to explain how the Betsie text-only programme works (see page 273).
The Eclipse Pottery website (page 267) has an external link to the 'Great Potters' website.

A web ring and web forums

A web ring is a group of websites linked together. These may comprise sites from individuals or businesses with a common interest, such as businesses that are members of a trade association, a company and its major shareholders or a business and its customers. Oxfam is linked in this way with other Oxfam organisations such as Make Trade Fair, Oxfam Publishing and Oxfam Unwrapped.

A web forum is an online conference, in other words a service in which messages may be sent and read by all. The Tell Shell forum, mentioned on page 264, is an example.

assignment focus

- To achieve P4, you need to describe key business opportunities arising from an online presence.

  You might identify the different ways in which your website might provide new opportunities for the business. Describe each point giving examples.

- To achieve M3, you need to explain how an online business presence facilitates greater freedom of business operation.

  Here you should explain how a web presence allows a business more choices in the way in which it carries out its business operations. This might involve factors such as where the business is located, the type of business activity and market it is engaged in.

- To achieve D1, you need to evaluate the extent to which the website you have created may both attract customer interest and facilitate greater freedom of operation, supporting the achievement of your business aims and objectives.

  Here you are to consider the extent to which the website will generate customer interest and freedom of operation. You must then make a reasoned judgement as to how effective the website will be in supporting business aims and objectives.

Glossary

accessibility: meeting audience needs effectively using readable, legible text; sounds; images, etc.

added value: value of business output less the cost of bought in inputs

advertising agency: marketing business that will design, plan and implement an advertising campaign

advertising: paid for impersonal communication or message intended to inform or persuade an audience

AIDA: Attention, Interest, Desire, Action

AIO inventory: questions to find consumers' activities, interests and opinions

appraisal: a system for gaining feedback on employees' performance, by looking at what a job is, how well it is performed and what action should be taken in future

attitudes: emotions, feelings, etc. for or against a product

B2B: business to business, e.g. wholesaler, retailer

B2C: business to consumer

benchmarking: process of identifying then improving on best practice in another organisation; best practice is the standard or benchmark

blog: short for web log. A personal online diary

body language: non-verbal communication comprising gestures and facial expressions (e.g. smiles) which can help or hinder communication

brand: used by a supplier to identify their products from those of competitors. It may be a name, a symbol or a term. Brands are often given a particular image or value

branding: giving a product a distinctive identity through trademarks, design, packaging, etc.

break-even point: the level of production and sales at which a business covers its costs so that there is neither a profit nor a loss. It can be measured either in units or in revenue

broadband: a system that can carry many signals of varying frequencies. For the user the advantage is more information (text, audio, video, etc.) at greater speed

budget: an agreed plan that serves as a target for a future period, e.g. sales, production or revenue. It may be quantitative (units) or financial

business: an organisation that produces or distributes goods or services

business angel: an individual willing to risk funds by investing in a new or risky business venture

Business Link: an organisation that provides help and advice to businesses in a local area

business objectives: goals or aims of an organisation which are **SMART**

cascading style sheets (CSS): templates that can be set up when designing a website. They enable page features such as colour, font and size to be created and then shared by a number of pages, e.g. a single CSS may be used to apply a blue background and white text to each page in a website

cashflow cycle: the timing of cash inflows and outflows as a business produces and sells

cashflow problem: a shortage of working capital (available cash) to pay bills.

central government: the government at Westminster, as opposed to local government

centralised control: where all strategic decisions are taken by managers at the top of the organisation

Chamber of Commerce: an organisation serving the needs of businesses within a locality

charity: a business operating on a not-for-profit basis usually to provide a service for a good cause

coaching: an expert helps others to develop specific skills

communications media: press, radio, TV, etc. used for promotion and advertising

competitive pricing: pricing policy in line with competitors, non-price competition becomes important

compulsory competitive tendering (CCT): by law, local authorities must allow outside firms to put in bids (or tenders) to provide council services (such as refuse collection). The contract will be awarded to the lowest tender. In some cases this may be the local authority in others a private firm

contingency plans: plans drawn up in case the unexpected happens

continuous improvement: when organisations constantly seek to improve working practices

contract of employment: legal agreement between an employee and employer which sets out terms and conditions of a job

cookie: a file that loads to the hard drive of your computer when you visit a website. Next time you visit they are able to identify you, e.g. 'Hello Roger'. Most web browsers give the option to refuse cookies

copyright: exclusive legal ownership to e.g. music, text, software (Copyright Act 1988)

copywriter: person who writes the words (known as 'copy') for an advertisement

corporate communication: any form of communication between an organisation and its stakeholders

corporate identity: personality of an organisation created through its corporate communication and behaviour

corporate image: view that an organisation projects of itself to its stakeholders (consumers, employees, etc.)

corporate message: features of a product or organisation most stressed in its advertising and promotional activities

corporate performance: extent to which an organisation achieves its aims/objectives such as quality, customer service, profitability, etc.

cost plus pricing: adding a percentage or mark up to the cost to obtain the price

costs: the value of those resources consumed (or used up) in production over a trading period. In this sense fixed assets are not costs since they remain useful into future periods

critical path analysis: sequence of activities which show the shortest time in which a project can be completed. Critical tasks must be completed before subsequent tasks can be started.

cross-platform compatibility: the ability of software to run on more than one type of processor or operating system

culture: the set of beliefs, values and attitudes that shape and drive an organisation

cyberspace: mythical place through which internet information travels on its journey to and from users

decentralised control: where strategic decisions are taken by divisional managers further down the organisation, e.g. a business may have different divisions for geographical areas or for different products

demographic segmentation: splitting consumers into similar groups based on demographic features

demographics: features of the potential buyers such as age, gender or income

direct marketing: communication from the seller direct to the buyer such as mail, text or e-mail

direct selling: selling directly to the buyer, e.g. door to door and home parties

Disability Discrimination Act: states that it is illegal to discriminate against someone because they have a disability

disciplinary procedure: formal systems which must be followed when staff are disciplined. Beginning with an informal verbal warning, the process could end in dismissal of an employee

distribution channel: means by which goods reach the final user, can include retailers and wholesalers

domain name: the web address used by an organisation. It is used as a way of locating information and reaching other users. In an e-mail address, for example, everything following the @ is the domain name

DTI: Department of Trade and Industry

e-commerce: electronic commerce, i.e. all commercial transactions conducted via the internet. This includes selling, banking, investing and bill paying

elasticity: responsiveness of demand to a change in price

encryption: use of mathematical algorithms to make data unintelligible to all but the intended recipient. Sensitive data, such as credit card numbers, is protected in this way

endorsements: gaining favourable support from 'celebrities' or other organisations for a product/service

equal opportunities: legislation, such as the Race Relations Act and Equal Opportunities Act, which make it illegal to discriminate against someone on the grounds of race, colour, religion, etc.

ergonomics: study of the relationships between people and the machines, equipment and facilities they use

e-tailers: electronic retailers, i.e. online retailers

ethics: principles that guide our actions. Unethical behaviour will harm people, animals or the environment

EU: European Union

evolution: gradual change

exception analysis: management approach which uses the abnormal or exceptional differences between planned and actual results, e.g. planned (budgeted) and actual costs/revenues, etc. as the focus for management action and time

externalities: the social costs (or benefits) borne by society rather than by the business that causes them

firewall: software that filters out certain unwanted or undesirable intrusion from the outside world. It is used to prevent breaches in security

fixed costs (or overheads): costs that do not rise or fall with changes in output and sales. Fixed costs are usually related to time periods, e.g. rent

flat structure: few layers of management

focus group: market research interview method, a small group is assembled to discuss a particular topic

formal communication: communication which follows the formal lines of authority in an organisation

franchise: an arrangement under which one business (the franchisor) allows another business (the franchisee) to supply its products

Freedom of Information Act: states that anybody can request information from a public authority in England, Wales or Northern Ireland and has the right to receive that information (subject to certain restrictions)

FTSE-100 (the 'footsie'): an index showing changes in the share prices of the 100 most valuable companies listed on the London Stock Exchange

functional activities: the different departments within a business such as: R&D, production or operations, distribution, marketing, human resources, finance, administration, MIS

functions: activities within an organisation such as administration, personnel finance, etc. separate departments may be set up to carry these out

Gantt chart: chart or matrix which shows how project activities have to be achieved by a set time

geographic segmentation: dividing consumers into similar groups based on where they live

global: world-wide

goods: tangible items – we can touch, feel and see them

grievance procedure: formal systems which must be followed when staff have a grievance/complaint for unfair treatment against an organisation or another worker

hierarchies: layers or grades of formal management with clear lines of authority and control

HTML: Hypertext Markup Language used to write web-pages. It is compatible with all computers and software and so enabled the huge recent growth in internet use

human resources management: helps the organisation pursue its goals by planning, recruitment and development of an appropriate workforce

incentives: methods of motivating employees into working more effectively, may be monetary (bonus) or non-monetary (perks such as a company car)

industrial sectors: consist of the primary sector, secondary sector and tertiary sector

informal communication: ways of communicating which do not follow the formal lines of authority in the organisation, commonly called the grapevine

infrastructure: the services that support a business

innovation: putting an invention to commercial use

intellectual property (IP): an organisation's intangible assets such as trade marks, patents, copyrights logo, brand name, etc.

international: over more than one country

internet service provider (ISP): a company that provides software to allow a computer to connect to the internet, e.g. BT, AOL, Virgin

Investors in People (IIP): a national government-backed quality standard, awarded to organisations for effective investment in the training and development of their staff

Javascript: a language used to create interactive elements on websites, e.g. it may capture the name and address typed by a user and store it on a customer database

job description: written document setting out the duties, responsibilities and reporting procedures of a job

leasing: an arrangement where a business hires out an asset (e.g. a building or equipment) to another business

lifestyle: the way we live, our friends/family, activities, interests

limited liability: the amount an owner must pay creditors if a business fails is limited to the amount they have invested in the business

lines of authority: management positions in the organisation hierarchy, showing who is responsible for whom and who reports to whom

liquidity: the ability of a business to turn its assets (items owned by a business) into cash

livery: distinctive uniform or colour scheme used to distinguish a product or organisation from its competitors

local business: a business serving the immediate area

local government: the local council with headquarters at the town hall. It is responsible for local services such as education and road maintenance.

logistics: control of the movement and storage of raw materials (in-bound logistics), through production to the packaging, storage and distribution of the finished goods to the buyer (out-bound logistics).

logo: identity mark or name used to distinguish a product or organisation from its competitors

margin of safety: the amount by which estimated sales exceed break-even sales. The sales a business can lose and yet still break even

market segments: specific part of the market defined by particular characteristics such as age or income (consumers) type of retail outlet (business)

market share: proportion of a total market (often measured by sales value) held by a business or product. A market leader has a larger market share than competitors

marketing mix: the combination of the four 'Ps' of Price, Product, Promotion, Place, which are within the control of the business

matrix structure: a team/project structure with vertical and diagonal lines of authority, i.e. more than one boss

media mix: combination of media (press, TV, etc.) used to reach a particular segment

mentoring: someone with experience supporting someone with less experience

merger: (or amalgamation) involves combining two organisations to form a single business. This is agreed by management and shareholders of the businesses concerned

metatags: can be used to describe the contents of a website. They enable search engines to index the site and locate it when users make searches

monopoly: a business that it can dominate a market because it has little or no competition. In the UK a business with 25 per cent or more market share is regarded as a monopoly

multilingual support: providing translation or interpreting facilities for an audience

multimedia: use of images, sounds, video to create a presentation

national: across the nation. This may be a country such as France or a group of countries such as the UK

netiquette: internet ethics, e.g. use the spell-checker, don't ask before reading the FAQs (frequently asked questions)

NIC (National Insurance Contributions): deducted from wages to pay for benefits such as the state pension

niche market: a small or specialised market segment, e.g. expensive sports cars

OHP: overhead projector used in presentations

online presence: a website

online: activities on the internet

operations: the day-to-day work involved (i.e. business operations) carried out by operatives

Glossary

organic growth: growth achieved by re-investing profits.

outsourcing: buying from an outside provider, e.g. a business may use a security firm rather than employing their own security staff

partnership: business with between two and 20 owners

patents: an exclusive legal right to sell, use or make an invention

PAYE (pay as you earn): income tax deducted from an employee's pay. This is a main source of government income

PDA: personal digital assistant

penetration pricing: prices are initially set low to gain a foothold in the market

PESTEL: the external forces that affect businesses. They include: political, economic, social, technological, environmental and legal factors

physical resources: premises and facilities used by an organisation

portals: a website, such as Yahoo, that offers free entry to many other sites by posting pages full of links

press/news release: statement given free to newspapers and news media

primary data: data collected for the first time

private limited company: a business owned by shareholders and run by a board of directors

private sector: those businesses not run by the state but by private individuals. Profit is a usual motive of the private sector

privatisation: changing state-owned businesses into privately owned business. This involves selling the shares to private buyers

product: features and benefits associated with goods and services, one of the four Ps

product development: changing a product to increase its appeal to existing or new customers

product mix: the range of products provided or produced by an organisation

product positioning: using the marketing mix to create an image for a product by emphasising particular benefits or features

product range: the total number of product/service lines and items sold or produced by a business

production: the process for transforming inputs such as materials, labour and capital into goods and services

profit: the surplus or additional money created when goods or services are sold at a price higher than the cost of producing them; sales revenue – total production cost (variable + fixed costs) = profit

promotion: process of informing, persuading or influencing businesses or consumers into making a purchase

promotional mix: combination of methods such as advertising and public relations used to promote a product

public relations: an organisation's relationships with its stakeholders intended to create a favourable impression

public sector: the part of the economy owned by local or national government

public spending: money spent on goods and services by the government

publicity: unpaid form of attracting attention to a product/person, by using the media; may be favourable or unfavourable

qualitative information: attitudes or views about a product/service, 'soft' information

quantitative information: numerical or 'hard' information

search engines: search the World Wide Web to locate pages with a given content, e.g. Google, MSN, Yahoo, Ask Jeeves

secondary data: data collected using existing hard copy or electronically published sources

segmentation: splitting whole markets into smaller units (segments) in order to target promotion and other marketing activities at specific groups of people

service: an action providing a benefit such as banking or education

shareholder value: the value of each share. This should increase if the company makes profits

SMART targets/objectives: precise quantifiable targets that are: specific, measurable, achievable, realistic and timed

SMEs: small and medium enterprises

social costs: costs to people in general resulting from business activity

sole trader: business with one owner

spam: unrequested information sent to web users by businesses wishing to advertise their products

stakeholders: the people and communities who have an interest in a business because they are affected by its activities

strapline: slogan or phrase associated with a product or organisation

strategic planning: setting up corporate/organisation-wide plans to achieve goals and objectives at some specific time in the future

strategy: plans by which a business will achieve its long-term objectives

SWOT: an assessment of a business under the headings: strengths, weaknesses, opportunities and threats

tactical planning: plans for departments/functions such as finance, marketing or finance

tactics: plans worked out by managers for achieving strategic objectives

take-over: one business taking control of another by buying sufficient shares

target markets: segment or group classified by age, gender, etc. which is the focus of specific marketing activity

trade association: an organisation representing firms operating in the same industry

uniforms: corporate clothing worn to create a professional image

unlimited liability: where the owners of a business must pay in full all money owed to creditors

URL (uniform resource locator): used to identify a website address, web page, a file or a server on the internet

USP (unique selling point): the reason why customers go to one business rather than another, e.g. quality or low prices

variable costs: costs that change proportionately as output rises and falls i.e. twice the output means twice the cost

VAT (value added tax): is a tax on the value added during production. A business pays input tax to suppliers of goods and services. It reclaims this by charging output tax on the sales of goods and services to customers. Any excess is sent to the Department of Customs and Revenue

venture capital: loan or share capital made available to new businesses or those that have a significant amount of risk

verbal communication: face-to-face or telephone communication where specific skills such as listening are needed

viability: the extent to which a business is likely to succeed

voluntary sector: The part of the economy in which businesses have at least some volunteer workers. These are not-for-profit businesses providing a service to a group in society

WAP: wireless application protocol that permits mobile 'phones and pocket computers to read e-mail and web-based information

web browsers: request and read pages from the World Wide Web, e.g. for example: Netscape Navigator, Internet Explorer

web-authoring tools: help users to design websites without the need to understand a programming language, e.g. Flash, Dreamweaver

web-based presentation: the layout, structure and design of an organisations' website and other online activity

working capital: money needed to run the business from day to day

World Wide Web Consortium (W3C): organisation which provides standards on web accessibility

Index

Page references in *italics* indicate figures or tables

accountability 73, 84
accountants 51, 229
accounts, annual 227
added value 17, *17*
administration *37*
advertising 133–4
  agencies 141–3, *142*
  cod of advertising practice 181
  media 144–50, *147*, 148
Advertising Standards Authority 173
agents 130
aims, corporate 18–20, 35, 53–4
  and promotional objectives 106–7, *107*
AIO (attitudes, interests and opinions)
    inventory 113–14
animation 184, *184*
annual reports 9, 227
appraisals 87
Arriva 27, *39*
Arsenal FC 16
asset value 30
assets 22, 95, 223
authority 55, 73, 84
averages 177

banks 15, 215, 229, 253
bar charts *176*, 177, 178
benchmarking 62, 63
body language 101
Boots Group plc 46–7
borrowing 215
brands and branding 117–18, 140
  and online presence 265, 277
break-even forecasts 21–6, 233–6
budgets 93–4, *93*, 160
building societies 6, 7
buildings, maintenance and refurbishment
    77–8
business angels 215
Business dynamics 217
Business Link 50, 217
business plans 58, 223, *224*
  action plans 58–60
  Eclipse example 239–46
  evaluation 236–7
  financial 41–5, 230–6
  legal 226–8
  managers and 67
  marketing 219, *219*
  monitoring and future planning 60–4,
    237

operational 223–5
  self-development 229–30
  SWOT analysis 45–7, *46*
business to business (B2B) 109, 111, 139,
    250, *251*
business to customer (B2C) 109, 111,
    135, 139, 251, *251*
businesses 1–2
  failures 204, *204*
  functions within 34–40, *34*, *36–7*,
    72–3, *73*
  ownership of 4–8, 5
  purpose of 11–13
  researching 9–10
  stakeholders 14–16
  strategy 18–33
  survival and growth 41–51
  types and range of activity 2–4
buyers (procurers) 17

call centres 38, 258
campaigns, promotional 151–60
capital 214
  working 95–6
cascading style sheets (CSSs) 268, *268*
cashflow
  cycle 95, 231–2, *233*
  forecasts 42–5, 95, 231
  and online presence 276
CCT (compulsory competitive tendering) 37
chains of command 55, *71*, 72, 84
Chambers of Commerce 229–30
charitable status 7, *211*
chat rooms 264
cinema advertising 146, *147*
Co-operative Financial Services 31
co-operatives 5, 6–7, 50
Coca-Cola 103
communication 67, 100, *101*, 165
  barriers to 168–9
  components of 165–8, *165*
  corporate 191–7
  formal and informal 100
  non-verbal 101
  online 256, 257
  verbal 100
  see also information; promotion
communities and business 16
Companies Acts 1985 & 1989 227
company directors 14, 35
competition 47–8, *47*, 62, 276–8

competitive pricing 126
compulsory competitive tendering (CCT) 37
Computer Misuse Act 1990 98
Consumer Safety Act 1987 226
consumers *see* customers
contingency planning 227
continuing professional development (CPD)
    102, *103*, 229
continuous improvement 64
contract law and the internet 274–5
contracts of employment 82–3
cookies 257
copyright 97, 97–8, 218
Copyright, Designs and Patents Act 1988
    97–8
copywriters 142
cost centres 94
cost leadership 47
cost plus pricing 126
cost, selling at or below 11–12
costs 21–2, 25, 41, 225
    advertising 143, 146–7, *147*
    minimising 26–7
    presentation 190
CPD (continuing professional development)
    102, *103*, 229
creativity 67, 206
critical path analysis (CPA) 61
CSSs (cascading style sheets) 268, *268*
culture, organisational 89
current assets and liabilities 95
customer service 20, 278
customers 14
    legislation protecting 226, 274
    loyalty 109, 110, 117–18, *118*, 265
    and online presence 256, 257, 259–65,
    277

data 162
    capturing and storing 257
    primary and secondary 163–4
    see also information
Data Protection Act 1998 172–3, 273
dealers 129
debt funding 215
delegation 67
demand-based pricing 126
deregulation 5
design departments *36*
designs, protecting 96, 97–8, 218
differential pricing 127
differentiation 47, 123–4
direct mail 138, *147*
direct marketing 138–9, 147
direct reply advertising 139
direct selling 128, *128*, 265
directors, company 14, 35
Disability Discrimination Act 1995 181

disciplinary procedures 86
discounts 126, 139
distribution 18, *36*, 127
    channels of 128–32, *128*, *130*, *131*
    and online presence 275, 277
    of services 132
documents 182–3
domain names 271
door-to-door distribution 138
dot.com companies 252

e-commerce 18, 251–2
    see also online business
ECGD (Export Credit Guarantee Department)
    216
employees 14
    contracts of employment 82–3
    grievance and disciplinary procedures
    85–6
    health and safety 83
    incentives and rewards for 90–2
    in industrial sectors *36*
    Investors in People and 88, *88*
    legislation relating to 226
    liaison with others 85
    and lines of authority 84
    and online presence 276, 278
    organisational structures and 68–73
    outsourcing 37–8, 225
    performance management 87
    performance monitoring 87
    recruitment and retention 80–1
    supply of 81–2
    teams and teamwork 84, *85*
employer associations 15
Employment Act 2002 226
empowerment, employee 91, 92
encoding process 166
endorsements, celebrity 194
enterprise
    business failures 204, *204*
    business plans 223–37, *224*, 239–46
    and business trends 207–9
    entrepreneurs *49*, 201–3, 204–5, *205*
    innovation and creativity 206
    legal status 210–11, *211*
    marketing strategy and tactics 219–22
    protecting ideas 97–8, 217–18
    SMEs and UK economy 205, *205*
    sources of finance and support 50–1,
    213–17
environment, business 46, 48, 62, 207–8,
    208
Environmental Protection Act 1990 228
Equal Pay Act 1970 226
ergonomics 83
ethics 30–3
European Working Time Directive 2002 226

exception analysis 64
exhibitions 135–6
Export Credit Guarantee Department (ECGD) 216
externalities 16, 32

factoring 215
Federation of Small Businesses 230
feedback 168
field tests 123
finance
    break even forecasts 21–6, 233–6
    budget management 93–4
    cashflow 42–5, *230*, 231–2, 233
    function *37*
    generating extra 94–5
    plans and planning 41, *41*, 230, 237
    provision for emergencies 96
    raising 45
    records 227
    sources of 213–17, *213*
    working capital 95–6
Financial Services Authority (FSA) 173
firewalls 272
fixed assets 22, 223
fixed costs 21
flat organisations 68–9, *69*
focus 48
franchises 6, 130, *211*
Freedom of Information Act 2000 173
functions, organisational 34–5, *34, 36–7*
    control of 39, *39*
    interdependence 40
    objectives 56, *56*
    and organisational structure 72–3, *73*
    outsourcing 37–8

Gantt charts 61, *61*, 159, *159*
goods 1, 2, 119
    see also products
government
    advice and support 216–17
    and business activity 16
    and public sector business 4, 13
    spending *13*
    statistics 10, 209
graphics 178
Greenpeace 8–9
grievance procedures 86
growth 27–30, 41–51, 53

health and safety 78, 83, 226
Health and Safety at Work Act (HASAWA) 83, 226
hierarchies 34–5, *34, 71*, 72
human resources (HR) *37*, 79–80, 225
    see also employees

ICI *39*
image
    corporate 191, 192–6
    product 109
incentives, for employees 90–2
industrial sectors 2–3, *3, 259*
inertia in business 48
information 161–2
    accuracy and suitability 173–5
    internal and external 163
    legislation and standards 172–3, 181
    life-expectancy of 164
    online 261–2
    presentation 179–80, 182–91
    primary and secondary data 163–4
    processing 175–9
    purpose of 169–70
    sources 9–10, 170–1, 180, 229–30
    types of 162–3
    validation 172
    see also communication
Innocent Drinks 202–3
innovation 67, 206
insurance 227
integration, growth and 27
intellectual property (IP) 96–9, 273–4
internet 171, 247–9, *248*
    searching 171
    web-based presentations 185–6
    see also online business
internet service providers (ISPs) 195, 271–2
interpersonal skills 100–1, *101*
interpreters 186
Investors in People 88, *88*

job descriptions 80, 84

Kraft Foods Inc. 63

leadership 73–4, 89–90
leaflets 154
leasing 215
legal planning 226–9
legal status (of businesses) 49, *49*, 210–11, *211*
licenses 228
limited liability companies 6, *49, 211*
line graphs *176*, 177, 178
lines of authority 55, 71–2, *71*, 84
literature, corporate 195
livery 192
loans 215
local government 16, 228
logistics *see* distribution
logos 15, *15*, 117, 192, *192*, 277
loyalty, customer 109, 110, 117–18, *118*, 265

machinery 77
magazine advertising 145, *147*
mail order 138
management 65
    authority and accountability 73
    and business performance 103
    consequences of effective/ineffective
        74–5, *76*
    functions and responsibilities 65–7
    leadership and judgement 73–4, 89–90
    levels of 55–6, *55*, *60*, *65*, 65, 162
    and organisational structure 68–73
    of resources 76–99
    skills 100–2
management information services (MIS) *37*,
    163
managers 14
    liaison between 85
    objectives 19
    roles 55, 66–7
    see also management
Manchester United 19
margins of safety 24
market capitalisation 30
market research *36*, 121, 220
market segmentation 114–17, 120
market share 27, 28–9, 75, 109–10
market trials 122–3
marketing *36*
    strategies and tactics 120, 219–22,
        219, 236
    see also promotion
marketing mix 105, *119*, 219, 222
    distribution 127–32
    price 125–7
    products and services 119–25
    promotion 132–40
mass markets 220–1
matrix organisations 70–1, 70
media, advertising 144–50, *147*, *148*,
    154–6, 194–5
memoranda *166*
mergers 27, 48
message, corporate 193
MIS (management information services) *37*,
    163
mission statements 18
mock-ups 158
motivation 90
multimedia presentations 183–5
mutual organisations 5, 6, 7

National Trust 8, 50
newsgroups 264
newspaper advertising 145, *147*, 148–9,
    150, 156
niche markets 142, 220–1, 260
not-for-profit sector 7–8, 13, 50, *259*

Objective One funding 217
objectives, corporate 18–20, 35, 54–5, *54*,
    56, *56*
    promotional 106–18
online business 247
    advertising 146, *147*
    corporate communication 195
    creating and maintaining websites
        266–75
    direct selling 128, *129*
    impact on customers 259–65
    opportunities 275–9
    potential advantages 256–9
    purpose of online presence 255
    range of 250–4
operational planning 59–60, 223–5, 237
organisational structures 68–73
outsourcing 37–8, 225
overhead projectors (OHPs) 190
overtrading 48, 222
owners of businesses 14

packaging 140
partners, commercial 15
partnerships 5, 14, *49*, *211*, 225
patents 97–8, 218
Patents Act 2004 98
PDAs (personal digital organisers) 263
penetration pricing 125
percentage change 177
performance, corporate 53, 75
    monitoring 61–4
performance-related pay (PRP) 91
personal selling 136–7
personnel departments see human resources
PESTEL factors 46, 48, 62, 207–8, *208*
phishing 254
pie charts 177–8, 178, *178*
place *see* distribution
plans and planning *see* business plans
plant and machinery 77
point-of-sale (POS) displays 139
portals 278
positioning pricing 126
positioning, product 124
posters 145
PPPs (public-private partnerships) 5
premium pricing 125
presentations 182, *182*
    audiences 186, *187*
    costs and benefits 190–1
    face-to-face 186–9
    facilities 189–90
    multilingual support 186
    multimedia 183–5
    web-based 185–6
    written 182–3
press releases 135

pressure groups 15, 264
prices and pricing 47, 125–7, 265
primary industrial sector 2, 3, 3
Prince's Trust 217
private limited companies (ltds) 6, 6, 211
private sector 5–7, 5, 11–12, 259
privatisation 5, 7
procurement departments 36
procurers (buyers) 17
producers 18
production 1, 36
products 1, 2, 119
    development of new 120–3
    differentiation 109, 117, 123–4
    extending life of 124
    failure of 123
    online 254–5, 260, 262–3, 277
    positioning 124
    presentation 140
    price of 125–7, 265
    raising awareness of 107–8
    range 120
profit centres 94
profits 11, 29
    maximisation 26–7, 126
    profitability 230, 233–6
project-based organisations 70–1, 70
promotion 105
    adverting agencies 141–3
    advertising 144–50
    campaigns 151–60
    methods of 132–41
    presentation of information 182–91
    promotional objectives 106–18, 107,
        148–9
    straplines 193
PRP (performance-related pay) 91
public limited companies (plcs) 6, 6, 211
public relations 134–5
public sector 4–5, 5, 12–13, 20, 259
publicity 133, 134
purchasing departments 36
push and pull promotion 109

Race Relations Act 1976 181
radio advertising 146, 147, 150
Railtrack 7, 31–2
range (statistics) 177
recruitment, employee 80–1
relationship marketing 110
reports 167, 182
repositioning, product 124, 124
Research & development (R&D) 36
resources 59, 76
    financial 92–6
    human 79–92, 225
    physical 76–8, 223
    technological 96–9

retailers 18, 129, 130, 265
retention, employee 81
revenue 21, 26, 41
rewards for employees 90–2
risk 223, 227

Sale and Supply of Goods Act 1994 274
sales function 36
    see also marketing
sales promotion 139
sales revenue 21, 25, 26
screen readers 272
search engines 258, 273
secondary industrial sector 2, 3, 3
security 78, 254
segmentation, market 114–17, 120
selling process 136–7, 136, 137
services 1, 2, 20, 119
    distribution 132
    and online presence 260, 262–3, 278–9
    raising awareness of 107–8
    see also products
Sex Discrimination Acts 1975 & 1986
        181
shareholders 6, 14, 29
shares 29, 75
Shell Livewire 217
skimming pricing 125–6
Small Firms Loan Guarantee Scheme (SFLGS)
        216
Small Firms Training Loans (SFTLs) 216
SMART objectives 18–19, 35, 54, 56, 57
SMEs (small and medium enterprises) 205,
        205
social costs 16, 32
socio-economic groups 170, 170
sole traders 5, 14, 49, 211, 225
solicitors 50, 229
sourcing departments 36
span of control 71–2, 72
sponsorship 137–8
staff see employees
stakeholders 14–16, 20, 76
statistical analysis 177–8
stocks 223
storyboards 157, 158
straplines 193
strategy, business
    action planning 58
    aims and objectives 18–20, 35, 53–7
    breaking even 21–6
    ethics and 30–3
    growth 27–30
    monitoring performance and future
        planning 60–4
    profit maximisation 26–7
    service provision 20
structures, organisational 68–73

suppliers 15, 261
supply chains 17–18, *18*, 128–31
internet and *129*, 257, 275–6
supply and demand 11, *11*
Supply of Goods and Services Act 1982
226, 274
SWOT analysis 45–7, *46*, 221, *221*

tactical plans 58–9
take-overs 27, 28, 48
tall organisations 69–70, *69, 70*
target audiences/markets 112–13, 149,
193
targets, performance 63, 75
taxation 227
teams and teamwork 84, 84–5, 85
tele-marketing 138
television advertising 144–5, *147*, 150
tertiary industrial sector 2, 3, *3*
Tesco plc 12, 28, 40, 57–8, 87
trade associations 229
trade marks 97, 218
Trade Marks Act 1994 98
trade promotion 139, 154–5
Trades Descriptions Act 1968 226, 274
trades unions 15
trait theories 89
trends, business 207–9
Tropicana 111
trusts 8

uniforms 192–3
unique selling points (USPs) 47, 123–4,
222
Usenet 264

value chain 17–18
variable costs 21
venture capital trusts (VCTs) 214
verbal communication 100
voluntary sector 7–8, 13, 50, *259*

WAP (wireless application protocol) 263
waste 77
web rings 279
websites 255, 266
creating 185–6, 269
firewalls 272
launching 270–2
legal constraints 273–5
maintaining *262*, 272
planning 266–8
potential advantages of 256–9
suitability for use 272–3
testing and usability 269–70, *270*
see also online business
wholesalers 18, 130
workforce *see* employees
working capital 95–6
World Wide Web Consortium (W3C) 273